BRITISH AND AMERICAN AIRCRAFT IN RUSSIA PRIOR TO 1941

Vladimir Kotelnikov

Translated by Kevin Bridge

Helion & Company

Helion & Company Limited
Unit 8 Amherst Business Centre
Budbrooke Road
Warwick
CV34 5WE
England
Tel. 01926 499 619
Email: info@helion.co.uk
Website: www.helion.co.uk
Twitter: @helionbooks
Visit our blog at blog.helion.co.uk

Published by Helion & Company 2022
Designed and typeset by Farr out Publications, Wokingham, Berkshire
Cover designed by Paul Hewitt, Battlefield Design (www.battlefield-design.co.uk)

Translated by Kevin Bridge

ISBN 978-1-915070-88-3

British Library Cataloguing-in-Publication Data.
A catalogue record for this book is available from the British Library.

Contents

List of Abbreviations

ADD Long-Range Aviation (*Aviatsiya Dalnego Deystviya*)

DVR Far Eastern Republic (*Dalnevostochnaya Respublika*)

EON Special Purpose Squadron (*Eskadrilya Osobogo Naznacheniya*)

GUAP Main Directorate of the Aviation Industry (*Glavnoe Upravlenie Aviatsionnoi Promyshlennosti)*

GU GVF Main Directorate of the Civil Air Fleet (*Glavnoe Upravlenie Grazhdanskogo Vozdushnogo Flota*)

GUSMP Main Directorate of the Northern Sea Route (*Glavnoe Upravlenie Severnogo Morskogo Puti*)

GVF Civil Air Fleet (*Grazhdanskiy Vozdushniy Flot*)

LII Flight Testing Institute (*Lyotno-Ispytatelniy Institut*)

MAGON Moscow Special Purpose Air Group (*Moskovskaya Aviagruppa Osobogo Naznacheniya*)

NII GVF Scientific-Research Institute of Civil Air Fleet (*Nauchno-Isseldovatelskiy Institut Grazhdanskogo Vozdushnogo Flota)*

NII VVS Air Force Scientific Testing Institute (*Naucho-Ispytatelniy Institut Voenno-Vozdushnykh Sil*)

NKAP People's Commissariat for Aviation Industry (*Narodniy Komissariat Aviatsionnoy Promyshlennosti*)

NOA Scientific-Experimantal Airfield (*Nauchno-Opytniy Aerodrom*)

OAGS Special Liaison Air Group (*Osobaya Aviagruppa Svyazi*)

OELID Department of Operations, Flight Testing and Refinements (*Otdel Ekspluatatsii, Lyotnikh Ispytaniy i Dovodki*)

ODVF Society of Friends of the Air Fleet (*Obshchestvo Druzey Vozdushnogo Flota*)

OTB Special Technical Bureau (*Osoboye Tekhnicheskoye Byuro*)

RKKVF Workers' and Peasant's Red Army Air Fleet (*Raboche-Krestyanskiy Krasniy Vozdushniy Flot*)

RVS Revolutionary Military Council (*Revolyutsionniy Voenniy Sovet*)

STO Council of Labour and Defence (*Sovet Truda i Oborony*)

TOZ Tula Armament Factory (*Tulskiy Oruzheyniy Zavod*)

TsAGI Central Aero and Hydrodynamics Institute (*Tsentralniy Aerogidrodinamicheskiy Institut*)

UMVL Directorate of International Air Routes (*Upravleniye Mezhdunarodnykh Vozdushnikh Liniy*)

UVVS Air Force Directorate (*Upravleniye Voenno-Vozdushnykh Sil*)

VVS RKKA Workers' and Peasants' Red Army Air Force (*Voenno-Vozdushniye Sily Raboche-Krestyanskoy Krasnoy Armii*)

Introduction

The book in your possession is about the fate of British and American aircraft in Russia between the years 1906-1940, and their influence on aircraft manufacturing in the country.

Five periods can be identified in this timeframe, all of which have their characteristic features. The first is from the birth of aviation in Russia up to the outbreak of the First World War. Then, Russian aviation was almost completely under the influence of the French. The proportion of aircraft acquired in Great Britain and the USA was very small. These flying machines had no bearing on aircraft manufacturing in Russia.

The second period encompasses the years of the First World War. Russia fought this war on the side of the Entente. The front needed a large number of aircraft, significantly more than the still poorly developed indigenous factories could produce. Purchasing of aircraft increased sharply in America, but the aircraft types selected were, for the most part, unsuccessful, and were all but unused in combat. Deliveries of aircraft from Great Britain began in 1916. Up until this point the Russian Army had predominantly been using French aircraft. Large batches of British aircraft arrived in Russia after the abdication of Tsar Nicholas II in February 1917, under the Provisional Government. Comparatively few British reconnaissance aircraft and fighters made it to the front line before the Bolsheviks took power at the end of October. Up until that time the factories in Petrograd and Moscow had been engaged in preparing to manufacture Sopwith 1½ Strutter and DH.4 aircraft under licence.

The third period is the Civil War. The red forces, led by the Bolsheviks, fought the whites, supporters of the previous regime. In different parts of Russia governments of all sorts of denominations were formed – from advocates of absolutism to liberal democrats, and they created their own armies. In addition to them, there were the blatant criminals who were looking to take a little of the power and the money in all the confusion. Great Britain played an active role in this war on the side of the whites, acting both as part of the white forces, and assisting the white armies, supplying them with arms and equipment, as well as military advisers and instructors. In terms of white aviation, British aircraft were predominant over French machines. The reds had significant numbers of British aircraft as well, both those that had been obtained from the old army, and trophy machines. There were also British aircraft that had been manufactured in France. The Americans also sold aircraft to the whites, but these were very few in number. The reds only acquired a handful of examples of these aircraft, which were captured beyond the Ural Mountains.

The fourth period was the post-war resurgence of aviation in Soviet Russia (subsequently the Soviet Union). During the Civil War very few aircraft were manufactured in Russia, and the available airplanes were patched up. When the fighting came to an end, only obsolete and worn-out aircraft remained in service. As production could not grow rapidly, the Soviets resorted to purchasing the equipment from abroad. The largest number of these aircraft was acquired from Great Britain. They enabled the old flying machines to be taken out of service. The manufacture of British aircraft in Russia, however, had a far greater significance. The 1½ Strutter and the DH.4 were the first to be assimilated into production without assistance from the West, and preparations for manufacturing these aircraft had begun under the Provisional Government. At that time indigenous modifications began to be undertaken to trophy Avro 504s (as the U-1) and DH.9As (as the R-1).

The last of these became the most widely produced aircraft in Soviet military aviation almost up until the mid-1930s. It was these types that enabled import of aviation technology from abroad to be rejected. A lead article in the *Dayosh Motor* magazine in January 1925 stated: 'it is impossible to build a powerful Red Air Force fleet using aircraft purchased from abroad'. In fact, by the mid-1920s the Soviet Air Force was almost exclusively operating indigenously manufactured aircraft. Apart from that, some aircraft types had been purchased in Great Britain in small numbers so they could be studied.

The fifth period was one that saw rapid development of Soviet aviation and aircraft manufacturing. From the beginning of the 1930s the factories were producing original aircraft designs, which did not bear the imprint of having been borrowed, as they had done previously. Licences were obtained abroad for engines, as well as various kinds of equipment, but overall, the aircraft were purely Soviet. Between 1930 and 1940 a very limited number of British flying machines arrived in the Soviet Union. They were destined solely for studying the experience of the foreign colleagues. After they had been examined and tested, individual components, and some successful design solutions were copied, but not entire aircraft.

At the same time in the Soviet Union there was a great deal of interest in the state of aircraft manufacturing in the USA, which had quickly assumed the position of a world leader. American aircraft manufacturers could not break into the Soviet market for a long time because of political restrictions imposed by the government. Under President F. Roosevelt, however, the 'flood gates were opened'. Soviet aircraft designers were frequent visitors to the USA. They began to view America as a more developed partner in the aviation field. In the end this led to a large-scale campaign on the part of the Soviet Union to acquire licences for a whole series of new American aircraft, both military, and civil. Although only one aircraft type was put into mass production at Soviet aircraft factories (the famous DC-3), and a further two were produced in limited numbers, the significance of these acquisitions was enormous. Along with the drawings and the examples of these aircraft, there was new equipment, documentation on advanced technology, and unfamiliar materials and components, which became examples for Soviet specialists. All this went a long way to developing aircraft manufacturing in the Soviet Union in the years leading up to the Second World War. This period actually came to an end after the outbreak of the Soviet-Finnish War, which caused a rapid deterioration in relations between the USSR, Great Britain, and the USA.

The structure of the book overall corresponds to the periods set out above. The first three periods are intertwined so closely with one another that they have been combined into a single chapter. In terms of the fifth period, separate chapters have been created for English and American aircraft, in view of the large amount of material. Within these chapters sections have been created on the individual types of flying machines, or the families they belong to. In cases where the history of a given aircraft, or family of aircraft, has gone beyond chronological boundaries, for the sake of completeness this has been given in full, which has in some cases meant going to the end of the 1940s.

The author would like to extend his sincere thanks for the help in preparation of this book to the following persons (in Russian alphabetical order): E.N. Arsenyev, N. Eastaway, S.M. Kaminsky, S.D. Kuznetsov, V.G. Kulikov, O.Yu. Leiko, M.A. Maslov, E.A. Melnikova, C. Owers, B.L. Osetinsky, G.F. Petrov, V.G. Rigmant, G.O. Sloutskiy, A.A. Firsov, N.V. Yakubovich, A.A. Yurgenson. Aircraft scale drawings and colour side views were prepared by Andrey Yurgenson.

1

The Period from the Birth of Aviation in Russia up until the End of the Civil War

Originally, the author wanted to divide this section into three: the period leading up to the First World War, the First World War itself, and the Civil War years. Then the author understood that this was all closely connected. The aircraft that Russia acquired prior to the First World War frequently participated in combat activities against the Germans, Austrians, and Turks. The same types were supplied to the tsarist regime, then to the Provisional Government, and finally to white generals, who were supported by the Entente nations. At the same time these aircraft were taken by red aviation from the storages belonging to the old army, and were then augmented with trophy aircraft, captured from the whites. In the Civil War both sides would often use one and the same aircraft types, which fought against one another. In view of the fact that everything was so closely intertwined, the author decided to combine it into a single chapter, grouping it into sub-sections on the aircraft families, and the companies that created them. Texts about the DH.4 and DH.9 reconnaissance aircraft and the Avro 504 have been deliberately placed outside the boundaries of this chapter. This is linked to the fact that they played an important role in Soviet aviation in the first half of the 1920s. Their significance was greater at that time than during the Civil War.

How did this all begin? The first proposal to supply aircraft to the Ministry of War of the Russian Empire came from America. In spring 1906 Wright brothers sent a letter to St Petersburg with such proposal. This letter, however, was given little attention.

Only in 1909 did the Russian generals decide to acquire Wright biplanes, not in the USA, though, but in France. This country had rapidly broken into the ranks of the world leaders in aviation. At that time France made the world's best aircraft, and the best engines. Unsurprisingly, it was France that was Russia's main and long-term partner in the creation of Russian aviation. The majority of the equipment for land-based military aviation was imported from there. Engines and instruments were purchased there, and it was in France that the first pilots were trained. Russia's aircraft factories began to work under French licences, the French created branches at their enterprises, which for the most part produced engines. British aviation at that time conceded quantitatively, and qualitatively to French aviation. Correspondingly, purchases from Great Britain were few in number. The only aircraft brought from there was a small batch of Bristol Boxkite training aircraft in 1911. In America, although it was the birthplace of aviation, progress was also slower than in France. Russian representatives were only interested in the G. Curtiss hydroplanes. In December of that year an example of this aircraft was ordered. Up until the outbreak of the First World War the Russian fleet acquired a batch of Curtiss floatplanes, albeit a small batch.

By the start of hostilities in July 1914 Russia had quite a significant air fleet. With the rare exception, however, of the famous *Ilya Muromets* bombers designed by I.I. Sikorsky, these were aircraft either brought into the country from France, or which had been manufactured at indigenous aircraft factories based on French examples. Combat operations on a scale not seen before dramatically increased the requirement among the country's armed forces for flying machines. The Russian aviation industry, which was still poorly developed, could not meet this demand. The Tsarist Government turned to the allies, Great Britain and France, for help. In 1914–1915, however, their aircraft factories were overflowing with their own rapidly developing aircraft. Russia had to get by on its own resources for a while. The first attempt to copy a British design – the Sopwith Tabloid, not an especially military aircraft, relates to this period. This aircraft was manufactured but was not put into series production.

The Russian Navy were counting on the acquisitions they were making in the USA, which at that time had yet to join the war. They purchased a few batches (more than fifty aircraft in total) of Curtiss flying boats. At the start of the war, they were used quite actively on the Black Sea. However, the majority of contracts were for the Curtiss K, which performed poorly in operations and was quickly taken out of service. They were soon overshadowed by the M-5 and M-9 flying boats designed by D.P. Grigorovich. From 1916 onwards, no more American aircraft were acquired.

Large-scale deliveries of aircraft from the allies began in 1916. Aircraft were delivered by sea via Arkhangelsk and Murmansk. Significantly fewer British aircraft were delivered than French, and not one of these types was widely used in Russian aviation. The FE.2b reconnaissance, and BE.2e spotter aircraft did see limited use on the front line. The Russian factories were also building, for the most part, French designed Nieuport, Farman, and Voisin aircraft. They constituted the bulk of the aircraft among front line aviation detachments and groups.

Only one British aircraft became truly widespread in Russia, and that was the Sopwith 1½ Strutter. This successful aircraft was sent from both Great Britain and France, where it was produced under licence. The Sopwith became a clear demonstration that the level of British aircraft manufacturing had grown. By that time other new aircraft had been put into battle on the Western Front – reconnaissance aircraft, light bombers, and fighters. British designers were comparable on their own terms with French designers, and in some ways they had already begun to surpass them. It was no accident that the 1½ Strutter began to be manufactured in France as well. Unfortunately, they only began to arrive in Russia in spring 1917, and the country by that time was under the Provisional Government. Comparatively few of these aircraft made it to the front line. From the Sopwith Triplane fighters that also arrived in the autumn of that year, only a handful of these machines were used in combat.

The rapid progress achieved by British aircraft manufacturers led to the Russian factories starting to acquire licences for British aircraft, and in doing so they destroyed what had been up until that time almost a monopoly among the French industrialists in the Russian market. Preparations were made to produce that same 1½ Strutter, and the new de Havilland DH.4 reconnaissance aircraft. An almost complete set of documentation was delivered for the former, and a partial set for the latter.

The Provisional Government, which was led by A.F. Kerenskiy, began negotiations to supply American combat aircraft in summer 1917, but they never completed this order. In October, the Bolsheviks took power in Petrograd, and then across a large swathe of the territory of Russia. The demoralised Russian Army almost collapsed. The Germans, the Austro-Hungarians, and Turks went on the offensive. A period of political and economic chaos ensued. On the fringes of the country local governments started to appear one after another that had the widest variety of political affiliations. Finland, the Baltics, the Ukraine, and the Caucasus fell away. By December 1917 the detachments under the Cossack Ataman G.M. Semyonov launched combat operations against the Bolsheviks in the Transbaikal region.

Following the insurgency of the Czechoslovak Corps, which was organised by British and French intelligence operatives, the Civil War flared up. This corps had been formed in Russia and was made up of soldiers and officers of the Austro-Hungarian Army who were prisoners of war and was readied for deployment to the front line. After the revolution, the corps retained its neutrality for some time, but in summer 1918 they fought on the side of the whites, capturing important junctions on the Trans-Siberian Railway.

Admiral A.V. Kolchak had massed his entire army in Siberia, in the south the Armed Forces of the South of Russia, under the command of Lieutenant General A.I. Denikin, was steadily being formed. The Entente nations sent their troops to Russia. Great Britain was the most active of all the other nations in the intervention. Without formally declaring war on Soviet Russia, from March–August 1918 they *de facto* captured the North-European region of the country, and in the autumn they captured part of Azerbaijan, Georgia, and Central Asia. In these areas puppet governments were formed with their own armed forces. From November 1918 the British Navy conducted operations against the Russian Baltic Fleet, which included using hydroplanes.

The Americans took part in the intervention in the north and in the Far East, but the scale of the American interference was much reduced; their aircraft were not drafted into operations in Russia.

Only the European part of Russia remained under the control of the Soviet Government, the Council of People's Commissars. A stubborn struggle for power began. The country was divided into the reds, the supporters of the Bolsheviks, and the whites, their enemies, among which were the most diverse forces – from fanatical supporters of autocracy, to liberal bourgeois democrats. Russia was caught up in the Civil War for some considerable time.

The Entente actively supported the whites. British units, including aviation units, fought on their side directly. In autumn 1919, following the elections, which the conservatives lost, the British Government decided to withdraw its forces. British support for the white armies, however, first and foremost General Denikin, and then Lieutenant General Baron P.N. Wrangel, who replaced him, continued up until spring 1920. In total the whites were supplied with several hundred British aircraft (according to calculations by British historians this figure was 134). These were more modern machines than those that had been sold to Russia prior to the October revolution. The whites had been supplied with a number of the DH.4, DH.9, and RE.8 reconnaissance aircraft and light bombers, which had proved themselves well in the West, as well as Camel, and SE.5 fighters. Considerably less of the F.2B, Pup and Snipe fighters arrived. These aircraft, however, had been taken from the storages that were left over from the First World War. Some of them arrived incomplete, and with non-functioning armament. They were not gifts either: supplies of different sorts of raw material and grain were required in response.

As they withdrew, the British squadrons left their Fairey III and Short 184 hydroplanes in Russia. Apart from that, the whites used some aircraft that were manufactured in

Britain and which had been captured from the reds or stolen by deserters (the latter were by no means a rarity at the start of the Civil War).

American supplies to the whites were limited to just 28 unarmed LWF V biplanes, which were sold to the Czechoslovak Corps. Subsequently, the Czechs sold some 18 of these aircraft to Kolchak's army. These machines saw limited use on the front line.

The reds got a considerable proportion of Russian Army aircraft, and the majority of storages in the rear. A great many 1½ Strutters were in them, and by the beginning of the Civil War they had become one of the most widespread aircraft types in the Workers' and Peasant's Red Army Air Fleet (RKKVF, *Raboche-Krestyanskiy Krasniy Vozdushniy Flot*). The British aircraft were subsequently captured by the Red Army as trophies. In view of the fact that the aircraft factories in central Russia could not provide the red units with the required number of airplanes, anything that could get airborne was sent to the front line, including trophy aircraft. Rarely was a detachment (which had six aircraft in its line-up) was comprised of one and the same aircraft type. Both sides employed British and a small number of American aircraft, right up until the end of the Civil War.

Pilot N.E. Popov standing next to the Wright biplane, 1910.

1.1 Wright Airplanes

The famous Wright biplanes became the first American airplanes in Russia. None of these aircraft, however, was manufactured in the United States of America.

As already stated above, back in the spring of 1906 the Wright brothers offered their aircraft to the Russian Ministry of War. In their letter they even agreed to abstain from selling their aircraft to other states for some time, if the Russians were the first to conclude an agreement. In the Russian Ministry of War, however, this approach by the Americans was ignored.

Two years later the ministry nevertheless decided to acquire Wright A aircraft, not in the USA though, but in France, where the Ariel company were manufacturing them under licence. They paid 15,000 roubles for one aircraft, but during flight-testing in 1909 in France this machine crashed; the pilot was killed. The company offered to produce two new aircraft to replace it.

In April 1910 the aircraft, together with their accompanying pilot N.E. Popov (who was Russian but was a permanent resident in France) arrived in St Petersburg. The aircraft had been fitted with 30hp Wright engines, which had been produced under licence by the French company Bariquand et Marre. Almost immediately Popov took part in the 'aviation week' events in the Russian capital, first in one aircraft, and then in another. The aircraft had to be changed because of failures, they both sustained damage in different forms.

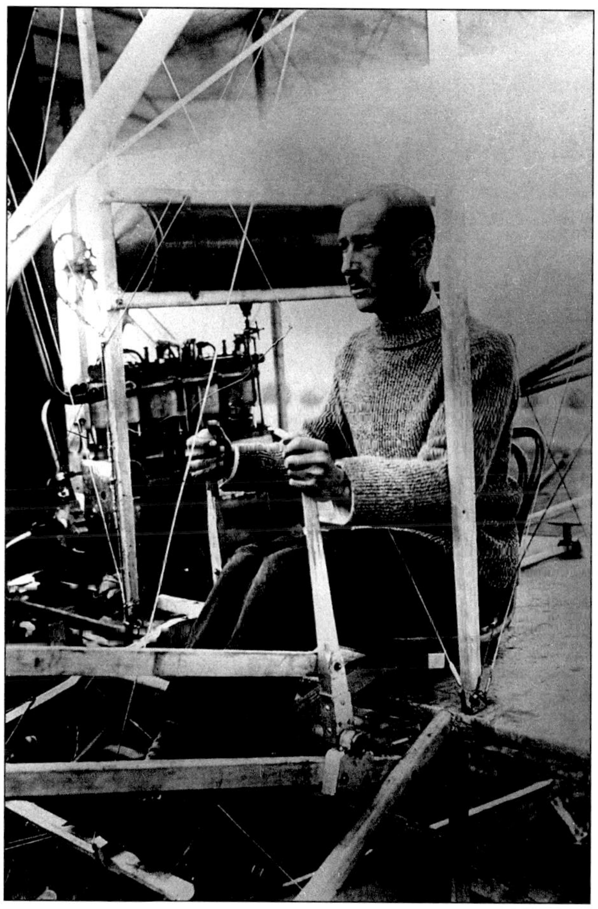
N.E. Popov sitting in the pilot's seat: the 30hp Wright engine is clearly visible.

The Wright A airplane were already considered by many to be obsolete, and conceded significantly to new French designs. They criticised the launch from a special rail and the landing on skids that would often break. The Aero i Avtomobilnaya Zhizn magazine wrote: 'it is just a shame that Popov is flying such a clumsy and obsolete flying machine as the Wright biplane ... Compared to the newest, more refined aircraft, the Wright biplane looks just as strange as a bicycle with one large, and one small wheel, against modern bicycles.' Nevertheless, Popov took second place overall and won prizes for the longest flight duration, and the highest altitude.

A French-made Wright airplane airborne at the Aviation week in St Petersburg in April 1910. Note the attendee's number in this competition visible on the fin.

The Wright A aircraft were intended to be used to train Russian pilots, who had gathered for training at Gatchina outside St Petersburg, where the School of Aeronautics was situated. This plan, however, did not come to fruition. On 21 May Popov performed a demonstration flight in front of the students at the school. Just before he landed, the engine failed, the machine fell sharply from an altitude of approximately four metres and struck a hillside. The airplane and the engine were completely destroyed; the pilot was seriously injured. A journalist from the Vozdukhoplavatel magazine wrote: 'as it crashed the flier's head punctured the underside of the aircraft'. Popov sustained a broken thigh, as well as injuries to his head, and his rib cage. A doctor, who happened to be nearby, administered first aid to him. Without waiting for an ambulance carriage, the injured Popov was loaded into a horse drawn cab and taken to the palace hospital. Popov made a full recovery approximately six months later.

Popov's accident on 21 May 1910 in Gatchina; on the upper left is a portrait of the pilot.

The French flight instructor Gobert began to fly another aircraft. However, almost immediately shortcomings with the machine came to light: its low power-to-weight ratio, poor stability, and control difficulties. The Ministry of War did not order any more Wrights in France.

In autumn of 1912 V.M. Abramovich made a flight in a Wright airplane from Berlin to St Petersburg. While he was a Russian national, Abramovich was the chief-pilot of the German company Flugmaschinen Wright, which just like Ariel company had acquired the rights to produce the American biplane. The Germans had updated the aircraft design significantly. The German Wright was given an elongated tail truss with an altered tailfin, and wheels in addition to the skids. The aircraft was fitted with what was for its day a powerful 90hp NAG engine. This version was sometimes referred to in Russia as the 'Abramovich Wright'.

Abramovich competed successfully in the 3rd military aircraft competition, which was held in St Petersburg. This led to a contract being signed with Flugmaschinen Wright in November 1912 for delivery of six combat, and two training aircraft, with a total cost of 114,000 roubles.

V.M. Abramovich in the Wright biplane fitted with an NAG engine.

Abramovich with Russian officers at the airfield in St Petersburg, autumn 1912.

Pilots standing next to an 'Abramovich Wright' biplane at the flying school in Gatchina.

The aircraft were ready by the summer of 1913. They were accepted in Berlin at a ceremony attended by *Shtabs-Kapitan* Gotovskiy. After they had been test-flown the aircraft were packed in crates and sent to Gatchina. They were used there for some time as training aircraft.

Attempts were made to set up production of the Wrights in Russia too. In March 1910 the Riga-based *Motor* factory acquired a single aircraft in Germany. Under the leadership of engineer T. Kalep this factory produced its own biplane in Riga that was based on the German machine. This aircraft differed from the prototype in the design of the tailfin, and the fitting of wheels on the skids. The Wright engine was not just copied, but was updated, bringing its output up to 35hp. M. Trautman made the first flight of this version of the Wright, manufactured in Riga, on 11 January 1911. The airplane, however, was not

This 30hp Wright engine, manufactured in Riga, is exhibited at the Central Museum of the Russian Air Force in Monino.

successful, orders were not forthcoming for it, and only the one example of this machine existed.

1.2 Curtiss Hydroplanes

In March 1911, the naval attaché Vasilyev wrote from Washington to St Petersburg about the work of G. Curtiss, who had successfully produced floatplanes. In January of the following year Lieutenant I.I. Stakhovskiy in Antibes (France) was able to familiarise himself with this American aircraft (he even flew on one of them as a passenger) and recommended they be acquired in place of the French Voisin Canard, which was planned as the initial choice.

Prior to this, however, in December 1911, the Main Engineering Directorate of the Russian Army ordered a two-seat floatplane from Curtiss that was also fitted with a wheeled undercarriage. The aircraft was intended for familiarisation, and this was the first amphibian to be seen in Russia. The hydroplane arrived in St Petersburg by sea, where it was assembled in the presence of company representatives. American pilots H. Robinson and E. Gode test-flew the aircraft. In May 1913 Captain Aleksandrov participated in the third 'aviation week' event in St Petersburg flying this aircraft.

It is entirely natural that the navy would be interested in hydroplanes, rather than the army. On 29 February 1912 the Russian navy ordered three first floatplanes from Curtiss: one single-seat Curtiss D, and a pair of two-seat Curtiss E aircraft. A further two orders followed on from this one, on 3 August 1912 and 2 June 1913. All these aircraft were destined for the Black Sea Fleet.

The first three Curtiss airplanes were unloaded at the port of Libava (now Liepaja). They were later delivered by rail to Sevastopol. Two Curtiss E aircraft arrived there in July, whilst in September it was the turn of the Curtiss D.

The Americans, pilot Ch. Witmer and mechanic J. Hallett, assisted the Russian naval pilots in their assimilation of the first three aircraft. On 10 July the first Curtiss flew over Sevastopol. Witmer immediately set about training the Russian pilots. On 28 July *Michman* V.V. Utgof made the first solo flight. Two days later the first accident took place. That same Utgof struck the cruiser *Kagul*, but the aircraft itself only sustained minor damage and the pilot was unhurt.

The Curtiss hydroplanes turned out not to be very stable in flight, but they handled well. Their seaworthiness was assessed as being sufficiently high.

In total, the Black Sea Fleet received six type E aircraft, and two type D machines. Deliveries of these floatplanes came to an end in autumn 1913.

In that same year the transport ship *Dnepr* was converted into a hydroplane carrier as an experiment. A 'shed', or hangar, was built on its deck. The ship was designed to carry three Curtiss aircraft. On 26 August the first machine

The Curtiss amphibian, a single example of which was purchased in 1912.

Pilots of the first hydroaviation unit of the Baltic Fleet stand next to a Curtiss amphibian.

A two-seat Curtiss E floatplane on a beaching trolley.

A Curtiss D hydroplane flying alongside a cruiser.

was loaded onto the deck of the *Dnepr*. Attempts to lower the aircraft onto the water and take off, however, were not successful: either the canvass on the wings got wet, or the engines were flooded.

In that same month the American hydroplanes were demonstrated to Tsar Nicholas II, who had visited Sevastopol on his yacht *Shtandart*. Five aircraft took part in these demonstration flights.

In January 1914 attempts were made to accommodate the Curtiss machines on the cruiser *Kagul*. The aircraft were successfully raised onto the deck, and were lowered down onto the water, but no information is available concerning flights in these aircraft. Evidently, at that time hydroplanes were only operating from shore.

The pilots trained reconnaissance, mine detection, surface ship and submarine hunting, and bombing missions. On 24 February 1914 Lieutenant N.A. Ragozin dropped a live bomb for the first time on a training target, a circle of floating barrels. From 13 July in connection with the deterioration in the international situation the Curtiss aircraft began constant sea patrols around Sevastopol.

By that time seven aircraft remained – one had been seriously damaged whilst landing in fog on 14 February 1914 and was written off. The other floatplanes were already very worn out and had been repaired more than once.

On 19 July 1914 the First World War began. The value of the American aircraft in combat was not so high. Their low speed, small payload, very low service ceiling (just 500–700m) did not place them in the best light. Russia though had to use what was to hand.

Lifting a Curtiss D hydroplane onto the cruiser Kagul.

A Curtiss N flying boat in Sevastopol.

In August, two aviation units were formed with two Curtiss aircraft in each. One of these was sent to Batum (now Batumi), while another was sent to the Danube estuary. By the middle of August, they had been returned to Sevastopol.

On 16 October the German battleships led by the battlecruiser the SMS *Goeben* fired on the city. *Michman* B.D. Svetukhin took off on a reconnaissance mission. He spotted the *Goeben* as it was traversing the Khersones lighthouse. On that day naval pilots flew a further 25 reconnaissance flights, but they did not make any attempts to bomb the enemy ships.

At the beginning of November 1914 four hydroplanes remained in service, and two of them were fitted with bomb racks. By the end of the month just one serviceable aircraft was left.

The final Curtiss floatplane on the Black Sea was lost at the beginning of 1915. The wing destroyed in flight, the aircraft crashed into the sea, and the mentioned above pilot Svetukhin was killed.

By that time other Curtiss aircraft were operating on the Black Sea, and they were flying boats. Back when the third contract had been signed for floatplanes a single Curtiss F flying boat was included in it. This was a biplane with an engine mounting beneath the upper wing and which was fitted with a pusher propeller. Its flight-performance characteristics were a significantly improvement on those of its floatplane predecessors. Acceptance tests with this airplane took place in Sevastopol on 16 September–13 November 1913, and it was G. Curtiss himself who flew the aircraft. On the first

A Curtiss F and an M-5 belonging to the Aviation Training Unit of the Black Sea Fleet on the shore near Kacha.

Black Sea pilots on board of a Curtiss K flying boat.

A Curtiss K flying boat at the naval pilots training base in Baku.

A crew standing next to a Curtiss K flying boat, Sevastopol.

day he flew three familiarisation flights from the Bay of Kilen. The passengers took turns: the first was *Podpolkovnik* Muruzi, the second was Lieutenant Stakhovskiy, while the third was *Michman* Urgof. The *Vozdukhoplavatel* magazine wrote: 'the Curtiss distinguished itself in all three flights in terms of how smooth it was to fly'.

Russian pilots acknowledged that the aircraft was stable and was responsive to the controls. In terms of manoeuvrability and speed there was just no comparison with types D and E. It was much more comfortable for the crew as well, who sat in what was a cockpit, albeit a primitive one.

Successful tests led to an order for a further six flying boats. They differed from the one tested at Sevastopol in terms of their angled keel underside, as opposed to a flat

A Curtiss OX-5 engine, which, evidently, arrived in Russia along with one of the flying boats. It is now on display at the Central Museum of the Russian Air Force in Monino.

A base of the Black Sea Fleet hydroaviation at the Bay of Kilen in Sevastopol; in the foreground is a Curtiss E hydroplane, and further back is a Curtiss D.

underside, which was designed to enhance their seaworthiness. This batch of aircraft arrived in Sevastopol in March 1914 and the handover of Black Sea Fleet aircraft was completed in May.

A Curtiss K flying boat on the Bay of Kilen shore in Sevastopol.

Operations with the Curtiss F flying boats on the Black Sea revealed a series of shortcomings in their design. The hull bulkheads turned out not to be strong enough, as did the struts between the wings, and the propellers. The aluminium sheets, which formed the external skin on the underside, suffered very badly from corrosion. Therefore, some of the aircraft were subject to modifications. The flying boats received a new skin made up of copper plate or galvanized iron, new reinforced bulkheads were prepared, and the control cables were replaced with thicker examples. The flight instruments were modernised, specifically, the aircraft were fitted with compasses.

Following the outbreak of the First World War at the end of August 1914 an order was placed for a further five Curtiss F flying boats. However, in October the Black Sea Fleet only had six serviceable Curtiss hydroplanes. They all had bomb racks and bomb release mechanisms. On 24 November, one of these aircraft spotted the German light cruiser the SMS *Breslau* that was sailing towards Sevastopol accompanied by Turkish ships. Two Curtiss aircraft attacked, bombing the ships. They did not score any direct hits, but the enemy, who had lost the element of surprise, chose to turn back.

The flying boats were constantly patrolling the sea around Sevastopol. In August–September 1914 attempts were made to accommodate the Curtiss aircraft on the cruisers *Kagul*,

Members of the commission and trainee pilots on the day they take their exams; Kovedyaev and Essen are sitting in a Curtiss E biplane.

Almaz, and *Pamyat Merkuriya*. The vibration as the ship was firing its guns, however, turned out to be a problem, and this had a destructive effect on the fragile design of these aircraft.

This was solved by fitting out special seaplane carriers, which were known at the time as 'hydro-cruisers'. Three of these appeared in the Black Sea Fleet: the *Imperator Nikolay I*, the *Imperator Aleksandr I*, and the *Almaz*. Having taken 11 flying boats (which included six Curtiss F aircraft) on board they set sail for the coastal waters off Turkey. On 17 March 1915 aircraft launched from these hydro-cruisers bombed the port of Zonguldak. The crew under the command of Utgof, who was already a lieutenant, succeeded in blowing up a power station. Five aircraft bombed the *Irmingard* transport ship which was anchored at the port, and it sank. Destruction and fires were also prevalent around the railway station. All the Russian aircraft returned safely to their hydro-cruisers.

In addition to the deliveries from the USA, manufacturing of Curtiss F flying boats was also arranged in Petrograd. The factory belonging to the First Russian Society of Aeronautics, which was owned by S.S. Shchetinin, handed over one aircraft that had been written off, as an example. Based on the drawings that were reverse-engineered according to the dimensions of this aircraft, five similar flying machines were manufactured. They were also sent to the Black Sea.

In July–August 1915 the Curtiss aircraft, operating from the hydro-cruisers, participated in escorting the battleship *Imperatritsa Mariya* on her voyage from Odessa to Sevastopol, and then in naval exercises with a seaborne assault on Belbek. After that the American aircraft were replaced by the more modern M-5 flying boats designed by D.P. Grigorovich, which had better flight-performance characteristics.

Another Curtiss flying boat type operated on the Black Sea, the Curtiss K with a longer wingspan and a more powerful 150hp engine. The first order for two of these flying boats was placed with the Americans on 31 August 1914. Then a further five contracts followed, and in total these were for 46 aircraft.

Deliveries were made through Arkhangelsk and Vladivostok. By 16 May the first batch of flying boats had arrived in Sevastopol. During testing it emerged that the engines had been subject to insufficient refinement, so they had to be improved in situ. The fuselage, side floats, and the tailfin turned out not to be strong enough. The handover of these aircraft was delayed but, in the end, naval aviation did accept 10 aircraft.

Considering the shortcomings that had come to light, the Curtiss K airplanes were not accommodated on the hydro-cruisers. They only operated from coastal bases and what is more they did not give a good account of themselves. Accidents and fatal crashes followed one after another. On 2 March 1916 one of the flying boats made an emergency water landing at sea and sank; the crew were rescued. On 1 April another aircraft was destroyed on take-off in Kazachya Bay.

Pilot G.A. Fride sitting at the controls of a Curtiss E hydroplane.

The only land-based Curtiss KPL which arrived in Russia

The Curtiss K airplanes that were destined for the Baltic Fleet were not accepted into service. One flying boat ended up on the Caspian Sea region: at the beginning of 1916 this aircraft was transferred to a training base for naval pilots in Baku. There it made just three flights, after which it went in for repair. The majority of the 48 Curtiss K aircraft acquired by Russia never actually took to the skies. They were kept in various storages and gradually fell into disrepair. These aircraft did not see service in the Civil War.

On 12 April during a reconnaissance flight the nose of the engine crankshaft failed. The propeller broke through the crankcase, damaging the fuselage, and the aircraft left wing. What is more, as it bounced off it broke through the rudder control rods. Pilot I. Ozol, however, was able to land safely.

Following this incident, relations with the company immediately deteriorated. A decision was made to store the American aircraft.

On 29 August 1914 Russian representatives in America signed an agreement on the purchase of two large twin-engine Curtiss H-4 flying boats. They were required to pay 25,000 roubles for each of them. The order though was subsequently cancelled, and on 25 February 1915 it was resurrected. The requirements for these aircraft were changed several times. In total in Russia three H-7TB flying boats were assembled that were fitted with 160hp engines. They were shipped from the USA in April 1916. On 7 July the aircraft arrived at Sevastopol in disassembled condition. The first flight took place on 22 September and ended in a landing accident. On 12 October the second aircraft took to the skies. Unexpectedly, it entered a spin and crashed into the sea. Only *Podporuchik* Kasatkin, who had been sitting in the co-pilot's seat, survived.

Following the February revolution, the Provisional Government took Curtiss to court. In view of the political turbulence in Russia, however, the deliberations were protracted. In the end the settlement was not favourable.

Aside from the flying boats, Russia also imported from the USA a single land-based aircraft – a Curtiss KPL (acronyms for 'K Pusher Land') acquired in 1915. It had wings, an engine mounting and a tailfin from a K type flying boat, and which were built onto a modified fuselage and a wheeled undercarriage. Subsequently, a few batches of KPL fuselages were ordered for the flying boats that had already been purchased, of these some were fitted with ski undercarriage. A dozen of these fuselages arrived, not one of which were employed.

1.3 The Bristol – the First British Aircraft in Russia

The first British aircraft to end up in Russia were two-seat (where necessary they could accommodate a second passenger) Bristol Boxkite biplanes. They were larger copies of a well-known aircraft designed by Henri Farman. This machine was fitted with French 70hp Gnome rotary engine. The Ministry of War of the Russian Empire acquired nine (other sources give a figure of eight) of these aircraft for study purposes. One of them was shown at the First International Aeronautical Exhibition in St Petersburg. An article in the *Aero i Avtomobilnaya Zhizn* magazine noted that the Bristol differed 'in terms of the exceptional solidity of its construction'. In design terms it was a true copy of the Farman, and the English did not introduce anything new to this aircraft. Russian specialists noted the excellent serviceability of this aircraft and the strong undercarriage. The *Vozdukhoplavatel* magazine noted that 'in terms of the care taken over the finish and the choice of materials they probably exceed French standards'. British aircraft arrived at flying schools in Gatchina and Sevastopol, where they flew in 1911-1913.

At the aforementioned exhibition in St Petersburg a Bristol monoplane of 'some kind' was also present, which was fitted with a Gnome 50hp engine.

In Russian archive documents there is a mention of a 'Bristol aeroplane with a Gnome 80hp engine'. In May 1916 *Praporshchik* Gofman of the 27th Corps Air Unit flew this aircraft. It is possible to assume that this was a Bristol Scout.

Bristol aircraft were used during the course of the British intervention. In the autumn of 1918, the 72nd Squadron that was engaged in operations against the Turks just outside Baku had a detachment 'C' in its strength which was equipped with some kind of 'Bristol monoplanes'. Interestingly, in this case the British were not supporting the whites, but the reds! Since it was actually red units that were defending the city from the Turkish and Azeri nationalists. The enemy, however, turned out to be the stronger. Their forces broke through to the city and began to rob and slaughter the Armenians. The British pilots set fire to their aircraft, and evacuated.

Other combat aircraft manufactured by this company subsequently found their way into Russia right at the end of the Civil War. Forty F.2B fighters fitted with 275hp Rolls-Royce Falcon III engines were sold to the Polish Armed Forces. During the Polish-Soviet War in 1920 one of these fell into the hands of red army troops. On 15 October 1920 a Polish pilot of the 9th Squadron made an emergency landing due to a shortage of fuel behind Red Army lines and, having evaded capture, he returned safely to his own unit. The aircraft was captured and following some small repairs was handed over to the 1st Reconnaissance Squadron, 2nd Air Wing of the Western Military District, where it remained until the end of 1922.

A Bristol Boxkite biplane at the First International Aeronautical Exhibition in St Petersburg, 1910.

A Bristol Boxkite biplane at the flying school in Gatchina

A Bristol F.2B airplane from the Red Army 1st Combat Air Group, autumn 1920. The famous pilot I.U. Pavlov is sitting on the wheel.

A line-up of airplanes serving in the 2nd Air Wing at Post Volynskiy airfield just outside Kiev, September 1922. The first airplane on the right is a Bristol F.2B.

Subsequently, Soviet Russia acquired two fighter versions of this aircraft in Britain with the aim of studying them. As of 1 December 1922, one each of these aircraft were listed in the 4th Separate Fighter Squadron and the 2nd Fighter Squadron, 2nd Air Wing of the Western Military District. In December 1923 one serviceable and one unserviceable aircraft were listed in the inventory of the RKKVF fleet. By mid-1925, one fighter remained in service of the 4th Squadron. Subsequently, all the remaining F.2B aircraft were used as study aids at flying schools.

1.4 Airplanes of the Royal Aircraft Factory

At the end of 1916 eight (other sources put this figure at seven) two-seat FE.2b biplane fighters, manufactured by the

Royal Aircraft Factory and fitted with 160hp Beardmore engines, arrived in Russia. This batch was intended more for study and evaluation. Several airplanes in spring 1917 were assembled and tested at Khodynka Moscow airfield. By that time the FE.2b was already showing its age as a fighter. It was very heavy and demonstrated mediocre flight-performance characteristics, but it could easily replace the archaic French Voisin reconnaissance aircraft in Russian aviation. The order, however, never reached England. All the FE.2b aircraft were later transferred to a Moscow flying school.

One aircraft of this type survived up until the end of the Civil War. In 1922 it was used at the Theoretical School of Aviation, and later ended up in the air unit of the Higher School of the Red Air Fleet. This aircraft was listed as being at this location up until 1924, more than likely as a non-operational study aid.

The two-seat BE.2e reconnaissance aircraft and light bomber fitted with 150hp RAF.1b engine appeared at the end of 1916 when the Russian government acquired 30 of these airplanes. Russian pilots liked this aircraft, it stood out in terms of its excellent stability, light handling, and its ability to perform aerobatic manoeuvres. In July 1917 BE.2e aircraft joined the strength of the 2nd Artillery Air Unit, 11th Air Division, attached to the 11th Army of the South-Western Front. Five reconnaissance aircraft joined this unit, they were fitted with radio sets and were intended to correct heavy artillery fire. In the course of two months of operations the unit lost just one aircraft, and this was for non-combat reasons. On 28 August the BE2.e flown by the unit commander *Podpolkovnik* Vamelkin and observer *Shtabs-Kapitan* Bonch-Bruevich crashed. They flew into a storm cloud, and a gust of wind at an altitude of 500m put the aircraft into spin. The pilot pulled the aircraft out of the spin with difficulty, but at that moment a piece of the starboard aileron broke off. The crew perished along with the aircraft.

After two months of intensive operations three of the five BE.2e airplanes of the 2nd Artillery Air Unit required heavy repair. The airplanes were directed to the 3rd Air Depot workshops. On 20 October 1917, a further six of these aircraft were to be found at this location.

In the Civil War period both warring factions were operating a few BE.2e aircraft. Specifically, one airplane was used by the 28th Air Unit under the reds. Six BE.2e aircraft belonged to the 1st Photographic Unit. In April 1919 this was merged to become part of the School of Aerial Photography and Photogrammetry.

The Head of Aviation in the Tambov region A. Muratov had a single BE.2e (serial number 1215). Attempts were made to use this aircraft to combat local insurgents, but on 17 March 1921 during a flight over a river the engine failed. The pilot glided the aircraft onto a smooth landing ground but the wheels caught on a dam. The lower wing was damaged, as were the propeller and undercarriage. Muratov himself and engine mechanic Maksimov sustained bruises. No further information was found on the fate of this biplane.

At the end of the war several BE.2e airplanes continued to serve in the RKKVF. Two of these machines flew with the 51st Air Unit, and one aircraft was serving in the training unit of the *Ilya Muromets* Air Ships Division. By the beginning of the 1920s the aircraft were already worn out and needed heavy repair. In November 1923 at the *Aviarabotnik* factory in Petrograd (St Petersburg was renamed Petrograd under Tsar Nicholas II in September 1914) a new set of wings were manufactured for one BE.2e.

An FE.2b biplane, which was inspected by the Russian military attaché in Britain.

Pilots standing next to an FE.2b airplane, Khodynka airfield, 1917.

An FE.2b biplane of the Moscow flying school.

A BE.2e airplane on ski undercarriage during testing on Khodynka airfield in Moscow.

By the mid-1920s these British reconnaissance aircraft were obsolete, and a start was made on finding another use for them. Some of these airplanes were handed over for study and propaganda purposes to the Society of Friends of the Air Fleet (ODVF, *Obshchestvo Druzey Vozdushnogo Flota*). For example, a single BE.2e on 17 July 1924 from the Higher Auxiliary Services School (the former school of Aerial Photography and Photogrammetry School) was transferred to a branch of the Northern Caucasus division of the ODVF. On the undersides and on the rudder of this aircraft the letters R.K.K.O.D.V.F. were written (these denote the Russian for the Workers' and Peasants' Red Society of Friends of the Air Fleet). On 28 March 1925 this aircraft was on the airfield next to the village of Gnilovskaya.

Over this period the BE.2e aircraft served in Soviet Russia as an agricultural aircraft. In autumn of 1924 in the village of Tushino outside Moscow (today this is within the boundaries of the city) tests were carried out into spraying

A BE.2e of the Moscow Pilots School, 1916.

Praporshchik N. Bragin (left) of the 2nd Artillery Air Unit standing next to his BE.2e airplane.

dry chemical pesticides from the air. The chemical pesticides were poured into a special tank located in the front cockpit. The aircraft was fitted with an *Aeropyl* device, designed by engineers Ya.M. Mikhailov-Senkevich and G.I. Korotkikh. The spraying was conducted from an altitude of 10–20m. One fill of the tank (up to 150kg) was enough to spray an area of approximately 27 hectares with pesticides.

The BE.2e was also used at flying schools; these aircraft could be encountered at various airfields across Russia up to 1925.

A BE.2e, which was used as an agricultural aircraft. A tank containing chemical pesticides was installed in the front cockpit. Pilot K.E. Dedushchenko, wearing a protective mask, is sitting in the rear cockpit.

The other British reconnaissance aircraft, the RE.8, found its way to Russia later on, right at the height of the Civil War. This was also a two-seat biplane fitted with 140hp RAF.4a engine. These airplanes were supplied to the white armies, and the reds just had their trophy examples. The British handed over the first batch of 25 aircraft to the Armed Forces of the South of Russia under General A.I. Denikin on 22 June 1919. In total, approximately a hundred RE.8s (other sources put this figure at around 80) were supplied to Denikin. The white artillery divisions of the 3rd, 4th, and 9th Air Units were equipped with these airplanes, as were the 1st and 3rd Don Air Units.

In order to convert the Russian pilots onto the RE.8 and other foreign aircraft, a British study centre was set up in Yekaterinodar. Instructors Smith, Had, and Ritchie re-trained their Russian colleagues over the course of approximately two months. Over this period several accidents and fatal crashes took place. In three instances on 19, 21 and 24 August it was the British pilots who actually crashed the aircraft. Specifically, Smith put an RE.8 of the 4th Air Unit out of action in an aborted take-off. The unit commander's report stated: 'The aircraft has been completely destroyed and is excluded from the air unit's inventory.'

Operations with the RE.8 quickly revealed a series of its shortcomings: it was difficult to control, had insufficient lateral stability, was prone to enter a spin as it lost speed, and there was an increased risk of fire, which was caused by design defects in the fuel system. There were recorded cases of fire in flight and of inability to exit spin.

Eight Russian pilots lost their lives in the RE.8, which led to a legitimate bias against this biplane. For example, on 21 November 1919 pilot of the 3rd Air Unit Senior *Unter-ofitser* Stadnichenko with engine specialist Timoshenko in the rear cockpit, during a cross-country flight from Borispol to Post-Volynskiy entered a fogbank and stalled at an altitude of 150–200m, crashing into the ground. Stadnichenko was

A BE.2e biplane, which was used as a training aircraft at the *Ilya Muromets* Air Ships Division, standing next to a tent hangar in Sarapul, summer 1922.

Pilot Moshin and mechanic Shmelyov posing next to a BE.2e on a ski undercarriage before departing for the Western Front, early spring 1920. The port and starboard parts of the upper wing are painted different colours – it is possible that the airplane was assembled from parts of two airplanes.

An RE.8 aircraft, which was captured by the Red Army in Taganrog in early 1920.

killed, Timoshenko was seriously injured, and the aircraft was completely destroyed.

An interesting story is linked to one of the RE.8s, which was operating in southern Russia: as the Volunteer Army was retreating from Kiev, the 3rd Air Unit's train was left without a locomotive. The unit's entire inventory was under threat of being captured by the reds. Then the fuselage of one of the aircraft was fixed straight onto a railway flat wagon and the engine was started. This improvised locomotive pulled the wagons along behind it.

The situation was not resolved so successfully every time. When the whites abandoned Taganrog the red army troops discovered eight RE.8s that had been left there by the enemy, of these five were disassembled and packed in crates, as well as some spare parts.

The RE.8s were also in the inventory of the Slavo-British Air Corps, which was fighting the Bolsheviks in northern Russia. In autumn 1918 the Murmansk based British 'C' Flight, which formed part of this corps, was equipped with these aircraft.

Initially it did not play any part in combat operations as the front line was very far away. From October, however, the Flight commenced combat operations. On 13 November one of the RE.8s was shot down by rifle fire from the reds. The pilot succeeded in landing the powerless airplane safely in a small clearing in the forest. The crew wandered around the woods for four days before they came across a local peasant, who led the Englishmen back to the whites' lines.

An RE.8 at an exhibition of the Northern-Caucasus Division of the ODVF in Taganrog, late 1920s.

With the onset of the cold weather the activity of the British pilots reduced dramatically. The liquid cooled engines would prove difficult to start in the cold, and due to overcooling they would be unreliable in flight. By summer 1919 only four RE.8s remained in service. They were used in June in battles against the red 6th Army. The airplanes performed missions to correct fire from gun batteries around Kitsa and bombed vessels on the Severnaya Dvina River. What became of these aircraft following the evacuations of the interventionists is not known.

Red aviation aircraft on the parking area; on the right is a BE.2e.

In total the reds as it turned had up to three-dozen trophy RE.8s, which were known in Russia as *Arieyt* using the English pronunciation. One aircraft from those captured in Taganrog was quickly restored. Pilot S. Smirnov at the end of April 1920 flew the first combat sortie in this airplane against vessels of whites in the Sea of Azov. He dropped four 10-pound bombs on them.

Later *Arieyts* joined units in the Moscow and Ukrainian military districts (specifically, the 20th and 51st Air Units, and the reconnaissance squadron of the 1st Air Wing), but they hardly flew because the aircraft were thought to have poor flight-performance characteristics and were considered a fire risk.

During the Polish-Soviet War in 1920, the Poles captured a single reconnaissance aircraft. A crew from the Soviet 22nd Reconnaissance Air Unit of the South-Western Front failed to return from their combat sortie on 5 June. As it turned out later the biplane made an emergency landing behind the front line near Kiev and ended up in the enemy's hands. The Poles later took this aircraft to Warsaw in a disassembled state but were unable to repair it in view of serious damage the aircraft had sustained. Thus, this RE.8 became a trophy for the second time, as it had previously been used to convert pilots flying for the whites in Yekaterinodar and was captured by the Red Army as they took Taganrog.

Gradually a large part of the RKKVF airplanes of this type entered long-term storage. Thus, on 15 November 1920 one RE.8 without an engine was listed in the 1st Air Depot workshops awaiting repair.

By December 1921 some 22 RE.8s remained in service, but only a few of them continued to be used. In view of the service life of the British RAF.4a engines coming to an end, and the lack of spare parts for them, the aircraft began to be fitted with available 160hp Austro-Daimler engines.

The final aircraft of this type were withdrawn from the Air Force units in 1923. Subsequently the RE.8s that had reached a non-airworthy condition were used as study aids at flying schools and in the work of the ODVF. Officially the

An SE.5a fighter of the 6th Fighter Air Unit on the airfield.

Red pilot N. Vasilchenko, who was twice decorated with the Order of the Red Banner, standing next to his SE.5a fighter; Moscow, summer 1921.

An SE.5a fighter from the Air Unit of the 1st Cavalry Army, summer 1920.

RE.8s were taken out of Air Force service on 15 December 1925.

The single-seat SE.5a fighters fitted with 200hp Hispano-Suiza 8A engines also found their way to Russia in the Civil War period. The first of these were sent to a location near Baku in September 1918. 'A' Flight of the No. 72 Squadron RAF was partially equipped with these aircraft, however during the ferry flight all three were destroyed.

Then the British government began to supply the army led by General A.I. Denikin with these aircraft. The first batch of 18 fighters arrived from Egypt in October 1919 and a further six machines arrived in the December of that year. In total white aviation in the south of Russia received 24 SE.5a airplanes. They were used for some time on the front line against the reds.

During the course of the Civil War some of these airplanes became trophies of the Red Army. The first six SE.5as were seized in December 1919 during the capture of Taganrog. These aircraft turned out to be brand new, but it turned out that the British had dispatched these aircraft with unsuitable propellers. In total the RKKVF took 15 airplanes of this type, which were known in Russia as *Esifaif*.

Several Soviet SE.5 fighters participated in combat operations against Poland in summer 1920. Two of these were in service with the 3rd Fighter Air Unit. One of them was flown by pilot Petrenko and another by pilot Agishevskiy. Following the end of the Civil War, units in the Western, North-Caucasian, and Ukrainian military districts operated these aircraft. By 1922 the British fighters that remained serviceable were transferred to join the Fighter Squadron of

The SE.5a fighter flown by pilot G. Alishevskiy of the 3rd Fighter Air Unit; Sokologornoe airfield, Southern Front, 1920.

An RAF.1A engine, removed from a BE.2e aircraft, on display at the Central Museum of the Russian Air Force in Monino.

the 1st Air Wing. The last of these was written off in 1924. Officially the SE.5 was taken out of service under the decree of 15 December 1925.

1.5 Vickers Airplanes

In August 1915 a prototype of the Vickers ES.1 Bullet fitted with a 100hp Gnome Monosoupape engine, developed a speed of 183km/h at an altitude of 1,500m. This was a small wooden biplane that was offered as a single-seat fighter. It immediately caught the eye of the Russian military attaché. This sort of speed really was exceptional for that time and an order was forthcoming from the Russian government for 50 aircraft. Then, a further two prototypes of the modernised ES.2 were manufactured. They were fitted with the more powerful 110hp Clerget engines, and Rhone J engines rated at this same output were subsequently tested. In August 1916 an aircraft appeared that was designated the FB.19 Mk.I, which was produced in small numbers. Then the company transferred to the Mk.II version with 120hp Rhone Jb engine. The British military, however, did not show any great interest in this airplane – they were of the opinion that the visibility from the cockpit was poor, and the armament was weak. The fighter was not suitable for operations on the Western Front. A small number of aircraft that were accepted were used in peripheral theatres of war or as training aircraft. Vickers, however, wanted more.

In the second half of August 1916 this new fighter was demonstrated by the British Major Sitwell, initially in Petrograd, and at the beginning of September, in Kiev. On 4 September 1916 Grand Prince Aleksandr Mikhaylovich, who was in charge of Russian aviation, ordered that two fighters be sent for service testing to the 3rd Aviation Company just outside Kiev. At the same time a testing commission was set up under the chairmanship of *Yesaul* V.M. Tkachyov. A further four Russian pilots, *Shtabs-Kapitans* S.K. Modrakh, Nikolaev, E.N. Kruten, and G. Yablonskiy, who had been recalled from the front for this purpose, joined the commission. The tests were conducted on the airfield belonging to the Air Observers School in Kiev. On 9 September one fighter was sent to the military flying school in Gatchina to continue testing.

Test conclusions put a 'very good' mark to the British fighter and a decision was made to place an immediate order. The Russian Air Fleet command decided to purchase 400 airplanes from Vickers and to obtain a licence to manufacture this aircraft at Russian aircraft factories. A necessary condition, however, was the delivery from Great

One of the FB.19 airplanes that were supplied to Russia.

Praporshchik V. Anders of the 18th Corps Air Unit standing next to his FB.19 fighter, 1917.

Britain of the required number of engines, as engine manufacturing in Russia was lagging behind.

By the end of autumn 1916 the first batch of FB.19 airplanes arrived in Russia via the port of Murmansk. Unexpectedly, however, it turned out 'that the Vickers aircraft (20 in number) have arrived without their machine guns, they have, on their port side of the fuselage, space to fit Vickers machine guns, but the fittings and the machine guns are missing'. Grand Prince Aleksandr Mikhaylovich was informed of this on 16 November from the Moscow Air Depot, which was where aviation equipment delivered from abroad was usually brought.

This error, which was either the fault of the Russian administrators or the British company led to unarmed fighters being sent to Russia, which were not suitable for combat operations. Only at a significantly later date were machine guns and synchronisers received. This circumstance delayed the arrival of these new aircraft on the front line by almost a year. Only in mid-summer 1917 were they handed over to aviation units.

Two FB.19 aircraft in mid-July were handed over to the Fighter Detachment of the 18th Corps Air Unit, 10th Air Division of the Western Front. *Praporshchiks* V. Anders and F. Konyukhov flew them, but these machines were not popular and by October they had amassed just a few flying hours. In autumn both these fighters were transferred to the 10th Air Division's base for storage.

The British fighters were used more intensively in the 9th Fighter Air Unit, 9th Air Division of the Romanian Front. Two airplanes were sent to this detachment from the Moscow Air Depot on 14 July

1917. The renowned Russian ace *Praporshchik* G. Suk flew one of these aircraft. In August 1917 alone, he flew dozens of combat sorties with a total duration of 25hrs 5mins. On 20 August Suk won a victory in his Vickers, having shot down an Austrian Brandenburg reconnaissance airplane. A week later in that same fighter he destroyed another Austrian aircraft, an Aviatik. The Russian ace gave the British fighter an excellent evaluation: 'I am now flying a different type of fighter ... [up until that point he had been flying a Nieuport 21– author's note] The excellent machine gun mounting, and the 'push' if you like, is that the speed and rate of climb up to altitude are enormous. In comparison with this the Nieuport is just a 'cow' ... this aircraft though is something else! It can catch any German and force them to engage in combat, and until recently in the Nieuport I would rarely catch them, and then only in a dive.'

An FB.19 aircraft with its original British registration number A1968 on the vertical fin. This airplane survived the Civil War and in 1922 served in the 2nd Squadron of the 2nd Air Wing; by that time the original Clerget engine had been replaced by a Rhone.

Two FB.19 fighters of the 9th Fighter Air Unit on the parking area.

Another FB.19 was used by the pilots of the 9th Fighter Air Unit only for training flights and not for a long period of time. In October, both aircraft were handed over to the 1st Air Depot of the Romanian Front.

Thus, only four Vickers airplanes actually took part in the First World War on the Russian Front. Several examples arrived at the Moscow flying school but the majority remained in store. In the Civil War years some Red Army air units were equipped with them, as were the Special Purpose Air Group and the 39th Air Unit.

At the beginning of the 1920s the RKKVF was experiencing a serious shortage of aircraft. The majority of those they had were obsolete and were extremely worn out. Attempts were made to solve this deficit in any way possible and the air depot storages were completely 'cleaned out'. At the beginning of 1921 around a dozen FB.19 fighters were found in the Moscow Air Depot storage. Six of them were handed over to the 2nd Fighter Squadron, 2nd Air Wing, while the 41st Air Unit and No. 2 Air Squadron of Moscow Military District received one airplane each. Two Vickers in January 1921 were listed as being in service at the flying school in Yegoryevsk; one of them was removed a short while later – evidently this aircraft had been written off.

One more fighter fitted with a Clerget engine, which had previously been captured by the reds in Zabaykalsk from Ataman G.M. Semyonov's troops, was used in the 18th Reconnaissance Air Unit. On 2 September 1923 pilot Bocharov destroyed this airplane during an emergency landing next to the Ussuriysk railway line.

On 24 June 1921 demonstration flights were undertaken in Kiev. A Vickers aircraft flown by pilot Krivosheev unexpectedly broke up in mid-air and the pilot was killed. On 19 October 1923 there were four Vickers aircraft in service of the Ukrainian Military District Air Force, one of these was fitted with a Rhone engine, and the other three were fitted with Clerget engines. British registration numbers of two of these aircraft are known – A1968 and 4072/32. All

Airplanes from the Special Purpose Air Group before being sent to the front line, August 1919. Note Sopwith Triplane (first on the right) and FB.19 (third on the right) fighters.

Red pilots standing next to an FB.19 aircraft from the Moscow Pilots School; this airplane is unarmed.

A disarmed FB.19 biplane of the Moscow Pilots School.

these airplanes, however, were recorded in the documentation as being 'unsuitable' and were to be written off. As of 10 October, the 4th Fighter Squadron in Minsk had a 'Vickers 19' on its strength, and the engine of this airplane was replaced with a Russian made Rhone-120.

All the Vickers aircraft were taken out of service on 15 December 1925. They were in storage for some time but on 13 January of the following year an order was sent around the various units that these aircraft were to be written off.

Another Vickers aircraft, which had caught the attention of the Russian military agents was the experimental FB.16A fighter fitted with 150hp Hispano-Suiza engine. On 12 February 1917 this aircraft was tested at the company's factory airfield by the aforementioned Russian ace *Shtabs-Kapitan* E.N. Kruten, who at that time had been on a visit to England. The pilot, however, did not like this airplane. He remarked on the fighter's poor handling: if the control stick was pushed actively, the pilot was almost thrown out of the cockpit, or it had the opposite effect of pushing firmly back in the seat if the stick is pulled. 'On take-off the aircraft needs to be kept close to the ground for some time, while it gathers speed and becomes responsive. The aileron response is poor, it is unable to maintain 30–40 degrees of bank, either the wing stalls or it enters a spin, and the manoeuvrability is unsatisfactory.' It is no surprise that after such unflattering flight-performance characteristics no order was forthcoming from the Russian government for this aircraft:

Pilot I.N. Polyakov (left) with his mechanic standing next to an FB.19 fighter on the Moscow Pilots School airfield, summer 1919. Note a Sopwith Triplane on the left.

1.6 Sopwith Fighters

The first Sopwith aircraft to appear in Russia was the Tabloid. A copy of this biplane was manufactured in December 1915 at the Lebedev factory in Petrograd. Several aircraft of this type successfully passed factory testing and were sent to the front line, to the 21st Corps Air Unit. These airplanes were completely unarmed. Service testing of the type demonstrated this unarmed aircraft's poor effectiveness in air combat. As a result, Lebedev did not receive an order for series production of the Tabloid.

At the end of the First World War and afterwards, in the Civil War period, a relatively large number of different types of Sopwith fighters were brought to Russia. The Triplane entered Russia in autumn 1917, when the Russian Front had all but ceased to exist. As its name suggests, this was a single-seat triplane of a mixed construction, fitted with 130hp Clerget engine.

Only a few documents survive from that period. One of them notes that on 23 October 1917 the Commander of the 1st Fighter Air Unit K.K. Vakulovskiy asked the division command for a Sopwith as a reward for his service in combat. What is more, he agreed to accept the Triplane which nobody wanted. Just how many of these aircraft were brought into Russia is not known, but the whites did not have any of these machines in service. On the other hand, several of these airplanes were operated by the 1st Fighter Air Unit under the reds. The last Triplane was destroyed there in January 1920 on a training flight. A further Triplane was serving in the 11th Fighter Unit. At least one aircraft belonged to the Moscow flying school in January 1921. In December 1923 a Triplane, carrying the number 252/P, was undergoing repair at the *Aviarabotnik* factory.

One of these fighter aircraft was handed over to the Central House of Aviation and Chemistry in Moscow as an exhibit. It was suspended from the ceiling in one of the halls there for some time.

A Russian-made Sopwith Tabloid biplane.

One of the first Triplanes to enter Russia; this aircraft still carries British markings.

The Triplane has been towed out of the hangar at Khodynka airfield, summer 1917.

This same airplane on the airfield; it later found its way to the Moscow military Pilots School, and then to the AGON.

In the 1950s, in one of the old hangars at Moscow Central airfield a Triplane was unexpectedly discovered in factory packaging (in a crate) in quite a reasonable condition. This aircraft was assembled and handed over to the Air Force Museum at Monino. Unfortunately, the original (British) livery was irrevocably lost following an unsuccessful painting of the aircraft at the museum. The fighter armament and most of the instruments disappeared, while the aircraft wheels are now not 'original'. Even in this configuration, however, the aircraft still remains the centrepiece of Monino exhibition. This airplane has been used many times as a prop for making films about the early period of aviation.

All other Sopwith fighter types entered Russia during the Civil War years. They either arrived with British aviation units that were supporting the combat activities of the whites in the north and south, or they were supplied to various white governments.

General A.I. Denikin, who headed the Armed Forces of the South of Russia, ordered 18 Sopwith Salamander fighters, but did not receive a single one of them. On the other hand, in the south of Russia a number of Sopwith Pup airplanes were used. They were single-seat biplanes of mixed construction. The Pup had three versions with different engines, and it is not known which of these versions was brought to Russia. Likewise, the number of these aircraft that arrived in the country is also unknown, but it is unlikely to have run into a large number of examples. It is possible that the Pups were supplied to the whites in place of the Salamanders they had ordered.

The Red Army captured two of these fighters in 1920 when P.N. Wrangel was already leading the white forces in the south. The reds operated these trophy aircraft. A single Pup in May 1919 was in service with the 14th Reconnaissance Unit which belonged to the 10th Army; it was flown by V. Kuzmin.

A Triplane on a ski undercarriage at Khodynka airfield.

A Sopwith Triplane serving in the Moscow Military Pilots School, Khodynka airfield, winter 1921. The head of the school flew this airplane.

The whites in the south also had Sopwith Camel aircraft, which was a development of the Pup. According to various sources, between 29 and 40 of these airplanes arrived, so it became the most widespread Sopwith fighter type to enter Russia. The aircraft that were sent to Russia, however, were not new and were quite worn out, so the head of the British aviation mission requested that Russian pilots 'do not perform aerobatics in these British aircraft'. This, of course, significantly reduced the value of the Camels as fighters.

The first large batch of these airplanes arrived at Novorossiysk aboard the HMS *Engadine* transport on 8 May 1919. The 6th Air Unit received most of these aircraft (more than eight), five went to the 4th Don Air Unit, while the 1st Kuban Air Unit received one aircraft.

On 28 September 1919 three Camels took off from Yekaterinodar bound for Beketovka, but only two arrived, as the third crashed on the way. The damaged aircraft was loaded onto a railway flat wagon and was taken back to Yekaterinodar for repair.

The whites used the British fighters primarily for attacking infantry and cavalry, as well as for reconnaissance. For this purpose, the aircraft were fitted with racks for carrying small calibre bombs.

It was not only Russian pilots who flew the Camels. Flight B of the No. 47 Squadron Royal Air Force was equipped with these fighters in 1919, and they supported operations by the whites around Tsaritsyn. The Commander of the Flight was Captain S. Kincade. Initially the Flight's fighters were tasked to escort DH.9 bombers, but, using the advantage the whites had in the air, the Camels would often strafe enemy forces on the ground, as well as ships and vessels of the Volga-Caspian Flotilla. On 30 September, two red pilots D.V. Shchyokin and A.S. Korotkov in their old Nieuports

Pilot Yu.A. Bratolyubov in the cockpit of a Triplane, 1918.

The Triplane was exhibited hanging from the ceiling of the Central House of Aviation and Chemistry in Moscow for quite some time.

A Triplane on display at the Central Museum of the Russian Air Force at Monino.

attacked three Camels, the pilots of which were distracted with their strafing of targets on the ground. The element of surprise helped – and as a result of this short battle a single British aircraft was damaged and broke off combat. Captain Kincade, however, fired at one of the Nieuports from a short distance away. The aircraft crashed into the Volga River; the pilot Shchyokin went down with his airplane. This was the British pilot's 41st victory.

The Commander of 221st Squadron RAF Major Andrews had a single Camel fighter, fitted with 150hp Bentley BR.1 engine. This unit, which was equipped with DH.9 biplanes, was delivered by the *Riviera* steamer to Batumi, and was then taken to Petrovsk by rail and operated from there over the Caspian Sea coast. Interestingly, the rotary engine on the Camel started well even in freezing conditions, whereas it took up to an hour to pre-heat the Puma engines in the DH.9s.

As they withdrew from Russian territory the British units would usually hand over the still serviceable aircraft they had to the whites. This was also the case with the Sopwith airplanes. By the time the Red Army had completed the liberation of the south of Russia, however, the majority of the Camels had either been lost in combat, or had been destroyed in accidents and fatal crashes, or had been written off as worn out. What is known for certain is that in November 1919 four Camels were left to the Red Army troops in Taganrog. Almost all the aircraft of the 6th Air Unit of Volunteer Army, which were surrounded close to Grozniy, had to be destroyed. Three pilots of this detachment flew to Georgia in March 1920, where their aircraft were interned and then came under Georgian aviation. It is known that a Georgian pilot destroyed one of these aircraft in an accident close to Tiflis (now Tbilisi) later that same year. After the Soviet power had become established in Georgia, the other two aircraft became part of the 47th Air Unit, which belonged to the Red-Banner Caucasian Army Air Force and deployed in Navtlug. This unit was commanded by M.S. Machavariani, a former *Polkovnik* in the Tsarist Army and then the head of aviation in the newly independent Georgia under the Menshevik government. In autumn 1924 this unit was re-equipped with new aircraft, and the outdated airplanes were, evidently, written off.

The reds put one Camel that had previously belonged to Wrangel into battle to repel the advance of Wrangel's army in autumn 1920. This airplane became part of a temporary air unit, which had carried out raids on white ships in the Sea

The Triplane from Monino has been used on a number of occasions as a film prop during the making of films about the early years of aviation.

An officer from the British Mission standing next to a Sopwith Camel fighter from the 1st Kuban Air Unit of the Armed Forces of the South of Russia; Yekaterinodar, summer 1919.

of Azov. In particular, pilot Sivoglazov participated in these raids, flying this fighter on 7–8 October 1920.

The British used a small number of Camels in northern Russia. Five fighters with their British pilots were based in summer 1919 at Lyumbushy airfield not far from Onezhskoe Lake. They were to ensure air cover for a British hydroplane base close to Medvezhya Gora. As the red pilots did not make any attempts to attack this base, however, the fighters were used for reconnaissance and ground attack missions. During the course of one of the raids on Petrozavodsk pilot R. Sykes made an emergency landing due to an engine fire close to Lizhma village. This event took place on different dates according to various sources – on 29 August, or 31 August, or 4–5 September. The airplane became a trophy for

The Sopwith Camel flown by the British pilot Sykes, which was captured by red sailors following a forced landing near Petrozavodsk, 29 August 1919.

A Camel fighter captured from the whites, and which belonged to one of the red air units.

A Camel of the 34th Air Unit of reds, this biplane was flown by pilot P. Karpukhin, summer 1920.

the reds and was taken to Petrograd. There, it was directed to the Baltic Fleet aviation, joining a fighter unit based at Noviy Peterhof. The British fighter flew there until 1922. In April 1921 another trophy Camel was transferred to Moscow from northern Russia. It is possible that it was in this aircraft on 10 November that same year that pilot Tsitsilinimo caused the aircraft to wing stall due to piloting error, went into a dive and crashed.

One of the fighters captured in Taganrog later came into service of the Black Sea air force, joining the 2nd Fighter

A Camel from the 6th Air Unit of the Armed Forces of the South of Russia that had been flown to Georgia; this aircraft came under Georgian aviation.

An accident with a Georgian Camel close to Tiflis (now Tbilisi), 1920.

A former Georgian Camel that became part of the 47th Air Unit of the Red Banner Caucasian Army, 1923; evidently the biplane's propeller is damaged.

Unit. On 9 February 1923 pilot N.P. Romashkin destroyed this aircraft in a crash. On 5 October another Camel serial number 762 was sent there to replace the one that had been written off. In April 1922, the Baltic Fleet hydroplane depot stored two Camels, serial numbers 4055 and 4065. In January 1923 a Camel serial number 72/393 was undergoing repair at the *Aviarabotnik* factory in Petrograd. The order to take the Camels out of service completely came on 15 December 1925.

The most modern type of Sopwith fighters that entered Russia was the Snipe biplane, which entered series production in 1918. This aircraft was fitted with a powerful 230hp BR.2

A replica of the Camel biplane that was acquired in the USA for the Technical Museum of Vadim Zadorozhniy in Moscow.

engine. The Slavo-British Air Corps in the Russian north received six of these aircraft, and three of them entered service with a Russian squadron. In summer 1919 during the advance of the whites along the Severnaya Dvina River, they were used successfully as ground attack aircraft. Red pilots, who had been flying their old Nieuports did not have the courage to engage the Snipe in combat.

The Sopwith Snipe fighter flown by *Poruchik* Yakovitskiy of the 1st Northern Air Unit, which was captured by the reds in Arkhangelsk in February 1920.

On 1 August 1919 the famous Russian ace *Polkovnik* Aleksandr Kozakov (by that time he was a Major in the Royal Air Force) was killed flying one of the Snipes. He took off in a fighter that had only just been repaired. As he gained altitude the engine 'cut out,' and the aircraft went into a spin from an altitude of several dozen metres. He did not have enough altitude and the aircraft crashed into the ground near one of the airfield tents. Kozakov passed away shortly afterwards at the crash site, he had broken his back. The magnificent funeral of this hero of Russian aviation took place in Bereznyak on 4 August. It was not only soldiers and officers from Russian units who took part in this event, but also representatives of the allied nations, and the local population.

After the British had left, the 1st Air Unit of the Northern Front was formed which was manned by the Russian pilots. Only two pilots in this detachment had participated in combat sorties flying Snipe fighter at the end of 1919: Commander of the unit *Poruchik* Prince Tumanov, and the naval pilot Lieutenant Yakovitskiy. As the Red Army advanced the aircraft that were still airworthy became their trophies. The Snipe which had been flown by Yakovitskiy fell into the hands of the red ace G.S. Sapozhnikov. It was in this aircraft that he was killed on 8 September 1920. A.K. Tumanskiy wrote in

The Snipe flown by red ace G.S. Sapozhnikov, which was decorated with the Ace of Spades emblem, summer 1920.

Pilot G.S. Sapozhnikov standing next to his Snipe, the Central Air Group, Northern Tavriya, August 1920.

his memoirs: 'Sapozhnikov flew a wonderful trophy British Snipe with the most powerful engine at that time, which produced 220h.p.' Officially, the reason for this accident was given the same one as in Kozakov's case – an engine failure on take-off. Sapozhnikov had only gained 20m, when the engine 'cut out' and the biplane crashed into the ground. The pilot died because the machine gun breeches broke through his rib cage. But in the recollections of eyewitnesses, however, there is evidence that Sapozhnikov had not yet sobered up from the evening before. His mechanic tried to stop him taking off but the pilot, threatening him with his Mauser, forced him to start the engine. The fighter went into a steep climb, stalled, and crashed.

In April 1921 two trophy Snipes were delivered from northern Russia to Moscow. One of the last aircraft of this type was listed as serving under the headquarters of the 2nd Squadron, the 2nd Air Wing, at the end of 1922. Officially the Snipe was taken out of service with the RKKVF in 1925, the same time with the other Sopwith types. Subsequently these aircraft were used as ground-based study aids, or exhibits. Just one fighter was, evidently, an exception to this. At the end of 1925 the Moscow GAZ-1 aircraft factory received a Snipe airplane from the military for training flights by factory pilots. It is not known when this aircraft was written off.

All the mentioned Sopwith airplanes operated on wheeled undercarriage in summer and used a ski undercarriage in winter. In northern Russia, however, the British interventionists also operated fighter floatplanes. On 1 August 1918, as they were capturing Arkhangelsk, hydroplanes operating from the HMS *Nairana* hydroplane carrier carried out air strikes on the city and on coastal defences of the reds. Aside from the bombers there were two Sopwith Baby fighters fitted with floats aboard this ship. This was a version of the aforementioned Tabloid fitted with an 110hp Clerget engine and two short floats; a third float was attached to the tail section of the fuselage.

Both Baby fighters were subsequently assigned to the British river flotilla, which was active on the Severnaya Dvina River. The flotilla, which was led by Captain Altam, was made up of a monitor, two gunboats, two launches, and a tugboat. The latter towed a small barge behind it, on which the two floatplane fighters were accommodated (there was, however, only one pilot for these two aircraft), as well as mechanics, spare parts, fuel, and oil. In the forward section of the barge there was a crane, which was used to lower the hydroplanes down into the water and lift them on board once more.

The British river flotilla began its combat operations on 14 September, tasked with aerial reconnaissance. There is, however, no information available on the combat operations carried out by these Sopwiths. By 31 October both hydroplanes were listed in the reports as having been written off.

1.7 Sopwith 1½ Strutter

Significantly more widespread in Russia than the Sopwith fighters were Sopwith 1½ Strutters – two-seat reconnaissance airplanes and light bombers. This biplane received its unusual name due to the fact that its each half-box section of the wing had a pair of standard struts, and a pair of angled short struts, which could be considered as 'half struts'. These aircraft were not only supplied to Russia by the allies but were manufactured by factories in Petrograd and Moscow. The first airplanes of this type appeared on the Russian Front in spring 1917 when the country was ruled by the Provisional Government. The pilots of the 9th Army Air Unit, 7th Army, were among the first to receive them. In August of that year the new reconnaissance aircraft entered service with the 18th Corps Air Unit (which received two airplanes), the 35th Corps Air Unit (a single aircraft), the 6th Army Air Unit (five aircraft), and the 17th Corps Air Unit (seven aircraft). Several airplanes remained in the reserve at the 3rd Air Depot. These were all British-built machines, which had been ordered at the times of Tsar Nicholas II.

By the time of October revolution, the Russian aviation had approximately 100 machines of this type. A significant proportion of these, however, did not make it to the front line. They were either in warehouses in the northern ports,

Sapozhnikov's Snipe with its undercarriage damaged following an unfortunate landing.

in Murmansk or Arkhangelsk, or in storages behind the lines. Thus, in autumn 1917 in the Central Air Depot in Moscow, there were listed approximately 70 different British reconnaissance aircraft, and for the most part these were the Sopwiths.

In December 1917, when the Bolsheviks were already in power, a steamer arrived in the port of Arkhangelsk, which delivered 46 1½ Strutters that had been manufactured in France, and had been paid for by the Provisional Government. These aircraft differed slightly from those produced in Britain. As the Russian Front had, by that time, all but ceased to exist, the allies had requested that these aircraft be handed over to Romania. The representatives of the new order, however, decided to use them to equip the Red Army. They succeeded in transporting a significant number of the airplanes and engines from Arkhangelsk, including approximately three-dozen Sopwiths, prior to the outbreak of the Civil War in the north.

Earlier, under the tsar, the excellent flight-performance characteristics of the Sopwith reconnaissance aircraft led to a decision on its series production in Russia. Its manufacture was entrusted to the V.A. Lebedev factory in Petrograd. On 24 March 1916 Air Fleet Directorate ordered 260 1½ Strutters from this factory, which were to be fitted with 130hp Clerget engines. Without an engine, propeller, and machine guns each aircraft was to cost 13,700 roubles. The military paid Lebedev an advance that amounted to half the cost of the order. The factory was to start handing over the aircraft four months after receiving the documentation, the sample airplane, and after the work order had been drawn up.

A British made 1½ Strutter in Russia, 1917. As with many aircraft of British origin it wore the original markings and registration numbers.

For this purpose, the Russian government acquired a licence for the 1½ Strutters, and the drawings and other documentation for this aircraft began to be sent from Britain to Petrograd which arrived at the Lebedev factory in March 1917. One of the airplanes that had been purchased (registration number N3437) was used as a template, it was dismantled and measurements were taken. Almost immediately, however, problems emerged over a shortage of the required materials, which in Russia were either absent, or

A 1½ Strutter that had arrived from Arkhangelsk following assembly, next to a hangar at Khodynka airfield, mid-1917.

A British made 1½ Strutter at an airfield.

A Sopwith 1½ Strutter with Russian markings at the Moscow Pilots School, 1917.

were in very short supply. On 22 June 1917 the Lebedev order was reduced to 140 aircraft, the first 30 of which were to be handed over on 16 October.

Then the process of 'russification' of the 1½ Strutters began. On 31 July the factory was given permission, with spruce in short supply, to use a standard pine for a number of components. Specifically, use of this material was approved for the spars and the frame of the wingtips. The wing skids (semi-circular hoops) were to be manufactured from ash. The Palmer wheels were replaced with single Lebedev wheels of 760x100mm in size. On 2 October the military approved manufacture of landing flap (airbrake) control wheels from ash instead of celluloid. That same October, it was proposed that the spars be made composite instead of one-piece. The factory, however, did not receive a response to this. There was a new revolution underway in the country – on 25 October the Bolsheviks captured the Winter Palace, where the Provisional Government was housed. Lebedev converted all the money he had into hard currency and fled abroad. By that time his factory had manufactured the majority of the required components, but no work had begun on assembling the aircraft. Overall, the fulfilment of the order stood at around 65 percent.

The state bureaucracy continued to work for some time under its own inertia. On 8 November a new letter arrived at the factory, which gave permission for the use of wire instead of single streamline wire (or RAF wire), or cables instead of double streamline wires, with fairings made from linden.

The Bolsheviks, having taken power, announced Russia's withdrawal from the war and the transfer of the armed forces onto a peaceful footing. The order for the 1½ Strutters was cancelled, at the close of the year the acceptance commission was disbanded. This led to the work in Petrograd stopping for a long time, only resuming two years later.

The imported, foreign-made aircraft entered service of the first Red Army air units. Thus, in the 1st Socialist (all the first red aviation units were named 'socialist') Reconnaissance Air Unit comprising 25 aircraft there were four Sopwiths. On 30 December 1917 this unit was sent to the front line. Initially, the subdivision observed German troops around the approaches to Strugi, Belaya, and Pskov. Subsequently, the unit took part in clashes with the Estonians near Yamburg, and then began to fight the white Finnish forces near Vyborg. The Sopwiths performed liaison flights, carried out reconnaissance, and also bombed the German assault forces that had landed in Finland.

Crash-landed French-built Sopwith 1½ Strutter, which was used by the whites in North Russia.

A 1½ Strutter of the 1st Kuban Cossack Air Division of Denikin's army, 1919

A British made 1½ Strutter of the 1st Southern Air Unit, which came under the command of the Great Don Army. This biplane was captured by the cossacks in autumn 1918 after an emergency landing of red pilot Kuznetsov. Note German Hansa-Brandenburg reconnaissance airplane on the right.

The 3rd Socialist Air Unit had been reformed from the Kronstadt fortress air unit, and it was commanded by I.M. Savitskiy. This unit had 14 aircraft in service, including five 1½ Strutters. In November 1917 it was deployed in Tsarskoye Selo, and later carried out reconnaissance at Yamburg and Gdov. The unit also took part in raids on German troops in Finland.

On 1 April 1918 pilot Petrov in a Sopwith completed a Petrograd–Moscow flight. Close to Klin he entered cloud and only maintained his orientation with difficulty. It was almost nightfall by the time the aircraft arrived in Moscow. 'I had to land by touch', the pilot later commented. After he had landed, all he had in the fuel tanks were a few drops of fuel.

In the Civil War years, the 1½ Strutters were very popular aircraft. The reds and the whites both flew these machines, while the reds had higher number of Sopwiths. They managed to put into service the majority of British and French aircraft which the Tsarist and Provisional Governments had acquired. By summer 1918 the Soviets had more than a hundred 1½ Strutters in use. In terms of their

Personnel of the 31st Air Unit of the reds at the landing ground close to the station of Kresty just outside Pskov, January 1919. A Nieuport 17 fighter can be seen on the left, and on the right is a Sopwith 1½ Strutter.

A Sopwith 1½ Strutter of the 25th Air Unit of the reds, Eastern Front, November 1919. The airplane is decorated with red flags and ribbons celebrating the second anniversary of the October revolution.

Red pilots near Sopwith 1½ Strutter, South-Western Front, summer 1920. Note a Lewis machine gun mounted on the centerplane of the upper wing in a French style.

numbers 1½ Strutters held third place after the Nieuports and Farmans.

An interesting story is connected to these 1½ Strutter aircraft. In 1918 Chairman of the Council of People's Commissars V.I. Lenin decided to 'spur on' the global revolution, which to him at that time seemed not far off. An enquiry was sent to the RKKVF – what options were available for delivering and dropping leaflets over the capitals of Europe (Berlin, Budapest, and Vienna)? The capacity of the fuel tanks in the *Ilya Muromets* was more than enough to fly there and back but in view of the low speed and service ceiling, as well as the insufficient manoeuvrability the four-engine giant was very vulnerable both to anti-aircraft artillery, and to fighter attack. The preference was for the 1½ Strutter, which could fly over foreign territory at a safe altitude from the point of view of potential fighter attacks. It was true that the return journey, in view of a lack of fuel, would be impossible for this aircraft. Volunteers were found, however, who were prepared to give their lives for the cause of world revolution.

Six aircraft were prepared in the space of 10 days: three were to be sent to Berlin, and three to Vienna. Each of them was to carry a 'useful political cargo,' one or two *poods* each (16–32kg) of leaflets in German with calls to start a revolution. A week, however, was lost waiting for good weather and a tail wind, and then the Bolsheviks signed the Treaty of Brest-Litovsk with Germany, so the idea of using

Aircraft flown by pilot P. Karpukhin of the 34th Air Unit, which was destroyed and partially burnt out in an accident, summer 1920.

Aircraft of the 3rd Reconnaissance Unit of the 5th Army, Eastern Front, at the landing ground close to Innokentyevka station (another source gives this location as Innokentyevskaya) near Irkutsk, June 1920. Note a semi-assembled 1½ Strutter, which is camouflaged with diagonal stripes.

aviation for the international propaganda was dropped as it was forbidden under the terms of the treaty.

The red Sopwiths participated in all the large-scale operations at the beginning of the Civil War. In May–June 1918 they had already appeared in Latvian territory, providing air support for the Red Army units. The aircraft conducted reconnaissance, bombed, and strafed the enemy. A single 1½ Strutter was shot down as it was bombing a bridge and the pilot made an emergency landing. Subsequently, this aircraft served in the Latvian Air Force up until the mid-1920s.

In July 1918 a red air unit commanded by V.V. Karpov arrived at a location near Tsaritsyn (now Volgograd), which had been attacked by the Don Army under General P.N. Krasnov. The unit had 11 Sopwiths in its strength and carried out reconnaissance, but also was involved into bombing operations and enemy units strafing.

That July Sopwiths participated in raids on Kazan. On 31 July 1918 the 23rd Corps Unit under the command of I.V. Satunin was sent east. Among the unit airplanes there was a single 1½ Strutter. On 5 August the train arrived in Kazan, having offloaded at Tatarskaya station. On 6 July Satunin and flight observer F.A. Kolosov flew the first combat sortie in this Sopwith. They conducted reconnaissance and dropped bombs on white steamers and barges on the Volga River. After this, however, they had to evacuate immediately – that night the whites entered Kazan.

K.A. Akashev, who commanded the red air forces in that area, later wrote that the Sopwiths had entered service in Russia only in 1917, and therefore there was a lack of pilots who had mastered this aircraft fully. In Akashev's opinion, the visibility for the crew in this aircraft was worse than in the Farman 30, and the Sopwith also conceded to this aircraft in terms of its bomb load.

Under initiative of Akashev, the aviation carried out several air raids on Kazan. Red aircraft, including five Sopwiths from three different units, bombed and strafed the centre of the city. The air raids continued up to capturing Kazan by the Red Army on 10 September. On 24 August 1918, a Sopwith of the 23rd Air Unit crewed by pilot Smetanin and engine specialist Mesbakh, whilst returning from a reconnaissance mission near Kazan, crashed on its own side of the front line for some unknown reason. One reconnaissance airplane was intendedly crashed by ex-officer Kudlaenko. After receiving another aircraft of this type at Alatyr, Kudlaenko defected to the whites.

In summer 1918 the Smolensk Air Group was formed of those pilots who had undergone training in England in 1917. It was made up of two units (12 aircraft in total). In November this group was deployed to the Voronezh Front. The Sopwiths, for the most part, were used as light bombers. They attacked targets a short distance behind enemy lines, specifically, railway junctions. For example, at the Talovo station the group succeeded in destroying a steam locomotive with a direct hit. There were failures however – one of the red Sopwiths emptied its bomb load on Khrenovaya station,

The crew standing next to a 1½ Strutter. Note a Lewis model 1915 infantry machine gun mounted in the rear cockpit.

A red Sopwith 1½ Strutter that has crashed into the forest.

Repairing a British made 1½ Strutter in the red army workshops.

which had already been captured by their own side. The pilots reported heavy losses among the whites. Fortunately, however, none of the personnel were injured, the only casualty of the raid was a cow.

Later on, this group supported the liquidation of the breakthrough by the white cavalry near Bobrov. The airplane dropped a mixture of small calibre bombs, and petrol canisters and tin cans with holes in them – the explosions and the terrible wailing frightened the horses. In course of this operation, pilots Shnel, Zhemchuzhin, Petrenko, and Medveditsyn distinguished themselves.

On 19 May 1919 the whites tried to perform a troop landing using three steamers near the village of Semikarakorskaya on the Don River, the location of the 37th Air Unit's airbase. When approaching the base, they opened fire with their cannons and machine guns. Being near the aircraft, mechanic Bazylik climbed into the rear cockpit of one of the Sopwiths and strafed the first vessel. He succeeded in hitting the bridge and the steamer lost control for a while, getting in the way of two others. In all the commotion among the whites, the aircraft were towed away from a dangerous location and a defence was organised. The pilots and mechanics gathered all the machine guns they could. Since no mounts were available for the aerial machine guns, one man would get down on all fours, while another would lay the barrel down on his back, and fire. The intense fire forced the enemy to take the dinghies carrying the soldiers back on board, and to withdraw.

On 21 September 1919 pilot Bratolyubov with his air observer Minikin spotted General

Shkuro's main forces near the village of Shatalovka. Bombs were dropped on the soldiers and they were strafed by machine-gun fire, but the Sopwith was also damaged by return fire. The pilot made an emergency landing north of the village. The crew set fire to the aircraft, but they were captured themselves and were later shot.

A 1½ Strutter serving in red aviation, which has been put on ski undercarriage.

In September 1919 the 16th Air Unit under the reds also operated Sopwith aircraft, which supported 10th Army operations on the South-Eastern Front. There, crews under pilots A.T. Sarkisov and A.E. Rossov distinguished themselves in combat against the white cavalry.

Red pilots standing next to a 1½ Strutter in the early 1920s.

The red 1½ Strutters also saw active service in the Urals and in Siberia. In combat against the forces of the Ufa Directorate the reds attained their first aerial victory of the Civil War in a Sopwith aircraft. On 16 September 1918 a 1½ Strutter flown by pilot F. Grab and his observer Schultz circled over an enemy airfield near Shamora station, they, however, did not find any aircraft there. On their way back they were attacked by a Nieuport 17 fighter. Schultz fired two bursts at this aircraft. The Nieuport side-slipped onto its wing and then crashed into the taiga. The downed aircraft belonged to the 33rd Corps Unit under the whites, and *Praporshchik* Vladimirov was at the controls, he was killed in the air. The Sopwith was holed by return fire in four places. For their aerial victory Grab and Schultz received a prize of 5,000 roubles.

By mid-1919 the reserves of materiel in the depots, which were captured by the reds, was beginning to dwindle. The shortage of aircraft, however, forced the reds to retain even completely worn-out airplanes in service. The machines had been repaired multiple times, and often one good airplane was assembled from two or three that had been damaged. This enabled the fleet numbers to be maintained, including the Sopwiths.

These aircraft participated in combat operations in spring and summer 1919 on the Eastern Front against Admiral Kolchak's army. Thus, on 25 May the reds launched a raid on an enemy airfield close to the village of Loktyzhma (near

Preparing a Sopwith 1½ Strutter for a flight.

Ufa). On 8 June the Sopwiths of the 11th Reconnaissance Unit dropped small calibre bombs (in total they dropped 90kg) on an artillery battery belonging to Kolchak's forces on the banks of the Belaya River. This battery ceased to fire which enabled the 25th Division commanded by V.I. Chapaev to cross the river successfully. For this achievement,

Aircraft from one of the red air units at the airfield; note two 1½ Strutters.

A landing accident with a 1½ Strutter, early 1920s.

pilots Savin, Yuzhak, and Tomashevskiy were awarded the Order of the Red Banner.

In July 1919 the 1½ Strutters participated in supply operations for the forces of the IV Army, which were surrounded by the whites in Uralsk. Three regiments and the headquarters of the 22nd Rifle Division ended up in this encirclement. The 26th and 33rd Air Units, which had been brought together under the Shipovsk Group, to which the 30th Air Unit was later added, were drafted in to supply the encircled forces. In total they had 16 aircraft but no more than five of them could be used for transport operations. They delivered the post, tobacco, medicine, and spare parts for the radio station. From time to time these aircraft would carry passengers – inspectors from army headquarters would be flown into the city, and personnel from divisional headquarters were taken out of the encirclement to report back and for orders to be drawn up. Sopwiths also conducted reconnaissance of the whites' positions. For example, on 9 July the Commander of the 26th Air Unit Labrents with his observer Shpak was conducting reconnaissance over the Shipovo area in a 1½ Strutter. Two days later the Commander of the 33rd Air Unit Lukandin, also in a Sopwith returning from Uralsk, spotted a convoy of carts belonging to the white forces, and then two cavalry companies and approximately 200 infantrymen, close to Lake Kamyshin.

During intensive flights the entire allocated reserve of fuel was quickly used up. The resolution of this issue was entrusted to the Emergency Commission for Combating Counter-Revolution and Sabotage (Cheka). They requisitioned anything that would burn from around the district – fuel, kerosene, ether, ethanol, and even cognac and moonshine. They mixed up a fuel substitute from these substances. Most surprisingly of all was that the engines worked on this fuel, although Labrents reported: 'the pilots are saying that it is almost impossible to fly on this mixture'. Flights to Uralsk continued for two and a half months, after which the whites retreated under pressure from the reds, and the city was liberated.

In the course of the defence of Orenburg the red forces were supported by a single flight – one 1½ Strutter and one Rumpler. One of air observers on the Sopwith would go on to become a famous designer, the creator of *Zveno* combined aircraft, V.S. Vakhmistrov. The airplanes of the flight conducted reconnaissance as well as dropping leaflets and the *Bednota* newspaper over enemy territory.

Sopwiths also fought in other locations. A unit (which was later named *Tsaritsynskiy*) consisting of four 1½ Strutters and three fighters were re-deployed to Tsaritsyn on 25 June 1918. In view of its intensive use, aircraft of the unit had lost its combat capability by September. The unit was augmented and re-deployed to other locations. In April 1919, already designated as the 16th Air Unit, it arrived at the Remontnaya station with just a single Sopwith. The commander of the 10th Army I.E. Yegorov gave them a task – to drop bombs on Rostov-on-Don, some 250km away. The unit commander V.I. Popov responded that he would fly there but would not be able to return. Yegorov was insisting, but meanwhile the 1½ Strutter was damaged on landing. Pilot Nazarchuk of the 40th Air Unit flew there but he did not return ... It later emerged that following an emergency landing he had been taken prisoner.

A 1½ Strutter built at the Moscow GAZ-1 factory (the former *Duks*).

The whites had a few 1½ Strutters, they were delivered from abroad to the white armies in very small numbers, but for the most part they were captured airplanes, or had been hijacked by turncoat pilots. Thus, on 27 September 1918 a Sopwith made an emergency landing in the steppe due to the engine failure and was captured by the Cossacks, it was later used by the 1st Don Air Unit under the whites. The 10th Air Unit operated in the Kurgan area on the side of the whites and included two trophy Sopwiths.

A 1½ Strutter, built at the GAZ-3 *Krasniy Lyotchik* factory (the former Lebedev factory), June 1921. Pilot Schmidt flew this airplane in the 39th *Zhelezniy* Reconnaissance Air Unit.

Admiral Kolchak's army had more Sopwith aircraft in its strength. In March 1919, following an emergency landing near Sarapul, an almost serviceable 1½ Strutter fell into the hands of Kolchak's troops. The Cossacks captured a further aircraft on an airfield as they were taking Lbishchensk in September of that year. The whites were not able to use this aircraft, however – the prisoners of war, observer Olekhnovich and engine-specialist Zherdin, escaped from capture just before dawn, started the aircraft's engine and attempted to take-off. They did not really have any understanding of how to control the aircraft though, so the biplane crashed on take-off and was seriously damaged. These brave aviators removed the machine gun and strafed a Farman airplane that was standing nearby. As the Cossacks appeared, Olekhnovich shot himself, and Zherdin managed to run away and return to his own lines.

A mechanic shows where the canvass is peeling off on the upper wing of a 1½ Strutter built by the GAZ-10 *Lebed* factory.

Kolchak, aside from the captured aircraft, had airplanes that had been sold to him by the French. A French air unit had appeared in Siberia back in July 1919. It amounted to 17 French-built Sopwiths. It was not subordinate to the

A group of red pilots standing next to a 1½ Strutter.

Locals standing next to the 1½ Strutter *Krasnoyarets,* which was used by the ODVF for a propaganda flight in 1925.

The white pilot in the damaged aircraft was forced to turn back. The other two Kolchak airplanes dropped their bombs but missed the red's balloon.

Three days later Captain Muromtsev, also flying a Sopwith, nevertheless destroyed this balloon. On the night of 10–11 October he dropped two bombs on it from an altitude of just 20m, in spite of ground fire. The balloon, which was full of hydrogen, exploded. Muromtsev's airplane returned back to base with dozens of bullet holes, and with the air observer wounded.

The whites also operated 1½ Strutters in significant numbers in the north. After the British interventionists had captured Arkhangelsk, 18 French-built Sopwiths were discovered in a store in Bakaritsa, which the reds had not been able to take with them. Out of these the whites were able to assemble 16 airworthy airplanes. They were used to equip the aviation detachments of the Slavo-British Air Corps. The unit led by *Polkovnik* A.A. Kozakov received six of them, and from 15 August 1918 this detachment was conducting reconnaissance missions from a site near to Obozerskaya station. Interestingly, on the other side of the front line the Kostroma Air Group (subsequently renamed the 18th Reconnaissance Unit), which was also partially equipped with 1½ Strutters, was fighting Kozakov's detachment.

On 12 November 1918, Captain Kossovskiy's Sopwith was shot down by an anti-aircraft shell fired from *Pavlin Vinogradov* steamer. The air observer was killed and the pilot survived but was captured and later shot. The ship's gunner, who had shot the aircraft down, was decorated with the Order of the Red Banner.

Russian pilots, on contrast to the British, continued to fly in winter. The airplanes were put on a ski undercarriage, and the rotary engines were started even in 30 degrees of frost. The British provided aircrew with electrically heated suits, for which a small wing-mounted generator supplied the current. Using these flying suits, the Russian pilots would undertake flights lasting up to two hours in very cold weather.

whites' command, but at the beginning of August a single flight of three aircraft was sent to the front, where they were conducting reconnaissance over the course of a month.

In September the French left. The aircraft were sold to the Main Engineering Directorate of Kolchak's army for 500,000 roubles each. They equipped several air units, either fully, or in part, specifically the 14th Air Unit. The white 1½ Strutters saw active service at the front line. On 7 October 1919 an air battle was recorded involving a red Sopwith against three machines of the same type operating under Kolchak. The whites were going to bomb a base belonging to the 5th Aeronautical Unit near the Zyryanka station, and they were spotted by the red pilot Baturin, who had vigorously attacked one of the enemy aircraft, strafing it. The bullets punctured the fuel tanks, injuring the air observer.

Although in spring 1919 new airplanes were delivered for the Slavo-British Air Corps, the Sopwiths continued to be used. They participated in supporting an offensive by the whites in May–June 1919.

The 1½ Strutter *Krasnoyarets* is mounted as an exhibit at the gates of the City Park in Krasnoyarsk, April 1930.

At the end of May aviation activity of the reds became a concern for the interventionist command, so they decided to strike one of the enemy's airfields. A.A. Kozakov developed a plan for the raid on an airfield close to Puchega station. Nine aircraft were to attack the base from low level using 20lb bombs and machine-gun fire. On Major Kerry's signal three Sopwiths from the Russian squadron would land on the airfield, and their crews would set fire to tents that housed the airplanes. For this purpose, each 1½ Strutter carried three canisters with fuel and torches made from tow. After the sabotage group had taken off, six DH.9s were to drop 250lb bombs on the runway and on the airfield structures.

Take-off on this unusual combat sortie took place at 1700 hours in the evening on 17 June. Immediately after take-off the engines gave out on the Snipe flown by British pilot Knight and the Nieuport flown by Lieutenant Beresnevich, so they were not able to participate in the raid. Only Major Kerry's fighter remained to provide cover for the sabotage group of Sopwiths. These circumstances changed the plan, and the landing part of the raid had to be cancelled.

The strafing with machine-gun fire, however, turned out to be sufficiently effective. Six Sopwiths strafed the aircraft and tents from low-level. The DH.9s dropped bombs on the airfield and the vessels in the red river flotilla. A Nieuport standing on the airfield burst into flames after being hit by incendiary bullets, and barrels of fuel on the edge of the airfield exploded. Bullets and bomb splinters took another Nieuport and Spad in the tents out of action. After this raid the activity of reds from Puchega airfield ceased for a considerable time.

Following the withdrawal of the interventionists from the Russian north, the last 1½ Strutter served the whites in the Murmansk air division under *Polkovnik* Barbas.

The number of 1½ Strutters in the red air fleet was reducing gradually due to combat losses, accidents, and crashes. Thus, on 13 March 1920 the engine failed on one Sopwith, and the air observer P.S. Pivin was killed during an emergency landing. On 18 April of that same year there was a case of an in-flight fire. Pilot P.I. Pokhazchikov and air observer V.G. Sergeev were killed.

A dismantled 1½ Strutter is taken to Kabul on converted arba carts, September 1921.

Sopwiths were operated by the reds in the south during the final attempt by Wrangel's army to break away from the Crimea. For instance, there were three 1½ Strutters in a Combined Combat Unit under the command of V.I. Chulkov. On the morning of 3 June 1920, they bombed the harbour in Kerch and were attacked south of the Cape of Ak-Burun by a Nieuport biplane, flown by *Shtabs-Kapitan* Denisenko. The red pilots had decided that this fighter was one of theirs and paid the price for it. An oil pipeline on Chulkov's biplane was ruptured and he had to make an emergency landing near the Vasyutino village. On 15 July, however, Chulkov again encountered Denisenko in flight. This time flight observer Zemulen immediately gave him a burst of fire. With its higher speed the fighter shot past and Chulkov again gave him a burst of fire from the nose machine gun. The hit Nieuport ditched in the Kerch Strait.

In autumn of that year the red aviation provided assistance in repelling the advance by Wrangel's army along the coast of the Sea of Azov. Pilot Petrov was flying one of the Sopwiths. On the morning of 7 October 1920, he spotted the whites some 40–45km away from Taganrog and counted 14 vessels that were at sea in support of them. That same day an air raid was carried out on these ships. No direct hits were achieved but the raid pushed the enemy further back from the shore. A second strike was carried out the following day.

The 1½ Strutter used for reconnaissance during operations against the Basmachi, Kizyl-Tepe airfield, 1923.

The 1½ Strutters also participated in the closing stage of the Civil War. Several airplanes were in service with aviation of the Far Eastern Republic (*Dalnevostochnaya Respublika*, DVR) which was created as a buffer between Soviet Russia and the troops of Japanese interventionists. It was in one of these aircraft that pilot Kalitnikov bombed the headquarters of the white Ataman Semyonov in Chita. As of 15 June 1921, there were four Sopwiths in the DVR air force. Two of them subsequently participated in the advance on Mongolia against forces of General-Lieutenant Baron R.F. Ungern von Shternberg that had settled there and were yet to be finished off. Baron declared himself the ruler of Mongolia, but did not last long.

When the combats against large white troop formations had almost finished, the 1½ Strutters began to be used for the suppression of local uprisings against Bolshevik power. In March 1921 the reds flew the British aircraft in their suppression of a revolt at the Baltic Fleet base at Kronstadt. The Sopwiths bombed and strafed the city and the moorings of the ships.

They were used just as actively in summer and autumn 1921 in the suppression of a peasants uprising at Tambov region, which had been dubbed *antonovshchina* after the surname of the leader of the insurgents, socialist-revolutionary A.S. Antonov. Three air units, as well as a special-purpose flight formed part of the Combat air squadron under the command of S.Ya. Korf. Among the flight crews was a group of voluntary pilots from Germany. The flights were undertaken from Tambov and Borisoglebsk airfields. In the 20th Air Unit among the other aircraft there were two 1½ Strutters, which were flown by crews under B. Schmidt and Soome, likewise there were two in the 39th Air Unit flown by Danilov and Bolyagin. The airplanes conducted reconnaissance, bombing missions, and strafed concentrations of insurgents. Especially successful were the combat actions of pilots on 11 April 1921. A large unit of the Antonov's troops captured the village of Rasskazovo, taking approximately 300 prisoners and trophies. Three hours later this unit began to withdraw but came under fire from three fighters and three reconnaissance aircraft (including two 1½ Strutters). The column was attacked with bombs and machine gun fire. The majority of the red soldiers escaped and the enemy sustained considerable losses. The worn-out engines on both Sopwiths, however, became unserviceable.

The enemy did not have any specific anti-aircraft defence, although they could fire rifles and machine guns, but the Sopwiths did not sustain any combat losses. On one occasion a bullet severed one of the bracing wires on the stabiliser of an aircraft of the 39th Air Unit, piloted by Ya.I. Yuzhak (his air observer was S.P. Lukin). The airplane's handling deteriorated, but the pilot was able make emergency landing. The Antonov's troops tried to capture an aircraft and its crew. This situation was saved by a Farman-30, which dropped bombs on the insurgents and strafed them with machine gun fire. This biplane landed alongside the Sopwith, the crew helped to get the engine started on this aircraft, and both biplanes returned to base successfully.

In another occasion, on 22 July 1921, during a test flight of a repaired aircraft at this same detachment the airplane's wing box broke down and it inadvertently entered a spin at an altitude of 1,000m. As a result, the 1½ Strutter crashed into the ground, the pilot Bolyagin and mechanic Tabarovskiy sustained serious bruises and concussion.

The 1½ Strutters also served in naval aviation, which in the Civil War period came under the navy command (not the RKKVF). It is known that on 23 November 1918 pilot Koptev of the 1st Fighter Unit (on the Northern Front), flying a 1½ Strutter, entered spin and destroyed the aircraft. Later, the 1½ Strutters saw service on the Black Sea and in the Baltics.

On 1 December 1920 in the Baltics, in a fighter division deployed to Peterhof, there were three 1½ Strutters, but two of them unserviceable. On the Black Sea on that same date there were two aircraft in the fighter air unit in Nikolaev, though only one of them could get airborne.

There were four aircraft in the Black Sea Fleet in October–December 1920. One of them was at Ochakov, one at Nikolaev, and two at Taganrog (as part of the Air Division of the Azov Sea). In 1921 two 1½ Strutters were listed in the fighter division of the Baltic Sea Air Brigade.

This 1½ Strutter, hijacked in January 1919 by an Estonian pilot who had deserted from the Red Army, formed the basis of Estonia's military aviation.

The Turkestan Front in Central Asia was always considered a secondary front. In winter 1919, a single air unit was re-deployed there to assist in combats with local insurgents (the Basmachi). The Sopwith that became part of this detachment was brought disassembled to Petroaleksandrovsk (some 80km from Khiva), where it was assembled and test flown. Half way to the designated landing site the pilot lost his way and circled for about an hour, regaining his orientation. It then emerged that he had been circling over a kishlak (small settlement), where the red commanders were holding talks with representatives of the local Basmachi chief, Djunaid-khan! As they had been afraid of the threat from the air, the Basmachi agreed to major concessions. Individual Sopwiths participated in an advance on Bukhara. The aircraft were worn out considerably. Mechanic A.A. Tokarev wrote in his report: 'Our Sopwith airplane ... is old and shabby, it has had up to 70 patched up repairs of all kinds, and the main spars and the pedals have been eaten away by mice.' When this airplane crashed in Gissar, three mouse nests were found in the wings!

This type, which was considered fast and reliable, was used more than once for important flights. For example, on 20 April 1920 a Sopwith piloted by B.I. Rossinskiy took off from Moscow and made a flight on a route Moscow–Nizhniy Novgorod–Kazan–Samara. It delivered Deputy Head of the Active Army Aviation V.S. Gorshkov. Rossinskiy then returned to Moscow, where he brought the Deputy Head of Aviation of the Turkestan Front N.G. Smirnov.

Russian-built 1½ Strutters participated in the concluding phase of the Civil War. In mid-1919 the former Lebedev factory, which had been renamed the GAZ-3 *Krasny Lyotchik* (Red Pilot), received a new order for 25 aircraft. In August the factory informed that it had commenced assembly of the first batch of 10 airplanes. The leading machine was already at a state of approximately 85 percent completion. The re-counting of the existing backlog revealed the components for approximately 100 biplanes in various states of manufacture.

Since the original British example had already been broken up for parts, the majority of which were lost due to the considerable time past, the *Krasny Lyotchik* factory requested that another imported machine be transferred to them from the *Duks* factory (by that time this factory had been renamed the GAZ-1). Furthermore, it emerged that the bomb racks were missing on this aircraft (which at the time were known as 'bomb-throwers'). The *Duks* factory, however, did not hand over their 1½ Strutter, since their intention was also to put this type into series production (more on this below).

In view of a lack of components, including instruments, engines, and propellers, the actual delivery of the completed Sopwiths in Petrograd only began in summer 1920. By 1 June the factory had presented 10 aircraft, of which eight successfully completed the incoming inspection. The process then continued. Thus, on 8 October, the military officially accepted two biplanes following test flights, while one of these aircraft was fitted with a Clerget engine as planned, but the other had 120hp Rhone Jb. The 32nd Air Unit subsequently received both these airplanes. By 4 June 1921, of the 25 1½ Strutters ordered GAZ-3 had presented 18, of which 16 were test flown. Some of the aircraft had already participated in combat operations.

In March 1921 a Petrograd-built aircraft, flown by pilot Shuman, completed testing at the Scientific Experimental airfield in Moscow. As it turned out, the Russian 1½ Strutter demonstrated 'excellent flight-performance characteristics'.

By 1 January 1922, 20 airplanes had been assembled at the GAZ-3 factory and handed over to the military; by that time the order had been reduced to 22 machines.

In Moscow, the 1½ Strutters were manufactured at the GAZ-1 factory. In April 1919, engineers N.N. Polikarpov and V.V. Bartoshevich requested a Sopwith from the Moscow Air Depot 'for photographing and checking against the drawings'. In summer of that same year, earlier than in Petrograd, the factory rolled out its first 1½ Strutter, which became a reference example. It is possible that it was this aircraft (registration No. 2379) that ended up in the 1st Separate Reconnaissance Air Unit in November 1919. On 20 December, the enterprise received an order to manufacture 25 aircraft, and more were to follow. A task was defined to produce 60 Sopwith aircraft by 1 May 1920. However,

An accident with 1½ Strutter, when a red pilot overshot on landing and crashed into a forest, Eastern Front, winter 1918–1919.

shortage of raw materials, semi-finished products, and components was getting in the way of this. To speed up the process some 25 sets of components were sent from GAZ-3 to Moscow in 1920. Incoming inspection, however, revealed a significant discrepancy in the dimensions, the components were not compatible with one another. As a result of overheating during welding, the eyelets on the cable shoes began to crack when the bracing cables were tightened.

The first series production 1½ Strutter in Moscow was presented to the military inspectors at the very end of 1921. As of 1 December 1923, nine aircraft had been assembled, of which six were accepted – the rest did not have engines.

The manufacturing quality of the Moscow and Petrograd-built 1½ Strutters turned out to be very poor. They differed in that they were larger and heavier than the original and also in terms of their poor quality (a crumbly, unseasoned timber had been used and the outer skin was peeling away). In February 1921 the GAZ-3 factory had to recall some of these aircraft from the units and depots for repair. On 10 March, an entire decree was issued to withdraw the Russian-made 1½ Strutter from the air force units. In view of the shortage of aircraft, however, this was clearly not fulfilled.

On 31 March 1921, the *Duks*-assembled aircraft were inspected by a commission led by I.S. Prishchepov, Head of the acceptance department under the Directorate of Aviation Supply. The commission proposed strengthening a number of components, specifically, introducing fuselage spars without machined recesses, replacing a series of metal plates, and increasing the cross-section of the bracing wires.

On 19 June, in the aforementioned 39th Reconnaissance Unit, a partial destruction of the upper wing of the aircraft occurred in flight; the pilot managed to land safely. On the following day a further two Petrograd-built 1½ Strutters of this unit were inspected. It emerged that the fuselage spars and wing ribs were manufactured from a poorly dried crumbly wood using a poor-quality adhesive, in addition the wood screws in the joints were too short. In the following month, in that same detachment which saw action in Tambov region, incidents were recorded when bracing wires separated in flight. As a result of such failure, one airplane made a forced landing in the enemy occupied area. A deformation of the ribs was found in one of the 1½ Strutters.

Nevertheless, Russian-built Sopwiths were used actively in air force units and augmented the imported aircraft. For example, a single 1½ Strutter manufactured at the GAZ-3 factory was listed in service of the 3rd Naval Fighter Unit on 1 January 1922. As of 13 December 1923, the 1st Separate Air Unit of Leningrad Military District had four 1½ Strutters that had been manufactured at the GAZ-1 factory.

In 1920 the Red Army air fleet was supplemented by several 1½ Strutters which had been captured during the incursion in Transcaucasia. These aircraft previously belonged to the Georgian aviation.

At that time, it was rare for any unit in the RKKVF to be equipped solely with the same aircraft type. For example, as of 8 October 1921, the 3rd Air Unit in Irkutsk had five aircraft in service. Of those, two were 1½ Strutters – one Russian-built and the other of the British manufacture. On the other hand, on 29 October the 50th Reconnaissance Detachment had solely Sopwiths in its strength, nine in total.

Soviet aviation continued to support operations against the Basmachi in Central Asia. The local insurgents conducted a partisan war in the steppes and mountains, fighting in comparatively small mobile cavalry groups. Airplanes turned

Preparing a 1½ Strutter for a sortie to bomb Polish forces, 1920.

out to be invaluable in conducting reconnaissance and supporting troops on the ground. They also bombed and strafed concentrations of Basmachis. These operations were seasonal, and the enemies would disperse to warmer areas for the winter. Sopwiths featured among the aircraft drafted into these military operations.

At the beginning of November 1921 Red Army units conducted operations against Kurshermat's group, which had been active between Kokand, Namangan, and Andizhan. They were supported by the 18th Air Unit, which had several 1½ Strutters in service. The airplanes would hunt out the bandits in the dense undergrowth, flying between three and four sorties per day. They set fire to the dry reeds with incendiary bombs, driving the enemy in a certain direction. One Sopwith was forced to land amongst the reeds close to Namangan. Pilot Nikolin and observer Bronnikov abandoned the aircraft and returned to their own lines. The Basmachis noticed the reconnaissance aircraft on its descent and organised a search, but they did not find it. When the district came under the complete control of the reds, the Sopwith was located from the air; it was just left there among the reeds.

In June 1922 a flight of four aircraft (two Nieuport fighters, and two 1½ Strutters) was sent to the southern districts of Bukhara region. They were brought to Qarshi, assembled there and then ferried by air. As a result, one fighter managed to reach Termez, and a Sopwith got to Derbent. From there, attempts were made to undertake combat sorties, but the range of the Nieuport turned out to be too small and in reality it was the 1½ Strutter that operated alone.

In 1923 the Sopwiths were operated in Central Asia by the 4th Reconnaissance Air Unit. The detachment was accommodated on the steppe near the small railway station at Kizyl-Tepe. This location was not entirely safe, by night the gunners would man the machine guns in the rear cockpits of their biplanes. It was from this location that several sorties a day were flown, reconnaissance was conducted, and the bandits they encountered were bombed and strafed. Thus, on 22 April two airplanes successfully struck a group consisting of around 500 men west of the Shur-Kul Lake. The enemy opened fire with rifles, but they did not inflict any damage on these aircraft.

On 4 May the Basmachis attacked the Kirmene railway station, killed the stationmaster, telegrapher, and red army soldiers that were guarding the airfield. They poured kerosene onto the station building, set it on fire, and rode away in an unknown direction. The station watchman managed to escape the massacre, reached Kizyl-Tepe by foot and reported what had happened. Pilot N.N. Starodumov on his Sopwith found the Basmachis close to a mountain pass, after that the entire unit attacked the group.

The flights did not always end successfully. On 27 November 1923 pilot S.I. Baskakov during a reconnaissance sortie made a forced landing near Lake Makhan. Basmachis from the Dzhura-Alim's group encircled his aircraft. The crew were in a firefight for two hours; the pilot was killed, and air observer Shitikov shot himself with the last round in his revolver. The bandits set fire to the aircraft along with the bodies of the crew.

In the rest of Russia military aviation had gone onto a peacetime footing and was limited to training flights and participation in manoeuvres. Furthermore, however, losses of aircraft and pilots continued. Thus, on 11 June 1921, whilst climbing to altitude the commander of the unit I.P. Klyuev was involved in a fatal accident. At an altitude of 80m his engine failed, the Sopwith entered a spin; the pilot had no time to recover. On 24 July another airplane crashed in the mountains. Pilot Mikhasov was killed, and the engine mechanic, who sat in the rear cockpit, came away with bruises.

On 14 January 1923 the Head of the Moscow Central airfield G.S. Smirnov was killed in a Sopwith while performing a training flight. Sitting in the rear cockpit as a

A crew standing next to a 1½ Strutter, Southern Front, 1920.

passenger, was the airfield duty officer, G.M. Smirnov, who was also a relative of the head. After take-off the pilot began to rapidly gain altitude, but the engine rpms were dropping drastically. The aircraft stalled and crashed into the ground. The pilot was killed, and his passenger survived, but with broken arms and legs.

Two fatal crashes were recorded involving 1½ Strutters in the 6th Separate Air Unit in Ukraine, which occurred in 1923. The first of those was on 9 May close to the village of Cherkasskiye Tishki, where aircraft No. 302 crashed. The crew made up of pilot Kolobaev, and air observer Yengalychev were killed. The crew also perished in the second incident. The reason for the first fatal crash remained unknown, but when investigating the second, the commission quickly came to the conclusion that as assembly workers were short of a special control cable, they had replaced it with telephone wire which gradually stretched.

As of December 1923, 46 1½ Strutters were in the strength of Soviet units, but two dozen of these were listed as unserviceable. A further nine were at various training establishments, but the state of the aircraft at these locations was deplorable as well: five airplanes were actually not airworthy. A further two serviceable Sopwiths were stored in military depots, while 13 reconnaissance airplanes were undergoing repairs at the enterprises of *Promvozdukh* trust.

In 1923 in Germany a small batch of Heinecke backpack parachutes was acquired. Officers of the *Reichswehr* provided training in how to use this equipment. Thus, in Moscow the instructor was *Oberleutnant* W. Triebner, who had trained around 40 men. They made training jumps from a balloon and an old Sopwith aircraft. Following testing at the Scientific-Experimental Airfield, the Heinecke parachutes were rejected, it was thought that their landing speed was too high.

Evidently, the Sopwiths fought in combat for the last time in an operation in Khorezm in January 1924. The Basmachis made two attempts to take Khiva, the capital of the Khorezm Republic, which existed at that time. Three aircraft were sent to assist the defenders – one was a 1½ Strutter, the others were a DH.9 and a single Yu-13 (Junkers F.13). Only the latter aircraft made it, the two others made emergency landings due to engine failures. The Sopwith flown by pilot F. Likhovitskiy was destroyed on landing at Chardzhou.

By the mid-1920s the 1½ Strutters were already obsolete, and apart from that, a large proportion of these biplanes were completely worn out. At the end of January 1925 four Sopwiths were still listed at the Higher School of Air Observers in Leningrad, but they were indicated as 'dilapidated' in the documents.

The final 1½ Strutters were found in air force units even in the mid-1920s. Officially, this type was taken out of the Air Force strength in December 1925.

The military airplanes that had been taken out of service were transferred to the ODVF. This was done in accordance with a decree issued by the Council of People's Commissars, which enabled the handover of 'non-airworthy aircraft of the Red Air Fleet that belonged to types that had been withdrawn from service'. In exchange the ODVF was to draft in its members to level out the ground on military airfields, or the society was to pay for the aircraft. Specifically, the ODVF received the final 1½ Strutters manufactured at the GAZ-3 factory. For example, reconnaissance airplane No. 1786, following several years of service, was recognised as being only suitable for propaganda flights over airfields, and it was

Photo of pilots and personnel of RKKA VVS unit along with the People's Commissar for Military Affairs of Belorussia (standing in the centre) with a 1½ Strutter in the background, Minsk, 1922.

transferred to the Novgorod division of the ODVF. One aircraft in September 1926 was brought to Blagoveshchensk in the Primorye region. It was planned that propaganda flights would be made in this aircraft around the nearby towns and settlements.

In May 1925 five Sopwiths were delivered to the Krasnoyarsk region, and a little later the sixth was added. In September an aircraft named *Krasnoyarets* (citizen of Krasnoyarsk) made a propaganda flight around the Minusinsk region and Khakassiya. The airplane visited 15 towns and settlements. In the course of the flight the crew found themselves in mist, rain, and snow. At various locations they gave demonstration flights, dropped leaflets, and gave rides to passengers. The arrival of the first aircraft in this region attracted considerable interest. The local officials declared the day of the *Krasnoyarets* arrival a holiday. In the town of Minusinsk an orchestra and a group of 5,000 citizens waving flags greeted the Sopwith. In Ust-Abakansk 'one native woman' (this was how they were described in the press) who had been alarmed by the sight of a flying machine that they had never seen before, suffered a heart failure. In September, a telegram arrived from Novosibirsk from the leadership of the ODVF that all aircraft of this type were to be withdrawn from service. By that time the *Krasnoyarets* remained the only serviceable example out of the six airplanes. At the end of the month the leadership of Siberian division of the ODVF allowed flights in this machine to continue, but they were punished for it. On 19 October the airplane was dismantled and handed over for storage. It was subsequently reassembled once again and mounted as a gate guardian at Municipal Park in Krasnoyarsk.

Although by that time the Sopwith had become hopelessly obsolete and was only suitable as a museum piece, several examples of this aircraft were put into storage and were still kept in the depot of the Siberian Military District in December 1927.

A single 1½ Strutter was gifted by Soviet Russia to Afghanistan. In September 1921 a special purpose flight under the command of V.V. Goppe was sent to this country. Initially, this flight was comprised of three airplanes, but the Farman 30 was destroyed during a test flight on the Soviet side of the border. A Nieuport fighter and a Sopwith reconnaissance aircraft remained. The plan was to deliver these to Kabul overland in a semi-dismantled condition. To begin with, the fuselages were towed on their own wheels, and the wings were transported in arba carts that were linked together, and camels carried barrels of fuel and oil. As the convoy passed over the mountains the road deteriorated more and more – it was narrow, winding, and obstructed by rocks. In some places it was no more than a path with steps. The cargoes were either placed on horseback or were carried by Afghan peasants rounded up by the Shah. Attempts were made to attach the wings, which had been packed away, onto four donkeys, but they could not get them to move in unison. Subsequently, three elephants carried the biggest boxes. The journey to Kabul took a month and a half. Assembly work started on these aircraft in Kabul and the Afghans began to be trained. A *coup d'état* occurred, however, and the personnel in the flight had to leave Kabul immediately. What happened to this 1½ Strutter remains unknown.

1.8 Trophy British Hydroplanes

British hydroplanes were not delivered to Russia, prior to, or during the First World War. They only appeared in the Civil War years, when the interventionist units joined the white armies.

The British hydro-aviation actively joined combat operations in the north. On 1 August 1918 during the capture of Arkhangelsk by the interventionists Fairey Campania aircraft from the floatplane carrier the *Nayrana* carried out raids on the port, city, and on concentrations of red troops. One of these airplanes dropped bombs on an artillery battery on the island of Mudyug with some success, this battery ceased firing. At that time on the *Nayrana* there were five Fairey hydroplanes and two Baby fighters on floats.

During the navigation season of 1919 there was a plan to supplement the British river flotilla on the Severnaya Dvina River with a unit of land-based aircraft with a wheeled undercarriage, but no suitable site was available where these airplanes could be base as impenetrable taiga stood on both banks of the river. The closest most suitable location was approximately 70km from the river. Two large barges were included in the flotilla, which became mobile bases for the hydroplanes. The barges were converted and hangars, workshops, and facilities for aircrew and personnel were fabricated onboard.

Twenty-four hydroplanes were housed on these barges, which were delivered using the seaplane carrier HMS *Pegasus*: a dozen Fairey IIIBs and the same number of Short 184s. Both of these types were large, single-engine biplanes fitted with floats. According to the recollections of the flotilla commander, he had between two and four aircraft at his disposal on a daily basis.

Combat operations commenced in May when the river overflowed in its upper reaches. The pilots were given their objectives, and for the most part, these involved conducting reconnaissance. They also flew missions to bomb ships belonging to the red flotilla on the Severnaya Dvina River, as well as troops on the front line, and in fortified areas. These aircraft corrected the flotilla's artillery fire and observations were made on the state of the river channel. The latter enabled minefields to be detected in good time and to identify a safe passage along the river.

In June, whilst making an emergency water landing one of the Fairey IIIBs were destroyed. A launch that rushed to the scene was able to rescue the crew, however, and also towed the damaged aircraft to shore.

July was a time of particularly heavy fighting, when the whites began an advance alongside the river in the direction of Kotlas. The British flotilla was ordered to support combat activity by troops between Troitsa and Topsa, having neutralised the red river flotilla. Furthermore, the hydroplanes were used very intensively. They flew bombing missions all day, leaving the mechanics just enough time to fuel them, and to attach the bombs.

On 8 July a Fairey IIIB flown by Lieutenant Hilton was strafed by ground fire and the fuel tank was ruptured. Nevertheless, the crew dropped their bombs and returned safely back to base. On 14 July Lieutenants Marshall and Lansdown took off in that same aircraft on a combat sortie. Their hydroplane came under heavy anti-aircraft fire from gunboats, was damaged (fuel leaked out from punctured fuel tanks) and landed close to enemy lines; the crew were captured. The tender *Trud* towed the trophy aircraft to positions of the Northern hydroaviation division of reds. This was the first Fairey to be captured by the red army troops. The Baltic Fleet Revolutionary Military Council 'campaigned persistently' for the handover of the 'British aircraft captured by the *Onflotiliya* [Onezhskaya Flotilla – Author's note]' to the 1st Hydroaviation Division in Oranienbaum. This request was supported by Western Front command. On 30 July the Head of the 2nd Hydroaviation Unit Zverev left Petrograd for Kotlas to accept the aircraft. It was dismantled and delivered to Petrograd.

In July, the advance of the whites, supported by the British interventionists, continued. Most of vessels in the red Severodvinsk flotilla sustained significant damage and withdrew upstream or were scuttled. The M-9 and M-20 flying boats of the reds, which had been a part of the Northern Air Division flotilla, only flew occasionally and as the enemy drew near, they withdrew under the protection of their own anti-aircraft batteries. The British hydroplanes, despite the bad weather, flew sorties systematically to bomb and correct artillery fire from the flotilla and from land-based batteries.

The British also sustained losses – on 20 July a bomb exploded on a Fairey after it had taken off on a sortie. The pilot Rankin was rescued, but his air observer drowned. During a test flight of an assembled Short 184 aircraft pilot Le Moin entered a spin and perished in a crash, his mechanic Quantrelle suffered severe concussion.

Some of the British hydroplanes were sent to Onezhskoe Lake. On 6 June 1919 in the area around the Medvezhya Gora (in the northern part of the lake) seven officers arrived from Murmansk, together with 30 soldiers, and four Fairey IIIC aircraft. On that same day they began to assemble the airplanes. As evening drew in, the first aerial photographic combat sortie was carried out. Some 35 minutes later the aircraft returned with its propeller punctured – it had come under fire.

The British had to combat the red flotilla which included several destroyers. On 6 June a single Fairey attacked three small launches close to Shunga, having dropped its bombs and strafed with the machine gun. The launches withdrew to the

Construction work at the British hydroplane base close to Medvezhya Gora. Note Fairey IIIC floatplane in the background.

The view from the water of the British hydroplane base at Onezhskoe Lake, summer 1919. Short 184 and Fairey IIIC hydroplanes are visible.

south, returning fire. On 8 June in that same location, near Shunga, British pilots dropped their bombs on two steamers.

Reconnaissance and bombing flights were conducted almost every day, weather permitting. Bombing and strafing from the air turned out to have a demoralising effect on the enemy flotilla. The red vessels would, as a rule, turn back and disperse after an attack.

Another important mission was the raids on the railways. Specifically, on 12 June an armoured train was bombed. In some cases, the British made their bombing runs from low-level, using delayed-action fuses. The actions of the British

British Fairey IIIC floatplanes on the shore of Onezhskoe Lake, autumn 1919.

A Fairey IIIC floatplane on take-off.

pilots led to the reds halting their movements along the railway line by day, they only moved by night.

The access routes, piers, and slipways for lowering and recovering the hydroplanes as well as hangars and facilities for aircrews had been completed at Medvezhya Gora by mid-June. Furthermore, red prisoners of war were used widely as slave labour. The hydroplanes continued to fly for the whole of June on reconnaissance and bombing missions against the red flotilla and the railway line. They even began to operate by night (in that period the white nights were in full swing).

By the new summer offensive, aviation on Onezhskoe Lake has been significantly augmented. On 26 July seven pilots and the same number of hydroplanes (two Short 184s and five Fairey IIICs) arrived. On 4 August a further six Shorts were delivered on barges from the Severnaya Dvina River, but they did not take part in combat missions.

In the first part of August, British pilots supported the white offensive on Petrozavodsk. They bombed and strafed Tolvoya and

Preparing a Fairey floatplane for flight.

The Fairey IIIB floatplane captured by the reds on Onezhskoe Lake, summer 1919.

The same aircraft in service with the 1st Hydroaviation Division of the Baltic Fleet in Oranienbaum.

Petrozavodsk, even using chemical weapons. The fighting continued until 10 August, when it emerged that the British expeditionary corps were preparing to evacuate, The British airplanes continued their activities on the Dvina River till the end of August and on the Onezhskoe Lake almost until the end of September 1919. By 10 September the British flotilla on Severnaya Dvina had withdrawn to Troitsa, and then began to retreat steadily by river back to Arkhangelsk.

The majority of the serviceable aircraft were returned to England, but some of the floatplanes were left to the whites. Following the departure of the interventionists the resistance did not last long. Among the trophies captured by the reds were also several British hydroplanes, including at least six Fairey IIIBs and IIICs, and three Short 184s. All these airplanes were later brought to Petrograd.

On the Black Sea the British hydroplane carriers HMS *Ark Royal* and HMS *Pegasus* with hydroplanes on board were patrolling until November 1920. In May of this year the hydroplanes from HMS *Pegasus* carried out several air raids on the positions of reds. On 7 May four Short 184s bombed an airfield in Temryuk and damaged one 1½ Strutter. On 12 May two airplanes attacked shipping in a port of Temryuk.

The British and whites also used Short 184s on the Caspian Sea. On 17 November 1918 units from the British 14th Division captured Baku. The British forces requisitioned 25 Russian merchant ships, which were in port at the time, and formed a military flotilla from these vessels. The small tankers *Aladir Husseinov* and *Orlyonok* were converted into hydroplane carriers, and were intended to serve the 266th Squadron, Royal Air Force. The first batch of personnel, and aircraft was delivered by trucks via Iraq and Iran, and then by ship across the Caspian Sea to Petrovsk (now Makhachkala). The second group travelled by sea from the island of Lemnos into Batum (Batumi), and from there they moved by train via Tiflis (Tbilisi) to Baku.

The British arrived in Petrovsk on 1 March 1919 and began to build a base in this location. On 12 March the hydroplanes were delivered there. According to one source, there were 10 of them, while other sources put this figure at six. In April, the airplanes were assembled and test flown.

Another Fairey, which became a trophy of the Red Army in the north; previously this airplane was flown by the British Captain Park. This aircraft went on to serve in the Baltic Fleet aviation.

A Short 184 floatplane on the shore of the Severnaya Dvina River.

A Short 184 is lowered down onto the water using a crane in Petrovsk.

One of the Shorts was damaged on 25 April – it was blown against the side of a ship by a strong gust of wind. Repairs on this machine continued until July.

The *Aladir Husseinov*, which had been renamed by the British into the *Yussanoff* was ready to go to sea on 10 May. Two days later word came through that the reds had captured the city of Fort-Aleksandrovsk (today this is known as Fort-Shevchenko). On 13 May, after loading two Shorts on board, the *Yussanoff* departed for the island of Chechen, where it arrived by evening of that same day. The following day a reconnaissance flight was conducted along the northern coast. The enemy was not spotted, and no bombing targets were discovered, so the aircraft just strafed villages on the coast with machine guns.

On 15 May red ships were spotted at sea. The British flotilla, augmented by Denikin's armed steamers, set off to meet them. The *Yussanoff* was also part of this flotilla. Following several unsuccessful attempts, on 20 May one of the Shorts biplanes managed to perform a bombing raid on Fort-Aleksandrovsk. However, not one of the bombs hit the targets. The engine on the second aircraft failed on take-off, and the airplane crashed into the water; the crew were rescued safely. A second raid by the first Shorts was also unsuccessful, as the pilot was forced to turn back due to engine trouble. The reason for this turned out to be water in the carburettor. Subsequently, poor quality petrol would prevent the completion of combat sorties on more than one occasion.

On 21 May the hydroplanes several times attacked the vessels of Astrakhan-Caspian flotilla of the reds. The aircraft succeeded in finishing off the damaged destroyer *Moskvityanin* with a direct hit; apart from that, the strafing from the air forced the launch *Schastliviy*, which was dead in the water, to be abandoned. The successful attack is attributed to pilot Sadler.

The *Yussanoff* floating base with two Short 184 airplanes on deck, May 1919.

The following day this crew's luck changed. After setting off in search of red ships at sea, the aircraft ran into fog on the return leg. The pilots water-landed and proceeded as a skimmer. The wind and the waves, however, capsized the aircraft. The crew caught hold of the floats. Only in the evening of the following day they were picked up by the steamer *Aziya*.

On 27 May the *Yussanoff*, with its aircraft, participated in a seaborne landing of troops at Fort-Aleksandrovsk, which ended in the capture of the city. After this, the vessel was drafted in to reconnoitre the Volga delta. On 29 May the British aviators completed four sorties to bomb enemy barges and tugboats, which had been spotted in the lower reaches of the river.

During 13–18 June the vessel was in for repairs (the ship's boilers were cleaned), and she then departed to the Ural estuary. Here on 21 June the hydroplanes were lowered into the water. They conducted several reconnaissance flights along the banks of the river. Combat sorties also took place on 24 and 25 June. Furthermore, bombing and machine-gun fire damaged a paddle steamer, two tugboats, and several motorboats of the reds in the Volga delta. On 28 June, in an attempt to lighten a Shorts hydroplane, which was unable to take off, the crew jettisoned one bomb and, unexpectedly, it exploded. Miraculously the aircrew survived, but the aircraft was blown to bits.

On 8 July the *Yussanoff* returned to Petrovsk. Her speed had reduced down to five knots, and on 11 July British command took the decision to transfer the hydroplanes from this vessel onto the *Orlyonok*, which was dubbed as the *Orlyonoch*. On 17 July this vessel left Petrovsk for the first time with two Shorts on board. The following day both aircraft were lowered into the water close to the island of Tyuleniy to carry out reconnaissance missions. Later on, they flew sorties around the island of Dolgiy, and in the Volga delta. On 24 July during an attack on a tugboat the aircraft

A Short 184 on a beaching trolley at the port of Petrovsk.

A Short 184 hydroplane captured by the reds in the village of Ganyushkino on the shores of the Caspian Sea in January 1920.

A trophy Short 184 on take-off. Note that the aircraft is carrying both Soviet and British markings.

flown by pilot Sadler was damaged by machine-gun fire from a vessel. The bullets passed through the aircraft's port lower wing, damaging the fuel pump and pipeline. The pilot turned his damaged aircraft to the south-east. Twenty minutes later the engine failed, and the British had to make an emergency landing. Launches towed the downed hydroplane to the carrier.

On 27 July the *Orlyonoch*, with two Shorts on board, set off for Guryev. In the Ural River estuary, the plan was to hand both hydroplanes over to white pilots. Of all the Russian pilots, however, only Captain Yegorov had expressed a desire to fly the Shorts. Having received his briefing and after spending two days performing training flights, on the third day Yegorov decided to fly a bombing mission by himself. The Russians refused point blank to attach the bombs to racks under the wings, which came as some surprise to the British. The observer carried the bombs with him in the cockpit, placing them habitually on his knees. This was what Russian pilots had done throughout the war, flying with Russian-built weapons. Whether Yegorov and his companion were relying on Russian 'luck,' or they were simply unfamiliar with the British bomb system, remains unknown. Shortly after take-off the bombs exploded, blowing the aircraft and the aircrew to pieces. The introduction of these new British aircraft ended there – nobody among the whites wanted to fly the second hydroplane.

The *Orlyonoch* returned to Petrovsk on 31 July 1919. On 1–26 August she participated in combat operations with a single aircraft on board. On 8 August it was mobilised for an operation to drive the Bolsheviks out of Ashuradeh, in the south-eastern of Caspian Sea. The vessel spent the rest of August convoying the ships captured from the reds to Petrovsk. When news came through of the British parliament's decision to withdraw forces from Russia, the *Orlyonoch* covered the evacuation from Baku to Iran, along with other vessels in the flotilla.

On 26 August this carrier was handed over to the whites along with the aircraft, the *Yussanof* was transferred to them too, in October 1919 she was renamed the *Volga*. The following day all the British pilots left Petrovsk. The whites were left between two to six hydroplanes in various states of repair. No information is available concerning their use by pilots in Denikin's army. In January 1920 the Short 184 aircraft, registration number N9085, was captured by the reds in the village of Ganyushkino.

As they withdrew from Baku the whites loaded a variety of equipment on their ships and vessels and took them to the port of Anzali in Iran, which at that time was occupied by the British. The demands on the part of the red command to return everything back were ignored. Then, the Soviet flotilla approached Anzali and began strafing military targets. The British garrison abandoned the city without a fight, leaving the artillery batteries and the various warehouses with no defence; and the warehouses were immediately looted by the local population. The whites also fled, after putting on British clothing to disguise themselves. The vessels and ships from Anzali were taken by reds to Baku. This included the *Volga*, which arrived there on 23 May with two hydroplanes on board. It is possible that one of these was the Short 184, registration number N9078.

The British floatplanes captured in the north and south were used for some time by Soviet naval aviation. Thus, a single Short 184, which had previously belonged to the

266th Squadron, ended up in the hydroaviation division of the Volga-Caspian Flotilla. In Astrakhan it was loaded onto the barge *Kommuna*, which was the division's hydroplane carrier. The further fate of this aircraft is not known.

At least six Fairey and three Short airplanes arrived on the Baltic Sea. The first of these was Lieutenant Marshall's former aircraft, which at the end of 1919 was already listed as being part of the 1st Hydroaviation Division at Oranienbaum. The rest of the hydroplanes were captured in 1920 at Medvezhya Gora, on the Segezha River and on the island of Popov (near Kem). They were taken to Petrograd in the second half of 1920. The airplanes needed repair and were entering service gradually. On 1 December in the 1st Hydroaviation Division there were two Faireys (of these one was serviceable) and two Short aircraft (only one of these was likewise serviceable). On the Black Sea a single Short was listed on that date as being part of a combat flight in Odessa. In that same month, a further two airplanes were handed over to various units. Interestingly, these aircraft retained their Royal Air Force registration numbers, which were applied to the aft section of the fuselage. The engines in all these airplanes were very worn out and were not able to develop their full output.

In March 1921 trophy British hydroplanes participated in suppressing the rebellion of sailors in Kronshtadt. Three Faireys and a single Short aircraft took part in the combat sorties. They flew from Gutuyev Island where sufficient area of ice-free water surface was available. The first sortie, which was flown by A.A. Taskinen's crew on 11 March, was not successful, the homemade anti-freeze boiled away in the cooler– it was a mixture of water, ethanol, and petrol. The following day the pilots did manage to drop bombs on Kronstadt. During an attempt to repeat this raid the aircraft came under fire from the ground. The bullets torn several of the undercarriage bracing wires, which resulted in an emergency landing a kilometre away from the airfield. In the next days, the aircraft bombed the city, as well as fortifications, and ships at their moorings. On 17 March M.Ya. Lindel dropped four one-*pood* (around 16 kg) bombs on the battleships that were frozen in the ice, and achieved one direct hit. A cloud of steam formed above the vessel. Naturally, a bomb like that was not going to seriously damage a battleship, so it has been suggested that the explosion ruptured a steam pipe of some kind. On 15–16 March, pilot O. Kalvits tried to bomb Kronstadt from a Short 184 aircraft. No information is available about the 15 March sortie, while on the next day the engine overheated almost immediately after take-off, and the pilot had to return to base.

As of 15 September 1921, a single Fairey was operational in the 3rd Hydroaviation Unit, and a further two more in the 4th Unit. In autumn of that year clashes took place with groups of Finnish nationalists on the border with Karelia. The rebels demanded separation from Russia and annexation to Finland. In connection with this, the 4th Reconnaissance Hydroaviation Unit was deployed to Onezhskoe Lake, which included two Faireys, a single Short 184 and three M-9 flying boats. It was also supplemented by the 1st Hydroaviation Detachment with two more Faireys in its strength. Due to the freezing cold the mechanics could not put the Short 184 into service, while one Fairey crash landed in a dense fog. The other airplanes were used for reconnaissance missions.

Loading a Short 184 hydroplane, serial number N9078, onto the *Orlyonoch*, July 1919. In May 1920 this airplane was captured by the reds.

As of 1 January 1922, the 'English hydroplanes' were listed in the 1st Hydroaviation Unit: two were fitted with Rolls-Royce engines (Fairey Nos. 9449 and 2233), and one with a Sunbeam engine (Short No. 9193). One of the Faireys (No. 9449) crashed on 22 January 1922. As of 1 May, the Short 184 No. 9193 and the Fairey No. 2233 remained in the detachment, the rest of the fleet was comprised of Russian M-9s and M-20s airplanes. A further two British hydroplanes were listed in a transport detachment as of that same date – they were Fairey No. 9231 and Short No. 9024.

The Fairey IIIC served in the Baltics up until spring 1923. Starting from April, Savoia 16bis flying boats began to arrive from Italy, and Soviet naval aviation began to be converted onto this type.

In autumn 1923 there was arranged a campaign aimed on checking the condition of the outdated aircraft, so to write

A Short 184, serial number N9078, is being rolled onto the *Kommuna* barge, the floating base for the Hydroaviation Division of the Volga-Caspian Flotilla, Astrakhan, summer 1920.

them off. In the 1st Reconnaissance Hydroaviation Unit in the Baltics, a commission inspected the two Short 184s – Nos. 1381 and 9024; the latter had previously belonged to a training unit. In accompanying documents, it was noted that the first aircraft had been captured from the British, and then in 1920 was sent for repair to the Black Sea Fleet workshops. The aircraft was not airworthy any more: the engine was missing, the wooden sections were dilapidated, and the canvass was rotting. The conclusion stated: 'This aircraft is not suitable for further service.' The second hydroplane was also written off 'due to frequent repairs and storing in the open air'.

The last Short remained at the 2nd Reconnaissance Hydroaviation Unit until the end of 1923.

At least two Shorts were in service on the Black Sea. One hydroplane was stored for some time in a dismantled condition and then underwent repair in Odessa. Furthermore, it was fitted with a non-standard cooler, the performance of which turned out to be unsatisfactory – at high revs the Sunbeam engine would quickly overheat. Nevertheless, this aircraft was handed over to the special-purpose hydroaviation unit.

On 7 October 1921 pilot V.V. Mikhaylov with mechanic N. Srybniy, in that same hydroplane, took off from Odessa for the Tendra Spit. In the area near Ak-Mechet the engine began to misfire, so the pilot made an emergency landing close to the Yevpatoria lighthouse. The peasants helped to drag the aircraft to shore. After an inspection of the Sunbeam, it emerged that the spark plugs were covered in oil. The following day the aircraft took off again, but the engine gave out a second time. The landing was not successful, the hydroplane nosed over, the crew were thrown out of the open cockpit into the water; Srybniy was killed. The aircraft quickly sank. Mikhaylov, who clung onto a float that had broken off, signalled to the steamer *Dmitriy*. Having investigated the fatal crash, a commission came to the conclusion that the piston rings in the engine had worn.

As of 1 May 1922, however, in the 4th Hydroaviation Unit, Short No. 9086 with Sunbeam engine was still extant. It is not known if this aircraft was airworthy. It is more than likely that this machine was written off in 1923.

1.9 The *Wilson-Sturtevan*

The LWF V American biplane was known under this strange name in Russia. The reason for this is that the aircraft was fitted with 140hp Sturtevant model 5 engine, but where the *Wilson* comes from is still a mystery. It is possible, that this was somehow linked to the fact that the President of the United States of America at that time was Woodrow Wilson.

In spring 1918 the command of the Czechoslovak Corps, which had been formed in Russia of prisoners of war and officers of the Austro-Hungarian Army, came out on the side of the whites, under the influence of intelligence agents from the Détente countries. Instead of an agreed evacuation to France via Vladivostok, the soldiers in the Czechoslovak trains captured cities along the railway line. The corps built up a significant level of independence, and their headquarters decided to acquire aircraft for themselves. They ordered the airplanes from the USA.

In December 1918, two steamers delivered to Vladivostok crates containing these aircraft in dismantled condition. The airplanes were brought by rail to the station Vtoraya Rechka, which was where the Czech pilots were initially based, and then to Okeanskaya, where the aircraft finally began to be assembled. Only there did they discover that the aircraft were of different type than they had ordered. The crates contained obsolete and worn out LWF V airplanes – 28 of them in total. It was already too late, however, and they had to use what they had.

On 7 March 1919, an LWF V took off for the first time from the ice on the Ussuri River, but during a turn it entered an uncontrolled dive, and crashed. Both aircrew members suffered serious injuries.

Shortly after this the Czechoslovaks sold 18 flying machines on to the army under Admiral A.V. Kolchak,

A celebration at the hydroaviation division in Oranienbaum, 1923. Note a trophy Short 184 in the background.

which at that time controlled the whole of Siberia. They had a large number of pilots, who had escaped from the European part of Russia, but they did not have enough aircraft for them. The principal engineering directorate in Kolchak's army acquired LWF Vs for 13,000 USD each. The former owners did not lose on this deal, as they had acquired them for 12,700 USD each.

The combat value of these American aircraft was not significant, since they did not carry any machine-gun or bomb armament. They could only be used as reconnaissance planes or for training purposes.

These airplanes joined the newly formed 14th and 15th Air Units. Familiarisation with these new machines was protracted and difficult. The low level of reliability in the worn-out engines was particularly irksome. Over the summer of 1919 two fatal crashes took place. In both cases the aircraft caught fire in the air, and the crew were killed. Three serious accidents are worth adding to this list.

By August the 14th Air Unit were converted onto the French-built Sopwiths. The LWF Vs that once belonged to it had been sent away to other units. Three aircraft ended up in a Manchurian air unit, which was based in Chita, and a further three – to a flying school in Kurgan. Two aircraft were put in storage in a warehouse, where they remained until the Bolshevik forces arrived.

At the end of July 1919, the 15th Detachment arrived at the front with seven American aircraft. The *Sturtevans* were used as reconnaissance airplanes, following the movements of the red troops. In view of their frequent failures and the lack of fuel, the unit only flew 15 combat sorties in the course of a month and a half. In September, the reds surrounded the airfield near Aktyubinsk, on which the unit was based. The pilots had to burn the aircraft that were left without fuel.

After having sold a large proportion of the LWF Vs to Kolchak's troops, the Czech Corps were left with nine aircraft. They joined the 1st Air Unit, which was commanded by Captain Skala. The unit was based at Okeanskaya. Six biplanes were assembled and readied for flights, and the other three were retained for spares. On 6 May 1919 the air unit set off for the west. Their train caught fire close to Khabarovsk, so one aircraft was lost and several were damaged.

On 31 May the Czechoslovak pilots arrived in Omsk. There the American aircraft joined a Czech flying school, which up to that point had only had two aircraft in service. They succeeded in bringing only three LWF V aircraft up to flying condition. Between June–July 1919 these aircraft flew approximately 350 training flights.

Due to the retreat of Kolchak's forces, the school was soon moved to the Far East. On 19 September flights resumed in this new location, in Nikolsk-Ussuriysk. At that time five aircraft were in operation there. On 25 November one of these airplanes crashed due to engine failure in flight. The crew were not injured, but the wrecked aircraft was written off. The following day flights had to be stopped due to the cold weather. The Czechoslovak LWF Vs did not fly any more in Russia. In connection with the evacuation of the entire corps in January 1920, the flying school personnel and four biplanes were loaded onto the steamer *Silesia* in Vladivostok, which sailed for Marseilles. The personnel and equipment were delivered from there to Prague by train.

These obsolete and worn-out aircraft did not find any use in Czechoslovakia. In November they were officially written off. At present, a single restored LWF V is on display in the National Technical Museum in Prague.

Following the rout of Kolchak's army by the reds, the Manchurian air unit was transferred to the white Ataman G.M. Semyonov, who was fighting in the Transbaikal region. The unit did not, however, get to the front line, and neither did it participate in any combat operations. One of former Kolchak's LWF V ended its days serving in the air unit of the

An LWF V at the airfield

An accident with one of the LWF V aircraft serving in Kolchak's Army

The sectioned fuselage of the LWF V was displayed at the Central House of Aviation and Chemistry in Moscow, 1927.

A trophy LWF V serving with red aviation.

An LWF V that was brought out of Russia by the Czechoslovak Corps is now an exhibit at the National Technical Museum in Prague.

Far Eastern Republic. As of 15 June 1921, among eight aircraft in service in the republic, there was listed a single *Sturtevan*. It is possible that in 1920–1922 this airplane participated in battles with the *Zemskaya Rat* – the forces of the bourgeois government, located in Vladivostok, and which collaborated with the Japanese interventionists.

Two Kolchak's LWF V which had belonged to a flying school in Kurgan became trophies of the reds. They were considered unsuitable for combat and were transferred to civil aviation. It was decided that the *Sturtevans* would be converted to agricultural aircraft, and chemical spray equipment was fitted. Even in this capacity, however, they were not widely used. An indigenously built aircraft – *Konyok-gorbunok,* designed by V.N. Khioni was better suited to the specific requirements of the agricultural aviation.

The further fate of these trophy *Sturtevans* is not really unknown. On 31 March 1921 a commission led by Iordan, which had been revising the engine inventory of the air force, recommended that the Sturtevant engines be retained only for experimental operation. The only other fact known is that in September 1922 a single *Wilson* aircraft, fitted with a *Sturtevan* engine, was present at repair Factory No.2. It is possible that it was this aircraft that later joined the flying school in Borisoglebsk where it was used for some time as a trainer.

The last of these airplanes were taken out of service in accordance with a decree of 15 December 1925. One *Wilson* ended up in the House of Aviation and Chemistry in Moscow, where it was turned into an aid for studying aircraft fuselage construction.

2

The Period of Soviet Aviation Resurgence

Following the end of the Civil War the Red Air Fleet was in a critical condition. Russia's aircraft factories were, to a great extent, paralysed by economic decay, and many of them had stopped working completely. Far fewer aircraft were produced than under the tsar regime.

Nevertheless, in 1920-1923 the factories managed to introduce the de Havilland DH.4 light bomber and reconnaissance biplanes into series production using documentation received from Britain under a licensing agreement which had been concluded at the times of the Provisional Government, as well as utilising trophy examples captured from the whites. Less than a hundred of them were built, however, which for a huge country was a drop in the ocean.

A very varied fleet of native and foreign flying machines was in service with Soviet aviation, and in some cases they were down to single aircraft of the type. The majority of them were obsolete and completely worn out and had been repaired on many occasions.

As there were no particularly high hopes of a rapid roll out of indigenous production, the country turned to making purchases from abroad, and there was a solid basis for this. After the end of the First World War the enormous orders placed with aircraft manufacturing plants were cancelled immediately. A large number of airplanes that were no longer required had built up in storage, which countries were prepared to sell for a very reasonable price. Foreign aircraft production companies were taking on any orders they could find, if only to give their factory assembly workshops something to do, and to empty out their stores.

A decree from the Revolutionary Military Council (RVS, *Revolyutsionniy Voenniy Sovet*) of 26 March 1921 stated: 'In view of the enormous role aviation played in the Civil War ... the Russia's RVS considers it absolutely necessary to purchase a significant amount of aviation equipment from abroad, since production in the country itself is falling at such a rate that losses are not being recovered at all'.

The Soviet Government began to purchase airplanes from Italy, France, and the Netherlands, and a little later on – from Germany. As strange as it may seem, however, the vast majority of aircraft were purchased in Britain. Relations between Soviet Russia and Britain at the time were very strained. Business is business though and initially these purchases were made through intermediaries in Sweden, and later on they were made directly. They were brokered through ARCOS – All Russian Co-Operative Society, which had been established as the official buying and selling agency of the Soviet government in the United Kingdom.

British Martynside F.4 fighters and de Havilland DH.9 reconnaissance aircraft entered service with the RKKVF, which in April 1924 was renamed the Workers' and Peasants' Red Army Air Force (VVS RKKA, *Voenno-Vozdushniye Sily Raboche-Krestyanskoy Krasnoy Armii*). The latter type was used very widely, they were not only imported as ready-made aircraft but individual, dismantled airframes were also acquired, which were assembled at Soviet factories and fitted with different types of engines. In Soviet Russia production subsequently began of an indigenous version of the DH.9, designated the R-1. These aircraft were fitted with M-5 engines (a copy of the American Liberty engine), and the R-1 was the most widely used aircraft in the VVS RKKA for a long period of time.

Similarly, production of the Avro 504K biplane was arranged in Petrograd, and its Soviet version was designated the U-1. These biplanes were fitted with M-2 engines (a copy of the French Rhone 9J) and all the country's flying schools flew these airplanes up until the beginning of the 1930s.

In Moscow a small number of MF-4 fighters were produced which represented somewhat inferior versions of the Martynsides.

The British companies suggested the Soviet Government to acquire other flying machines as well. For example, in 1922 the management of Vickers Limited sent a letter to Moscow in which they announced their readiness to sell a batch of five Virginia twin-engine bombers (fitted with Condor or Lion engines, to the customer's the choice), although they would be unarmed, and would not have any photographic or radio equipment. The lead time was defined as six months after the signing of the agreement. The agreement, however, was never concluded, and it is possible that this was in view of the high price.

In April 1924 that same Vickers company proposed establishing production of its aircraft in Russia, and Rolls-Royce also bought into this as they were prepared to arrange manufacturing the engines for these airplanes. The British proposed an offer of credit amounting to 60 percent of the cost of these orders. The choice of aircraft types and engines, it was proposed, was to be made by the Soviets. The Head of the Foreign Department of the Air Force Directorate (UVVS, *Upravleniye Voenno-Vozdushnykh Sil*) G.K. Linno wrote to the RVS: 'the proposal should be examined as one with significant meaning and weight … '. The Soviet Government was to have provided a factory, which the British would then fit out. The negotiations continued up until November 1924, and proposals were examined involving the formation of a mixed stock company (and moreover, Vickers to invest two thirds of the capital) and with the factory leased on concession. In the first few years the airplanes were to be produced from imported components, and then they would be manufactured independently. No agreement was reached on this, however, and the priority was given to the German Junkers company (which was secretly being financed by the Ministry of War in Germany).

In summer 1925, the British Gloster company offered their Grebe III fighters fitted with Jupiter engines. On 22 July of that same year the Scientific Committee of the UVVS discussed this proposal and the recommendation was that it be turned down.

The airplanes purchased in Britain comprised a significant part of the VVS fleet in the first half of the 1920s. The aircraft that had been produced by the Soviet factories, on the basis of copying British designs, played a significant role for a much longer period. The U-1 trainer, and particularly the R-1 served for many years. The latter was produced in large numbers up until 1932 and was operated by flying schools up until 1935 when it was superseded by the R-5 designed by N.N. Polikarpov.

By the end of the 1920s the VVS RKKA had almost totally transferred to indigenously produced types, although the aircraft and engines, in many cases, were copied from foreign examples. There were still very small numbers of foreign aircraft in service but in the first half of the 1930s they were all replaced by original Soviet designs.

Aside from the types mentioned above, in the first half of the 1920s several British machines were purchased as examples to study. These included NT.2b Norman-Thompson flying boat, Vickers Viking IV amphibious aircraft, Avro Baby and DH.53 light airplanes, Vickers Vimy Commercial and DH.34 passenger planes, as well as Handley Page Hanley I torpedo bomber. After familiarisation, some of them were operated by Air Force units. The torpedo bombers were used in experiments with the first Soviet air-launched torpedoes.

After the 'ARCOS raid' and the break in Anglo-Soviet relations in 1927, acquisition of aviation materiel in Britain ceased for some time. Soviet Russia did not purchase any aircraft in America in the 1920s at all. Aircraft engines and their components were acquired, as well as instruments and various items of equipment but there were no plans to purchase any American aircraft at that time. This situation remained in place up until the beginning of the 1930s, when the Soviet Union set about a rapid development of their military and civil aviation.

2.1 The *Deaichfor* (DH.4)

This is how the DH.4 biplane became known in Russia, with a pronunciation that more or less equates to the original English, and it became the first de Havilland aircraft to arrive in this country. This two-seat light bomber and reconnaissance biplane, which appeared on the Western Front in spring 1917, quickly gained popularity and was produced in series. The Provisional Government in that same year ordered 50 DH.4s from Britain, fitted with FIAT 240hp A.12 engines. The reason the Italian engines were chosen was that they were not in such short supply in Russia as the optional Pumas were. An order was placed in Italy for a large number of A.12s and some of them had already arrived in Russian Army stores. The British, however, were not able to deliver the aircraft within the timescale. Agreement was reached to extend the deadline to spring 1918 and the size of the order was increased up to 75 biplanes. They were actually produced but by that time the Bolsheviks were in power in Russia and the British Government decided that there was a greater need for new aircraft on the Western Front. The Royal Flying Corps accepted all of these machines.

A DH.4A aircraft with an enclosed cabin for passengers was used by the British aviation mission with the army of General A.I. Denikin in the South of Russia.

An accident with one of the DH.4s serving in a British reconnaissance flight in the Russian north, 1918.

A Russian-made DH.4 fitted with a Fiat A.12 engine.

the DH.4s for conversion training, having fitted them with 200hp RAF.3A engines and dual controls. The British flying instructor, who had arrived along with the aircraft, was in charge of the training.

The DH.4s were also operated by 'A' Flight of the No. 72 Squadron RAF which supported movements of General Dunsterville's troops around Baku in September 1918. During the British retreat under pressure from the Turks the serviceable aircraft were burnt down. The 'fours' were also used by 'A' Flight of the No. 47 Squadron RAF, which had been sent to Russia to assist the forces of General Denikin. When the whites were forced to evacuate Novorossiysk and head to the Crimea two serviceable DH.4s were left in this unit. The British Military Mission used another aircraft that had been converted into a limousine (with an enclosed aft cabin). Evidently, the British supplied some more airplanes of this type to the white armies, including the improved DH.4Bs fitted with 400hp Liberty engines.

Some of the de Havillands became trophies for the Red Army, and five DH.4Bs were captured at different fronts. Several airplanes, in different states of airworthiness, were handed over to the GAZ-1 factory (the former *Duks* factory). A single DH.4B underwent testing at the Scientific-Experimental Airfield (NOA, *Nauchno-Opytniy Aerodrom*).

Pilots of the 49th Air Unit of the reds (the 14th Army, Southern Front) I.G. Savin, A.I. Tomashevskiy and I.I. Yuzhak standing next to a DH.4 aircraft fitted with a Fiat engine.

As the aircraft ordered from Britain by the Provisional Government had not been received, a decision was taken to manufacture DH.4s fitted with FIAT engines independently

A collision between a DH.4 and a Nieuport fighter at Khodynka airfield in Moscow.

An accident of pilot D.M. Vershinskiy on 18 June 1921 at Tambov airfield. This airplane was in service with the 6th Air Unit of the Combat Air Squadron of the Forces of the Tambov Governate and participated in the suppression of a peasant uprising.

A line-up on the Air Fleet Day at one of the airfields of Ukrainian Military District at the beginning of the 1920s. Note two DH.4s with ace of clubs emblems on the rudders.

in Soviet Russia, thanks to the documentation on this aircraft that had arrived in Russia in autumn 1917 in accordance with the licensing agreement. From spring 1918, the Main Directorate of the RKKVF began to request that the Central Directorate of Army Supply release funds for this undertaking but the Soviet economic system was in its infancy at that time. The Central Directorate of Army Supply and the Supreme Council of the National Economy fought for a long time for control over the aviation factories and the issue remained unresolved, despite the obvious need to augment the military aviation fleet which had been significantly depleted following the collapse of the Eastern Front. Things only began to move forward in August, when L.D. Trotskiy who was the party official in charge of the armed forces visited the front line near Kazan. K.E. Akashev, who was commanding Soviet aviation in this region, advised Trotskiy of the shortage of aircraft and requested that 20,000 roubles be allocated for setting up production of the DH.4 with the FIAT engines that were available. Trotskiy immediately sent a telegram to Moscow to issue the funds. On 20 August, the Head of the Main Directorate of the Air Force sought permission to manufacture a single aircraft at the *Duks* factory.

On 19 September the Technical Committee under the Head of Supply announced that the drawings for the DH.4 were sufficient, and the lack of drawings for some parts was not a significant issue. On 30 September a work order was written out for the manufacture of a single DH.4, which was in fact a prototype example.

On 26 December 1918 a board examined a proposal to order 70 airplanes with the 'available 230hp FIAT engines', and this issue was handed over to the Technical Committee for their consideration. An agreement was subsequently drawn up, dividing this quantity into three individual series – 30, 20, and 20 biplanes.

A group of designers, led by N.N. Polikarpov, were engaged in the 'reshaping' of the airframe of the British aircraft using materials that were available in Russia. In view of the shortage of personnel in the Technical Department all the engineers and technicians at the factory were drafted in to modify the drawings. In particular, the American spruce was replaced by Russian pine, which had lower strength parameters. This forced a recalculation of the strength of the entire structure, and suitable Russian steels and fastenings were selected. It was suggested that initially these machines would be fitted with the A.12 engines, which would subsequently be replaced by the more powerful Liberty engines, similarly to the DH.4B.

The military set the delivery date for the first batch of reconnaissance aircraft as the middle of 1919. The first airplane was actually assembled in July of that same year, but the numerous defects and the need of refinement of the engine mount in the situation of economic decay, when there was a shortage of absolutely everything, led to this Soviet de Havilland was ready for flight only in May 1920. By 1 June the factory presented representatives of the RKKVF with seven DH.4s, and on 2 June pilot Gorshkov made the first flight of the leading aircraft (serial number 2262). On 15 June, the second biplane took to the air. In reality, the first series comprised 23 aircraft. The Moscow-built de Havillands had Hazet type engine coolers located along the sides of the fuselage near the cockpit.

By that time, GAZ-1 factory had received the second order for 20 reconnaissance aircraft, and by September 1921 some 26 airplanes had been assembled in total. The shortage of engines, components, and various materials caused significant delays to the work. For example, the military acceptance committee accepted the first example of the second order 'provisionally' ... without wheels! Production of the 'fours' was ceased in 1923 and in total 60 (other sources put this figure at 66) aircraft of this type had been completed.

In the records, the Russian-made aircraft were often designated as ΔH.4 – the first letter was taken from the Cyrillic and the second from the Latin alphabet. This was how the aircraft was identified in the official technical description, published in 1923.

As the aircraft engine would overheat in the warmer regions, a cellular radiator positioned under the fuselage nose section was added to the two Hazet coolers. It did not retract and was supported at the rear using a pair of struts. These coolers were also fitted to the earlier produced biplanes.

A DH.4 biplane flown by pilot A.I. Lapin is put back onto its wheels after a ground loop at Khodynka airfield in Moscow, summer 1922.

The last airplanes were produced under the factory designation ΔHΔ, which the military did not use in their records. They differed by a single set of controls (the biplane could only be flown from the front cockpit) instead of dual controls. The main fuel tank was divided by a bulkhead into two, and the fuel supply tank was repositioned to the upper wing center section, similarly to the DH.9 configuration. Fuel was transferred into the supply tank by two pumps driven by aerovanes. The biplane cell was reinforced by the introduction of thicker outer struts and dual (instead of single) bracing wires. One bracing wire was added in the aft cockpit and the shape of the upper fairing of the fuselage was changed slightly.

In terms of quality, the airplanes produced at GAZ-1 were inferior to the British examples – the assembly process was negligent and poor-quality materials were used. Returning these aircraft for that reason back to the repair department of the Central depot or to the factory became standard practice. For example, airplanes serial numbers 2316 and 2321 were returned in September 1921 due to defects and sub-standard workmanship. Moreover, it emerged concurrently that the first of them had not even passed the factory testing!

The airplanes fitted with the FIAT engines would glide poorly due to incorrect trim. However, after four dead-stick landings pilot Yuzhak managed to define an angle of incidence for the stabiliser that improved this situation.

The Italian engine itself was not famous for its high reliability either. They would often suffer from valve break-off where the valves would fall into the cylinders. The carburettors would often fail as well. Incidents of the engine

A DH.4 at an exhibition organized by the *Aviakhim* society, Leningrad, 1920s.

catching fire in flight were not uncommon. The aircraft type was even given the nickname 'the British hearse'.

In 1923 one of the last examples of the Soviet DH.4 was modified by installing the inter-plane struts of a teardrop shaped cross-section instead the ones with a circular cross-section used before. This, however, had no bearing on the series-built aircraft.

As there was a concern that the reserve of Italian engines in the stores would soon run out, the search began for an alternative power plant. In 1921, a decision was taken to use the German 260hp Maybach engine which was also an in-line water-cooled type. In that same year the GAZ-1 factory was given an order for 20 of these biplanes, and plans were in existence to produce 35 of them fitted with these same engines in 1922. Production, however, progressed at a slow rate, and there was no hurry to introduce the German engine. Only in 1924 a single Moscow-built DH.4 was actually converted to accommodate the Maybach. It was on this aircraft that a new thicker wing profile proposed by V.V. Kalinin and V.L. Moiseyenko had been tested. By that time, however, production of the DH.4s had ceased, and the results of the experiment were purely scientific.

The airplanes manufactured in Moscow augmented the small numbers of trophy British-built machines in RKKVF units. For example, one of the first two DH.4s built at GAZ-1 factory were handed over to the 2nd (the former 39th) *Zheleznіy* Reconnaissance Air Unit of the 2nd Squadron, where it served until the end of 1922. DH.4s were in service in 1921–1924 with units in the Ukrainian, Leningrad, and Siberian military districts. Among these were the 1st Reconnaissance Squadron of the 2nd Air Wing; the 6th Combat Air Unit of the Tambov province forces; the 1st, 3rd, 5th, 12th, 13th, 15th, 16th, 17th, and 48th Separate Reconnaissance Air Units; and the 1st, 3rd, and 5th Separate Reconnaissance Squadrons.

The DH.4s succeeded in participating in the concluding stage of the Civil War when the large-scale alignments of white troops had already been routed and serious combat operations were only to be encountered in the Far East. In certain locations, however, uprisings of those opposed to the new ruling party would break out.

In January 1921 during the suppression of an uprising in Karelia an air unit was redeployed to this region from the south. This unit had some trophy DH.4s fitted with Puma engines in service and was accommodated on the ice on the estuary of the Vyg River. However, they did not have necessary equipment to pre-heat the water and oil. The commander requested a steamer, but this was refused. As a result, the water was heated in barrels on bonfires, and the firewood was gathered from the nearby forest. The Pumas gave a poor account of themselves in the sub-zero conditions and the oil would often be subjected to overcooling, especially when the engines were tested on the ground. These airplanes performed reconnaissance missions, bombed villages, and strafed the enemy using their machine guns. The operation was completed by mid-February.

In Ukraine military units under the anarchist N. Makhno continued to be active, initially, he had supported the reds but then began to fight against them. Troops were deployed to fight him, which were augmented by aviation forces. On 30 May 1921 a crew of the 48th unit made an emergency landing during a reconnaissance sortie behind the lines of the 'dad' Makhno. The pilots were rescued but the enemy forces set fire to the aircraft. A further two airplanes in this unit were destroyed by Makhno's forces when the cavalry attacked the airfield.

Four DH.4s were in service with the 6th Air Unit of the Combat Air Squadron, and this unit was attached to forces under the command of M.N. Tukhachevskiy, who had participated in the suppression of the peasant uprising in the Tambov province. The combat activities were held there from May till September 1921 when the uprising was put down, and the red pilots made widespread use of high explosive and incendiary bombs against poorly armed peasants and unarmed population. They would strafe the civilians with machine gun fire from low-level flight. The unit did not incur any combat losses in the air, which is hardly surprising as the insurgents were not able to put up any significant resistance.

An unfortunate forced landing of a DH.4. 1920s

A DH.4 aircraft flown by pilot Voronovich ground looped on landing at an airfield in Minsk, 1922.

Pilots T.V. Suonio, V.L. Galyshev (who subsequently became a well-known polar aviator), Yermolayev, and Brekke flew these DH.4 biplanes.

This airplane type was in service in other locations as well. On 2 August 1921 an air day was held in Simferopol. It was marred slightly by an emergency landing of a biplane flown by pilot Karabanov, as the Italian engine in his machine had failed in flight. The aircraft was sent for repair, and Karabanov himself was only slightly injured.

On 23 September of that same year pilot S. Lyalin and his flight observer B. Lobach-Zhuchenko set off on a reconnaissance sortie on a route Orenburg–Iletsk–Orenburg looking for white Cossack units moving around the steppe. The airplane's engine, however, failed on take-off at an altitude of 50m. The machine was completely destroyed and written off, but the crew survived.

A number of DH.4s were handed over to flying schools, where they would regularly be broken down, sometimes with serious consequences. On 22 August 1921 during a long-range flight from Podosinki to Moscow, a cadet of the Moscow flying school Bykov made a left turn with a very steep bank angle, so his biplane tumbled downwards and crashed into the ground. Bykov was killed, as was the commandant of the airfield in Podosinki, who was in the rear cockpit. On 9 May 1922, at the Moscow school, cadet pilot Leyland lost speed at an altitude of approximately 200m, entered s spin, and could not recover from it. Along with the pilot, the engine specialist Rozhkov was also killed.

In September 1921, a radio-telephone designed by A.N. Kovalenkov was fitted to a single DH.4. It was very heavy unit weighting 64kg which could only provide communications over a distance of about nine kilometres. During testing on 30 September, a connection was established with the radio room of the NOA.

In summer of 1922, a unit equipped with DH.4 aircraft fitted with Liberty engines was re-deployed to Qarshi in Central Asia to support forces fighting the Basmachi. The pilots had to work in very difficult conditions – the aircraft engines would overheat in the hot conditions, and the landings on the loose sandy runways led to ground loops. Only a few combat sorties were flown, including just one successful bombing attack in the area around Gissar. Then there was a terrible fire, which destroyed all the unit's equipment, with the exception of a single airplane.

In December 1923, the RKKVF units had 20 DH.4s fitted with FIAT engines in their strength, but 13 of them were unserviceable. Several airplanes served in different flying schools; the proportion of serviceable aircraft was higher there – seven out of nine. A further two biplanes were in storage, and nine were listed as being in for repair. The records indicate a further three airplanes (all of which were serviceable) fitted with Liberty engines (evidently, the trophy machines) – two were in the air units and one at a flying school. A fourth DH.4 fitted with a Liberty engine was in for repair.

These aircraft were scattered across different air units. For example, on 12 November 1923 the 15th Reconnaissance Air Unit in Gomel had two DH.4s fitted with FIAT engines, and on 13 December 1923 the 1st Separate Reconnaissance Air Unit of the Leningrad Military District had one DH.4. On 14 October of that same year a single reconnaissance aircraft with a FIAT engine was in the 5th (previously the 13th Kazan) Separate Reconnaissance Air Unit in Vitebsk.

The military service of the DH.4 ended for the most part in mid-1925, at that time the numbers of this type in the VVS were in single figures. For example, a single DH.4 produced by the GAZ-1 factory was in service at the NOA. The order to withdraw these airplanes from service was signed on 15 December 1925, although in practice, individual examples continued to be used for some time. In January 1927 for instance, there was one DH.4 fitted with a Liberty engine in the 28th (the former 7th) Squadron based outside Leningrad. In 1927, five aircraft were listed in the reserve at the 5th permanent air base of the Siberian Military District. Then, the serviceable biplanes were handed over to the flying schools and training squadrons. Several aircraft ended up in the *Aviakhim* organisation (Society for the Assistance of Aviation and Chemical Construction), where they initially flew propaganda flights within the confines of the airfields, and then became ground based study aids. The last DH.4s were written off there in 1929.

2.2 De Havillands – Red And White

Another de Havilland type, which was used much more widely in Russia, was the DH.9. This reconnaissance aircraft and light bomber, built in large numbers in Britain and Canada, along with the Sopwith 1½ Strutter, was the most extensively operated British aircraft in Soviet Russia. The DH.9s were built there with Puma engines, while the DH.9As were equipped with more powerful Liberty power plant and had a larger wingspan. More than 160 DH.9s and DH.9As participated in Russian Civil War, and the majority of these (118 airplanes) saw action in the south.

The first machines of this type appeared in the south of Russia at the beginning of 1919 – these biplanes were in the strength of several units which were directed to support the White Army under General A.I. Denikin. On 31 December 1918, 'A flight of the No. 17 Squadron RAF was sent from Saloniki, and it was followed by the No. 221 Squadron which was loaded onto HMS *Riviera* and HMS *Empress* steamers on Moudros island. These units were equipped with DH.9s powered by Puma engines, and the No. 221 also had several improved DH.9As with Liberty engines.

The No. 221 Squadron under the command of Major G. Andrews began to be offloaded in the port of Batum (now Batumi) on 3 January (other sources put this date as 5 January) 1919. Two aircraft were lost during the offloading of the final batch as a result of a storm. Then, the personnel and equipment were transferred to Petrovsk by rail, which shortly before this had been captured by Denikin's troops. By 14 January, the first airplanes had been assembled and had carried out test flights, but the commencement of combat operations was delayed by cold weather and a blizzard.

By the end of January all the aircraft were ready. During one of the test flights on 28 January Captains Griegson and Gayford crashed one aircraft but they escaped with only light bruises.

On 3 February the first combat sortie took place – four DH.9s took off from Petrovsk, bombing Kizlyar and the village of Kalinovskaya. Close to Shchedrinskaya village they attacked a red armoured train; one aircraft was damaged from return of fire from the ground, and crashed on landing. On 5 February the squadron officially became part of the Armed Forces of the South of Russia, which was commanded by General A.I. Denikin. On that same day a single airplane attacked Grozniy, causing a fire, and strafed concentrations of infantry and cavalry on the edge of the city.

Then the DH.9As took to the skies for the first time – two aircraft took off on a reconnaissance mission. To the south

Aircraft of the Slavo-British Air Corps at Bereznik airfield, summer 1919. Note a single DH.9 and two DH.9As.

of Astrakhan, the pilots noticed a cavalry unit, and dropped bombs on them, photographing the result. One of the explosions occurred next to a group of cavalrymen. The following day it emerged that they had bombed the whites by mistake. An enraged cossack officer arrived, after which a decree was received from general headquarters to stop all flights until further notice.

Overall that day had not been a successful one, two biplanes had been hit by ground fire, one of them was destroyed during a forced landing, and the

Personnel of the 'C' Flight of the No. 47 Squadron RAF in front of a DH.9 during the battles near Tsaritsyn.

DH.9 airplanes from 'C' Flight of the No. 47 Squadron RAF, summer 1919. The biplane in the foreground was subsequently handed over to the whites and came under the 2nd Air Division of the Armed Forces of the South of Russia.

This DH.9, registration number D3149, from the No. 47 Squadron RAF subsequently served in Denikin's aviation, and in autumn 1919 it was captured by the reds.

A DH.9 of the No. 221 Squadron RAF in Petrovsk, 1919.

Red pilots D. Shchyokin and A. Korotkov standing next to the wreckage of a DH.9 of the No. 221 Squadron RAF, which they shot down over Astrakhan on 16 June 1919.

General P.N. Wrangel visiting the 1st Air Unit, Crimea, summer 1920. Note a DH.9A on the right.

other crashed before it reached the airfield and was set on fire by its own crew.

The squadron was reassigned to perform a different mission – reconnaissance of the ice on the northern part of the Caspian Sea. The British pilots were tasked with spotting any attempts by the Bolshevik flotilla to leave a delta of the Volga River. In view of the insufficient range of these airplanes, the reconnaissance had to be conducted from a forward base on Chechen Island, approximately 100km north of Petrovsk. At the end of April, the ice dissipated, and the red flotilla captured Fort-Aleksandrovsk on the north-eastern bank of the Caspian Sea. By that time, Major De Ville had been made squadron commander, and Andrews, who had caught typhus, was sent back to Britain.

The principal objective for the British pilots from May 1919 onwards was to bomb Astrakhan and its surroundings. The airplanes would take off from Petrovsk on these missions; the flight distance there and back was approximately 600km, and what is more the majority of the route was over the sea. There was an intermediate airfield on Chechen Island. On 14 May during the course of the raid on Oranzhereynoe, which is some 60km south-west of Astrakhan, eight bombs were dropped. Moreover, a lucky direct hit destroyed a barge belonging to the Astrakhan Hydroplane Air Division.

Not all these flights ended successfully – for instance, on 16 May during an unfortunate landing on Chechen Island one of the de Havillands crashed. The aircraft exploded and was burnt out, and the pilot and observer perished in the flames. Four days later an old DH.9 was destroyed in this same location, the pilot survived.

On 22 May the No. 221 Squadron participated in an attack on Fort-Aleksandrovsk. The British flotilla as well as hydroplanes of the No. 226 Squadron were drafted in for this mission as well. All the crews coped with this task and landed safely, while during the raid several ships and port structures had been damaged. As a result, only four destroyers of reds managed to find their way through back to Astrakhan. This operation became a good example of coordination between the naval and air forces.

A DH.9 airplane of the 5th Air Unit, which was captured by red army soldiers in the workshops in Simferopol, 1920.

A group of red pilots of the 9th Army standing next to a trophy DH.9, summer 1921.

On 31 May three crews carried out a raid on Astrakhan – the de Havillands, after circling over the city, dropped four bombs as well as leaflets and then turned for home. Red pilot P.V. Stolyarov tried to catch them up in his Nieuport but was unsuccessful. On 5 June the same raid was repeated. Two aircraft of the No. 47 Squadron RAF were scrambled to intercept: S.G. Kalan took off in his Nieuport, and M.V. Fisher in a Sopwith 1½ Strutter. They, however, were not able to catch the enemy and it became apparent that the use of these biplanes for ground alert interception would not ensure success. Therefore, the city defenders decided to organise a permanent air patrol the red pilots lay in wait for the enemy in the skies for more than a week.

Only 10 days later did this tactic bring any success, on 16 June during a raid by four DH.9s on the Baldinsk bridge across the Volga River, D.V. Shchyokin and A.S. Korotkov intercepted the enemy at an altitude of 2,100m. With an accurate burst from his Nieuport 23 Shchyokin damaged radiator on the enemy aircraft, and the DH.9As overheated engine soon jammed. The British pilots made emergency landing some 30km south-west of Astrakhan, set fire to their aircraft, and tried to escape into the steppe but they were captured. Subsequently, Lieutenants Ingram and Mentler were sent to Moscow and it is possible that they were later swapped with the help of the Red Cross. According to Soviet documents, these same red pilots a few days later shot down another DH.9, but the British sources do not corroborate this fact. The British airplanes returned from the next raid on Astrakhan on 19 June without incurring any losses.

On 21 June, new squadron commander Colonel Gordon arrived from Baku, and the next day six new DH.9As were delivered. Raids on Astrakhan by groups of four or five machines continued systematically over the whole of July with the same intensity, all the personnel had worked without a break for more than two months and were very tired. In mid-August vessels arrived in Batumi to evacuate the British. The combat activity of the No. 221 Squadron began to decline. General Denikin's forces launched a successful advance on Moscow while the significance of the southern sector of the front had reduced. Another important factor was the active Bolshevik campaigning among the Azerbaijan citizens, which could have led to an insurgency. A

Airplanes of the 34th and 25th Air Units, which were attached to the 1st Cavalry Army, in Yekaterinodar, September 1920. Note DH.9 biplanes in the background, which were captured in autumn 1919 from Denikin's army.

DH.9 airplanes (in the foreground) belonging to one of the air units of the reds.

A DH.9 from one of the air units attached to the 1st Cavalry Army.

realistic threat arose of being cut off from Baku and coming under attack from the insurgents in Petrovsk. The situation was becoming more serious by the day, and then it emerged that the British parliament had decided to withdraw their forces from Russia.

On 1 September 1919 the No. 221 Squadron RAF was disbanded and all the personnel were evacuated by sea. The six DH.9s that did remain in service were handed over to the 5th and 7th Air Units of the Volunteer Army, which had become part of the Armed Forces of the South of Russia.

There were DH.9 and DH.9A aircraft in the No. 47 Squadron RAF as well – on 10 June airplanes from 'C' Flight took off to fly to the area around Tsaritsyn. Combat operations, however, were delayed by rain and a bridge that had been blown up, which blocked the movement of ground crew. Flights from the airfield near the village of Gniloaksayskaya began from 23 June. British pilots carried out strikes on jetties in the Volga River as well as vessels and barges on the river and concentrations of red troops. In one case, a headquarters building was destroyed by a direct hit from a bomb, and around 40 people were killed. Sorties were also conducted against the city where fierce fires would often break out as the houses were, for the most part, made of wood. The small numbers of red pilots of the 7th and 4th Fighter Air Units did not mount any significant resistance to the British. On 30 July, after the whites had captured Tsaritsyn, the 'C' Flight was re-deployed to Beketovka, from where raids were launched on Kamyshin to the north-east. At the beginning of July, a new group of 13 British personnel arrived and they were incorporated into the 'C' Flight but were used on another sector of the front line close to Chyorniy Yar, where troops were holding out against the 11th Army of the reds, which had advanced from Astrakhan. On 25 July, after dropping bombs on barges and on the station, the biplane flown by G. Hatchett was attacked by a red Nieuport. In an accurate burst from his turret-mounted machine gun observer Simmons damaged the fighter, which side slipped onto its wing, descended sharply, and made a forced landing.

An unfortunate landing of a Soviet DH.9

On 30 July, three DH.9s dropped 19 bombs on barges on the river close to Chyorniy Yar. Captain Walter Anderson's crew photographed the results of this bombing mission, and was escorted by another de Havilland flown by William Elliot. To carry out his mission the pilots descended to an altitude of 1,000m. The DH.9 flown by Elliot was hit by intensive machine gun fire from the ground, the crew made an emergency landing behind red lines some eight kilometres from the front. A cavalry unit of the reds immediately headed from to the place where the aircraft had landed. The observer Lieutenant Laidlaw opened fire with the Lewis machine gun as the pilot was setting fire to the aircraft. Anderson came to their aid on his DH.9, even though there were bullet holes in the aircraft fuel tank. The aircraft landed next to them, Elliott and Laidlaw climbed into the rear cockpit, and the flight observer, John Mitchell, got up onto the lower wing, grabbing hold of the bracing wires. With his fingers, he plugged the holes in the fuel tank. Captain Anderson took off the overloaded machine with difficulty before the eyes of the astonished cavalrymen, who were hoping to capture the crews and their airplanes. For the entire return trip Mitchell stood firm on the lower wing, covered in fuel, he stood there for 50 minutes; any spark, flying out of the exhaust pipe, could have turned him into a flaming torch. This unusual flight was completed successfully, Anderson and Mitchell would be nominated for the Victoria Cross but supporting documentation was lost during the evacuation from Russia.

A DH.9A belonging to one of the Red Army air units.

TsAGI engineer V.P. Vetchinkin inspects the vertical tail of a trophy DH.9. This airplane was captured by the Red Army in the south and was transported to Moscow for a study.

A DH.9A from the Special Purpose Air Unit under the Combat Air Squadron of the Tambov Governate. This airplane was flown by the crew of Rudkov and Rutkovskiy.

At the beginning of August 1919, the Soviet Volga-Kama flotilla (by this time it had been renamed to the Volga-Caspian Flotilla) arrived on the Volga River from the Eastern Front. It comprised up to 40 combat vessels (destroyers, gunboats, monitors, and floating gun batteries) and approximately 70 auxiliary ships. The barge *Kommuna* formed part of the flotilla with 12 M-5, M-9, and M-20 flying boats on the deck. The *Kommuna* was towed behind the steamer *Samorodok*, with the 18th Aeronautical Unit based on the deck with a tethered Parseval aerostat. The other barge was a floating hydroplane carrier for a fighter air unit. Soviet command was

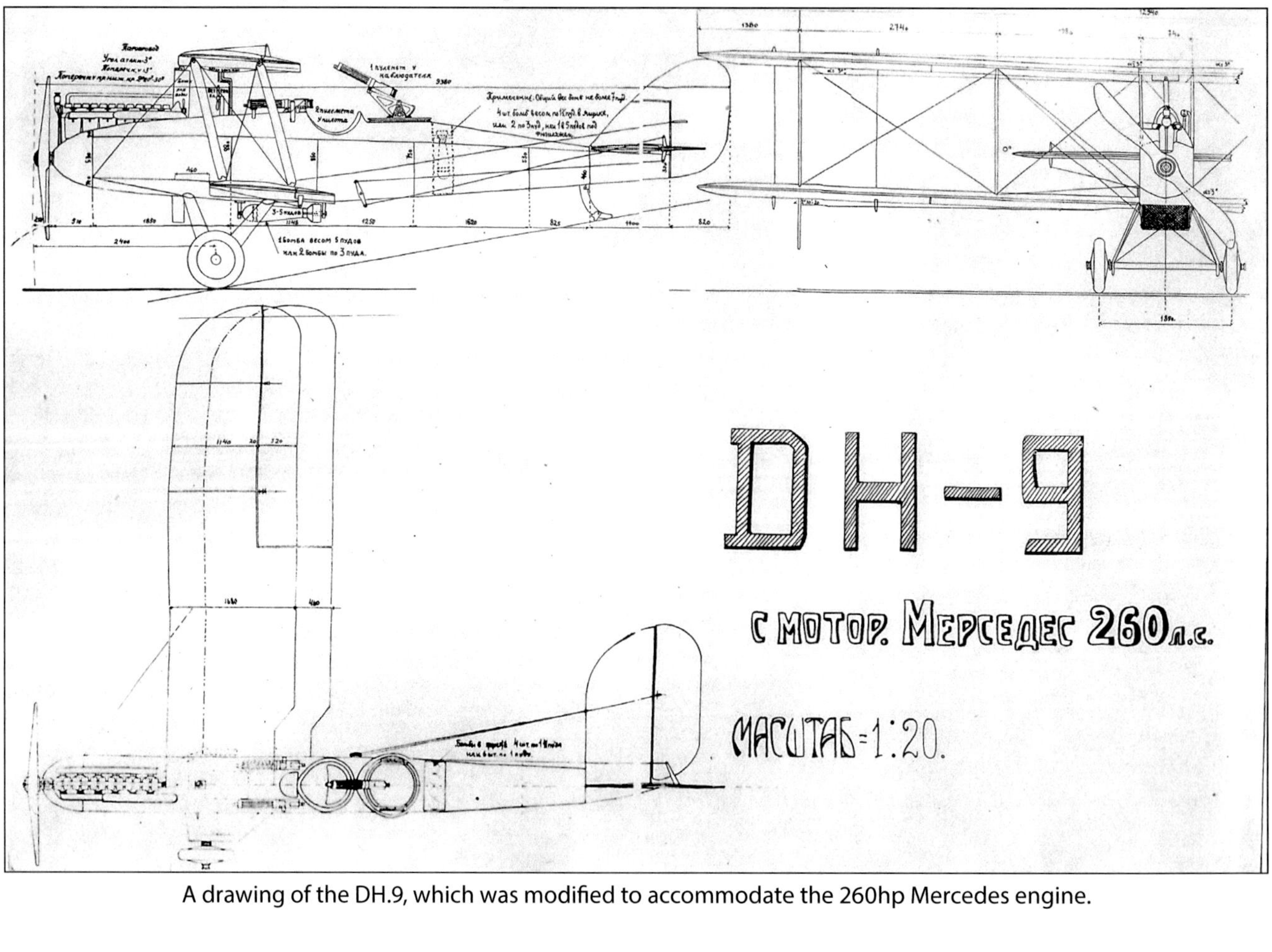

A drawing of the DH.9, which was modified to accommodate the 260hp Mercedes engine.

hoping to drive Denikin's forces out of Tsaritsyn with the help of the flotilla.

On 22 August 1919, the 10th Army of the reds began its advance, supported by the ships. The No. 47 Squadron RAF was concentrated in Beketovka and was tasked with attacking the red flotilla. On 28 August these aircraft flew the first sortie against the ships close to Dubovka. One bomb hit the gunboat *Bditelniy*, killing six and injuring 14. On that same day Captain Anderson close to the village of Shirokoye (north of Tsaritsyn) destroyed, by low-level bombing, a tethered aerostat of the 14th Aeronautical Unit, 10th Army. The victory was marred by the death of the flight observer Captain MacLennan, who was seriously injured by machine gun fire from the ships. He passed away after the aircraft had landed in Beketovka. Commander of the Caucasian Army General P.N. Wrangel issued a decree on 31 August 1919, decorating the British pilots with the St. George's Cross (Anderson was awarded 3rd Class, and MacLennan 4th Class). The St. George's Cross was very highly respected order in Russia – it could only be earned on the battlefield for demonstrating personal courage.

The red pilots tried one more than one occasion to shoot down the British DH.9s but without success. On 20 August, (other sources put this date as 16 September), Lieutenant Cronin's crew were attacked by a Nieuport close to Dubovka during a raid on Chyorniy Yar. An accurate burst of fire from the observer forced the fighter to descend steeply.

At the beginning of September, the Volga-Caspian Flotilla approached Tsaritsyn and opened fire on the city. At the same time the troops of the

A DH.9 fitted with Mercedes engine at the Turkestan Front, 1924. This airplane was fitted with Hazet type radiators on the fuselage sides.

A DH.9, which participated in a long-range flight to Kabul.

A DH.9 fitted with Mercedes engine of the 4th Reconnaissance Air Unit in Turkestan.

An unfortunate landing of a DH.9 fitted with Mercedes engine, Moscow Military District, the end of the 1920s.

A group of pilots standing next to a DH.9, mid-1920s.

A DH.9A on a ski undercarriage.

DH.9 and DH.9A biplanes of the 1st Separate Light Bomber Squadron named after Lenin.

10th Red Army attacked from the north-west, but aviation saved this situation. The DH.9s from the No. 47 Squadron and the Kuban Air Unit bombed the ships, and succeeded in destroying the lifting hoist on the *Samorodok*, and shot down an aerostat with machine gun fire. On the ground the advance on the city was beaten back, the reds retreated.

However, raids on Tsaritsyn by M-5 and M-9 flying boats based on the barge *Kommuna*, continued. In response, on 17 September two DH.9s took off to bomb the hydroplane carrier in Dubovka. Two Nieuports from the flotilla fighter squadron were scrambled to intercept. Pilot A.K. Tumanskiy was in such a hurry that he forgot to disengage the peg securing the biplane to the hard standing. After applying full power, he tore the peg out of the ground and took off in this configuration. The cargo, however, was rattling on the end of a rope, and made it difficult to control the aircraft in flight, so Tumanskiy was forced to return to base. Another pilot E.I. Pyatkevich, attacked a British machine but his aircraft was damaged by a return machine gun fire from the aft cockpit. The injured pilot was forced to make an emergency landing on the bank of the Volga River. During the further inspection, 32 bullet holes were found in Pyatkevich's Nieuport.

The British pilots scored two direct hits on the deck of the *Kommuna*, destroying five of the seven flying boats standing on the deck. Two men were killed, and eight were injured. Another bomb hit the floating base of the fighter air unit but did not explode.

According to some sources, at the peak of successes of Denikin's Army which was advancing to the north, the command of the No. 47 Squadron suggested carrying out a raid on Moscow using the DH.9As, but London banned this operation from going ahead.

At the end of September 1919, on the front line close to Chyorniy Yar, 'A' Flight of the No. 47 Squadron began its operations under the command of Captain Slatter. When the white cavalry put the red troops to flight and pinned them to the banks of the Volga, they themselves came under destructive fire from the southern unit of the Volga-Caspian Flotilla. Then the British pilots came to the rescue and flew several sorties against the ships, dropping more than a hundred bombs. They managed to sink a tug and to damage two armoured steamers, a further tug, and several floating gun batteries (a barge fitted with cannons).

On 10 October, the reds made a fresh attempt to recapture Tsaritsyn – the cavalry division under General Dumenko broke through the front line and headed for the city. The Volga-Caspian Flotilla opened fire once again and the No. 47 Squadron repeated their attacks on the ships, supported by the Kuban air unit of the whites.

The DH.9s bombed the shipping at low-altitude and then from very low level strafed them with machine gun fire, trying to take the gun crew out of action. They succeeded in sinking four small ships and damaging a few more. Having sustained losses, the flotilla retreated to the north.

The No. 47 Squadron ceased their combat operations at the end of October 1919. They were withdrawn back behind the lines and were attached to the British Aviation Mission. Specifically, the DH.9s operated liaison flights from the area around Novorossiysk out to the Crimea. The military situation began to change dramatically and the reds again went on the attack. Few British aircraft remained and they were very worn out, while in Rostov the reds captured the aircraft that had been sent to augment the British forces. Five more DH.9As were ferried by air to Taganrog but even there they became trophies for the Red Army.

A 'gift' DH.9A with the inscription 'The Ukrainian Chekist'. The aircraft belonged to the *Ilyich* Air Unit, summer 1924.

In January 1920 the remains of the No. 47 Squadron were re-deployed to the Crimea. There, from the airfield at Djankoi, they did play a small part in white combat operations. Thus, on 6 February two aircraft took off to bomb red units. In response, the reds bombed Djankoi twice. On 18 February 1920 Captain Grigson's crew encountered the enemy's Sopwith 1½ Strutter during a raid on Novo-Alekseevka. The British attacked this aircraft from above and damaged it – Sopwith made an emergency landing. The red pilots abandoned their airplane and walked to the railway station.

The DH.9 fuselage ready for transportation by rail.

On 22 February Major Collishaw's DH.9 was hit by ground fire over Chongar. He made an emergency landing, and unable to take off again, taxied around 30km back to his own unit through the snow.

In March 1920, the entire personnel of the No. 47 Squadron left Russia, many of the unit's pilots were decorated with Russian orders and medals. The airplanes, including several old DH.9s under repair in Sevastopol, were left to the whites.

Denikin's pilots had already mastered the de Havillands long before this date, as it was the British who had supplied these aircraft. Following the end of the First World War there were plenty of surplus airplanes at the British stores on Lemnos Island, in Thessaloniki, and on Malta. They were not

The airplane flown by unit commander I.F. Skvortsov after the undercarriage collapse on landing, Moscow Central airfield. Documentation for this DH.9 indicates that it is a trophy example.

Maintenance of the DH.9A 'Lugansk citizen awarded the Order of the Red Banner' from the *Ilyich* Air Unit, 1924.

A landing accident in a DH.9A 'The poor man of Odessa' from the *Ilyich* Air Unit. The pilot was Sokolov, Kharkov, 18 May 1924.

new by that time, and some had been repaired, but they were still suitable for flying combat sorties.

These airplanes were delivered to Russia by sea, and a depot for RAF aircraft was set up in Novorossiysk. There the aircraft were assembled, test flown, and then handed over to the air force units, both British and Russian. The British Military Mission was in operation there up until 1920, which was responsible for conversion of white pilots.

The aviation of Armed Forces of the South of Russia was in desperate need of materiel; the few French biplanes they did have (Nieuports, Farmans, Voisins, and some other types), which remained from the time of the Provisional Government, were already substantially worn out and were hardly suitable for air combat. Assistance from the British came just in time, as the first batch of four DH.9s arrived on the SS *Warpointer* on 29 April (24 April, according to other source) 1919. These airplanes were fitted with Puma engines, and they were handed over to serve with the 1st Air Unit (named after General Alekseev) of the Volunteer Army. *Praporshchiks* Ivanov and Yanchenko flew these machines, along with *Podporuchik* Grechishkin, and *Poruchiks* Yesipov and Desino. This unit, which was acknowledged as the best of the air units in the Armed Forces of the South of Russia, became the main one to operate the DH.9 prior to the end of the White Army's resistance in November 1920.

On 29 May of that same year the next batch of DH.9s were delivered to Novorossiysk on the British seaplane tender HMS *Engadine* (known in Russian documents as the *Ingodin*), and other deliveries followed this one. This enabled more units to be partially equipped with these biplanes – the 4th, 5th, and 7th Air Units in the Volunteer Army and the 1st Don Unit of the Don Army also received them.

Over the course of the summer Russian pilots were mastering the new type. Each of Denikin's air units had, among its personnel, the British flight instructors, observers, and two or three mechanics.

By summer 1919 the units began to participate in combat activity. One of the tasks of the 5th Air Unit was suppression of rebel highlanders in the Northern Caucasus. At that time five DH.9s were in the strength of the unit. The Chechens, led by their Imam Uzun-Hadji, launched an uprising in the area behind the white's lines using the slogan of a holy war with the infidels. They conducted raids on transport convoys and garrisons of Denikin's Army and would return with their loot to remote mountain villages unpunished, inflicting much havoc. Command, however, were not able to allocate sufficient forces to protect and were restricted to guarding the large cities of Grozniy and Vladikavkaz. To fight the insurgents, aircraft were used, and pilots carried out reconnaissance and bombed the villages. In the words of the Head of aviation of the Armed Forces of the South of Russia *General-Mayor* V.M. Tkachyov 'the Abreks were brought to obedience by the bombing of their impregnable villages'.

Personnel of the air unit during a celebratory line-up on 1 May 1925 at the airfield in the village of Nizhne-Gnilovskaya. The unit was equipped with DH.9A airplanes.

Personnel of the *Ilyich* Air Unit standing next to DH.9A 'The poor man of Odessa'. Standing in the centre is the Deputy Head of Aviation of Ukrainian Military District N.K. Kirillov, commander of the air unit K.A. Rudzit, and his deputy I.I. Nusberg, Kharkov, summer 1924.

On 18 June 1919 the 1st Air Unit took off from Yekaterinodar bound for the front line at Sinelnikovo. The unit had five DH.9s in its strength and came under command of *General-Mayor* A.G. Shkuro. For their combat sorties the unit were assigned an area Konstantinograd–Pyatikhatka–Nikopol. On their arrival at the front line, however, only three biplanes remained fully serviceable. On the airplane of the unit commander *Shtabs-Kapitan* A.K. Kaputovskiy the engine had to be changed following the ferry flight, and *Poruchik* D.P. Yesipov damaged his aircraft on landing. On 22 June following an engine failure the DH.9 flown by *Poruchik* K.A. Zhivago was also damaged in a forced landing near Lozovaya village. Only *Praporshchiks* M.I. Yanchenko and N.I. Ivanov were able to commence combat operations successfully. Overall, in the course of June the unit's pilots flew 19 combat sorties and dropped 1,087kg of bombs. A separate flight comprising Yesipov's and Ivanov's crews were attached to the 7th Infantry Division on 13–31 June, and this unit flew nine combat sorties set by the division headquarters. On one occasion the Head of Division Headquarters *Polkovnik* Evert flew as an observer on a reconnaissance sortie.

Combat activity was undertaken in difficult conditions: there was a shortage of fuel, tooling and spare parts, and the pilots were always complaining about the poor performance of the Puma engines. Although British Lieutenant Harris, who had been attached to the unit, blamed this on the lack of understanding among Russian pilots' of how to operate the engine. The commander of the unit ordered a commission be set up 'to rid the unit of these undeserved allegations'. The story concluded with Harris being expelled from the unit and he was sent behind the lines on 29 June.

In July 1919 General Denikin's forces began an all-out offensive against Moscow, and the Bolshevik power was hanging in the balance. White command, however, were not able to deploy aviation widely as there was a catastrophic shortage of aircraft. Just three air units had been attached to the forces advancing on Moscow – the 1st, 2nd, and 6th, in total around two-dozen airplanes. From 22 July, the 1st Air Division of the Volunteer Army consisting of the 1st and 6th Air Units played an active part in the battles in the main

A DH.9 fitted with Mercedes engine is rolled into the hangar in Alma-Ata; this airplane was used for aerial photography in Central Asia.

thrust, during the capture of Poltava, Belgorod, and Kursk. As of 31 July, the 1st Air Unit had 11 officers, 75 men, and six DH.9 biplanes in its strength; it was acting in cooperation with the ground troops of the corps under Lieutenant General N.E. Bredov.

Despite the lack of aircraft, the unit offer active assistance to the white forces. Over the course of June, excluding nine days when the airplanes were grounded due to the weather conditions, the pilots of the 1st Air Unit completed 36 reconnaissance and bombing sorties, dropping 25 bombs of 12 and 20 *funts* (Russian pounds) on the enemy. In August they flew 40 reconnaissance and bombing sorties and 14 liaison flights. In the course of this month 66 bombs were dropped on Red Army units, with a total weight of 720kg.

The aircraft gradually went unserviceable, and by 3 October just two airworthy DH.9s remained in the 1st Air Unit. Thus, on 3 July during a flight from Lozovaya to Sinelnikovo the biplane flown by *Praporshchik* I.S. Krotyuk entered a spin for some unknown reason and crashed. The pilot sustained serious injuries, but did survive. On 4 September in Nezhin *Praporshchik* Ivanov crashed another DH.9 on take-off that was heading for an overhaul. On 20 September in an explosion of a cellar storing trophy German bombs at Post-Volynskiy airfield (just outside Kiev) three airplanes were destroyed, among them was a single DH.9. A further two aircraft were so worn out that after they had arrived at the 1st Air Depot a decision was taken – the airplanes were beyond repair and were to be broken up for spares. As they were left almost devoid of materiel, the 1st Air Unit was withdrawn back behind the lines to re-form. The combat achievements of the unit commander *Shtabs-Kapitan* Kaputovskiy were mentioned in orders issued by command, together with those of pilots *Poruchiks* Yesipov and Zhivago, and observers *Poruchik* Kudimov and *Yesaul* Belofastov.

Kaputovskiy's feedback regarding the DH.9 is of interest: 'In terms of the load-carrying capacity and flight characteristics this airplane is very suitable for the real war. The speed given the standard revolutions per minute is no more than 100–110 *versts* (Russian *versta* is 1.067km) per hour, and the engine power ensures a rapid ascent (9–10 mins) to an altitude of 1,000m. The aircraft handles beautifully, but converting onto this aircraft is difficult for pilots. The Puma engine leaves something to be desired ... '

The victories attained by the whites were replaced with defeats, the resurgent Red Army began to press them along the whole front line from the Volga to the Dnieper, and the remains of the Armed Forces of the South of Russia were concentrated on the Crimean Peninsula. On 4 April 1920 Denikin conceded the reign of power to Lieutenant General Baron P.N. Wrangel (who had previously commanded the Caucasian Army) who re-formed the white units into the Russian Army. At the end of March, the army had 34 airplanes of different types, both Russian and foreign, in its strength. The principal strike force was 27 DH.9s and DH.9As (12 of them were unserviceable).

Despite the small numbers, aviation of Wrangel's forces well performed during the Yushun Operation in March 1920. Three divisions of the Red Army captured Perekop and advanced towards Yushun, deep in the Crimea, while the exhausted corps led by *General-Mayor* Ya.A. Slashchyov, for whom no reserves could be found, slowed their advance. All aviation of whites was concentrated on the airfield of Djankoi: the 8th Air Unit (four aircraft), the 5th Air Unit (five DH.9As), and a training unit from Sevastopol Flight School. On the morning of 8 March, they attacked red troops and their convoys, which began to retreat. The following day the white cavalry attacked from the flank, and Red Army units withdrew to Perekop.

On 28 April 1920 *General-Mayor* V.M. Tkachyov became the Head of Aviation of Wrangel's Russian Army, and under his leadership it took part in the final offensive. The 1st, 3rd, 4th, and 5th Air Units – 25 airplanes in all, were concentrated close to Perekop. The 8th Air Unit (five aircraft) was sent to the Chongar direction. On 7 June Wrangel's forces broke through the front line of the 13th Army of reds at Perekop. The Red Army command thought that the whites were no longer capable of advancing and was caught by surprise. Wrangel's army broke away from the Crimea and began to advance to the north and east.

A DH.9 without outer skin was exhibited at the Central House of Aviation and Chemistry in Moscow.

The white pilots carried out reconnaissance, and bombed and strafed the enemy operating in groups of three to six aircraft. Five de Havillands, which were led by Tkachyov himself, successfully bombed the 13th Army headquarters in Chaplinka.

White aviation partly assumed the functions of a mobile reserve force, making up for the lack of a cavalry. The airplanes would follow the retreating ground forces and convoys, and would bomb and strafe them with machine gun fire. The air raids on the crossings over the Dnieper River at Kakhovka, where red personnel and convoys had been concentrated, turned out to be especially successful.

The white pilots landed next to their divisional or regimental headquarters and artillery positions, providing up to date information, and they would then make short reconnaissance flights on the orders of their command and drop message streamers. Wrangel marked the efforts of the air force in his order of 4 June: 'One of the most important components of our combat activity was performed by our self-sacrificing pilots. The reconnaissance, bombing and liaison between separate groups of our own forces were perfectly carried out by the pilots. The air attack by our squadron on 26 May of the enemy's Vladimir group, which have tried several times to snatch victory away from us, made it possible to finally rout the enemy.

The work of the pilots deserves full recognition among our forces. On behalf of the service, I thank the current Chief of aviation group General Tkachyov and all the pilots and observers, who took part in this operation. To our eagles aviators, hooray!'

The white command noted in the reports that 'aviation ... with its bombs, has caused irrevocable panic among the retreating convoys and artillery, and apart from that, has strafed the withdrawing forces with machine gun fire. Furthermore, it was noted that our artillery was immediately opening a quick fire on what for them were invisible targets, being guided by the explosions of these aerial bombs. On that day aviation found its true path, it achieved what it had long set out to do – aviation functioned like a separate branch of the armed forces.'

The Red Army, however, tried to organise a counteroffensive. In mid-June the 1st Cavalry Corps under the command of D.N. Zhloba, augmented by the 2nd Stavropol Cavalry Division, as well as artillery, armoured vehicles, and an armoured train, took their turn to break through the front, and headed for Melitopol. If they were successful, they could break Wrangel's army into two unequal halves and cut them off from the Crimea, condemning them to die on the steppes of northern Taurida. *Podporuchik* Baydak, a pilot of the 4th Air Unit, however, discovered Zhloba's main forces on 15 June near Bolshoy Tokmak. A difficult situation arose: General Wrangel did not have any reserves and it would have taken a long time to re-deploy troops from different sectors of the front, but they were again rescued by Tkachyov's pilots – the Crimean Combat Air Group comprising the 4th and 5th Air Units. The following day aerial reconnaissance detected the first targets for bombing, and a dozen DH.9s attacked the red cavalry. Raid followed raid, and the mechanics just about had time to fill the aircraft with fuel, load them with bombs and arm the machine guns. Pilots dropped bombs from an altitude of 300m, and then from 50m, and sometimes lower than that, and they would then strafe the enemy with machine gun fire. Even when the ammunition had run out, they would circle over the cavalry, chasing the horses as they went mad with the sound of the engines. The battles with Zhloba's corps lasted until 21 June.

For their outstanding combat achievements, the commander of the 4th Air Unit *Polkovnik* S.K. Shebalin, a pilot from that same unit *Podporuchik* L.I Baydak, and *General-Mayor* V.M. Tkachyov were decorated with the order of St. Nicholas the Miracle Worker, and the unit was given the honourable title 'named after the military pilot *Polkovnik* Kozakov'.

This victory, however, only delayed the end of Wrangel's army for a few months. The final large-scale operation that the white pilots took part in was the battle against the advance of the 2nd Cavalry Army. On 15 August the army broke

A DH.9 fitted with Mercedes engine of the 8th Corps Air Unit standing next to a hangar in Vinnitsa, July 1926.

through the white's lines from the direction of Orlyansk. Aviation was again drafted in to make up for the shortage of significant cavalry reserves. The 2nd Cavalry Army incurred heavy losses at the hands of aviation, after which dodged the fight with much smaller cavalry of *General-Mayor* I.G. Barbovich, and took shelter at the Kakhovka stronghold. However, this came at a high price for the Crimean Combat Air Group. The unserviceable aircraft and the worn-out engines had significantly reduced combat capability of the group, and even bombs had to be rationed.

By mid-October 1920 white aviation in Crimea amounted to just 22 serviceable airplanes, whereas the reds had 84. By the time that significant red forces had been re-deployed from the Polish Front and the 1st Cavalry Army under the command of S.M. Budyonniy had arrived at Perekop, the whites only had one serviceable airplane. This can partially explain the comparatively easy victory of the reds. Then came the storming of Perekop, the breakthrough by the reds into Crimea, and the evacuation by sea of the remains of Russian Army.

The British and the whites used de Havillands in northern Russia as well. By the summer campaign of 1919, some 21 DH.9s fitted with Puma engines, and 12 DH.9As with Liberty engines were due to be delivered by steamers to Murmansk and Arkhangelsk. The arrival of British pilots was also anticipated.

By 19 May around half of what was expected had actually arrived, including a dozen DH.9As. By that time Slavo-British Air Corps already had seven DH.9s in service. The arrival of new materiel augmented the corps appreciably. In the course of the reorganisation, it was decided that three squadrons would be formed, comprising two units each. The famous Russian ace *Polkovnik* A.A. Kozakov commanded the first Russian squadron; previously he had been the commander of the 1st Combat Air Wing and was awarded the rank of a British Major. Units led by *Kapitan* S.K. Modrakh and *Shtabs-Kapitan* N.I. Belousovich formed part of his squadron. The Russian squadron received four DH.9s and three Snipe fighters. Subsequently there was a plan to form another Russian unit but there were insufficient airplanes for this to happen. Two other squadrons were purely British and were led by Majors Carre and Bowman.

The Russian and British pilots flying the de Havillands participated in battles with the Red Army in the Russian north – they conducted reconnaissance and carried out strikes on enemy positions. On 5 May 1919 aerial reconnaissance discovered a red airfield in Seltso with two aircraft on it. According to a report, on the following day: '... our airplanes bombed and strafed an enemy flotilla, scoring direct hits. Our aircraft were successful yesterday in their operation on the Vaga River, they dropped bombs on enemy positions and strafed them with machine gun fire, conducted observations for our artillery, and took photographs of enemy gun batteries. Bombs from our aircraft fell onto an enemy steamer on the Dvina River today'. The reds also had their own aviation in this area, as the records of 31 May state: '... our airplanes, and those of the enemy, have been very active. Air combats took place over Kitsa and Seltso without any specific results.'

At the end of May 1919, the reds arranged two new airfields close to the Severnaya Dvina and Vaga rivers. Their Nieuport fighters began to torment the pilots of the Slavo-British Air Corps. In the meantime, the reds tried to attack just the Sopwith 1½ Strutters and RE.8s but they did not have the courage to take on the DH.9s.

The de Havillands took part in the raids on Puchega airfield on 17 May 1919. In particular, they seriously damaged two M-20 flying boats that were standing in a hangar on a barge.

Aviation was effective against the river flotilla of the reds – on 19 June the 'Floating battery No. 5' (a big barge with two naval six-inch cannons) was sunk by a direct hit of a bomb dropped by one of the DH.9s. Five de Havillands participated in this raid, bombing steamers, tugs, and barges close to the Island of Selets. The following day DH.9 crews

A trophy DH.9, which was used in the 1st Military Pilots School. Student pilot I.K. Bubenets had an accident in his first solo flight on this airplane, May 1926.

struck the red flotillas again, supported by artillery fire from British gunboats. At the same time, the Slavo-British Air Corps and the British units went on the offensive along the banks of the Severnaya Dvina and pushed the enemy back some 10–15km to the south. Severodvinsk flotilla of the reds retreated in a hurry, covered by fields of floating mines in the Vaga and Severnaya Dvina rivers.

At the end of July 1919 news came through that the British Government had made a decision to withdraw its troops from northern Russia. Back in June, American soldiers had left Arkhangelsk.

As the British withdrew, they took all serviceable DH.9s with them, and the rest were dismantled for spares, or were simply broken up. After evacuation of the interventionists the whites had only one DH.9 on ski undercarriage left in Arkhangelsk. However, nothing is known about participation of this airplane in the concluding battles at the Northern Front. Most likely it remained in Arkhangelsk up until the arrival of the Red Army. The records show that a single airplane captured by the reds along with examples of other trophy aircraft was delivered to Moscow on 15 April 1921.

The red air fleet also used de Havillands, although in much fewer numbers than the whites did. In the Civil War years approximately two-dozen DH.9 and DH.9As were left to the Red Army. For the most part these were the aircraft captured during the offensive on Novocherkassk and Taganrog in March 1920. They belonged to the last batch to arrive in the south of Russia in November 1919. The majority of the aircraft that formed that batch fell into the hands of the Bolsheviks unpacked, still in their boxes. Several airplanes which were found in Yekaterinodar for some reason had been obviously chopped with checkers. Either the white cossacks wanted to make aircraft unserviceable, or the red cavalrymen were concerned that the planes would be flown away ...

Eleven trophy de Havillands were immediately handed over to the air group under the command of M.P. Stroyev, with the 24th, 36th, and 41st units formed part of this group. British airplanes comprised exactly half the air fleet in this wing, and the crews quickly mastered this type. Already in May 1920 the Stroyev's group had been attached to the 1st Cavalry Army, which was re-deployed to the Polish Front. In operations against Polish forces in the process of advancing towards Warsaw, the British aircraft were mostly used as reconnaissance machines, making the best use of their long range.

In 1920 there were some accidents involving DH.9s, which were related to piloting errors. On 4 June the aircraft flown by the unit commander A.M. Lipichev stalled and crashed into the ground. The airplane caught fire and then the bombs carried under the wings exploded. The pilot was killed instantly, and flight observer Maksimov passed away in hospital from the serious injuries he had sustained. On 30 June another DH.9 entered a spin and was unable to recover, pilot Voronets and flight observer Tretyakov were killed in this fatal crash.

On 15 November 1920, the 1st Air Depot had six DH.9s with Puma engines (serial numbers 3003, 4305, 4296, 2958, and 620, and 618). de Havillands serial numbers 1138, 4033, 2842, 2944, and 690 were listed as under repair, all without engines.

A certain number of trophy de Havillands participated in combat activity after the official end of the Civil War. For example, they were used during annexation of the Trans-Caucasian republics to the Soviet Russia. In Armenia power was transferred to the Bolsheviks peacefully in September–November 1920, but in February 1921 the supporters of the *Dashnaktsutyun* party organised an uprising and captured the capital city Erivan' (now Yerevan). Red Armenian units were pushed back to the border with Iran, and were in a desperate need of money in order to buy provisions. There were no suitable airplanes available, however, for the flight to Nakhichevan. Then, three unserviceable DH.9s were brought there from Baku and in the course of two days one aircraft was assembled from these three. During a test flight it emerged that the aircraft was drifting to the right and it was constantly trying to pitch down into a dive, but it was decided to leave it as it is. On 29 February 1921 the crew, consisting of B.N. Kudrin, and V.L. Melnikov, flew the important sortie in this DH.9 biplane – they brought 5,000 gold coins from Tiflis (now Tbilisi). These were placed into small sacks attached to the fuselage frames. Near Nakhichevan a special signal was laid out for them at the landing site, consisting of three white squares and an arrow. For their successful delivery of the funds, Kudrin and Melnikov were decorated with orders of the Red Banner.

Some DH.9s were in service with the Special Purpose Air Unit under the Combat Air Squadron of the Tambov Governate. They participated in the suppression of the aforementioned peasants' uprising in May–September 1921. It is known that pilot Rudnev flew one of these machines. Another location where combat activity continued was the Turkestan Front. Here the 4th Separate Reconnaissance Unit had approximately a dozen DH.9s that had been deployed to the area near Tashkent and used to fight the Basmachi in Central Asia.

In January–February 1922 DH.9s fitted with Liberty engines took part in the suppression of an uprising in Karelia. In sub-zero temperatures these aircraft proved themselves to be better than the DH.4, although they also suffered from a change in the tension of the bracing cables during significant spikes in day and night temperatures.

These biplanes were also active in other locations. One machine was lost on 4 March 1922 – pilot R.G. Piir fell out of the cockpit in flight. He did not have a parachute and was killed. The mechanic and passenger Adamchik remained in the rear cockpit, but they were not able to control the aircraft, and perished when it hit the ground.

In 1923, a radiotelephone system designed by A.N. Kovalenkov was tested in one trophy DH.9. It weighed 16kg, had a range of 35km, and was powered by a generator with an aerovane placed on the upper wing.

As mentioned above, after the end of the Civil War the Soviet Russia had a desperate need in aircraft for its young aviation. The indigenous aircraft industry could not even cover the losses due to accidents, while the available fleet was extremely worn out. The Soviet Government began to look for ways to acquire combat aircraft from abroad, including from Britain.

There were some difficulties in this, since the British Government did not recognise the Bolshevik regime in Moscow. This, however, did not present an obstacle for the private business. There were a large number of aircraft in stores in Britain that had become surplus after the end of the First World War. They included DH.9 airframes, which the British were ready to sell.

Soviet representatives acquired a batch of German Mercedes (Daimler) D.IVa engines from the Hirsch brothers in Sweden at a reasonable price. Formally their output was 260hp, but in reality the maximum was 285hp, and the nominal output was 250hp. Following Germany surrender these engines were due to be scrapped, but they were secretly taken out of the country, and subsequently sold to Soviet Russia for installation on the DH.9s in place of the Pumas.

The airframes were acquired in Britain via ADC company, whose engineers made the necessary changes to the aircraft drawings. This same company arranged modification of the fuselage forward section. Secretary of the Royal Swedish Aeroclub T. Gullberg took a role of intermediary in the purchase of the DH.9s.

The first 40 modified airplanes were delivered to Russia in May 1922. The assembly of aircraft and installation of engines was carried out at the GAZ-1 factory in Moscow from the beginning of August. On 14 August I.G. Savin made the first flight of the first Anglo-German hybrid (serial number 5817, which had been registered in Britain under the number H5817). The take-off weight of the version with the Mercedes amounted to 1,720kg, and it was fitted with British wooden twin-bladed Davis propeller of 2.795m in diameter. No data on the aircraft maximum speed was found in the records, but the recorded 'average' speed at the ground level was 170km/h. The service ceiling was defined as 3,580m, and it took 6mins 30secs for the aircraft to reach an altitude of 1,000m.

The pace of the work at the GAZ-1 factory could never be called fast – by mid-1923 five more airplanes had been completed, and a further 11 had been added by mid-1924. The assembly, evidently, was also undertaken at other enterprises and workshops. A batch of reconnaissance aircraft fitted with Mercedes engines joined the 2nd Squadron in Smolensk in September–November 1922, and on 17 October 1923 there were 11 aircraft listed in service there.

A single DH.9B with a 360hp Rolls-Royce Eagle VIII engine was acquired in Britain for familiarisation purposes. The airplane was tested at the NOA in May 1922, and in September it was used for a long-range 15-days flight on a route Moscow–Smolensk–Vitebsk–Gomel–Kiev–Odessa–Kacha–Kharkov–Serpukhov–Moscow. The pilot was the Head of the Air Fleet Training Schools B.K. Velling, and the passenger was the then Head of the RKKVF A.A. Znamenskiy.

In 1923–1924, 42 DH.9s with Puma engines along with 15 DH.9As with Liberty engines were purchased via ARCOS and delivered directly to Soviet Russia from Britain. The first 17 aircraft in this order arrived in Leningrad aboard *Saturn* steamer in October 1923. This enabled to equip three separate reconnaissance squadrons solely with de Havilland aircraft – the 1st (based at Ukhtomskaya airfield outside Moscow), the 2nd (based at Vitebsk in Belorussia) and the 5th (based in Gomel, Ukraine).

The highest number of the British planes was in the first unit, which initially was designated as the 1st Squadron of the 1st Air Wing and in 1924 following the death of V.I. Lenin it was awarded his name and began to be known as the 1st Light Bomber Squadron. In 1923–1924 the unit had 18 to 20 de Havillands in service, including three trophy examples captured in the south of Russia.

Based on the results of an inventory carried out in December 1923, the DH.9s with Puma (in Russia it was also designated DKh.9SP) were highest in number with 41 biplanes in service. Of those, 27 airplanes (with 11 serviceable) were in air force units, two in flying schools, and 12 in for

A trophy DH.9A following repairs at the *Promvozdukh* factory.

repair. Total number of DH.9s with Mercedes engines were 39 – 26 aircraft in air force (17 serviceable), two at flying schools, and nine in for repair. More advanced DH.9As with Liberty engines were not being handed over to flying schools at that time, out of a dozen machines 10 were in service (with seven serviceable) and two in for repair.

The 5th Separate Reconnaissance Squadron named after Ilyich in Kharkov was equipped with de Havillands a short time after the 1st Squadron. The ceremonial handover of the first nine DH.9As took place on 18 May 1924, and further four were added in June–July. In the documents they were listed as the 'British R-1s of 1918 production' (the Soviet version of the DH.9A, which used R-1 designation, is covered later in the book). The aircraft were considered a gift from the ODVF. The money for them was collected from the workers, and moreover this was not always collected willingly; sometimes by way of a decision by party organisations the funds were just deducted from wages. All such gift airplanes had their own names, which were written large on the fuselage. The names usually referred to the locations where the money was collected, or the professions of the doners: 'The Donetsk Miner', 'The Red Resident of Kiev', 'The Yuzovka Proletarian', 'The Odessa Region Proletarian', 'The Ukrainian Chekist', and so on.

In a report from this squadron, the speed and good handling of the de Havillands were praised, but the report also noted: 'the manoeuvrability for a reconnaissance aircraft is more than satisfactory'. The reserve of structural strength in this aircraft, however, was acknowledged as insufficient. The 5th Squadron flew the DH.9A for a comparatively short time, at the end of the year the squadron began to convert to the Soviet R-1 version.

One or two de Havilland airplanes were listed in each of the air units of the Leningrad, Ukrainian, and Siberian districts, among them were the 1st, 3rd, 6th, 10th, 13th, 14th, 17th, 20th, 24th, and 87th separate units.

From 1924 onwards, a certain number of DH.9s and DH.9As were handed over to the training schools – among them were the Higher School of Military Pilots in Moscow, the 2nd School of Military Pilots, the School of the Aerial Gunnery and Bombing *Strelbom*, and the Military Technical School. This type was also in service with the 83rd Training Squadron, the squadron of the Military Aviation Academy, and at the NOA. At the end of January 1925, the Higher School of Military Pilots and Observers had four DH.9s with Mercedes engines in service, which had been handed over from the *Strelbom* school, but they were listed as being completely worn out and only good for spares, as well as a single example with a Liberty engine.

During the course of the above-mentioned uprising in Khorezm in February 1924, eight additional aircraft were re-deployed to Khiva, including five DH.9s of the 2nd and 4th separate reconnaissance units. The airplanes conducted reconnaissance sorties, strafed and bombed Basmachi units. At the end of February, the reds attacked the ancient fortress of Khanki, and several bombing raids in a row helped to break down enemy resistance. A short time later, aerial reconnaissance spotted a cavalry troop of the 4th Cavalry Regiment, which were encircled and engaged in combat near the Ak-Yayla well with an enemy five times their numerical strength. The aircraft that came to their aid dropped crates containing belts of machine gun ammunition and medical supplies, after which they attacked the insurgents with bombs and machine gun fire, and the bandits had to retreat.

The combat activity in Khorezm continued until the end of April, and the majority of the bandits were routed or dispersed. In the course of this campaign three aircraft were lost; all three were in accidents, specifically as a result of a sandstorm.

The DH.9As were the backbone of the RKKVF up until the mid-1920s, when they were replaced with Soviet R-1 reconnaissance aircraft powered by the M-5 engines. As strange as it may seem the aircraft fitted with Puma engines turned out to be the more long-lived, although the majority of them were used for training purposes. Individual aircraft of this version were also used in the second half of the 1920s. For example, an accident report lists an accident at the Central Moscow airfield in 1927 with a DH.9 that suffered an undercarriage collapse on landing. On 1 October 1927 there were just nine DH.4s and DH.9As fitted with Liberty engines in the Air Force, plus 23 DKh.9SPs (all of the latter were just training aircraft).

In 1928 the VVS RKKA command decided to take all the de Havilland machines out of service. These airplanes were no longer in flying condition and could only be used as study aids. The last of them survived until October.

Having become surplus, starting from 1925 these disarmed biplanes were gradually handed over to the *Dobrolyot* (the Russian Society of Voluntary Air Fleet – an early Soviet Union air transport organisation, an airline which was formed in 1923 and existed throughout the remainder of the 1920s) which widely used them for aerial photography. For example, in April 1928 two DH.9s took off from Tashkent for cartographic photographing flights over the districts of Central Asia, followed by a third aircraft that had been undergoing repairs. In that same year the registration system of these aircraft was changed, and only four of these machines remained in the inventory records. The military offered *Dobrolyot* a further 28 de Havillands, but these were rejected. The final examples in the Civil Air Fleet (GVF, *Grazhdanskiy Vozdushniy Flot*) were written off in 1930.

A single DH.9 fitted with a Puma ended up as an exhibit at the Central House of Aviation and Chemistry in Moscow, it was hung from the ceiling, after having removed part of the outer skin from the fuselage.

2.3 Martynside Fighters

The first Martynside aircraft arrived in Russia along with the aforementioned British No.72 Squadron RAF – its 'B' Flight was equipped with G.102 Elephant biplanes. It was a wooden single-seat fighter fitted with 160hp Beardmore engines. It was actually two Elephants that were the first to be delivered to the Baku region; they were assembled and test flown on 25 August 1918. The aircraft of the 'B' Flight carried out reconnaissance, dropped bombs and scattered leaflets. Enemy aviation was absent, but the Turks still took Baku and the British were evacuated, having destroyed their airplanes. No other airplanes of this type participated in the Civil War.

In 1922–1923 Soviet Russia purchased from Britain a batch of single-seat Martynside F.4 Buzzard biplane fighters. The fighter was also made almost entirely of wood and was fitted with 300hp Hispano-Suiza 8Fb engine, while its armament comprised two 7.69mm Vickers machine guns.

The Buzzard was much newer than the Elephant, and series production was only rolled out from 1919 onwards. These aircraft did not participate in the First World War, and the RAF purchased less than 300 examples, which in fact never did end up in air force units. The British were very keen to get rid of them, they were ready to sell them off cheaply and to deliver almost immediately.

A Martynside F.4 fighter during testing at the NOA.

The intermediary, as had been the case with the de Havillands, was ADC company, and Soviet representatives concluded an agreement with them at the beginning of 1922. ADC acquired the fighters, which had been put into long-term storage at Royal Air Force stores. The first batch of 20 Martynsides arrived in Petrograd in May 1922 on the steamer *Miranda*, and the aircraft were assembled and test flown. The first to receive this new materiel was the 2nd Fighter Squadron of the 2nd Air Group in the Moscow Military District, which was subsequently renamed the 7th Fighter Squadron, and was based on Podosinki airfield close to Lyubertsy. On 1 December there were 13 Martynsides based there.

New aircraft arrived in September 1923, and the second batch comprised 21 fighters. By the end of the month, however, only 25 Martynsides were operational in the VVS RKKA, the majority of the aircraft of the second batch were yet to be put into service.

The 7th Squadron participated in the air parade in Moscow on 1 May 1924. Following intensive training flights the fighters flew over the Red Square in formation, spelling out the name 'Lenin' and a star.

In June 1924 one of the imported fighters underwent testing at the NOA, and the measured flight-performance characteristics turned out to be lower than those indicated in the company documentation. Given a flight weight of 1,113kg a maximum speed of 211km/h was obtained, and a service ceiling of 7,500m. The aircraft climbed to an altitude of 5,000m in 15 mins 50 secs. Such results were explained by the fact that the aircraft was far from new. The Soviet technical manual, which evidently relied on the British data, the maximum speed is given as 233km/h for a flight weight of 1,043kg, and a service ceiling of 9,140m.

In March 1925 at Moscow Khodynka airfield, one of the Martynsides caught fire during a test start-up of the

A Martynside (MF-4) at the Moscow Central Airfield, 1929.

engine. The reason for this was a ruptured fuel pipeline, the pilot, however, who was in the cockpit, pressed down on the pipeline and held onto it, while pilot Krylov, who had run up to the biplane, opened the cowling and put out the fire using a hand-held fire extinguisher and sand.

In May 1925 the Martynsides were used in what was quite peculiar propaganda campaign. These airplanes, which had been purchased abroad some time ago and had been used for several years, were ceremoniously presented to the aforementioned 7th Fighter Squadron as a gift from the water and railway transportation workers, who had raised around 750,000 roubles. Before the ceremony the aircraft were repaired and were given a fresh coat of paint. On their sides they carried names that were in the spirit of the time: 'Chekist,' 'Guardian of the Revolution,' 'The Red Railwayman,' 'Always at the Ready,' 'Proletarian Defence,' and so on. In August 1925 the squadron was awarded the name of F.E. Dzerzhinsky, and this was the only unit in the VVS RKKA to be equipped solely with Martynsides. In June 1925 their numbers in the unit reached 20, and later this figure increased to 25 (the standard strength for a fighter squadron at the time was 21 aircraft).

A Hispano-Suiza 8Fb engine and the water radiator on a Martynside airplane.

This was the feedback that the pilots of the 7th Fighter Squadron gave to the British fighter: 'It has sluggish manoeuvrability but changing the aircraft attitude is easy, it can perform a figure of eight manoeuvre in 18 seconds. The airplane is capable of performing all aerobatic manoeuvres, with the exception of inverted flight.' Among the advantages noted were the lack of pretentiousness regarding the quality of the airfields it was operating from, and the ease of servicing. The disadvantages in the report were listed as the poor downward visibility, the inconvenient use of the armament, and potentially low survivability in combat. The overall conclusion, however, was positive: 'The aircraft performance characteristics and durability are considered acceptable.'

From December 1926 the 7th Squadron became part of the 10th Air Brigade, and from December 1927 it was transferred to the 2nd Brigade of the Belorussian Military District.

The squadron pilots acknowledged that one of the principal defects of the type was the insufficient reliability of the power plant. There was a constant shortage of spare 300hp Hispano-Suiza engines, but at the end of 1925 factory in Aleksandrovsk (now known as Zaporozhye) began to produce them under the M-6 designation. The Soviet engines were heavier, they did not produce the same output, and had

The instrument panel on an MF-4.

The landing accident of the instructor of the 1st (Kacha) Military Pilots School S.S. Zizymov, Kacha airfield near Sevastopol, 10 May 1929.

a reduced service life, but they did enable savings to be made in hard currency that was in short supply.

In the mid-1920s the first designs for Soviet aircraft carriers appeared, and carrier-based aircraft were required for these vessels. In June 1925 the Tactical Department of the Operational Directorate of Naval Headquarters proposed organising testing of the Martynsides in conditions that were similar to those on the deck of a carrier. This was never undertaken, however, and in general the value of these machines as combat aircraft gradually reduced over time.

In October 1925 comparative testing was undertaken at Lipetsk base with the Martynsides and the Dutch Fokker D.XIII fighters. The latter were provided by the Germans who had brought them into the country for their secret military flying school, disguised as the 4th Squadron of the VVS RKKA. On 2 October a mock air combat was held, in which three Martynsides and three Fokkers took part. The

A Martynside fighter at the airfield.

Location of a fatal crash involving pilot V.S. Vsevolodov half a kilometre from the airfield of the Kacha school, 24 May 1929. The wings of the airplane folded up as it recovered from a dive. On the right is the Soviet M-6 engine, which replaced the original Hispano-Suiza.

air engagement was performed at an altitude of 1,500m, and was followed by the combat at altitudes of 2,000m and 4,600m and the aircraft competed with each other for their horizontal flight speed and manoeuvrability. Soviet pilots flew the Martynsides (only two of their surnames are known – Loginov and Shalilo), while the Germans flew the Fokkers, led by the Head of the flying school Major W. Stör, who was a First World War ace.

Since the D.XIII was approximately half a tonne heavier, to equal out their chances the machine guns were removed from the Dutch fighters and they were not completely filled with fuel. The Fokker demonstrated a clear advantage in terms of speed and rate of climb across the entire altitude range, and also turned out to be more manoeuvrable than its adversary. The report stated: '... in air combat when flying in a circle it would always get to the attacking position because of its ability to develop a higher speed in the turn ... '. The Fokker pilots were able to get away from the Martynsides by side slipping and using an upward spiral climb. Basing on the outcome of the testing, the conclusion was unanimous: the D.XIII 'in our conditions is more desirable than the F.4 Martynside'.

Starting the engine on a Martynside serving with the *Osoaviakhim* Pilots School in Kharkov, end of the 1920s.

From 1925 the gradual displacement of British fighters to training schools began. Eight airplanes were handed over to the fighter squadron at the Military School of Air Combat in Orenburg, and some were delivered to the 1st Military Pilot School in Kacha just outside Sevastopol. It was not only Soviet pilots who were trained on these aircraft – Germans, Chinese, and Iranians (they were known as Persians at the time) can be found on the lists of students.

In spring of the following year, the 7th Squadron sent 15 fighters for repair and only 10 remained in service. In view of the shortage of fighters, two old Nieuport 24s had to be reinstated back into service.

The Soviet Martynsides did not participate in any combat activities and the only losses incurred were solely attributable to accidents. For example, on 26 June 1925 during a training flight at a flying school a Martynside flown by student pilot Shaf collided with a Fokker D.XI fighter flown by Shishlov, both pilots were killed. On 10 August 1927 senior pilot Krylov of the 7th Squadron, Moscow Military District, crashed on Klementyevo airfield.

By the end of 1927, the majority of the Martynsides had been handed over to different training institutions. On 1 December 11 airplanes were listed at the Higher School of Air Combat; the 1st Higher School of Military Pilots, the 1st, 2nd, and 3rd Pilots Schools, and the Air Force Academy had a few examples each.

Oddly enough, but attempts were made to set up production in the Soviet Union of this, clearly obsolete, aircraft type. Engineering drawings were prepared at Factory No.39 in Moscow basing on the available aircraft examples. The factory did produce a few fighters fitted with M-6 engines. These airplanes were given the designation MF-4. They were made of different sorts of wood and differed somewhat in terms of the layout of their cockpit instruments (for instance, there were no clocks and turn indicator). The width of the fuselage was reduced, some components of the airframe structure were strengthened, and the wing spars were made wider. Apparently, this was more like an overhaul using individual assemblies from the original. In any case the first airplane even retained its British registration number 4280 (D4280). The MF-4 less its machine guns and some instruments weighed 915kg empty, against 815kg of the original. The flight weight was 1,182kg against 1,113kg correspondingly.

In May 1928 the leading aircraft underwent factory testing, after which on 26 June it was handed over to the Air Force Scientific Testing Institute (NII VVS, *Naucho-Ispytatelniy Institut Voenno-Vozdushnykh Sil*) and there it was flown by pilot V.O. Pisarenko. His report noted: 'the aircraft is stable across all flight modes ... .and it performs all the aerobatic manoeuvres satisfactorily, a little sluggishly, but this is inherent in Martynside aircraft type ... Take-off and landing are easy'. Pisarenko achieved a maximum speed of 212km/h in the MF-4. Testing was concluded on 20 October, and the conclusions in the NII VVS report stated: 'as a fighter, the aircraft is obsolete in view of its low horizontal and vertical speeds. It can be used as a trainer to fighter pilots. From the documents that have survived it is unclear whether the Air Force accepted the produced MF-4s. It is more than likely that they did not. The evidence of this lies in the fact that the overall number of Martynsides in the service lists had not increased by the beginning of 1929.

The number of British fighters in the Air Force was gradually reducing – on 1 October 1927 there were 30 of them, a year later only 22 remained, and two years later this figure was at 18. Thus, the 1st Military Pilots School in Kacha lost two airplanes from mid-1927 until mid-1929. The worn-out aircraft occasionally would just disintegrate in flight. For example, on 24 May 1929 a half a kilometre from the airfield of the Kacha school, the wings folded up in a dive on an aircraft flown by instructor V.S. Vsevolodov.

In the end, the situation was acknowledged as dangerous, and on 26 May 1930 the UVVS issued a directive: ' ... Find out where the MARTYNSIDES are and what condition they are in, as the MARTYNSIDES have to go'. Some 14 airplanes were found, and of those nine were serviceable, all of them were at flying schools. On 14 June the Martynsides were officially taken out of service with the VVS RKKA. Decisions began to be taken concerning what was to be done with them, and it was decided that the parts would be stripped from those that were in bad condition and used to fit out the serviceable aircraft, and these would be handed over to *Osoaviakhim* (*Obshchestvo sodeystviya oboronye, aviatsionnomu i khimicheskomu stroitelstvu* – Society for the Assistance of Defence, Aviation and Chemical Construction). On 4 July the Deputy Chairman of the RVS

I.P. Uborevich added his own resolution to his proposal, which read: 'I do not object'.

In October 1930, four fighters were in the list of the 3rd Military Pilots School named after Voroshilov in Orenburg. They were serviceable but not being used for flying. Two more were found at the 1st flying school, and three at the 2nd flying school, all of which required repairs. In that same month the order arrived mandating the handover of all airplanes to *Osoaviakhim*.

In November the first four unarmed fighters were actually handed over to this organisation, and other airplanes followed in their wake. One Martynside was delivered to the flying club at the glass factory *Proletariy* (Proletarian), while another went to the *Osoaviakhim* division of the Evening-study University for Workers, and two – to the flying club in the Eastern Siberian region. One aircraft arrived at the *Osoaviakhim* flying school in Kharkov.

The MF-4 loaded onto a railway platform.

On 1 January 1931 the last three machines remained with the Air Force, and these left for *Osoaviakhim* a short time later. There they were used up until approximately mid-1932 for training pilots in aerobatics, and then as ground based instructional airframes.

2.4 The *Avrushka*

This was the affectionate nickname given in the Soviet Union to the U-1 training aircraft, which was actually a copy of the British Avro 504K biplane. The latter type was built in series in Britain from 1917 onwards and was one of the last versions of the aircraft, which had been designed back in 1913. Originally the Avro 504 was considered a combat airplane and carried armament, but the final versions were made as trainers and were fitted with dual controls.

The first airplanes of this type appeared in Russia in the Civil War years, and initially they arrived in the north, where the Slavo-British Air Corps operated since autumn 1918. By the summer campaign of 1919 the steamers from Britain had delivered six Avro 504K aircraft fitted with 130hp Clerget engines. Then, evidently, further aircraft were delivered which initially were intended for a flying school. This could be described more accurately as a training group, since it continued training the pilots from other schools which had been forced to close because of the Civil War, as well as provided refreshment training to those who had experienced a significant interruption in flying. The school, however, did not complete training of any of their pupils. Due to increase of combat activities at the front, a decision was taken to use training aircraft for combat. In June 1919 each of them was fitted with a Lewis machine gun for the observer and bomb racks. In August there were two armed Avro 504Ks at Berezniki airfield.

At the end of July of that year these two Avros were attached to the flotilla on Onezhskoe Lake for performance of reconnaissance flights. They became a part of the unit for which an airfield had been created in the forest a few kilometres from the lake in Lyumbushy. In August 1919, one of the crews made an emergency landing on the Avro in the area near Petrozavodsk. The aircraft was captured by Red Army soldiers, dismantled, and sent to Moscow to the GAZ-1 factory. A commissar of the aircraft repair railway train, the former aviation mechanic S.V. Ilyushin (who later became the famous aircraft designer), escorted this aircraft. At the factory, the trophy was studied carefully, and engineering drawings were made with the aim of copying the airplane. This work was overseen by N.N. Polikarpov. Due to wartime difficulties, production of a Soviet Avro began much later, and at other factories.

After the British left Murmansk and Arkhangelsk in September 1919, a few dozen British aircraft were left at the disposal of white command in the north, including eight Avro 504Ks. They were almost never used at the front and following the liberation of Arkhangelsk by Red Army forces these machines became their trophies. The majority of the airplanes were in poor condition, so they were disassembled for spares, and a few aircraft were later used in the Moscow flying school.

Considerably more airplanes of this type arrived in the south of Russia in summer 1920 – in total more than 30 Avro 504Ks were delivered to General A.I. Denikin's army, but following the command transfer to General P.N. Wrangel the deliveries of aviation materiel ceased. Initially the Avros were considered training aircraft, and were intended for the

Avro 504K airplanes of the Slavo-British Air Corps, Bereznik airfield, August 1919. A Lewis machine gun has been fitted in the rear cockpit on one of the airplanes.

Trophy Avro 504K trainers on ski undercarriage, Moscow Military Pilots School, early 1920s.

use at flying school in Kacha. As they were suffering from a shortage of aircraft, however, in August 1920 the whites formed the 2nd Combat Air Unit, which was comprised of just these airplanes. At the time they were the most modern aircraft type that Wrangel had but they were not fitted with armament and their only role was as short-range reconnaissance biplanes.

The reds were preparing to put an end to Wrangel, who had become entrenched in the territory of the Crimea, so they reinforced their aviation forces considerably in this region. The whites also drew their aircraft towards the front line, and the 2nd Air Unit was accommodated on Fyodorovka airfield. The unit played significant role in the battles near Perekop, and then in the Crimea itself in September–October 1920. It is also known that several Avros were in service with the Don Air Unit.

Following the defeat of Wrangel's army some of the aircraft were left to the reds. According to the archive records, at least nine Avro 504Ks were captured in the south. The majority of them were in a serviceable condition and entered service with the RKKVF. On 15 November 1920, the 1st Air Depot had Clerget-130 powered Avros numbered 9747, 9749, 9752, 9754, 9756, and 9758. All these were the airplanes from the same batch produced by the Grahame-White factory after the end of the First World War.

The trophy airplanes were sent to the flying schools, and also to the air force units as trainers. For example, on 1 December 1920 a single Avro was operating in the fighter air unit in Peterhof.

The Avro 504K deserved high status amongst red pilots, and this is what A. Laitsinger wrote about it: 'this machine ... has a high rate of climb given a slow horizontal speed, and its qualities as a trainer, according to pilots, are wonderful: it forgives any mistakes, easily recovers from any attitude, is surprisingly benign, and most importantly, it is very easy to land, it performs three-point landings by itself'.

Operational experience with these trophy biplanes was so successful that a decision was taken to acquire a batch of them in Britain. Furthermore, the majority of the captured machines would quickly fall into disrepair, as the student pilots were regularly crashing them.

In May 1922 the steamer *Miranda* delivered them to Petrograd. The airplanes were assembled, while the order for this work had already been issued in October 1921. In August 1922 the new aircraft underwent testing and then were delivered to flying schools and air force units where they were used for aircrew training. The highest number (ten) of the Avro 504Ks went to Kacha, to the former Sevastopol military flying school. The school operated both trophy British aircraft and the ones recently purchased in Britain. At the end of 1923, the 1st Military Pilots School had 13 aircraft of this type in service, which were the newest and most serviceable among others. A further five biplanes served in the Moscow Military Pilots School (three of them were

An accident of an Avro 504K at the Moscow Military Pilots School, early 1920s. Note the star on the lower wing which has been painted over the Russian roundel

trophy aircraft that were received from the Sevastopol Pilots School in 1921). Two other airplanes of this type joined air force units: a single Avro 504K was in the 7th Separate Reconnaissance Unit, and the only Avro 504L with floats served in the 1st Reconnaissance Hydroplane Unit in the Baltic Fleet, which was based in Oranienbaum.

In order to provide the red air fleet with new aircraft, a decision was taken to commence production of the Avro in Soviet Russia without a licence. The Soviet version of the Avro 504K was designated the U-1. It corresponded fully to the British original, but was made of different types of wood, and the design of some of the assemblies underwent minor simplifications. Imported French 110hp Rhone J engines and 120hp Rhone Jb, as well as their Soviet copies known as *Ron-110* and *Ron-120* (later re-designated M-2-110 and M-2-120) were fitted to these biplanes.

The first U-1s were built at the GAZ-5 *Samolyot* (Airplane) factory (the former *Moska* factory) in Moscow in 1922. This enterprise received an order to produce 18 aircraft. These airplanes were fitted with *Ron-110* engines. The U-1 differed slightly from the Avro 504K in terms of its dimensions (the length of the Soviet airplanes was 250mm shorter) and the weight (it was 40kg heavier). In view of this heavy weight and the reduced thrust-to-weight ratio the flight-performance characteristics fell short in comparison with the British original.

The following year series production of the U-1 was launched at the GAZ-3 *Krasniy Lyotchik* factory in Petrograd. The Petrograd-built machines featured enhanced quality of production and lesser weight. Thus, the weight of the U-1 produced at the GAZ-5 factory was 612kg, while the airplane built at the GAZ-3 weighted 570kg. The normal flight weight was 838kg and 810kg respectively. Lighter weight of the aircraft enabled an improvement in flight-performance characteristics. According to the results of testing at the Scientific-Experimental Airfield, the maximum speed increased from 132km/h up to 142km/h, and the service ceiling also increased by 100m. The figures for the

A U-1 biplane during testing at the NOA.

The Deputy Head of the VVS Directorate Ya.I. Alksnis (centre) stands among pilots next to a U-1. Alksnis completed his initial flying training in Moscow on this particular airplane.

rate of climb also improved, as did the take-off run and the landing roll.

Since there was a shortage of the M-2 engines some of the aircraft were fitted with 80hp Rhone C engines (these power plants were manufactured in Moscow as *Ron-80*). The airplanes were listed in the records as U-1 with *Ron-80*, or as U-3. The empty weight of this version was 563kg, but in view of the insufficient thrust the maximum flight speed was limited to 120km/h.

In total in the period from 1923 till 1930, two factories built 664 examples of the U-1. From summer 1928 these airplanes (starting from serial number 2152) received reinforced spars (without milled sections) for the upper and lower wings, while the height of the front spar was also increased, there were fitted ribs of a different design, thicker cabane struts, and reinforced bracing wires. The aim of this was to bring the strength of the airframe into line with the new standards that had been introduced in the USSR. These reinforcements were carried out in the course of repairs to the earlier produced biplanes. Limitations were introduced on performing certain aerobatic manoeuvres for aircraft that had not been strengthened.

Some number of the U-1 biplanes were manufactured in 1923 at the *Remvozdukhzavod* factory (the former repair workshops of the 4th Air Depot) in Nizhniy Novgorod. In February–March 1924 they underwent testing at the NOA and were handed over for operational service.

A group of U-1 airplanes in flight.

At the same time, production of the naval training MU-1 aircraft was launched at the *Krasniy Lyotchik* factory (this airplane was redesigned similarly to Avro 504L). The type was initially dubbed as just the *Gydro-Avro*. It was decided that the British floats were not going to be copied for the MU-1, so indigenous ones were designed, which had been simplified and were not manufactured from expensive types of wood. This enabled to reduce their weight on 41kg, and the cost was reduced as well. The altered outer lines of the floats slightly improved the aircraft seaworthiness. Soviet engineers also decided not to use a tail float and the vertical fin, which were present in the original.

Evidently, the prototype example of the MU-1 was built with the French 130hp Clerget engine. It was then followed by an aircraft with M-2 engine, which underwent testing in May–June 1925. It is constituted a rare case when the machine weighed 10kg less than that stipulated in the specification. Following the tests, the fuel supply system was re-designed; now the fuel flowed from the upper tank into the carburettor simply under gravity force.

In 1924–1930, 73 MU-1s were manufactured in Leningrad. Low production standards and replacement of materials (the use of pine instead of spruce, ash, and mahogany) led to a 200kg increase in the overall weight of the empty MU-1 in comparison with the British original. In parallel with the U-1, strengthening was also introduced into the airframe of the MU-1 (starting from aircraft serial number 2237).

The majority of the U-1s joined flying schools, but air force units also received a few dozen of them in 1924–1926. Among the

An accident of the U-1 which was flown by student pilot Mironenko of the 2nd Military Pilots School in Borisoglebsk, November 1927.

A taxi training U-1 (with part of the outer skin on the wing removed) which was used at the Military Technical School in Leningrad, Komendantskiy airfield, February 1929.

A group of instructors and student pilots of the 2nd Military Pilots School standing next to a U-1 biplane.

A U-1 of the 1st (Kacha) Military Pilots School, November 1929.

An accident of the U-1 which was flown by student pilot A. Zhdanov in Borisoglebsk, September 1929.

A U-1 airplane on the parking area of Kacha airfield, January 1927.

units which got this aircraft were the ones under the direct control of the UVVS: the training squadron of the Air Force Academy (five aircraft), the Scientific-Experimental Airfield (two aircraft), and the 1st Separate Heavy Aviation Unit, and the training unit of the UVVS (two aircraft). There were five U-1s in the Separate Reconnaissance Training Unit of the Moscow Military District, and one each in the 1st Separate Fighter Squadron of the Leningrad District, and in the 2nd Light Bomber Squadron of the Western District. These biplanes were used in the military units exclusively for training the aircrew. By the end of the 1920s all U-1s had been withdrawn from the air force units, and they were subsequently delivered to flying schools only.

Occasionally the U-1s were used as liaison aircraft. For example, during exercises of Leningrad district in September 1930, a unit of six U-1s was formed to service a group of intermediaries at Detskoye Selo airfield. The airplanes had been borrowed from the Air Force School of Military Theory. Officially this unit was known as the Air Unit for Liaison of the Upper Command.

As the pilots were aware of the British origin of the aircraft type, they named it *Avrushka*, and this was both used for the old trophy or purchased machines and for the Soviet-produced biplanes. Many famous Soviet pilots first took to the skies in a U-1.

The aircraft itself was considered sufficiently reliable, which was more than could be said for the M-2 engines. In 1926 at one of the schools a failure occurred in one of the valve push rods. As a result of a forced landing the *Avrushka* lost its engine cowling, the propeller was broken and the forward part of the fuselage was damaged, the fuel tank ruptured and two inter-plane struts were broken. At this school, a further five similar accidents were also recorded over the course of six months. Incidents like these were noted in other locations as well. For new U-1s, carburettor failures were also commonplace when balls of tin would get into the carburettors. They would find their way there from the fuel tanks, which were not flushed out properly after brazing.

On 1 October 1927 there were 193 U-1s at the flying schools, after one year their number rose to 252, and two years

Photo from the report on the collision of two U-1s of the 2nd Military Pilots School, November 1926.

A result of hard landing of a U-1 in Borisoglebsk, autumn 1927

A collision between two U-1s at Borisoglebsk airfield, June 1929.

later there were 293 airplanes in service. This was the peak, however, and then the quantities began to reduce. On 1 January 1933 the Air Force had 144 U-1s in service.

Several aircraft were used for experimental purposes – in 1931 one such airplane participated in tests of the first Soviet rocket-assisted take-off units. Two small dry-powder rockets enabled the take-off distance to be reduced considerably. Development of these units was led by Leningrad Laboratory of Gas Dynamics, while the tests were carried out at the Komendantskiy airfield. Pilot S. Mukhin flew the U-1 that had been provided by the Military Technical School. In total during testing 33 take offs were completed with no failures or accidents.

In 1926 in Leningrad N.P. Blagin, using one U-3, tested the pneumatic actuators in the first Soviet pneumatically operated autopilot, which had been designed by R.G. Nirenberg. A cylinder with compressed air was carried under the fuselage above the undercarriage. On 30 October the engine failed in flight but the pilot was nevertheless able to land at the Komendantskiy airfield, even though he damaged the aircraft.

The majority of the MU-1 hydroplanes also ended up at the flying schools. For example, they were in service at the Military School of Naval Pilots named after L.D. Trotskiy. A significantly high number of failures were commonplace for the flying schools. Thus, on 19 May 1926 an MU-1 flown by student pilot Kritskiy collided with a steam launch in the Northern Bay of Sevastopol on water landing and broke the starboard cell of the biplane wing. In December 1927 there were 11 MU-1s in service at this flying school.

As was the case with their land-based brethren the floatplanes entered air force units in small numbers, as both liaison or training aircraft. Up until the end of the 1920s they were used in the 55th and 62nd Hydroaviation Units, the 87th and 88th Training Units, and in the directorate of the 9th Air Brigade.

At the end of 1920s the MU-1s were used as ship-borne reconnaissance aircraft. In 1926 the cruiser *Chervona Ukraina* (former *Admiral Nakhimov*) of the Black Sea Fleet had Yu-20 floatplane on board. The Yu-20 was an all-metal monoplane manufactured at a concessionary Junkers factory

This U-3 airplane (fitted with a *Ron-80* engine), which was built by the GAZ-5 factory, was used at the 1st Military Pilots School. In March 1926 pilot K.G. Lukyanov attempted a take-off in a strong wind, that resulted in a crash.

Assembly of one of the first MU-1 floatplane at the *Krasniy Lyotchik* factory.

An MU-1 floatplane prior to the factory testing.

An MU-1 at the Naval Pilots School taxiing at one of the bays in Sevastopol.

Instructors and mechanics of the Naval Pilots School standing next to an MU-1.

The result of the forced landing by pilot Bakanov in Sevastopol, September 1929.

An MU-1 biplane from the Naval Pilots School has been towed onto the shore.

An MU-3 (fitted with a *Ron-80* engine) after an accident, Sevastopol, May 1926. The airplane was flown by pilot M.N. Kritskiy.

Instructors and student pilots of the Naval Pilots School, standing next to an MU-1 airplane.

Student pilot V.A. Khmelnitskiy, flying on this MU-1 in December 1928, porpoised heavily during water landing. The float struts broke and the entire airplane was bent.

An MU-1 airplane taxiing out for take-off.

The Black Sea Fleet cruiser *Chervona Ukraina* at sea. Note a MU-1 reconnaissance airplane between the funnels.

An accident of the U-1 which was flown by student pilot Muravyev of the 1st Military Pilots School, June 1929.

in Fili (which back then was just outside Moscow). The cruiser was at the testing stage at this time and, when firing its main calibre guns during the tests, the wings of the Junkers broke off. The naval command requested a replacement from the UVVS and they were offered three MU-1s, as no other hydroplanes of similar dimensions and weight were found – almost all of the few Yu-20 monoplanes available had by that time used up their service lives. These three MU-1s comprised a flight of the cruiser's ship-borne aircraft.

Naturally, the training biplanes could never be considered fully-fledged naval reconnaissance airplanes due to their slow speed, short-range, and poor seaworthiness. One of the UVVS documents of December 1928 recorded sadly: 'Ship-borne aviation up until now still does not have an aircraft that fully meets the requirements of a naval reconnaissance hydroplane. As an interim measure the MU-1

In October 1926, this U-3 (fitted with a *Ron-80* engine) was used for testing autopilot pneumatic actuators designed by R.G. Nirenberg. A compressed air cylinder was mounted under the fuselage. Test pilot N.P. Blagin flew these tests, and in one of the flights, during landing approach at the Komendantskiy airfield in Leningrad, the engine failed resulting in a crash landing.

Tubular guides for the 82mm rocket projectiles fitted under the lower wing of the U-1.

The rocket projectiles being placed inside the tubular guides.

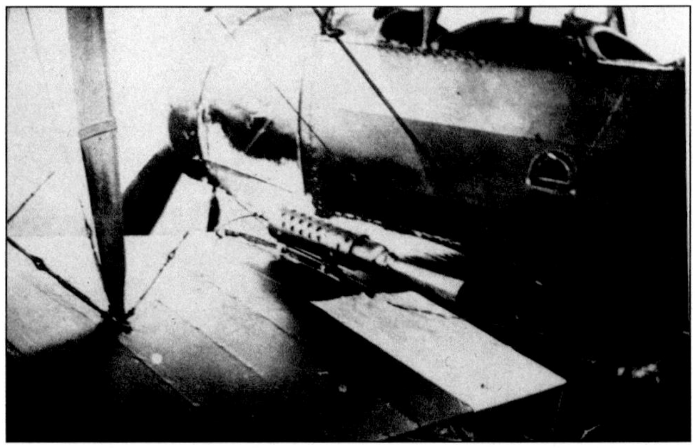

A port rocket-assisted take-off unit on the lower wing of the U-1. A thin strip of stainless steel was mounted instead of canvass on the upper surface of the wing behind the unit

U-1 aircraft from one of the aeroclubs in Ukraine. Note that all three airplanes carry gift inscriptions.

A female student pilot of the Moscow School of *Aviakhim* prepares to start the M-2 engine on the U-1 airplane, 1931

training aircraft are in service, which are entirely unsuitable for fulfilling the tasks of servicing the fleet ships.'

When in 1928 the *Chervona Ukraina* put to sea, there were two biplanes on board with a third remaining in reserve on the shore. There was no catapult on the cruiser, but the Avro would not have survived a catapult launch anyway. For take-off the aircraft was hoisted down onto the water using a crane, and this was how they were recovered following their flights. In the course of summer exercises, one MU-1 was performing reconnaissance flights on the open sea, and its crew got gratitude for successful completion of reconnaissance of the 'enemy's' forces. On 22 July 1929 an aircraft from the *Chervona Ukraina* lost speed in a steep turn and plunged into the sea, the crew were killed. It emerged that the flight commander Gureykin, who had been the observer, and was still studying to become a pilot, had been flying the aircraft. This incident became significant, so after this the Head of the UVVS P.I. Baranov banned initial training in air force units, which up until that time had been permitted. Pilots were now required to graduate from a flying school. Then the Yu-20 came out of repairs and the biplanes were handed over to the Naval Pilots School.

In the Baltics a single MU-1 was carried on board of the completed cruiser *Profintern*, (originally it was called

Pilots standing next to a U-1, mid-1920s.

The gift U-1 airplane with inscription 'Mari Worker'.

A U-1 biplane taxies out for take-off.

The ceremonial handover to *Aviakhim* of the gift U-1 biplane carrying the inscription 'The Female Worker' at the Moscow Central Airfield, 1 May 1930.

Svetlana). The hoisting crane for lowering the aircraft onto the water was mounted between second and third funnels where the storage area was prepared for the aircraft. In

Preparing a U-1 for flight at one of the aeroclubs.

The gift U-1 airplane carrying the inscription 'The Ukrainian Technician'.

Starting the engine on a U-1 at the *Aviakhim* Flying School in Kharkov, end of the 1920s.

summer 1929 during Baltic Fleet manoeuvres this aircraft carried out reconnaissance operations relatively successfully. Pilot Ivanov and observer Tarasov spotted the battleship *Marat* at sea, and dropped a 'cargo' onto it (the author has not been able to determine what this was). In autumn of that same year the *Profintern*, along with the battleship *Parizhskaya Kommuna* were transferred to the Black Sea.

For a short time three MU-1s each were assigned to the cruisers *Chervona Ukraina* and *Profintern*. The aircraft belonging to the ship-borne flights featured large markings in the form of a geometric white shape – either a triangle or a square was applied to the wings and fuselage. In autumn 1930 the *Avrushkas* were replaced by KR-1 flying boats (Heinkel HD.55s) acquired in Germany.

The U-1 biplane with inscription 'The Kharkov Pravda' (the name of newspaper) which was operated by one of the aeroclubs in Ukraine.

Towing an MU-1 following an accident on 2 July 1928. The Flight Commander of the 66th Air Unit, Baltic Sea Air Force, A.M. Konkin took off in this airplane from Oranienbaum to give a ride to representative of the patronising organisation. Unexpectedly, the passenger pushed the rudder pedal which resulted in a crash.

Filming at the aeroclub airfield in Izhevsk featuring a U-1 biplane with a gift inscription.

An accident with a U-1 at the school in Borisoglebsk, November 1926. According to a report, student pilot 'Tip-Ship-Zyp, a Chinese man' crashed this airplane.

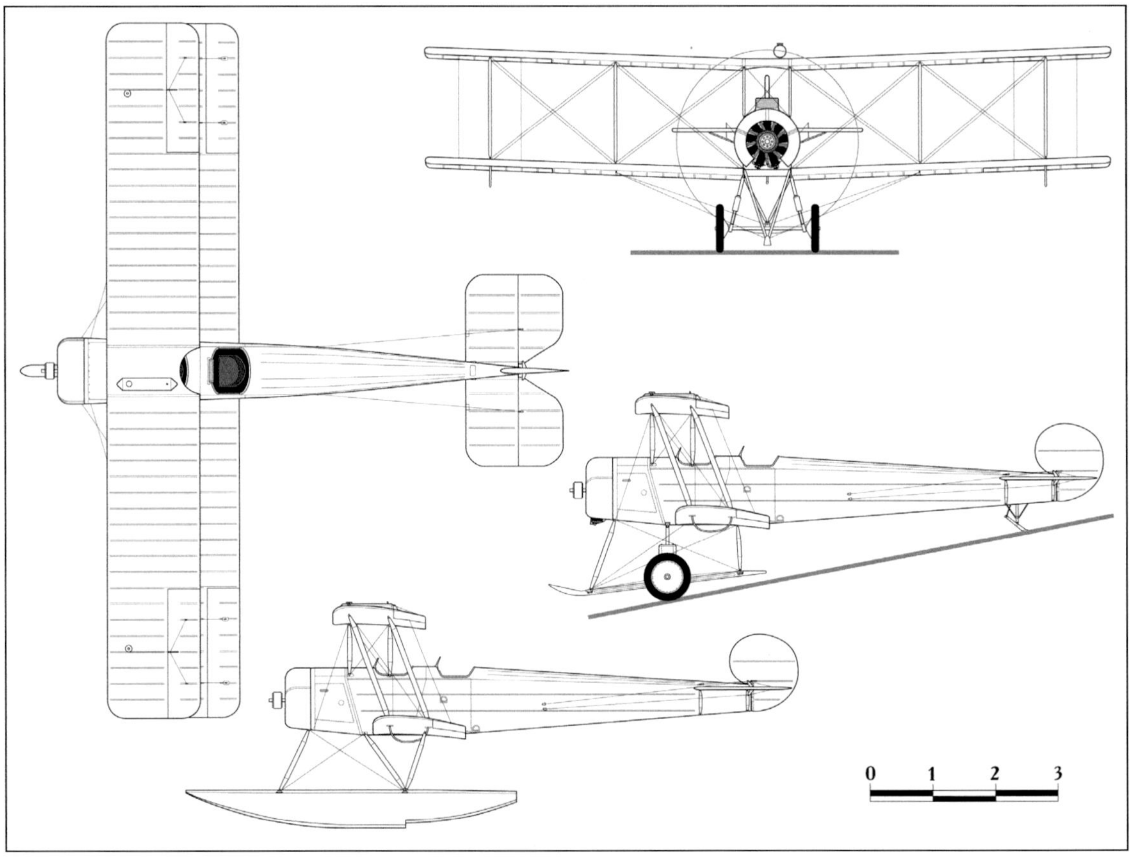

Three-view drawings of a U-1 trainer and side view of a MU-1 floated version.

Not a single U-1s survived in Russia, but an Avro 504K was acquired for the Vadim Zadorozhniy Technical Museum in Arkhangelskoe just outside Moscow.

Starting from 1930 the land-based U-1s began to be replaced by the newer U-2 training aircraft designed by N.N. Polikarpov and fitted with Soviet M-11 engines. By the end of 1932 the U-2 had become more widespread than the *Avrushkas*, although the latter flew at the Air Force flying schools up until 1934. Production of the M-2 engines by that time had stopped and they began to be in short supply. At the NII VVS, engineer Stoman developed a version of the U-1 accommodating the M-11 or M-12 engine (neither of these engines was rotary). This design, however, was never realised, as in August 1931 around 200 Rhone Jb engines were acquired cheaply in the USA. These engines had been stored since the First World War had come to an end. The engines were fitted to the U-1s during repairs at Factory No.47 in Leningrad. The MU-1s were also used to train naval pilots up until 1934 and were subsequently replaced by the Sh-2 amphibious aircraft.

When the U-2s were replacing the U-1s, the ex-Air Force aircraft were handed over to *Osoaviakhim*. This society paid for them not with money, but with the involvement of its members in the construction of airfields, in particular, in groundworks. Two *Avrushkas* that had been brought from Moscow were used in the first civil pilots school of *Osoaviakhim*, which was opened in Kharkov on 4 November 1928; they were subsequently augmented by several U-1s. In 1932 this school was transferred to Poltava. In June 1933 the Leningrad aero-club received four U-1s. These biplanes could be found at the flying schools up until 1935.

In the second half of 1929 three aircraft were handed over to the aviation department of the Joint State Political Directorate, but what role they performed and where is not known.

One instance of exporting this biplane type is known – in 1924 two Avro 504K aircraft (other sources say these were the U-1s) were sent to Iran.

2.5 The R-1 – Soviet Version of the DH.9A

Having achieved success in arrangement the production of the DH.4, the leadership of the military industry reasonably considered the idea of setting up the production of more advanced DH.9, which had proven itself well in the Civil War. On 24 October 1922 the Aviation Department of the Main Directorate of Military Industry requested the military to hand over one trophy DH.9A with a Liberty engine to GAZ-1 factory so the engineering drawings could be prepared using this aircraft at the sample. At the beginning of 1923 the design department of GAZ-1 factory headed by N.N. Polikarpov was tasked with copying the Liberty-powered DH.9A.

As a result, a development work began on an aircraft designated the R-1 (*Razvedchik-Perviy* – reconnaissance, the first). In February 1923 another well-known designer, D.P. Grigorovich, was made head of the design department of the factory, and held this post up until August 1924 when he in turn was replaced by Polikarpov.

The R-1 was not a precise copy of the DH.9A – Polikarpov thought that the design of the British biplane in many respects reflected the rush of aircraft development in wartime, so it had a number of defects, which could be eradicated. He, and subsequently Grigorovich, consciously introduced a significant number of changes to the design of the biplane. Furthermore, two tasks were identified: increasing the payload, and simplifying production of the aircraft. The I-section wing spars, which were milled from solid beams with lightening holes, conceded to box-shaped spars, the booms of which were milled half way along at the ends. As was the case with the DH.4, all different types of foreign timbers were replaced with the ones available in Russia. The load-bearing fuselage truss was changed – it was made statically determinate. The aircraft was given another wing profile, and in view of the increase in the size of the fuel tanks the fuel capacity rose by approximately 20 litres. The design of the structural joints was simplified, the complex cast components conceded to those manufactured from sheet metal. The R-1 had approximately a quarter fewer components than were in the DH.9A. The designers wanted to enhance the aircraft aerodynamics by replacing the enormous nose-mounted radiator for a pair of round Lamblin-type finned radiators. There were also changed the engine mount and cowling, the cabane struts, and undercarriage. The only part of the aircraft that was not re-designed was the tail fin – it corresponded fully to the original one on the DH.9. The aircraft project was presented to the Scientific Committee of the UVVS, which gave their approval.

The UVVS were not particularly warm about the idea of putting the Soviet version of the British biplane into production. They considered the aircraft obsolete and it was hardly worth producing it in large numbers. As it later emerged the military were seriously mistaken ... An order was nevertheless issued in January 1923 for the manufacture of a 'trial' R-1. The work on the prototype manufacturing began in July 1923, initially at the factory expense as no funds were forthcoming from the military.

The work was slow to progress, and the assembly and adjustments were only completed on 30 June 1924. However, the trial runs of the engine on that same day demonstrated that the radiators were not functioning satisfactorily. The water in the system was overheating. Initially it was decided that this was due to the insufficient productivity of the water pump, and this was replaced. The radiators were re-designed several times before they gave a more or less satisfactory result. In the end, however, the Lamblin-type radiators were rejected, and were replaced by nose-mounted honeycomb radiator, although it differed from the British design.

This airplane, however, was not the first R-1 to be manufactured – back on 15 March 1923 the factory had begun to hand over to the military acceptance committee the aircraft that were produced to a standard that was considered temporary. They had nose-mounted honeycomb radiators similar to those fitted to the British DH.9A. By 29 May some 25 of these reconnaissance aircraft had been handed over, and a further seven were in the final stages of assembly. In parallel, the GAZ-10 *Lebed* factory (the former Lebedev factory) in Taganrog was to arrange production of the R-1, and in fact the first order for 12 biplanes did fall to this factory, but the production began later than in Moscow, only commencing in January 1925.

R-1 serial number 318, built at the GAZ-10 factory in Taganrog in 1925

The handover of the gift R-1 biplane 'The Kolomna Worker' to the air force pilots, 1925. Note a single Lewis machine gun with a primitive gun camera on the mount in the rear cockpit.

Production at the GAZ-1 factory was also slow to get going, as the materials were difficult to get hold of so the factory would make use of whatever was to hand. Both American spruce and the Russian pine were used, and moreover, these timbers were dried or half-baked which were dried out at the factory itself. The gradual replacement of the timber type forced the airframe strength re-calculation and changes to the aircraft design. Initially metal was supplied from pre-revolutionary reserves, which then ran out. From December 1923 small batches of poor quality rolled metal began to arrive at the factory. This was the reason the axles for the wheels were made to be dual: one tube of a smaller diameter was inserted into another of a larger diameter. The factory was able to get away with this because no technical requirements for materials existed in the USSR at that time.

The aircraft manufacturers had to make themselves the radiators and the wire for the bracing. There was also a shortage of wheels, and they would be fitted to one aircraft after another to try them for size.

As a result, by January 1924 the production rate of the factory had fallen from 20 aircraft a month down to six. It later fluctuated from eight to 14 airplanes a month depending on delays in the supply of components. The workshops would either stand idle or would work feverish overtime. There was also a constant shortage of Liberty engines, and the factory

An R-1 biplane which was tested at the NOA.

could not hand over completed aircraft on which something was missing.

The Head of the Aircraft Production Department at Aviatrest (State Trust of the Aviation Industry which belonged to the Main Directorate of the Metal Industry) K.V. Akashev reported that the 'factories were faced with the need to completely halt the assembly of airplanes because all areas in the workshops, stores, hangars, and anywhere else were taken up with completed airframes that could not be handed over to the customer because they did not have any engines'. Approximately 100 aircraft were standing at the GAZ-1 factory awaiting engines, and the majority of those were R-1s. Assembly, paint and fabric skinning workshops of the factory were converted into stores, and an additional hangar was rented from *Dobrolyot* society at Moscow Central airfield. In June 1924 nine completed aircraft were rolled out onto the Central airfield, and assembly of the R-1 was ceased.

Officially, the aircraft acceptance by the military customer were going on from 15 August 1924 onwards. Ten airplanes were handed over to the military instead of the planned 42, after which a telegram arrived from the UVVS which ordered a cessation of the acceptance of unarmed airplanes. In fact, all the biplanes had been handed over to the air force units without their gun or bomb armament. The management of Aviatrest acknowledged openly that 'the factories are handing over flying boxes that have minimal combat value'.

According to the project, the aircraft armament was to have corresponded to the British prototype: the forward-firing machine gun on the port side with a synchronizer on the engine and a dual gun mount in a turret in the aft cockpit. There were no indigenous machine guns for aviation use in Russia at that time, so the British Vickers and Lewis ones were in service (these were for fixed and mobile gun mounts respectively). They were supplied to fit the British 7.69mm cartridge, and the reserves of these cartridges were running out. Therefore, the machine guns were sent to the armament factory in Tula to be converted to fit the Russian 7.62mm cartridge. Later these 'russified' versions of the machine guns were officially introduced into service under the names *Vikkers* model 1924 and *Lyuis* model 1924. The

Checking the process of hoisting the bomb to the underwing rack using a BL-1 winch.

Small bombs on the underwing racks of an R-1.

The aircraft designer D.P. Grigorovich (second from right) standing next to an R-1 at the GAZ-1 factory in Moscow, mid-1920s

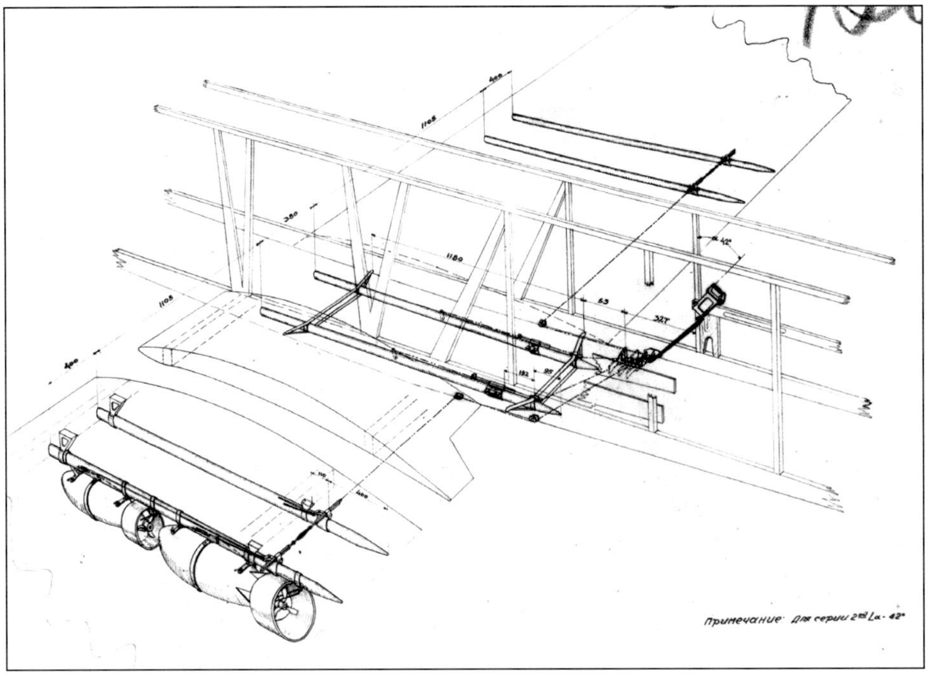

The layout of the Bombr-1 bomb armament set.

turrets and synchronisers were not produced at all at any factory in Russia.

Similarly, it was proposed to copy the bomb armament positioning from the British prototype – the bomb racks would be located under each wing and the bomb release mechanism with the primitive bombsight would be placed at the observer's station in the aft cockpit. However, the bomb racks and bomb release mechanisms were not being manufactured in Russia at that time either. Moreover, the military customers were not able to define the equipment type and its positioning on the airplane. Only on 7 January 1925 an agreement was signed with Aviatrest detailing the composition of the armament and equipment for different aircraft types, including the R-1. This document listed the set of components for various aircraft types but did not indicate specifically the component type, system, or manufacturing plant. For example, the list just stated a 'compass,' or 'clocks'.

The situation on the equipment and armament gradually sorted itself out, and in spring 1924 the D-1 (PUL-1) synchroniser appeared, which was designed by engineer Savelyev basing on a design that had been used on the Russian-built Nieuport fighters. In comparison to the Nieuports, however, the PUL-1 synchroniser turned out to be considerably more complex because the engine of the R-1 was located much further away from the machine gun. The PUL-1 was built in a hurry, as the UVVS was pressing to expedite. A prototype of the synchroniser was manufactured and tested – it turned out to be satisfactory, but no more than that. The designer himself considered the synchroniser unrefined. The military accepted the PUL-1 as a temporary type and agreed to put it into series production. Some 210 (other sources put this figure as 249) examples were produced, although the entire pre-revolutionary stockpile of high-quality steel was used up in their manufacture. This enabled installation of forward-firing machine guns to biplanes produced at the GAZ-1 factory from the end of summer 1924.

The Vickers machine gun was mounted on metal blocks attached on wooden brackets. The machine gun was belt fed, with 500 cartridges in a pull-out box. The GAZ-1 factory *post factum* supplied kits to retrofit the R-1s in air force units. Thus, in October 1924 some 25 kits were shipped to the 1st Light Bomber Squadron named after Lenin, and their installation was overseen by a factory mechanic.

Taganrog-based GAZ-10 factory handed over the first six aircraft without any armament at all, and then permission was obtained to complete a further 10 aircraft in the same configuration. After that the factory transferred to a standard accepted at GAZ-1, which included installation of the PUL-1 synchroniser. A short time later, however, the PUL-1 was

This photo from the accident report clearly shows the location of the bomb racks under the wing and fuselage.

The additional water radiator was mounted on R-1 serial number 2755, GAZ-1 factory, 1925.

The M-5B engine at the museum of *Salyut* factory in Moscow.

acknowledged as being unsuitable for combat service and newer types of synchronisers replaced the PUL-1.

On 21 August 1925 Aviatrest announced a competition for the best machine gun mount with synchroniser for the R-1, and received a whole series of proposals in response. The D-2 (PUL-2) was produced as a prototype back in March, but tested and rejected. The D-3 (PUL-3) was more successful – this was an original design created especially for the R-1 even before the competition was announced. Its prototype underwent extended testing at the gunnery range. On 13 May 1925 the PUL-3 was approved as the standard type, and then a batch of 30 examples was built. In June they began to be fitted to the R-1 but, in contrast to the prototype, series synchronisers worked intermittently. The reason for this turned out to be the poor quality of the steel used in their manufacture. The designers brought the defects to light and proposed a more refined version, the PUL-3bis. This example underwent testing and on 15 October 1925 it was put into production, but only a few dozen PUL-3bis units were completed. Nevertheless, they were fitted to biplanes both in Moscow and in Taganrog.

An R-1 airplane, fitted with an M-5 engine, at the factory, 1925.

The original PUL-6 synchroniser designed by N.P. Tryapitsin was in competition with the PUL-3bis. This unit comprised more than a third fewer parts and was 1.5–2.0kg lighter and easier to manufacture. This device underwent testing successfully and on 29 October 1925 it was accepted into series production. The first PUL-6 synchronisers appeared on the Moscow-built R-1s at the end of that same year. From January 1926 production of the PUL-3bis was ceased, and a factory in Kovrov was drafted in to manufacture

An R-1 during tests at the NII VVS.

On the early series R-1s, a British Lewis machine gun was mounted on the port side of the fuselage.

the PUL-6, so by the summer they were appearing on series R-1 biplanes. From 1 October these synchronisers were fitted to all aircraft that had been manufactured in Moscow, and a short time later to those produced in Taganrog.

All the above types of synchronisers were purely mechanical, but at the GAZ-1 factory experiments were being conducted with other design types. Engineer Savelyev developed an electro-pneumatic D-5 (PUL-5) synchroniser. It underwent factory testing but its reliability was considered insufficient, and the cost was excessive. The simple and reliable PUL-6 fully satisfied the customers.

During operation of a forward-firing machine gun the pilot would be doing the aiming, and for this purpose the simplest sight designed by Vakhmistrov was placed in front of the windscreen – a ring and bead sight.

From the end of 1924, turrets for a single Lewis machine gun began to be fitted in the aft cockpits of the R-1s. These turrets were foreign-built, most likely French, although it is not known whether these were purchased new or these were old ones taken from the stores. From the summer 1925, there appeared turrets that were manufactured at the

Tail fin of the R-1.

The ceremonial handover of one of the airplanes of the squadron 'Our Response to Chamberlain'. Among those present are the Head of the RKKA Headquarters S.S. Kamenev (standing, third from left), the Head of the VVS Directorate P.I. Baranov (to his right), and his Deputy Ya.I. Alksnis (seated, second from right). Note new PV-1 machine gun fitted to this airplane.

Tula Armament Factory (TOZ, *Tulskiy Oruzheyniy Zavod*), which had been copied from the French example. The aircraft factories were delivering airplanes that were unarmed and not fitted with sights, so this equipment was fitted directly at the air force units.

For a long period of time, the UVVS could not make up their minds what the ammunition load should be for the aft gun mount: six or eight magazines, each containing 47 cartridges. The number of magazines, in its turn, determined the dimensions of the magazine rack where they would be stored. In the end the decision was taken that six magazines would be sufficient.

In August 1925 a refined TOZ turret was fitted on aircraft serial number 2533. The turret had a clevis for the twin Lewis machine guns, and the Scientific Committee of the UVVS soon approved this mounting type. The TOZ committed to arrange series production of this unit in five to seven months, but in reality these turrets began to be fitted in Moscow and in Taganrog factories from October 1926. For the twin machine-gun mount an ammunition load of eight magazines was supplied, and this was later increased to 10 disks.

The aircraft with inscription 'Our Response to the Pope' was a gift to the VVS from Azerbaijan section of *Osoaviakhim*. How though did the Pope annoy the Azerbaijanis so much that they did this?

An accident with airplane serial number 2887 during an acceptance test flight at the GAZ 1 factory in Moscow, 1927.

Nose section of the R-1 with the nose-mounted radiator removed and the front of the M-5 engine clearly visible.

The PV-1 machine gun on the port side of the R-1 fuselage.

The Tur-4 turret with two Lewis machine guns.

The pilot's instrument panel on the R-1.

There were plans to use the metal wing spar on the R-1, but this was never implemented.

In the air force units, however, the preference was for fitting just a single Lewis machine gun in the aft cockpit due to the concerns related to the moved centre of gravity position.

Bomb armament of the R-1 would include D-3 bomb racks (later re-designated Der-3) under the wing and D-4 (Der-4) for carrying larger calibre bomb load under the fuselage. Both types of bomb racks could support carrying one bomb or two bombs in tandem, with a lighter fragmentation bomb carried in front, and a heavier high-explosive bomb positioned aft. The first batch of 30 D-3 kits was manufactured at the GAZ-1 factory at their own risk, without authorisation from the Scientific Committee of the UVVS.

The bombs were to be dropped using the SBR-5 or SBR-7 bomb release mechanisms designed by engineer Gorelov, and both of them were the versions of the British Browning mechanical bomb release mechanisms that had been captured as trophies during the Civil War. They enabled bombs to be dropped singly or in series with a set interval, as well as a salvo. The SBR-5 was later rejected, and the alternative was the SBR-3 bomb release mechanism designed by Savelyev, which was a simpler design but still allowed bombs to be dropped in a series.

On 11 June 1925 a commission headed by V.S. Vakhmistrov carried out an inspection and testing of the bomb armament on one of the R-1s. This aircraft had

An R-1, built by Factory No.31 (the former GAZ-10) in Taganrog, in 1930.

Two R-1 training biplanes from the Military Pilots School in Kacha, autumn 1927.

been allocated specifically for experimenting with bomb armament, and therefore it had been fitted with three different bomb release mechanisms: under the port wing was the Savelyev's, under the starboard wing was the Gorelov's, and the single bomb release mechanism (SBR-1) was for the fuselage-mounted bomb racks. The UVVS did not approve the report on the results of the tests, as they did not agree with the conclusions of the commission. On 30 June, however, a small batch of the above bomb racks and bomb release mechanisms was ordered.

By the summer of 1925 the Soviet bombsights only existed as prototypes and were of two types: designed by Nikolskoy (which was based on the British Wimperis), and a simpler unit designed by A.V. Nadashkevich. Subsequently, 25 examples of each of these designs were produced for thorough testing. The preference was given to the frame sight of Nadashkevich design, which was accepted into service as the AP-2. It was attached on the outside at the starboard side of the observer's cockpit, who would aim through a window in aircraft starboard lower wing.

The first 37 biplanes that were manufactured in Moscow under the plan for 1925–1926 (this timescale was measured from 1 July till 1 July next year) were not fitted with the bomb release mechanisms and cables for them, and the bomb racks turned out to be unserviceable because they were lacking certain parts. The next nine airplanes did not receive their bomb release mechanisms in time either. The bombsights were absent. Whatever was missing would later be sent to the units and would be fitted to the aircraft there. The early series R-1s carried bomb racks designed by L.D. Kolpakov-Miroshnichenko.

In September 1925 the UVVS refused to accept R-1s without complete set of armament. In that same month a full set of bomb armament, named the Bombr-1, was for the first time installed on aircraft serial number 2741; in October this airplane was tested on the range just outside Serpukhov where the School of Air Combat was located. The Bombr-1 included the Der-3bis (modified versions of the Der-3) and

A prototype of the R-1LD airplane fitted with Lorraine-Dietrich engine, 1925.

A prototype of the R-1SP biplane (R-2) fitted with Puma engine.

A series R-1SP at the airfield.

One of the two improved R-2s (the R-1SP), 1925.

The Bombr-1 was subsequently installed on all R-1s. The heavy bombs, for the standards of that time (16kg and 48kg), were carried only on the Der-4 bomb racks in view of the aircraft centre of gravity considerations. The bombs of no heavier than 10kg were carried on four Der-3bis bomb racks, and it was recommended that the entire bomb load be carried under the wing where possible. The R-1 range with bombs and a set of three machine guns was 275–300km.

The transfer to producing more combat capable aircraft was valued highly by the RVS: 'In the field of aircraft production the aviation industry has finally reached the stage of series production of combat reconnaissance aircraft ... '

The issues concerning the power plant were gradually being solved as well. The first series of the R-1s were fitted with Liberty engines which had been imported from USA and Britain. The British-supplied power plants underwent adjustment and check testing before shipping to Russia, so they could be fitted to the biplanes straight away. The American ones were purchased cheaply straight from the stores. Therefore, they were overhauled in Moscow at the GAZ-1 factory, where a special workshop was created for this purpose. However, there were constant shortages of these engines.

In November 1924 the UVVS, not wishing to 'put all their eggs in one basket' decided to acquire 40 biplanes with Liberty engines, and the same number with French Lorraine-Dietrich engines, and 90 airplanes with the British Pumas. The first two versions were entrusted to the GAZ-10 factory, and the latter to the GAZ-1. In practice, however, only aircraft with Liberty engines were produced at Taganrog, while the R-1 version with the Puma was actually put into production in Moscow.

Der-4 bomb racks, and SBR-7 bomb release mechanism. A commission headed by Nadashkevich carried out all the testing. The pilot for all flights was K.K. Artseulov, and committee members would take it in turns to fly in the aft cockpit – Nadashkevich, Dyakonov, and Seleznyov. The Bombr-1 set was officially approved on 19 December 1925.

R-1SP airplanes for the most part served as trainers. This landing accident involving an R-1SP took place in Borisoglebsk in September 1926

The GAZ-1 factory received an order to convert a biplane to accommodate a 230hp Puma engine back on 1 April 1924. These airplanes were planned to be used as trainers. An order for 150 Pumas was placed in Britain but the first 30 arrived only in July 1925, and then 40 engines were delivered each month over the next three months.

The design work on the Puma-engined version was headed by V.L. Moiseyenko, and a trophy DH.9 was planned to be used as an example. Then, a DH.9A with a larger wing area and an altered fuselage was chosen as a basis for conversion to another power plant, but in the end they arrived at an adaptation of the R-1.

Student pilot Belyaev ground looped this R-1SP, the 2nd Military Pilots School, July 1925.

This project, which was designated the factory as the 2US1, was put together very quickly. On 23 April the Scientific Committee of the UVVS approved its preliminary version. In comparison with the R-1, the engine mount, cowling and the radiator had been changed; the latter was accommodated under the nose section of the fuselage. Aside from the engine mount this version differed by smaller main wheels.

The first prototype of the R-1SP (later designated the R-2 or R-II) was just about ready by 1 August 1924, and two months later it was towed out onto the airfield. On 15 October, after the conclusion of factory testing the aircraft was handed over to the NOA. There, having completed its test flying by 9 December, the R-1SP was acknowledged as being successful and suitable for service in flying schools. However, the NOA report was very slow to pass through authority, and at the time when the first series production aircraft were standing at the factory it was still not known whether the UVVS would need to make any changes to the aircraft design or the equipment.

The first four production R-1SPs, which at the time were unarmed, arrived at the Moscow Central airfield in January 1925. One aircraft underwent a full program of testing, and the rest were subject to a shortened testing plan. The biplanes flew with three types of airscrews: one British design

The result of a collision between an R-1SP of the 7th Separate Reconnaissance Squadron and a Fokker D.XI fighter at Smychkovo airfield, August 1926.

An R-1BMW airplane fitted with a BMW IV engine.

The BMW IV engine of the R-1BMW with part of the cowling removed.

developed by Davis, and two indigenous designs created by Dyachkov at the GAZ-8 factory.

By early January the wooden sections of the airplanes of the first two series had been ready, but there was a shortage of engines and propellers. High production rate of the airframes manufacturing was due to the fact that the ready sections of the R-1s, standing at the factory without engines, were used. As a result, all the available areas at the enterprise again ended up full of half-finished airframes, which could not be handed over. On 10 January, management of the GAZ-1 factory decided to dismantle the wing boxes on 15 R-1SPs and to stop the assembly of a further 30 aircraft, which originally planned to be completed by the end of the month. The factory sent a complaint to the UVVS, which was obliged contractually to supply engines and propellers, requesting to pay for the airframes disassembly.

Only on 19 January did the military acceptance committee at the enterprise receive a list of changes that were being introduced on the basis of studying the aircraft prototype. It was proposed that the windscreen be moved forward, the throttle and the stabiliser control stick would be repositioned slightly, and both seats would be fitted with seat backs. The factory responded saying that this was only possible from the 41st aircraft onwards (as the stock for the forthcoming airframes had already been prepared), and that it would cost extra money, they should have thought about all this beforehand!

Then, less than a month later production was paralysed completely – on 12 February 1925 some 40 fully completed biplanes were stood in the workshops minus their engines and propellers, and a further 90 were at various stages of completion. The most interesting thing is that the UVVS was very well aware of the fact that the engines would never arrive from Britain before June!

The first Pumas were actually delivered at the beginning of June 1925, some 15 of them, and by the end of October all the

The first prototype of the MR-1 airplane fitted with Polikarpov-designed wooden floats, the Moscow River, October 1926.

A mechanic removes the beaching trolley wheels from the floats.

engines that had been ordered from Britain had actually been delivered.

The delays in the ordering of the engines had a serious impact on the process of handing over these biplanes. By 1 October 1925 the GAZ-1 was to have handed over 52 R-1SPs, but in reality by 28 November they had actually rolled out only nine completed aircraft. They had been fitted with synchronisers and bomb racks, but without bomb release mechanisms.

The series production R-1SPs biplanes were fitted with the Vickers machine gun on the port side, and in the aft cockpit they had a TOZ turret with a single Lewis. The PUL-7 synchroniser was especially designed for the Puma. It went through ground testing on 21–23 November 1925, and was officially accepted into service in November; by that time it was already in series production. Only 62 examples of this type of synchroniser were manufactured, however, far fewer than the number of R-1SP biplanes that were ever produced. This illustrates that around a half of these aircraft left the factory with incomplete armament, or without any armament at all. The R-1SPs were only fitted with the Der-4 bomb racks under the fuselage, and on some of the biplanes the factory had fitted the Der-3bis bomb racks under the lower wing. By 19 December 1925, when the biplanes were already in the assembly workshops, however, an order came through for these to be removed.

The R-1SP was produced in three series, consisting of 40, 50 and then a further 40 airplanes, of those 86 had been handed over by mid-1926 and a further 44 in the second half of the year.

Series production MR-1 built at Factory No.31 in Taganrog. The armament has yet to be fitted.

A prototype of the MR-1 on Munzel-designed metal floats, September 1927

An MR-1 on metal floats during service testing at the 55th Air Unit in Nikolaev.

Although these aircraft had been ordered as training biplanes, in view of a shortage of combat airplanes some of them were distributed around air force units and squadrons. For example, the 7th Separate Reconnaissance Squadron in the Leningrad District received R-1SPs, where they served

A series MR-1 prior to testing; the armament is still not installed.

An MR-1 of the 64th Air Unit is towed up onto the shore.

alongside with the standard R-1s. In February 1926 these aircraft participated in manoeuvres of the district troops. In May of that year the biplanes with the Puma engines joined the 28th Squadron, and the 1st and 41st Separate Air Units of that same Leningrad District. The aircraft were originally sent without the bomb racks, and these were only fitted in August.

Then the majority of the R-1SPs were handed over to flying schools, and only small numbers of them remained in the air force units, where they were used as trainers. For example, in January 1927 a single aircraft, that was a completely serviceable machine, served in the 1st Heavy Air Squadron. While in the same month all the R-1SPs were withdrawn from the 41st Air Unit, having been replaced by standard R-1s.

On 3 September 1930 there were 66 aircraft of this version in the Air Force (of those 32 were serviceable), and they only flew with the flying schools. This was facilitated by the fact that for the most part the biplanes with Puma engines had controls in both cockpits.

The planned versions with the Lorraine-Dietrich 12E engine did not progress any further than a prototype. The technical specification for its development was issued on 5 August 1924. The military designated this version the R-1LD, and at the factory it was designated the RD2.

The first assessments by the designers turned out to be disappointing, as almost all the flight-performance characteristics were worse than those with the Liberty engines. The service ceiling had reduced by 300m, the flight duration had been shortened by half an hour, and the rate of climb had deteriorated. The maximum speed alone was to have increased by approximately five percent.

Nevertheless, it was thought that this work had potential, and in line with the preliminary plan for 1925–1926, half of the biplanes produced at the GAZ-10 factory in Taganrog were to be completed with Lorraine engines.

For the designers, integrating a wide, triple-row engine of a large cross-section with the narrow fuselage of the R-1 represented a complex issue. In order to accommodate the carburettor that was on the rear of the engine the bracing struts of the engine mount were curved, which immediately affected its rigidity, and forced the tubes to be propped up in the middle from below using pyramids made from smaller diameter tubes. The engine cowling became much more complex in shape and design than it had been using the Liberty engine.

The R-1 was fitted with an automobile style front-mounted radiator, and the long forward section of the crankshaft passed straight through it. The available example of the 12E engine had a short forward section of the crankshaft, so it was fitted with an extender at the GAZ-2 *Ikar* engine factory.

An MR-1 of the 55th Air Unit on a shore parking area in Nikolaev; the airplane is fitted with machine guns and bomb racks under the wing.

In October 1924 work began on the manufacture of the R-1LD prototype, which was completed on 17 February of the following year. On 24 February the first attempt was made to start the engine on the biplane, and it failed as it emerged that the rods leading to the carburettor had been fitted the wrong way round.

On 6 March 1925 a Lorraine-engines prototype was taken to Moscow Central airfield. The factory testing was planned to be started from 10 March, but in fact they only began on 19 March. Four days later the biplane was handed over to the NOA.

During testing the radiator shook violently, so it had to be given additional support using struts, which led to another problem – rigid suspension caused destruction of one of the supporting rods as a result of vibration, which in turn led to a water leak.

The empty weight of the R 1LD turned out to be almost 100kg greater than of the series production Liberty-powered version: the take-off weight rose by approximately 30kg, and in conjunction with the deteriorating aerodynamics this had a negative effect on the flight-performance characteristics. They turned out to be lower than estimated, and the aircraft had lost more than 10km/h of its maximum speed and approximately 1,000m of its service ceiling. The rate of climb fell sharply too.

On 4 June 1925 an Aviatrest commission led by K.V. Akashev inspected the prototype fitted with Lorraine engine. The commission came to the conclusion that this engine was unsuitable for the R-1, so the works on the R-1LD were stopped.

Note the covered PV-1 machine gun and the bomb racks under the wing. Comparing to a standard R-1 there were only four bomb racks on the aircraft.

The successor to the R 1SP was the R 1BMW. By 1926 the reserves of acquired Puma engines had already run out, but the requirement for the cheaper version of the R-1 for training purposes had not disappeared. It was decided to replace the British engine with German BMW IV power plant, which was also an in-line water-cooled engine but its output was slightly less – 190hp. The project to modify the R-1SP around this engine was prepared by E.K. Stoman. The German engine was shorter, so the overall length of the fuselage was reduced by 49mm and the centre of gravity shifted forward slightly. The engine drove a two-bladed propeller from a Yu-20 aircraft that was 2.9m in diameter. The specification required the installation of a Vickers forward-firing machine gun and a single Lewis in the turret in the aft cockpit, but the aircraft actual centre of gravity position made this impossible.

Following a flight, this MR-1 of the Naval Pilots School in Sevastopol is pushed out onto a parking area. One of the sailors is hanging on to a ring under the tail of the airplane, trying to raise its nose.

A photo from the crash report of the MR-1 which belonged to the Naval Pilots School, May 1929.

An MR-1 of the 65th Air Unit is pulled from the water near the shores of Sevastopol, November 1929. The pilot L.N. Dmitriev flew into a buoy on take-off.

A prototype aircraft was manufactured in Moscow, and on 25 April–31 May 1928 it was tested at the NII VVS. Series production of the R-1BMW (also designated the R1-B4) was transferred to Taganrog, to Factory No.31 (the former GAZ-10). In Taganrog, a whole batch of 30 biplanes was quickly put into production, and in June 1928 the leading aircraft was rolled out and underwent testing on the factory airfield. The entire batch was handed over to the military by the end of the year, and the following year a further 51 aircraft were delivered. According to other sources in total some 83 R-1BMWs were built. These aircraft were used as transitional training airplanes at the flying schools.

The main version however, and from 1929 onwards the only version to remain in production, was the R-1 with the Liberty engine. Moreover, the majority of these airplanes received the Soviet versions of this engine, designated the M-5. At the beginning of 1922 six engineers of the Moscow engine-building factory GAZ-2 *Ikar* disassembled several trophy Liberty power plants and made engineering drawings on their basis. This work was headed by A.A. Bessonov. In contrast to the original engine, the dimensions of the reverse-engineered variant were done in the metric system. In May the work began on the manufacturing of the engine prototype, and on 22 August the UVVS placed an order to this factory for a series of 100 'Liberty' engines. In November 1923 the prototype engine underwent state bench testing, and the following year the first batch of five engines had been built, but they were handed over only at the beginning of 1925, after their defects had been eradicated.

The best engine from this batch was fitted to an R-1 that underwent flight testing in January 1925. In February–March pilot Inshakov and mechanic Tauson completed a long-range flight in this biplane on a route Moscow–Lipetsk–Kharkov–Kiev–Gomel–Smolensk–Moscow.

The Leningrad *Bolshevik* factory (the former Obukhov factory) was also arranging production of the M-5, and the first engines were assembled there at the beginning of 1925.

A floating crane pulls a sunken MR-1 of the 65th Air Unit out of the water in Nakhimov Bay. The pilot Ilyin was evading a destroyer on take-off, and his airplane overturned in the wind, May 1929.

R-1 flown by pilot Timofeev of the 1st Separate Combat (Ground Attack) Squadron in Kiev, June 1926.

In May of that year F.S. Rasstegaev flew an aircraft fitted with a *Bolshevik*-made engine on a long-range flight along the route Moscow–Smolensk–Vitebsk–Leningrad–Moscow. Under an order from the Head of the Air Force, this aircraft was given the name 'The Leningrad Bolshevik'.

The Soviet M-5s were manufactured from locally sourced materials and had slightly different set of flight instruments and equipment. The entire ignition system for this aircraft was imported, as were the fittings for the fuel pipelines, the fuel pumps, and many other items of equipment. The Soviet engines were a little heavier than their American counterparts. Thus, the M-5 manufactured at the *Ikar* factory weighed 424kg, which was 29kg more than the imported original. The production quality of the *Bolshevik*-made power plant was initially assessed as being superior, but in Moscow different refinements were rapidly being

A line-up of R-1s at an airfield.

Pilots study a combat mission they have been given by the commander of the 'Ultimatum' Air Unit N.I. Andreev, 1925.

introduced. For some series of the Moscow-built engines the

An R-1 of the 3rd Reconnaissance Squadron named after Frunze that has ground looped on landing in Kiev, May 1925.

crankshafts were imported from the USA, so such M-5s was a mixed version with metrical and imperial dimensions. The engines manufactured in Moscow were designated M-5I, and those manufactured in Leningrad M-5B, while the imported

R-1 airplanes support an attack by infantry and tanks during autumn manoeuvres of the Red Army, mid-1920s.

A group of pilots standing in front of an R-1 in the hangar.

American engines were known as M-5L. The Soviet-built engines were fitted to the R-1s from October 1925.

The delay in the manufacture of engines in the USSR comparing to the production of aircraft forced purchases from abroad to continue, but the number of M-5L engines used was steadily decreasing. Import of the Liberty continued up until 1930 but back then these engines for the most part had been converted into tank engines, as the aircraft were being fitted with the Soviet M-5s.

A collision between two R-1s in Rostov-on-Don, summer 1925.

The airframe of the R-1 was also being gradually updated. From the end of 1924 the situation with respect to supply had begun to improve slightly. Aircraft began to be fitted with British undercarriage axles made of chrome-nickel steel. In 1925 there was a change from the indigenous leather glue for wood to special imported glue. Even a little 'luxury' appeared – from autumn 1925 a soft cushion began to be placed onto the pilot's plywood seat. The glazing for the windscreen was initially made

Pilots of the 6th Separate Air Unit named after *Sibrevkom* (Siberian revolution commission) standing next to an R-1 airplane, Spassk, 1925.

An R-1 airplane with the gift inscription 'Combatant of the Cultural Front – from the Teacher's Newspaper'. The white tail is a distinguishing feature of the training air brigade of the Air Force Academy.

An R-2 is towed by a tractor at the NOA in Moscow.

of celluloid, which would rapidly become blurred. In 1925 triplex began to be used but it did not last long as the laminar glass would crack under temperature loads, so this forced a return to celluloid. In that same year there was a plan to fit these aircraft with lighting for night flights, but this idea was rejected, as necessary components were not available in the country.

The effectiveness of R-1 use as a reconnaissance and artillery spotter aircraft could have been improved if these biplanes were fitted with a radio set and a camera. Special aviation radios were only just at the design stage in the USSR at that time. Therefore, the lightest of the available examples, which were intended for the cavalry, had to be used. From mid-1925 the biplanes began to be produced with provisions for installation of an AK II radio set. It weighed 34.5kg and provided an opportunity to support communications with another aircraft over a distance of 2km, with the ground at 25km distance by telephone, and at 200km distance by telegraph. The radio set had a trailing antenna formed of a cable with a stabilising weight, and the generator with an aerovane situated on the lower wing together with a battery provided the electrical power. The factory fitted the series R-1s with a counterweight for the antenna and a mounting point for the AK II, but nobody though actually saw these radio sets on these reconnaissance aircraft.

In June 1925, in the electro-radio department of the NOA, a project was developed for installation of a lighter AK-23 radio set which weighed 25kg. The transmitter was housed in a plywood box in the aft cockpit, and subsequently some of the aircraft were actually fitted with the AK-23.

For R-1, installation of the Potte II camera was envisaged in the FOT I mount. However, the cameras were not fitted at the factories, while the UVVS approved the FOT 1 only at the end of 1925. The crews were quite satisfied with the unapproved equipment – if only it worked.

At the same time new issues had come to light. In autumn 1925 the GAZ-1 factory received timber of such poor quality that more than half of it was rejected immediately. The UVVS gave permission to use the earlier rejected spars that had deviations in the sizes of the booms, but this did nothing to rescue the situation. By the end of the year the reserves had

The Head of the Main Political Directorate of the RKKA Ya.B. Gamarnik (in the centre, with a beard) with pilots, standing in front of an R-1.

Pick-up of a message using a hook; the pack is suspended on a rope between two poles.

An accident with an R-1 of the 3rd Separate Reconnaissance Squadron named after Frunze during a night-time landing in Proskurov, August 1926.

run out, and in the final quarter of 1925 only a single R-1 was completed instead of the planned 65.

Aviatrest tried to speed up the production of reconnaissance aircraft in Taganrog. As a result, the factory had assembled 47 R-1s against planned 30 airplanes. The military, however, accepted only 15 of these biplanes and even this acceptance was provisional in view of the shortages of equipment and armament. In the end, Aviatrest failed miserably against the plan for that year.

The situation improved in 1926. In the meantime, the R-1 design underwent significant changes, which took it even further away from the original DH.9A. From 1926 onwards this biplane no longer corresponded to the new standards for strength that had been introduced in the USSR. The airframe was subject to a modernisation – the spars were strengthened, the position of the ribs was changed, and the ailerons were refined. The structure became lighter and at the same time, stronger.

Meanwhile the latest versions of the Liberty engine began to arrive from the USA, for which it was envisaged the synchroniser would be driven by an intermediate crankshaft, which rotated the distributing shaft. This same solution had been adopted for the M-5, and A.V. Nadashkevich designed a new PUL-9 synchroniser for this engine, which underwent flight testing in September 1926 and was approved on 28 October. Depending on the type of engine either the PUL-6 or the PUL-9 synchroniser would be fitted; complete introduction of the latter got underway somewhere around the end of the year.

On 3 May 1926 the UVVS demanded that the imported Vickers machine gun be replaced with a refined locally-built Maxim model 1908 machine gun. On the same biplane, on which the PUL-9 synchroniser had been fitted, a *Maksim-TOZ* was installed, which had been manufactured by Tula TOZ factory.

A visit to the 19th Air Unit by the Commander of Forces of the Siberian Military District Petin, Spassk, 1926.

In 1928, in place of the Vickers, the PV-1 machine gun was accepted into service; it represented an upgraded and re-designed air-cooled version of the Russian-made infantry version of Maxim machine gun. This modification was also done in Tula under the leadership of Nadashkevich. The rate of fire for the PV-1 was higher than that of the Vickers machine gun, while the weight increased from 11.7kg up to 14.97kg. Service testing of the new machine gun was carried out using an R-1 belonging to the 26th Squadron in the Northern Caucasus. Following the tests, the PV-1 began to be fitted to all series production R-1s, with the exception of those for export. They also replaced the Vickers machine guns on earlier built aircraft.

In autumn of 1926 the British 12.7mm Vickers machine gun was tested on a Nelson type mount with the same PUL-9 synchroniser. For a wooden biplane this armament turned out to be excessively powerful – the firing caused deformation of the outer skin and the spars.

A landing accident with an R-1 of the 7th Separate Reconnaissance Squadron in Trotsk, April 1926. Pilot Rozanov ran off the runway and clipped a house on the edge of the airfield.

In the first half of 1926 the new Der-6 bomb racks (designed to be accommodated under the fuselage) and the Der-7 (for installation under the wing) were submitted for testing. Along with the SBR-8 bomb release mechanism that was designed at the factory in Fili by the master gunsmith F.N. Shcherbakov, these were to have comprised the new Bombr-2 set. Its introduction was due to happen from 1 September 1927 as per the plan: this was more or less how it happened.

An R-1 airplane taxies out for take-off.

From April 1927 the German Hertz FI 110 optical bombsight was introduced into the aircraft configuration – it was attached to the starboard side in the stowed position, and in the operating position it would be set up in line with the centre of the aft cockpit, above an aperture in the floor. There was a constant shortage, however, of the imported sights. The supports for them were fitted to all airplanes but the Hertz sights, which were being fitted at the squadrons themselves, were by no means always available. In 1928 it was announced that their installation was mandatory but it is impossible to fit something that is not there. From the beginning

Pilots of the 5th Separate Reconnaissance Air Unit pose in front of an R-1.

Pilot P.F. Rotataev in the front cockpit of an R-1.

An accident with an R-1 of the 5th Separate Reconnaissance Squadron in Kharkov, the pilot was Li Dya-Muk, August 1926.

Aircraft of the 19th Air Unit at the landing ground close to Blagoveshchensk, 1927.

Pilot M.N. Karpuk of the 50th Squadron caught a tent with the wheels of his biplane on landing close to Darnitsa, June 1927.

An R-1 biplane in an experimental camouflage that was developed by Burche and Vorobyov-Moskvin, 1927.

of the 1930s, production of this sight was arranged in the USSR under the designation OPB-1.

Up until 1927 the pump that transferred fuel from the main tank in the fuselage to the feeder tank in the centerplane of the upper wing was powered by an aerovane. In place of this unit, a fuel pump was fitted on the engine. At the same time the area of the plywood outer skin on the lower wing was increased and a new standard control stick was introduced. Operations from unpaved airfields forced a strengthening of the undercarriage legs and the tailskid.

These improvements brought with them additional weight and a deterioration in the aircraft centre of gravity position. Thus, R-1s of the 11th series produced at the GAZ-1 factory became 87kg heavier than the standard that was set out in the technical specifications. As a result, the rate of climb suffered and a time lag appeared in spin recovery. The reinforcement of the undercarriage turned out to be insufficient given this increase in take-off weight: complaints were received about the axle bending. When landing in a cross wind the undercarriage would sometimes simply collapse.

In April 1927 there was a plan to fit 20 R-1s with protected fuel tanks manufactured by the French CEMAPE company. They had an external self-sealant made from layers of rubber and fabric. The sample fuel tanks underwent test-firing using Russian and British rifles. The experiment was a success, but the batch of fuel tanks was somehow never ordered from France.

The pilot standing next to one of the R-1 biplanes from the squadron 'Our Response to Chamberlain'.

Standing next to an R-1 airplane are (from left to right): the Assistant Commander of Aviation of the Ukrainian Military District F.A. Ingaunis, the Commander of Forces of the District I.E. Yakir, the Chairman of the Council of People's Commissars in the Ukraine V.Ya. Chubar, and the Commander of the *Ilyich* Squadron I.I. Nusberg, Kharkov, autumn 1927.

Initially, production of the R-1 was planned to cease in mid-1928, but the lack of success with the new R-4 reconnaissance aircraft forced to continue their manufacturing. On 27 August the UVVS sent Aviatrest a list of their desired refinements. In response, Factory No.1 (former GAZ-1) turned one of the aircraft that had undergone repairs into a standard for this new version. On this airplane, a 300mm stagger in the upper wing was introduced, the stabiliser motion was increased, the bomb racks position was moved forward, a new pilot's seat was fitted, which was designed to accommodate a parachute, and a toolbox was placed behind the aft cockpit. A further series of minor changes was brought in and the biplane was fitted with a camera and a radio set. All this was subsequently introduced on the series production R-1s.

The following year, seats with a "bucket" for a parachute (but of a slightly different design) appeared on series aircraft, however, there were not enough parachutes in the air force units, and folded covers were stuffed into the seat instead. Apart from that the framework of the pilot's windscreen was reinforced and an external foothold was built in to allow the pilot to get into the cockpit. A wooden undercarriage with a

R-1 biplanes at the Moscow Central airfield, second half of the 1920s.

The famous test pilot M.A. Volkovoynov is sitting in the front cockpit of an R-1, and in the rear cockpit is the Head of the VVS Directorate P.I. Baranov (who was not trained to fly).

steel axle was replaced with an all-metal undercarriage. This was not for long, however, only up until September, and then there was a return to the cheaper wooden design.

The R-1 at that time was being produced in three versions: the corps (short-range) reconnaissance airplane, the army (long-range) reconnaissance airplane, and the 3rd-class bomber. The first version was fitted with an AK-23 radio set or the newer VOZ III, two Lewis machine guns in the aft cockpit, and the bomb racks were either partially or entirely removed. The second version differed by the installation of a Potte I camera. The third one carried a single Lewis but did not have a camera or a radio set.

On the biplanes produced in 1928 the pilot's windscreen began to be manufactured from triplex, and the TOZ turret was replaced with a more reliable Tur-4 (although this was slightly heavier).

From 1929 onwards series production of the R-1 began to wind down, Factory No.1 assembled the final machines in the beginning of the following year. At Taganrog, series production continued for a further two years, and two versions were built there – the short-range reconnaissance airplane and the unarmed trainer. Some of these aircraft were fitted with the long tube of the OP-1 optical gun sight for use when firing the PV-1 machine gun. The relatively simple additional KP-5 (a ring and bead sight) sight was retained as a reserve. On aircraft of the last series a rear-view mirror was fitted as well as an ERO radio set (though by no means all airplanes were fitted with these).

In 1931 Factory No.31 at Taganrog assembled 266 R-1s instead of 302 as was envisaged by the plan, and at the beginning of the following year the final two airplanes were completed and at this point manufacturing of the type was ceased. The total number of biplanes produced is estimated at 2,457 examples.

The Soviet R-1s were equipped with a wheeled undercarriage for summer and ski undercarriage for winter. For naval aviation, however, and for the air units operating from rivers biplanes with floats were also built, which were designated MR-1, and which did not have any British analogues.

An accident with an R-1 of the 50th Squadron, June 1927.

An R-1 of the 19th Separate Air Unit, the Far East, September 1929.

Pilots of the 30th Squadron *Krasnaya Moskva* with the unfurled banner of the unit, March 1928.

Starting the M-5 engine by three people standing in a 'chain'

A failed landing of pilot V.I. Babikov of the 9th Separate Air Unit during exercises, Anapa airfield, 1928.

A landing accident in a strong wind with an R-1 from the 3rd Unit of the 20th Separate Squadron named after Frunze (hence the inscription on the fuselage), 21 September 1927. The pilot M.K. Belyaev flew a bombing mission with a group of other airplanes.

Two different types of floats were being developed at the same time – Polikarpov designed the floats out of wood while the German engineer Munzel used duralumin for his project. The first prototype MR-1 was equipped with Polikarpov's floats, and on 19 October 1925 it took to the skies for the first time, after taking off from the Moscow River. The airplane was piloted by V.N. Filipov. The Moscow River soon froze over and the hydroplane was transferred to Sevastopol on the Black Sea to continue testing. At this location the take-offs and water landings were attempted at different levels of sea state. When the pilot tried to land on waves one-and-a-half metres in height the float struts failed. The hydroplane began to sink, so the pilot and Polikarpov himself, who had been sitting in the aft cockpit, swam to the shore.

Subsequently a further three prototypes were built with Polikarpov's floats, while their struts were reinforced. The first of them was test-flown in Fili by M.M. Gromov in autumn 1926, and in February–April 1927 the aircraft was tested on the Black Sea, the test pilot was S.I. Komarenko.

Only one example of the MR-1 fitted with Munzel's floats was ever produced. This float was made of corrugated metal on the topside and smooth on the underside. The metal floats were lighter and had better aerodynamic characteristics. Ya.N. Moiseev tested the MR-1 with duralumin floats in September–October 1927. The aircraft was successful but for series production the choice had already been made in favour of Polikarpov's floats as they were the cheaper variant.

The 'standard' (the leading series production) MR-1 was assembled in Taganrog at the end of September 1927, and the first flight took place on 12 October. The speed turned out to be the same as that of the prototype, the service ceiling had reduced, but the rate of climb had improved slightly. The series production MR-1s had larger size of the vertical fin (to enhance directional stability), an additional radiator under the forward part of the fuselage. The tailskid and half-hoop-style underwing skids have been removed, and a shackle was fitted instead of the tail skid. The usual set of wheeled and ski undercarriage was added to these float-fitted biplanes, so they could be operated from shore or in winter, when the water surface was frozen over. Armament consisted of a single PV-1 and two Lewis machine guns, Der-7 bomb racks were fitted under the wing and the bombs were dropped using SBR-8

During a visit to Moscow by the Afghan *Emir* Amanullah in spring 1928 he had a brief tour to Moscow Central Airfield. This photo shows Afghan officers standing next to R-1 airplanes.

Pouring hot water into the engine cooling system, the 19th Air Unit, Khabarovsk, December 1928.

bomb release mechanisms. Up until the end of 1929 some 124 MR-1s were built.

The R-1 began to join the air force units from summer 1924, and apparently the 1st Reconnaissance Squadron in Moscow was the first to receive these biplanes. This period featured a rapid quantitive growth of Soviet military aviation. Across the entire country the funds were being collected for the production of airplanes. Messages were being published in the press: 'Workers at the Ivanovo dental orthopaedic laboratory decided to work and extra day assisting in the manufacture of the *Ivanovskiy Medrabotnik* (Ivanovo medical worker) aircraft,' or 'The collective farm named after Roza Luxemburg of the Novlensk village council, Nerekhta district, allocated 160kg of flaxseed for the manufacture of the *Rabochiy kray* (The region of workers) airplane'. These aircraft were considered the people's gifts and were presented to crews at official ceremonies. Such airplanes were given individual names which were painted on the fuselage sides: *Krasniy Voronezh – Ilyichu* (The red city of Voronezh – to Vladimir Ilyich Lenin), *Kizly Bukhara* (The red city of Bukhara), *Krasnogvardeyets and partisan Kievshchiny* (The Red Guards soldier and partisan of Kiev region), *Rabochiy-rezinshchik* (The rubber industry worker) and similar names.

The delivery of a significant number of new airplanes enabled to augment the existing air force units, to write off much of the old aircraft, and to transfer certain units (comprising 10 airplanes) into squadrons (comprising 31 machines), as well as forming new ones.

For instance, a diplomatic note received from the British Government in 1927 led to the creation of an entire squadron known as 'Our response to Chamberlain'. All the aircraft in this squadron were gifts, each of them carried the inscription *Nash otvet Chemberlenu* (Our response to Chamberlain) on the starboard side of the fuselage, and the aircraft individual name on the port side. For example, an R-1 *Stalnoy Put* (The steel way) was a gift from railway workers. Following the ceremonial handover, the squadron aircraft stood for a week in the open air at the Central Moscow airfield. After the rain,

The Head of the VVS of the Moscow Military District I.U. Pavlov inspects a unit equipped with the R-1s.

Mechanics carry out maintenance of an R-1. Note that the shutters in front of the radiator have been removed.

during large flooding close to Blagoveshchensk; the airplane conducted reconnaissance, carried passengers, and dropped food supplies in remote locations.

Amongst aircrew the R-1 did not enjoy a good reputation. The biplane was considered difficult to fly; it would enter a spin given the slightest mistake a pilot would make. The reason for this was the extreme rear positioning of the centre of gravity. However, at a time when more and more airplanes were being demanded from the factories, all the shortcomings of the R-1 were covered by its production simplicity and low cost. It actually cost just 14,806 roubles, which was more than half the price of the all-metal R-3. The Soviet leadership wanted to create a sizeable and powerful air force as soon as possible but they did not have the required funds available. This was why the R-1 was produced over such a long timescale, significantly longer than the DH.9A in Britain.

A group of pilots of the 22nd Squadron standing in front of an R-1 airplane at the airfield in Vitebsk.

There are some difficulties in assessing the number of the R-1s in service in the VVS RKKA at this period, as the designation R-1 was occasionally applied to imported DH.9As. For instance, the records of the 5th Reconnaissance Air Squadron of 1925 list 'R-1s produced in Britain in 1918' and 'R-1s produced at the *Duks* factory in 1924'. They were later split and counted separately. According to official statistics, by the end of 1925 there were 271 R-1s, plus 16 R-1SPs (R-2s) in the VVS RKKA.

They were based in the Moscow, Leningrad, Ukrainian, Siberian, and other military districts. Initially all the units and squadrons equipped with these airplanes were considered reconnaissance units, but from 1926 the light bomber and *boyevik* (ground attack) air units began to be formed. These, however, differed only in terms of the tactics they used, while the airplanes were the same for all of them.

Aircrew and technical personnel of the 13th Air Unit pose in front of an R-1, Karelia, 1928.

the paint and varnish began to blister, and the plywood began to warp. The aircraft had to be taken for repair straight away.

The 19th Air Unit *Dalnevostochniy Ultimatum* (Far-Eastern Ultimatum) received an R-1 in February 1925 and in autumn 1928 this biplane took part in rescue operations

In 1928 commander of the 50th Air Squadron I.V. Skrobuk and mechanics Sokolov and Lukovnikov fitted additional Vickers machine guns on the upper surface of the lower wing. The ammunition boxes were hidden away in the wing itself. Skrobuk himself tested this aircraft at the firing range close to Kiev and the biplane was then ferried to the NII VVS, where it was subject to additional testing. After this Factory No.39 in Moscow manufactured a batch of these gun mounts.

Later on, there appeared the machine-gun mounts designed by P.I. Grokhovskiy – six DA machine guns with disk magazines were fitted on the bomb racks under the R-1 lower wing. The firing was controlled from the aft cockpit. Ten sets of such mounts were manufactured and installed on R-1s of the 54th Air Squadron. Under the leadership of squadron commander Gorbunov they were tested during exercises close to Voronezh.

In 1926–1927, there was carried out a development of the R-1 ground attack version equipped with movable machine-gun mounts under the lower wing. A single 7.62mm *Maksim A2* or *Maksim TOZ* machine gun was to be positioned on each side with 500 rounds of ammunition each in drums. The barrels of these machine guns were designed to move 15° upwards and downwards, and 45° from side-to-side. At that, the number of bomb-carrying beams of the bomb racks was halved. The engineers of the Department of Land-based Aircraft Development of the Central Design Bureau working on the project calculated that for the prescribed ammunition load the diameter of the drum containing the machine-gun belt would be approximately half a metre. They asked the military to limit this to 250 rounds per machine gun, which could then be accommodated in a drum of 225mm in diameter. In reality, however, only Skrobuk's gun mounts entered service, and even then in small quantities.

By the end of the 1920s the R-1 were already considered obsolete type, but it was still suitable as short-range reconnaissance

R-1 airplanes of the squadron 'Our Response to Chamberlain' following completion of the propaganda flights, 1928.

The gift R-1 airplane with inscription 'The Red Khamovniki' flown by pilot Bedritskiy of the 30th Squadron at an airfield, May 1928.

The consequences of an unsuccessful pick-up of a message using the hook, area around Chita, 25th Separate Air Unit, pilot V. Shurov, July 1928.

Changing the M-5 engine on an R-1 airplane, the Far East, winter 1928/29.

aircraft. A report by the People's Commissariat of the Workers' and Peasants' Inspectorate, which inspected the Air Force in mid-1929 stated: 'our corps reconnaissance R-1 M-5 aircraft ... in terms of their flight-performance characteristics do not concede to the main foreign reconnaissance types, with the

Personnel of the 19th Air Unit at Grodekovo airfield before the start of conflict at the Chinese Eastern Railway, the end of autumn, 1929.

An R-1 at summer camps just outside Tambov, July 1929.

exception of rate of climb and horizontal speed'. The R-1 was called a corps reconnaissance aircraft because in the light bomber and army reconnaissance roles it was being replaced by new R-5 airplane. The plan was for this old biplane to be pushed out into army aviation, which was sizeable in terms of numbers of available aircraft but was considered secondary – a separate air unit was attached to each rifle or cavalry corps, which comprised of 10 biplanes.

Pilots of the 19th Air Unit standing next to an R-1 in Grodekovo, 1929.

The MR-1 floatplanes began to be delivered to the Air Force units (which at that time also incorporated naval aviation) in 1927. The 55th Air Unit in Nikolaev was the first to receive these airplanes. Subsequently the floatplanes entered service with the 66th Air Unit and the 62nd Air Squadron on the Baltic Sea, the 64th Air Unit in Sevastopol, and the 67th Air Unit in Kiev (as part of the Dnieper military flotilla). From 1928 training began on the MR-1 at the Naval Pilots School in Sevastopol which was transferred to Yeysk in 1931. In July 1930 there were 67 MR-1s in service with the VVS

RKKA, and by 1 January of the following year this figure had reached 71.

The first experiences of operating the MR-1 brought the airplane's many shortcomings to light. For instance, from the Baltic Sea it was reported that the fuselage was placed too high above the floats; the high centre of gravity position deteriorated the aircraft handling on water. The hinged joints of the struts with fuselage and floats led to a longitudinal oscillation of the fuselage on take-off and water landing, and as a result the joints would quickly come loose. The air force units suggested fitting Fairey-type shock absorbers to the struts, lightening the floats, and installing the bracing wires running from the wings to the fuselage.

The Black Sea units reported that after each flight the MR-1 joints required inspection, following 10–15 flights the floatplane had to be put into a hangar for a thorough check and for minor repairs, after 50–75 flights it had to be sent back to the factory for major overhaul. On average, the mean time between overhauls for the MR-1 was half that of the land-based R-1. Furthermore, the overhaul of the float-equipped version cost six times more than of the wheeled one.

The high position of the fuselage led to the aircraft turning over under a crosswind. The metal leading edges of the propellers deteriorated quickly, the other metal components rusted from the seawater, and the wooden ones rot. The aircraft was difficult to fly and was upset by even a small swell. A report from the Black Sea indicated: 'Operation of the MR1-M5 airplanes is only possible from hydroplane bases on rivers with a well-trained aircrew'. Summing up, the Black Sea pilots even wrote: 'The aircraft, in essence, is neither a naval airplane, nor a combat one.'

In mid-1928 Aviatrest engineers developed a plan to introduce reinforcements to the aircraft structure. It was planned to add a number of plywood plates, and to increase the area of the existing ones. The main task was to introduce additional struts running from the floats to the lower wing. The prototype of the modified MR-1 was manufactured in Taganrog, and in May 1928 it was sent to Sevastopol for testing.

The modification of the earlier-built aircraft was carried out at Factory No.45 in Sevastopol, and the first MR-1s with additional struts arrived in the Baltic region in December 1928.

These changes enhanced the strength of the airframe but they could not eradicate the airplane's high centre of gravity position, or the difficulty in handling the aircraft. For example, in November 1929 in one of the bays close to Sevastopol the wind caused an MR-1 flown by pilot L.N. Dmitriev of the 65th Air Unit to drift on take-off and crash into a buoy, the damaged hydroplane sank.

In September 1929 in the Baltic region the 51st and 66th Air Units operated the MR-1 (the latter also operated a single Dornier Wal flying boat).

An MR-1 that was converted in winter from floats to a ski undercarriage, next to the camouflaged barge *Amur*, the hydroplane floating base.

MR-1 aircraft of the 68th Air Unit at the Amur River prior to the start of combat activities.

One of the MR-1 airplanes is towed onto the deck of the barge *Amur*.

An MR-1 taking off from the Amur River on a reconnaissance mission.

One of the MR-1s on the water alongside the floating base the *Amur.*

The crew of flight commander N.A. Sokolov is leaving for a combat mission.

R-1 airplanes in flight over Manchuria.

In 1932 the question of converting some of the R-1s into ambulance version was considered. Possibly, the intent was to draw on the British experience, as they had operated refined DH.9s in the Far East for transporting the injured and the sick.

The true value of the R-1s was tested both in long-range flights and in combat. In 1925 these airplanes participated in the Great Eastern Long-range Flight on a route Moscow–Peking. Among six airplanes that took off from Moscow were two R-1s and a single R-2. The latter, in view of its low flying speed, was allowed to take off an hour early at each stage. Both R-1s, which were flown by M.M. Gromov and M.A. Volkovoynov, continued their journey and completed the long-range flight in Japan. Gromov was farthest to fly, landing in Tokyo, while Volkovoynov was forced to land near Shimonoseki in an area that had been designated as a forbidden. The Japanese demanded the aircraft be dismantled and removed, and this was duly completed. Both R-1s were delivered to the port of Tsuruga, and from there, by sea, to Vladivostok.

In July 1926 P.Kh. Mezheraup, in an aircraft named *Krasnaya Zvezda* (Red Star), completed a long-range flight on a route Moscow–Ankara. At the same time another R-1 flown by Ya.N. Moiseev, with the inscription *Iskra* (Spark) on the fuselage side made a visit to Tehran.

The R-1 mostly saw combat in foreign lands, and moreover, in the majority of cases, this was as part of varied foreign air forces. Soviet Russia was actively looking for allies in the eastern nations captured in the revolutionary unrest, and they were given financial support and weapons.

From spring 1924 onwards deliveries were made to Persia (Iran). Initially, four DH.9As assembled in Russia were sold to this country, which were followed by two R-1s. The latter were ferried from Baku to Tehran in May 1924 by N.N. Vasilchenko and P.I. Lozovskiy. In that same year these aircraft were used against the Kurds, Lurs, and Arabs who had risen up, and one year later against the Turkmenis and again the Kurds. Soviet aircrew participated in these combat operations.

R-1 airplanes of the 19th Air Unit at an airfield.

Pilots standing next to an R-1 prior to a sortie from Spassk airfield.

Pilots, mechanics and engine specialists standing next to an R-1, 1929.

The R-2 airplane flown by pilot A.N. Ekatov at one of the intermediate landing grounds during the Great Eastern Flight, 1925.

On 27 October 1925 the GAZ-1 factory received an order to assemble a batch of 'special purpose' airplanes, and this included airplanes destined for Iran. On 27 November the Iranian acceptance inspector Amin-zade arrived in Moscow. He demanded a series of changes be made to the aircraft equipment: a second battery was to be fitted, as well as a coupled holder for machine guns in the rear turret and an emergency hand-operated fuel pump in the observer's cockpit. The export versions of the R-1s featured the bomb

Ekatov's R-2 prior to a flight from Peking to Haifan.

The R-1 flown by M.M. Gromov after landing in Okayama (Japan).

The ceremonial welcome of Gromov's crew in Tokyo.

The R-1 with inscriptions 'Spark' and "Aviakhim / USSR' in which pilot Ya.N. Moiseev and mechanic P.V. Morozov completed a long-range flight from Moscow to Tehran.

An R-1 of the 9th Air Unit, Rostov-on-Don, January 1930.

Airplanes of the air brigade of the Air Force Academy at the Moscow Central airfield, 1930.

racks that were copied from British originals, as well as synchronisers with adapters that enabled foreign-built machine guns to be fitted.

In 1927 the GAZ-1 manufactured a further three R-1s for the Persians under a special order. Initially it was planned to fit these machines with the Soviet M-5 engines but *Praporshchik* Mokhti-khan, who had arrived to accept these aircraft, categorically objected to this and the airplanes were fitted with Liberty engines instead, which had been acquired in Britain. These biplanes were delivered to Baku, where they were assembled. Iranian pilots trained in the USSR ferried them further. *Poruchik* Amin-zade crashed one R-1 on take-off in Baku after engine failure, and he himself sustained a few bruises. Only *Podporuchik* Shtaudakh Issa-khan had succeeded in reaching Tehran non-stop.

The result of emergency landing made by pilot N.N. Chikhalenko of the 2nd Separate Air Unit near the village of Nikolaevka in the Leningrad region. The engine failed in his airplane during exercises, February 1930.

MR-1 aircraft of the 68th Air Unit near the shore of the Amur River, beginning of the 1930s.

R-1 aircraft under repair in workshops.

In 1928 a further five biplanes were sold to Iran. The Iranian R-1s actively participated in combat operations in 1928: initially against the Basmachi under Dzhunaid-khan who had crossed the border from Soviet Central Asia, and then against the Baloch tribes led by Dust-Mukhammed. *Feldwebel* Ibrahim-khan tried twice to fly from Tehran to the front line in an R-1, but each time he turned back due to worsening weather. On his second attempt, he crashed the aircraft in an emergency landing on the return journey. In April 1928 a Soviet pilot in an R-1 delivered General Nakhichevani to Lorestan.

In Baluchistan, Iranian pilots flew reconnaissance missions in Soviet aircraft, bombed and strafed the insurgents. The communication with the ground troops was one-sided: messages would be formed of strips of black material on white canvass of special shape (a semi-circle for the infantry, a triangle for the cavalry, and a circle for the artillery). Whether the Iranians made use of banner dropping is not known. *Feldwebel* Ibrahim-khan who was mentioned above, did actually reach the front line in another airplane in the summer of 1928 and achieved certain success. His award of the Order of Sepah and one hundred toman (the local currency) are testimony to this.

In mid-1929 the Iranians had nine R-1s, of which one was suitable for training purposes only. In the same year a further six aircraft joined the air force fleet. The Soviet side offered Iran the possibility of further deliveries of the R-1s. In 1930 the military attaché A.A. Langovoy was stubbornly convincing the Iranian minister of the court to purchase another batch of these machines, emphasising their low cost and simplicity of servicing and repair, but the Iranians chose the more up to date R-5s.

According to records of the People's Commissariat for Foreign Affairs, in September 1924 six R-1s were delivered to the Afghan leader Amanullah (in Soviet documents he was known as the *Emir* or *Padishah*). They were ferried along a route Tashkent–Termez–Kabul via the Hindu Kush mountain range by Soviet pilots led by P.Kh. Mezheraup. Photographs, however, show that one of these machines was an R-1SP (R-2) with a Puma engine. It is even possible that all these airplanes were of British origin, assembled in the USSR. All the participants of this long-range flight were later awarded the Order of the Red Banner. The Afghans awarded Mezheraup and pilot V.V. Goppe the Order of the Sun, and the others were awarded medals. Mezheraup returned to Russia, while the other pilots and mechanics remained serving the Afghan *Emir* as foreign volunteers paid under contract.

On 5 October Soviet crews flew their first combat sortie, dropping bombs and leaflets on the Pashtuns who had risen up in Khost province. A further three sorties followed. According to a report by the Soviet ambassador in Kabul L.N. Stark, these sorties 'had an enormous political impact'. Indeed, the majority of Afghans at that time had never seen an airplane!

In July 1925 another six R-1s were sent to Afghanistan, and they were ferried from Termez to Kabul by a group of aircrews led by V.F. Kaminskiy. Only four airplanes reached their destination, one was forced to land in the desert, and another in the mountains in Afghan territory. Both of them were later repaired, and G.M. Bondaryuk ferried them to Tashkent. As a replacement, in October two other R-1s were delivered to Kabul. The first four airplanes were handed over ceremoniously to the Afghans on 31 July 1925. The *Emir* Amanullah himself participated in the ceremony, and took to the skies as a passenger. The minister of war Vali-khan was also taken up for a ride, as was the commander of aviation Ehsah-khan (who was not qualified to fly by himself).

The gift R-1 airplane with inscription 'Electric Power', Leningrad Military District, beginning of the 1930s.

A collision between two R-1s of the 2nd Separate Air Unit at Krasnogvardeysk airfield, February 1930.

A result of emergency landing of an R-1 of the 17th Air Unit near the village of Yachniki in Ukraine. This was necessary because of a rupture in the expansion tank of the engine cooling system, August 1930.

In 1927 the Afghans had about a dozen of Soviet biplanes, and they were flown for the most part by foreign pilots.

At the end of 1928 Amanullah used his air force against insurgents who were approaching the walls of Kabul. From 17 December the R-1s bombed the enemy units. This helped

An airplane from the 1st Unit of the 28th Squadron picks up a message using the hook. The message was prepared by a reconnaissance group during autumn exercises of the forces of the Leningrad Military District, September 1930.

A result of emergency landing of an R-1 flown by pilot N.P. Kamanin of the 40th Squadron, on a street in the village of Novo-Nezhino, 29 August 1930. The M-5 engine initially overheated and then failed. N.P. Kamanin subsequently became a Hero of the Soviet Union and Lieutenant General.

A fire on starting the R-1 engine at the landing ground at Monastyrishche during exercises, September 1930.

to repel the enemy from the capital for a time, but did not save Amanullah, who was soon forced to abdicate. On 15 January 1929 the leader of the insurgents Khabibullah became *Emir*, so he inherited all the aircraft of his predecessor. Amanullah, however, could not come to terms with his defeat, and he gathered units from among his devotees and began to fight

An R-1 that was fitted at the NII VVS with American turbosupercharger manufactured by General Electric company.

The R-1 carrying two prototypes of winter *aviabuses* under the lower wing, which were designed to be dropped onto snow from low altitude flight.

Khabibullah. The R-1s flown by Afghan crews made several combat sorties against Amanullah's forces. In the end, in this battle between two contenders the winner was a third one: in October 1929 power in the country was transferred to Nadir-shah. He was left with few airplanes, and only a couple of those were able to take to the skies. Nevertheless, following this event the R-1s operated in Afghanistan for some years.

In 1925–1931 these biplanes were also delivered to China, and the aircraft was sent both to the Government of China and to their People's Revolutionary Army, as well as to General Féng Yùxiáng who was active in the north of the country. In total more than 30 airplanes were delivered to the Chinese. In the first Eastern campaign of February–June 1925 the People's Revolutionary Army used three R-1s with Soviet crews under the command of V. Sergeev. They conducted reconnaissance and provided liaison. In the second Eastern campaign, in October of that same year, just a single biplane took part although it did make its contribution to the capture of the Weizhou fortress, dropping bombs and leaflets.

In October–November 1925 GAZ-1 factory manufactured another batch of R-1s for the Chinese, and the

Air-droppable fuel tanks with parachutes were mounted on the R-1 bomb racks under the wing.

aircraft featured additional radiators for the hot climate that were fitted under the nose section of the fuselage.

The heavy operating conditions and the poor supply of spare parts led to the fact that in June 1926 there were just six biplanes left in service with the People's Revolutionary Army (and of those, only two airplanes were serviceable). In the Northern campaign of July–November 1926 three R-1s were used. Of those, two got into accidents during the ferry flight, so initially in reality only a single aircraft flown by pilot A.M. Kravtsov participated in combat. Ten days later a second airplane had been restored to flying condition. These two biplanes dropped 3,200kg of bombs on the enemy during combat close to Wuhan. Following the capture of Wuhan this tiny unit was active near Nanchang, but they run out of bombs, that had been delivered from Russia, by the end of this campaign.

By the end of 1926 the People's Revolutionary Army had approximately a dozen R-1s, but only half of them were combat capable. During a sortie in the province of Jiangxi pilot Remezyuk and mechanic Kobyakov were captured following an emergency landing. They were held prisoner in Guangzhou but were released in September.

Following a coup under the leadership of General Chiang Kai-shek in April 1927, four small units ended up in his hands, these were mostly equipped with R-1s. At approximately this time the Soviet crews began to be replaced with Chinese aircrew. Chiang's aviation began to be used in combat both against those generals on the fringes of the country that had broken away from central power, and against communist units. Soviet military assistance was no longer forthcoming for him.

In the meantime, deliveries to northern China continued. In Xinjiang the ruling *duban* (governor) had broken away from the country's central government, but he formed a friendship with the USSR and secretly joined the All-Union Communist Party of Bolsheviks. In December 1931 two series production R-1s were delivered for him from Alma-Ata to Ürümqi, and there two Chinese pilots and two mechanics were waiting who had arrived from Mukden. They were familiarized with the new aircraft, but Soviet pilots ferried these machines to Hami.

A *gruzovoz* (cargo container dropped by parachute) designed by N.P. Blagin is mounted under the R-1 fuselage.

An R-1 fitted with an 'Airborne firing range' system designed by P.I. Grokhovskiy. This airplane was able to launch subsequently several targets of different types.

In Hami a school was set up for training pilots and mechanics. On 4 March 1932 the Chinese pilot Li Siyaotan was the first to fly the R-1, although he did have an accident with the aircraft on landing. After having gone through the training course, in the summer the Chinese pilots were sent to assist the troops who were fighting the Muslim insurgents. The Soviet instructors did not participate in these combat actions.

A further three R-1s were sold to the Xinjiang *duban* in January 1932. The batch also included two K-5 passenger aircraft and three U-2 trainers. They were delivered by rail to the station at Ayagoz in Central Asia where they were assembled. The further part of the journey to Hami was done by air, which was no mean feat.

A landing accident with an R-1, in which K-3 (VAP-3) chemical spray equipment was being tested, Ukhtomskaya airfield, the pilot was N. Vasilyev, 7 January 1930. The VAP-3 was secret equipment so they had been removed before any photos were taken.

An R-1 trainer of the 3rd Military Pilots School, Orenburg, July 1929.

An R-1 from the flight training squadron of the Air Force Academy, which had ground looped, is being put back onto ski undercarriage. Student P.E. Kudinov made an emergency landing near Kryukovo railway station in the Moscow region.

Student pilot I. Plavinskiy crashed the R-1 training aircraft on landing. Such photos were put up on the 'board of shame' at the flying schools.

Starting the engine of an R-1 at the 14th Military Pilots School, Engels, 1933.

An R-1 trainer collided with a medical vehicle during taxiing, Borisoglebsk, August 1930.

Pilot Volnychenko, who was checking the way on one of the sectors of the route, became disorientated, as a frozen lake covered in snow resembled a flat plain. During an emergency landing the aircraft put one wheel into a pit and stood on its nose, damaging the radiator. Volnychenko and his mechanic Chekalov got to the nearby town of Barkul by foot but nobody spoke any Russian there at all, and the pilots did not know any other languages. The only way they could communicate was through gestures and drawings. They nevertheless reached agreement, and the radiator was brazered and fitted to the R-1 in the ambient temperatures of -30°! A crowd of local people tramped down the runway for take-off and the aircraft flew on to Hami without incident.

Instructors and student pilots standing next to an R-1 training aircraft on Ostraya Mogila airfield, 1935.

Starting the engine on an R-1 at an aeroclub by three people standing in a 'chain'.

A civil R-1 (P-1) in flight over Tashkent, 1927. The letter Ш ('Sh') in the registration indicates that the aircraft is a trainer.

The misfortune for this crew, however, did not end there. On the way back there was a covering of snow at Ürümqi and on landing the biplane bounced the entire length of the runway and ended up in a snowdrift. As a result, the propeller, radiator, and ribs in the port wing were damaged.

The process of ferrying the aircraft was postponed until the summer. The aircraft left the town of Bakhty on the Sino-Soviet border only on 28 July 1932, although they did land

A cart with fuel is pushed to the R-1 which is participating in a long-range flight.

safely in Ürümqi. It is known that one R-1 from the previous batch crashed in Xianjing on 8 July (the crew survived), and another biplane was destroyed in a fatal crash on 23 October (in which the Soviet instructor Antipov was killed).

The R-1 was also in service in Mongolia. Initially six airplanes, which had already seen some service in the USSR, were handed over to the Mongolians. One of these biplanes crashed in a short time and two were dismantled for spares. In fact, the only Mongolian air unit (named after Damdin Sükhbaatar) at that time was a part of the VVS RKKA. The aircraft and equipment were Soviet, as were the aircrew and the ground crew, while the Mongolian aviation was commanded by a Buryat, a citizen of the USSR. The biplanes wore the standard Soviet camouflage and red star insignia, to which the Mongolian Soyombo symbol was later added on the rudder.

In April 1930 two R-1s flown by Soviet pilots Grebnev and Lazuko made a long-range flight from Ulan-Bator–Kobdo. They flew over a terrain with few landmarks, using poor maps, and were landing on unprepared runways. In Kobdo, they participated in the May Day military parade, dropping leaflets and taking the local inhabitants up for a flight. Following their return to Ulan-Bator, the pilots were awarded the Mongolian Orders of the Red Banner and silver cigar cases.

In September 1931 Mongolian aviation had three R-1s, three R-5s and a single Junkers F.13. In March of the following year a further four R-1s were delivered from Moscow. A short time later the first Mongolian pilots were trained. In Mongolia, these aircraft participated in border conflicts against the Japanese and Manchurian troops in 1935–1936.

The Soviet Air Force itself for the first time used the R-1 during combat operations against insurgents in Chechnya. Gangs operated there, hiding in the mountains and supplied with weapons and ammunition from abroad through British intelligence. They attacked settlements, border posts and

This R-1 had been written off and was used as a target at the firing range for air-to-ground firing.

Mongolian pilots standing next to an R-1 airplane.

small garrisons, and also robbed columns carrying a variety of cargoes. At the beginning of July 1925, the 3rd Separate Reconnaissance Air Unit, which was based at Gnilovskaya airfield close to Rostov-on-Don, was ordered away from participating in the manoeuvres and received order to re-deploy near Grozniy. From there, they flew reconnaissance and bombing missions. The latter were carried out using the principle of 'lots of noise and no losses' – they chose targets that were stand-alone support structures, hitting them with small-calibre high-explosive bombs, and also flew over the settlements at low level. The task was to intimidate, not bomb the population. In September the leader of the Chechens *Imam* Gotsinskiy surrendered to Red Army troops. In that same month the 3rd Air Unit returned to their previous location in Gnilovskaya.

The R-1 was also used in Central Asia against the local insurgents, who were known as the Basmachi. The latter included those ideologically opposed to the Soviet regime and those who were unhappy with the reforms, as well as just bandits. There were detachments of a dozen insurgents, and of several hundred, and sometimes thousands. They were, however, poorly armed, and there were not even enough home-made weapons to go around, and machine guns were very few and far between. Occasionally the Basmachi would be supplied with guns and ammunition from Afghanistan, with the participation of British intelligence. However, these units were highly mobile, they would travel on horseback and by camel.

The Soviet aviation used in Central Asia the all-metal, German-designed Yu-21s, but the bomb load of these airplanes was meagre. Therefore, when more bombs needed to be carried a decision was taken to use the tried and tested R-1. This was the case during the combat testing of the chemical fragmentation bombs, which had previously been tried out on those same R-1s. A location where it is always warm and dry is an ideal testing ground for chemical weapons, while the remoteness of the area and the low-level of education among

Two R-1s and a single U-2 of Mongolian aviation.

Soviet pilots and flight observers that served in Afghanistan, with the Commander of the Afghan Air Force Mohammad Ehsah-khan; in the background is an R-1 biplane.

One of the R-1 biplanes of the Afghan Air Force.

the local population made it easier to maintain secrecy. The nature of combat operations enabled aircrews to operate against live targets with almost no resistance from the enemy, just like on a testing range.

In April 1928 a special purpose group under the command of Orlovskiy arrived in Tashkent. The personnel in this group had been selected for the most part of the 30th Squadron *Krasnaya Moskva* (Red Moscow), which was considered one of the best in the Air Force. At the beginning of May the group transferred to Termez, from where they began to fly bombing sorties against Dzhunaid-khan in the Karakum desert. However, the effectiveness of using small-calibre chemical ammunition against a fast-moving cavalry was very small.

It soon emerged that the R-1 was not much suitable given the local operating conditions: they often broke down on the uneven rocky airfields; the sun and heat degraded the canvass outer skin and led to deformation of the structural timber. In total the group lost three of the 13 R-1s to accidents and fatal crashes, and possibly the fourth was also written off. No combat losses were sustained given that the enemy had no anti-aircraft defences. At the end, the UVVS came to the conclusion that it would be more rational to send the all-metal R-3LD airplanes to Central Asia.

On a much larger scale the R-1s and MR-1s were used during combat at the Sino-Eastern Railway in 1929. In July of that year the forces of General Zhāng Zuòlin who ruled Manchuria captured the railway that belonged to the USSR and arrested Soviet soldiers. In response, the formation of the Special Far Eastern Army began. Two of its groups, the Transbaikal and Far Eastern were to have moved towards each other along this part of the railway. There were two air reconnaissance units in the Transbaikal group, the 6th and the 25th, both of which operated the R-1s. As reinforcement, the 26th Light Bomber Air Squadron, which also operated the R-1, was re-deployed from Lipetsk by air.

The Far Eastern group had in its strength the 40th Air Squadron which was based in Spassk from the beginning of autumn 1929, and the 68th Air Unit that was attached

Soviet flight-observer P.F. Mushtaev in an Afghan uniform standing next to an R-1 airplane.

The Afghan crew of an R-1 prior to take-off for a bombing mission.

Replacing the M-5 engine on an R-1 biplane in the Soviet aviation school in Kabul, 1925.

to the Amur Military Flotilla. The 68th Air Unit had 14 MR-1 floatplanes in service, four of which were on board the barge *Amur*.

On 12 October the forces of the Far Eastern group began the Sungari Operation. The objective of this operation was the town of Lahasusu, where the Chinese military flotilla was based. After air reconnaissance, the Soviet aviation carried out bombing raids on enemy fortifications and warships. The Amur Flotilla landed the troops, half a day later the Lahasusu garrison surrendered, while the Soviet pilots had sunk four Chinese ships.

Following this success, the Soviet flotilla moved up along the Sungari River. The floatplanes were conducting reconnaissance and provided escort cover for the ships from the air (Zhāng Zuòlin did have aircraft in this region, albeit a very small number – five Breguet 19s). On 30 October alone the MR-1s flew 17 sorties. On the next day the battle for Fujin city began. A pair of hydroplanes, led by the commander of the unit E.M. Lukht, dropped bombs on the enemy's largest gunboat *Jiang Hen*, which capsized and sank. After that the aviators dispersed a unit of cavalrymen who were attempting to hamper the troops landing. Apart from that, on that same day Soviet aircraft sank the armed steamer *Jiang An*, along with a barge. Not one of the R-1s was shot down by the Chinese.

The Transbaikal group began its operations on 17 November. On the morning of that day 20 biplanes bombed enemy fortifications near Zhalainuo'er village. On that same day two air raids were carried out on the airfield at Mudanjiang. Four aircraft were destroyed there along with two hangars and anti-aircraft gun. Then airplanes for two days were attacking infantry and cavalry on the ground. Army divisions of the Transbaikal group quickly reached the Manchuria station, encircling a relatively large alignment of Chinese. On 20 November enemy forces tried to break through this encirclement but aviation and an armoured train that arrived just in time put a stop to this. In one case the R-1s acted as chasers, directing the enemy towards a row of trucks armed with machine guns. Then the counterattack forced the Chinese to surrender. After that the Soviet troops moved towards Hailar and captured it on 29 November. By the end of the month the entire length of the China Eastern Railway had been purged.

The new year of 1930 dawned, and the new R-5s began to enter service with the VVS RKKA. They were superior to the R-1s in every respect – speed, service ceiling, and bomb load. In addition, this new type was much easier to fly. The R-5 was, first and foremost, sent to the light bomber squadrons. Production of the R-1 however, continued and their numbers grew in the Air Force. The peak of their numerical strength came in January 1931 with 1,517 R-1s plus 20 R-1SPs, and 79 R-1BMWs.

These well-mastered biplanes were used for planned training of aircrew, participating in regular military parades, and support of army and navy exercises. In August 1930 the R-1s participated in the world's first airborne assault, which was carried out during manoeuvres of the Moscow Military District in the area near Klochkovo village. The parachutists jumped out of a French Goliath aircraft, and three reconnaissance biplanes of the 35th Air Squadron dropped the armament (carbines and light machine guns) with ammunition. Every R-1 carried two cargo parachute bags. The airplanes were subsequently used in a similar way in exercises of the Leningrad Military District.

In March 1931 a pair of R-1s caused an international conflict. Two biplanes of the 28th Air Squadron, which was based near Leningrad, lost their way and entered Finnish territory where defensive structures had been built along the Viisijoki River. The Finns thought that the reconnaissance biplanes were photographing their fortified area. The Finnish Embassy in Moscow filed a protest. The culprits were quickly found, but it was concluded that these young pilots were not guilty of any major crime. The command only regret was that they had not actually been able to photograph the Finnish pillboxes.

By the beginning of 1931 standard chemical armament had appeared on the R-1. Experiments with spraying equipment had been undertaken already in 1926. Such unit represented a tank containing a mixture of toxic agents (usually a mustard-lewisite mixture in kerosene). The first

Iranian R-1s, which were used in Luristan.

known unit of this type that was designed for the R-1 was the VAP-2. Not much is known about this equipment – aircraft of special air unit sprayed targets on the testing range at Podosinki (now part of Moscow) using these units. In summer 1929 a new VAP-3 unit was tested which was allowing the mixture to be dropped as a salvo. In September of that same year the 56th Air Squadron used them in exercises close to Gomel. This equipment, however, was not considered successful. In December 1930 the VAP-4 with a gradual discharge was accepted into service. The R-1s would carry two 82-litre VAP-4 tanks under the lower wing. The liquid was pushed out of the tanks under pressure by the oncoming airflow. For these biplanes the weight of these tanks was excessive: two full VAP-4s weighed 240kg, while the bomb load of an R-1 was limited to 200kg.

Nevertheless, by the beginning of February 1931 the personnel of five ground attack air squadrons had undergone training on operating this spray equipment, but none of the squadrons had more than 10 VAP-4 kits in service. Only by the end of May the 56th Air Squadron was fully equipped with the VAP-4s. In total less than a hundred R-1s received chemical equipment, and the reason for this was the transfer to the new R-5 biplanes.

By the end of 1931 the old biplanes had been replaced by the R-5 in all light bomber squadrons. The following year it was the turn of the reconnaissance units. By 1 January 1933 the Air Force had 1,297 R-1s and 62 biplanes fitted with BMW IV engines remained in service, with the former were either in army aviation, or at training schools. For instance, in the Air Force of the Special Red Banner Far Eastern Army (which had been awarded the Red Banner honorary title for their victory at the China Eastern Railway) only three corps units were still equipped with the old aircraft type – the 6th, 18th, and 19th (30 R-1 biplanes in total).

This same process was underway in naval aviation – by January 1932 there were 17 MR-1s in naval units, and a further 29 were at the Naval Pilots School. They began to be replaced with S.62bis flying boats imported from Italy (in the USSR they were designated S-62Bs), and then by their Soviet copy the MBR-4. One of the last to hand over their MR-1s in June 1933 was the 67th Air Unit of the Dnieper Flotilla, after they had converted onto the R-5a and the Sh-2. By the end of the year the MR-1 had been completely withdrawn from naval aviation units.

Iranian pilots standing next to their R-1s in Luristan.

By the end of 1934 the VVS RKKA units had converted fully onto the R-5, individual R-1s only remained in very few units and they were used as liaison and training biplanes. Thus, on 1 January 1935 there were just four of these old biplanes across the entire area of the huge Ukrainian Military District. A month later there were still 1,110 such airplanes in the Air Force, but 1,067 of them were listed in flying schools while 565 were not capable of getting airborne.

At the beginning of 1930s the R-1s were often used for a variety of experiments, which included dropping of new bomb types, testing of cameras and parachute equipment.

In November 1930 a unique weapon was tested on the R-1 – so-called 'air mines' designed by the engineer A.E. Maisel. These winged craft had a propeller but did not have an engine. The source of energy was a high-revving flywheel, which had been spinned up on the airplane by an aerovane via a gearbox. It did not have a control system and maintained a straight flight thanks to the gyro spinning wheel. Two types of mines – ZAM (Barrage Aviation Mine) which was designed to hit airplanes and airships, and a larger PBM (Gliding Bomb-Mine) intended to destroy ground targets – were dropped from R-1s at a testing range close to Yevpatoria. The former type of mine would fly horizontally until detonation using a time-fuse, while the latter would glide with a gradual descent. The accuracy of fire for both types turned out to be quite low.

In July 1930 tests of the 76mm dynamo-reactive (recoilless) cannon designed by L.V. Kurchevskiy were carried out on an R-1. The cannon was placed near the middle

Soviet mechanics Matynenko and Matsunov standing next to an R-1 aircraft in Kabul.

pair of interwing struts, and was fixed to them using twine. The cannon was fired on the ground. After the first shot the canvass on the stabiliser and fuselage ripped, and a half-a-metre hole appeared in the fuselage side. After the second shot, the fuselage frames, one of the stabiliser ribs and the elevator rib cracked. Following the fourth shot the 'aircraft was rendered completely useless'.

The first experiments in the USSR with flight refuelling were also carried out on the R-1. The project was developed at the NII VVS starting from November 1929 under the leadership of A.K. Zapanovanniy. The tanker aircraft, instead of the machine guns, carried in the turret a container with a 30m-length hose on the end of which was a 'loading drogue' – a 3.5kg weight. Under the same protective cover, aside from the hose there was a telephone cable intended to equal out the difference in the electrical potential between the two aircraft. As the turret rotated, the cable would extend out through a hole in the floor. The gunner in the aft cockpit of the aircraft being refuelled had to catch the drogue, put the end of the hose into the refuelling nozzle and connect the jack plug on the telephone cable with a socket in the fuselage.

In total 26 test flights were undertaken. The pilots maintained an elevation of approximately 12m for the tanker above the second R-1. Initially the crews were just training in catching the drogue, then they started to transfer water, and finally, fuel. On one occasion the drogue punctured the upper wing of the aircraft being refuelled, and then the propeller of the latter cut off around three metres of the hose. The further experiments were carried out on the more up to date R-5 and TB-1 airplanes.

One of the first projects of the famous inventor P.I. Grokhovskiy at the NII VVS was the so-called: 'Airborne firing range'. This was an R-1 that had been converted into a target tug to train aerial gunnery. It carried six hoses and six gliding plywood targets, but this biplane was not put into series production.

Grokhovskiy later created 'the airborne cable dispenser', although this did not actually dispense anything but laid out telephone cable whilst flying at an altitude of approximately 100m. An R-1 could lay a line of around 2,500m in length, at the end dropping a telephone receiver along with a telephonist on a parachute. The first successful experiment of this technology took place on 1 January 1931.

In the summer of 1931, on the Amur River the 68th Air Unit experimented with dropping 'R' (*Rybka* – small fish) aerial bottom mines using the MR-1. These were the first Soviet mines with contactless (magnetic) fuses. They were later put into series production.

One of the last experiments conducted on the R-1 was the installation of a turbo-supercharger purchased in the USA and manufactured by General Electric company. This was the first time a turbo-boost device was used in the USSR. The first flight of the modified R-1 took place on 23 July 1935 and pilot Kaverin flew this aircraft. The flight ended in a fire on the ground following an engine shut down as the turbo-supercharger had burst into flames. The fire was suppressed, however, and the airplane repaired. In July–October 1935 pilots Kaverin and Uronichev made 17 successful flights of the R-1 with the turbo-supercharger.

The Soviet de Havilland actively served as a military training aircraft up until 1936, when the R-5s were replaced by the SB and R-Zet airplanes. Once the R-5s had become surplus, they were handed over to flying schools in ever increasing numbers. The old R-1s were no longer required and were written off.

At the beginning of the 1930s the R-1s were also used in aviation of the border troops of the Joint State Political Directorate (subsequently the People's Commissariat for Internal Affairs). For example, the 1st Separate Unit, which was formed in Tashkent in June 1932, operated these biplanes. They were used to patrol the border in sparsely populated areas. Later the R-1s were replaced by U-2s and R-5s airplanes.

In the end of the 1920s and beginning of the 1930s the R-1s were used for a short period of time in civil aviation. In June 1929 the *Dobrolyot* society acquired 10 aircraft from the Air Force, which were converted to spray agricultural

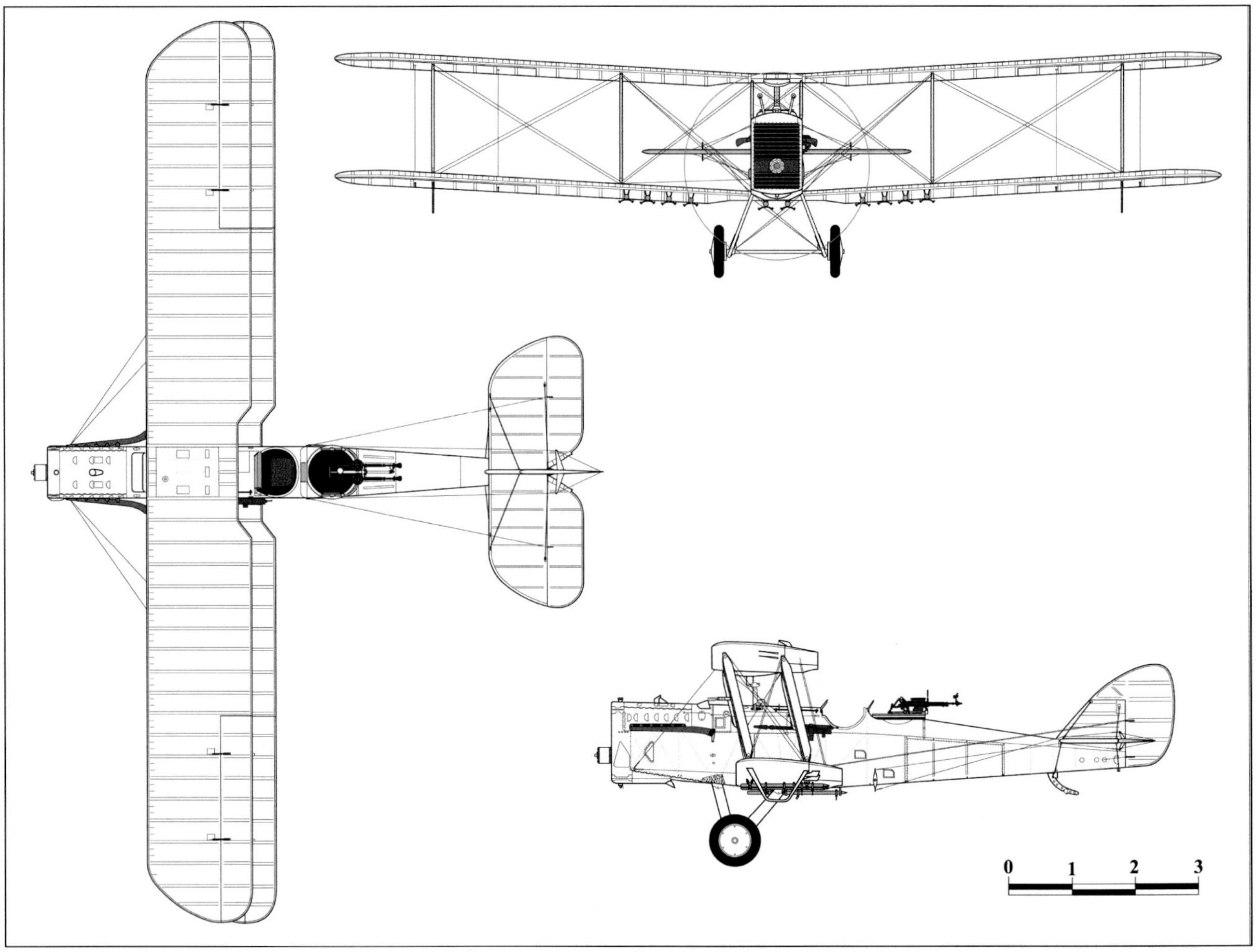

Three-view drawings of an R-1 airplane fitted with PV-1 and DA machine guns.

chemicals. These machines were tried out for the fight with locusts in Central Asia but their work left something to be desired. A further 10 R-1s came under the *Pravda* (Truth) air unit, which delivered the central newspaper matrices from Moscow to Leningrad. They were, however, quickly replaced by R-5s. Quite a number of R-1s served in the flying and technical schools of the GVF. On 1 August 1931 there were 86 unarmed R-1s serving there, which from 15 August began to be designated P-1. The P-1s almost never operated on the GVF routes, and only a few airplanes worked in the Ukrainian and Transcaucasian directorates, carrying mail, light cargoes, and on rare occasions they would carry passengers.

Ten R-1SPs in 1931 were transferred to *Osoaviakhim* flying clubs, and evidently a few years later they had all been written off.

2.6 British Passenger Aircraft

In the 1920s two examples of passenger airplanes were acquired in Britain for familiarisation purposes by Soviet Union. The Soviet civil aviation had only just been created and there was no series production of aircraft of such purpose in the country.

The first acquired aircraft was the relatively large DH.34 biplane which had a wooden construction and was designed to carry eight passengers (a ninth seat was provided for a 'cabin-boy', a young lad who would perform the role of a steward) with a crew of two. The aircraft was fitted with a single 450hp Napier Lion engine in the nose section of the fuselage. The engine rotated a three-blade wooden propeller. The engine mount was made easily detachable, so it could fold down on hinges for servicing and repair. Aluminium fuel tanks were located under the upper wing close to the first pair of struts, which should have reduced the risk of fire.

At the beginning of 1922 Soviet representatives ordered one such aircraft. It was delivered by sea to Petrograd, from where it was taken by rail to Moscow. There the de Havilland was assembled at workshops at Moscow Central airfield (at the time it was named after L.D. Trotskiy). On 9 August 1922 V.L. Melnikov made the first flight in the DH.34 with six passengers on board. The biplane made several circuits at an altitude of 300m at a speed of approximately 160km/h. Melnikov then characterised the take-off run and landing roll as 'short', and also noted on the ease with which the differential ailerons were used, which 'reduced the yaw of the aircraft'. The pilot also added that the de Havilland differed advantageously from the Fokker, which he had previously

A DH.34 airplane with its original *Dobrolyot* registration markings.

A DH.34 following assembly in Moscow. Note that the aircraft weight and payload markings (in the left lower corner of the photo) are in Russian, which evidently have been done back in Britain.

A DH.34 passenger airplane at the Moscow Central airfield, 1922.

A DH.34 in the workshop of the *Promvozdukh* repair factory.

flown, in terms of the fortuitous positioning of the pilot's cockpit, the responsiveness of the controls, the opportunity to perform tight turns, and the enhanced rate of climb.

Initially, most likely the intention was to use this biplane on the *Dobrolyot* society routes, and the airplane was given the civil registration number RR12. However, the military quickly showed an interest in this airplane, and it was decided that it would be used to train pilots of heavy aircraft. There were none of such airplanes serving in the Air Force at the time, but the twin-engine Farman F.62 Goliath biplane bombers had been ordered in France, and negotiations were ongoing with the Germans to supply the three-engine all-metal K.30 monoplanes (which were subsequently designated the YuG-1 in Russia). Aircrew and ground crew needed to be trained on these airplanes in good time.

The British aircraft was subject to various modifications. In order to increase the flight range in January 1923 an additional fuel tank, which had been manufactured at the *Aviarabotnik* factory, was fitted in the fuselage. Evidently, it took up the passenger seat space because in June the factory manufactured cushions which were to be placed on the passenger seats positioned on top of the fuel tank. The biplane was handed over to the separate unit of heavy aviation, which was based at the Central airfield. On 1 December 1923 the DH.34 was listed on the inventory of this unit and was in a serviceable condition. It was still there in November 1925.

In spring 1926 the unit was re-deployed to Leningrad, re-formed into a heavy squadron (the 1st Heavy Air Squadron) and was equipped with Goliaths. The DH.34 was used in the squadron's training unit. A year later, however, the modern German YuG-1 airplanes began to arrive to the unit, the Goliaths were transferred to the training roles, so the British biplane was no longer of use to the military.

Back at the end of autumn 1926 the DH.34 was returned to civil aviation fleet and received registration R-RUAP. The aircraft was transferred to the *Ukrvozdukhput* organisation (or *Ukrpovitroshlyakh* in Ukrainian). The primary base for the latter

A DH.34, following its transfer to the military, stands next to a tented hangar. The red stars are not visible but the vertical tail has been repainted in white.

A DH.34 following repair and refinement.

A Vimy Commercial following its arrival in Moscow, 1922.

A Vimy after a test flight, Moscow Central airfield, August 1922.

A Vimy at an airfield in Russia.

was in Kharkov, although the details of the aircraft service at this location have not been found. In March 1929 the airplane was re-designated to CCCP-212 in line with the new designation system, which means that the de Havilland was still airworthy. The exact date on which this aircraft was written off is not known, but at the end of 1930 the fuselage of a dismantled machine was already lying next to the hangars at Kharkov airfield.

In the same year of 1922 when the DH.34 was acquired, a twin-engine Vickers Vimy Commercial passenger biplane was purchased in Britain. It was a heavy airplane for its time

A Vimy during its use by the Air Force Academy, after the aircraft refinements, 1924.

which differed from its predecessor, Vickers Vimy bomber, by a large fuselage that was formed of a short, oval-shaped cylinder with a rounded nose. The aircraft was of a mixed construction but was made predominantly of wood – in the forward section of the fuselage the wooden frame was covered in plywood while a metallic truss in the aft section was covered in canvass. The wings were all wooden. The aircraft was designed to carry 10 passengers with a crew of two.

The Soviet representatives acquired the aircraft serial number 43, and it was the last to be completed. The manufacturer has used this machine for various tests, including a new mount for the 450hp Lion II engine. The nacelles for these engines were box-shaped and mounted on the lower wing. The airplane also received a new biplane cell from the Virginia bomber, with a larger wingspan and wing area. The aileron balancing horns on the upper wing on this biplane did not extend beyond the wingtips as they had done for the series production passenger version. It was planned to introduce these changes on the military transport version, which was known as the Vernon. On completion of testing the airplane was dismantled and sold to Soviet Russia. It was indicated that the biplane was designed to carry 12 passengers so the layout of its passenger cabin corresponded to the Vernon. The mix of the features of the Vimy Commercial and the Vernon led to some Soviet documents referring to the biplane as a Vimy and others as a Vernon.

On 4 April 1922 the shipment arrived in Petrograd by sea, from where it was directed to Moscow. There the airplane was assembled and on 10 August A.V. Pankratyev from *Dobrolyot* made the first test flight in this machine from the Moscow Central airfield. On board were also a mechanic and nine passengers. The biplane flew a wide circuit at an altitude of 700m, and the flight lasted approximately 20 mins. The *Samolyot* (Airplane) magazine wrote: ' ... Muscovites could see this large airplane flying over the city'. The pilot later

A Vimy Commercial prior to a flight.

A group of leaders of the Air Fleet pose with pilots and guests against the backdrop of the Vimy with its engines running. Among those photographed was the Political Bureau member V.G. Kuybyshev (in the centre of the second row) and the famous pilot K.K. Artseulov (on the far right in the second row).

remarked on its good handling as well as the ease with which take-off and landing were performed.

The Vimy, however, did not stay with *Dobrolyot* for long, and just as they had with the DH.34 the military got hold of this machine. Pankratyev was sent to undergo conversion training on the German Yu-13, while the British airplane was transferred to the training squadron of the Air Force Academy, and the students performed familiarisation flights in this machine.

In August 1923 the Vickers underwent modifications – additional fuel tanks were manufactured for it (forward and aft tanks) which were accommodated in the passenger cabin. These tanks augmented the main tanks that were suspended on straps underneath the cabin floor. The new fuel tanks were placed on wooden supports, and on top of these new seats with metal frames were fitted. The oil capacity was also increased by adding two oil tanks.

Group images of personnel in front of a Vimy at a Russian airfield.

A Vimy Commercial in the workshop of the *Promvozdukh* repair factory.

On 29 January 1924 the Vimy was handed over to the NOA, and an extensive program of the aircraft testing was carried out. The principal interest was in whether this biplane could be used as a bomber, as a significant number of aircraft of this type had been converted in China into substitute bombers which had been used in internecine wars between ruling cliques. After these tests had been completed the Vickers was returned to the training squadron.

In June 1925 the Vickers was transferred to a separate heavy aviation unit, and initially the Vimy was the only twin-engine aircraft in its service; in the unit documentation it was listed as a military training aircraft.

As mentioned above, at the beginning of 1926 the unit was moved to Leningrad and was re-formed into the 1st Heavy Air Squadron led by Squadron Commander Chekalov. After the squadron had received their Goliaths the Vimy remained in service with the training unit. In July 1926 the British biplane went in for repair following an accident, after which it disappeared from the inventories.

Pilot E.I. Gvayta with representatives of local government following an emergency landing in Tilburg (in the Netherlands).

E.I. Gvayta next to the Avro Baby after landing at the Moscow Central airfield, June 1922.

An Avro Baby following its arrival in Moscow; the airplane still retains its British registration numbers.

2.7 British Light Airplanes

Following the end of the First World War a trend appeared for small, single or two-seat aircraft with low-powered engines – up to 50hp. They were seen as a means of mass transportation, as sports machines, or as cheap training and liaison aircraft. In Russia such airplanes were known as *aviettes* to reflect the name they had been given in French. Before starting production of such aircraft in Russia, it was decided to review foreign examples. Two British light airplanes were chosen: the Avro 534 Baby and the de Havilland DH.53 Humming Bird.

The former was a small two-seat wooden biplane with a water-cooled 35hp Green engine. A nose-mounted water cooler was fitted in front of the engine, and there was no oil radiator, the oil was cooled in the tank suspended under the engine. The engine turned a twin-blade wooden propeller. The biplane was given a rounded rudder, which characterised Avro aircraft, while there was no vertical stabiliser. The undercarriage was a very simple design with a tailskid made of oak at the rear. The undercarriage legs were not fitted with shock absorbers, and the beam axle was simply suspended on the undercarriage legs on belt loops.

A prototype of the Baby was manufactured in April 1919 and following an accident the aircraft was significantly refined. Specifically, the fuel capacity was increased to 105 litres after an additional 65-litre fuel tank was fitted under the pilot's seat. This brought the flight duration up to between nine and ten hours given favourable conditions. As a result of alterations, the centre of gravity position changed, so the wheels were moved forward slightly. On 31 May 1920 pilot Hinkler flew this small diminutive biplane non-stop from Croydon to Turin, spending nine and a half hours in the air.

Series production of the type was started but in fact the airplanes were custom built and differed from one another. The seventh production Baby found its way to Soviet Russia and this was the first aircraft to make a journey by air from Britain to Moscow.

The Main Directorate of the Air Fleet (*Glavvozdukhflot*) issued an order to acquire this airplane, as the Baby was in the list of prospective aircraft for a potential study. Diplomatic relations with Britain in this period, however, did not exist, and therefore, a non-trivial approach was used: pilot E.I. Gvayta was sent to Britain, who purchased the light airplane as a private individual. He was an educated person, knew two foreign languages and did not look as a 'cannibal Bolshevik' at all. The Baby was configured specifically for him, and the example that had made the long-range flight to Turin was taken as the template. The fuel capacity was increased and the undercarriage wheels were moved forward. The engine carburettor was provided with a pre-heater, and the intensity of the oil cooling was increased by passing air pipes through the tank. In addition, a series of reinforcements were introduced into the airframe, and a baggage compartment was arranged behind the pilot's seat. However, it was forbidden to put anything in this compartment when the fuel tank was full, as

An Avro Baby in the Higher School of Military Pilots in Moscow.

the changes that were introduced had had a negative effect on the biplane's handling. Gvayta wrote: 'It is tail heavy ... it is hard to keep the aircraft flying straight'.

This light airplane received the British registration code G-EBDA which was written on the fuselage sides. On 9 July 1922 Gvayta took off from the factory airfield at Hamble. At Lympne on the English Channel coast he completed the border checks and cleared customs. A route via the Netherlands, France, Germany, and Poland was planned. It seems that the pilot did not have any visas and the aircraft was not insured, but this was not disconcerting to anyone. Gvayta was escorted on the first stage of the journey by the aforementioned British pilot Hinkler in an Avro 504 biplane, and they encountered rainfall over Holland. One spark plug failed and the engine began to operate on three cylinders. Over Tilburg the engine failed completely. After gliding from 200m altitude Gvayta made an emergency landing on a wet field, the aircraft ground looped and broke the rudder. Hinkler flew over the crash site, examined everything closely and then turned back. On the second day he returned with a new rudder. In order to take off, the airplane had to be towed more than 10km onto a military airfield. Following the repair, Gvayta continued on his way, crossing the border with Germany. Due to a lack of fuel, he was forced to land close to Munster, and there he was arrested by police. The pilot was held up in Munster for a week before the Soviet embassy arranged him permission to fly to Berlin to resolve this issue. Most likely, a preliminary agreement had been in place with the Germans, but they were waiting for him in Berlin and not in Munster, where the local government knew nothing of this flight. On 24 June the Soviet pilot received the required paperwork, and on the following day he took off from Berlin.

From there he set off for Konigsberg, he flew over Poland without stopping and landed for the refuelling in Vitebsk. From there his route took him to Moscow: on 27 June 1922 the biplane landed at Moscow Central airfield. The diminutive Baby had covered a route of 2,755km (Gvayta himself described a journey of 2,600km).

A DH.53 prior to the long-range flight Moscow–Serpukhov–Moscow; standing next to the aircraft is pilot Yu.I. Piontkovskiy.

Actually, Gvayta had acquired not just one but two Avro 534s in Britain. It is not known whether the second one was manufactured on the basis of the first or this was a standard variant with a Green engine. The second airplane had been manufactured earlier, and back in May had been sent by sea in a dismantled condition. In the end the steamer had delivered it to Sevastopol. Both Soviet Babys ended up in the 1st Military Pilots School in Kacha, and from there they went to the Higher School of Military Pilots in Moscow. There the British light airplanes operated in 1923–24. Subsequently, one of them was destroyed, while another was handed over to the 2nd Military Pilots School in Borisoglebsk. It was listed there until it was written off in 1928.

The second type of British light airplanes was purchased for the Sports section of the ODVF. The Humming Bird represented a kind of 'airborne motorcycle' – a single-engine wooden monoplane in such a configuration which allowed to fold the wings for storage. This light airplane was completed later than the Baby – in autumn 1923. Such monoplanes were later put into series production, powered with different engines, and even briefly stayed in service with the Royal Air Force as liaison aircraft.

The Soviet Union received a single example of the DH.53 which was fitted with a 26hp Tomtit engine. The airplane was acquired through intermediary company ARCOS. The machine underwent acceptance testing in Britain, and was then dismantled, packed away for transportation and delivered to Leningrad by sea. From there the DH.53 was transferred to Moscow. In March 1925 the airplane was handed over to the Air Force Academy which had plans to study and test it.

Students at the academy fully dismantled and assembled the aircraft, while the engine was bench tested. According to Soviet records the maximum output of this engine was not 26hp but 24hp.

Head of the flight operations section of the Air Force Academy V.M. Zernov in the cockpit of the DH.53.

The students of the academy also carried out flight-testing; the Head of the flight operations section V.M. Zernov made a number of flights, as he had graduated from a flying school in Britain in 1917 and then worked as an instructor at Gatchina flying school. The test program envisaged defining of the maximum speed, service ceiling, and the take-off and landing runs.

The light airplane flew both with the standard propeller that had been brought from Britain as well as with the propeller designed by the engineer Kuznetsov, which had been produced in the academy's workshops. The latter turned out to be worse and this was particularly evident in the increase of the take-off run. With the original propeller the characteristics also turned out to be a little lower than they had been set by the British test pilots. The service ceiling was particularly affected, this did not exceed 1,830m, and climbing to this altitude took 50 minutes. The stability and controllability were assessed as satisfactory.

In April 1925 the Humming Bird was handed over to the Sports section of the ODVF, and on 14 July of that same year it was demonstrated at the aviation parade in Moscow. The airplane flew over the participants of a rally, which had been organised on the Central airfield. It is possible that it was then that the DH.53 was demonstrated to the People's Commissar for Military and Naval Affairs M.V. Frunze. Student of the academy A.S. Yakovlev provided comments on this aircraft for him (he went on to become the famous aircraft designer). Subsequently the ODVF became part of the *Aviakhim* organisation, and the sports aviation department began to come under that organisation as well.

In March 1927 the DH.53 completed a long-range flight Moscow–Serpukhov–Moscow. The light airplane was flown by Yu.I. Piontkovskiy, and the aforementioned A.S. Yakovlev had participated in the organisation of this long-range flight. He later wrote in the *Aviatsiya i Khimiya* (Aviation and chemistry) magazine: 'The aviette quickly got airborne and after climbing to an altitude of 500m set course for Serpukhov'. Piontkovskiy was hindered by a strong headwind, which caused turbulence. The pilot was even concerned that the wings would be torn off. The Humming Bird covered a distance of 100km in two hours and on the return leg the oil pump began to play up. After having covered a distance of 30km Piontkovskiy returned to Serpukhov. Following repairs, he set off again but the wind direction had changed, it was again blowing head on. The return journey also took approximately two hours. This was the first time a light airplane had flown beyond the boundaries of an airfield in the Soviet Union.

The author has not been able to establish when this airplane was written off.

2.8 British Flying Boats and Amphibians

Along with the earlier described Vernon, the same vessel also delivered another aircraft manufactured by Vickers – the Vickers Viking IV amphibian. This aircraft had a biplane layout; both wings had the same wingspan, the lower wing laid on the hull and the upper wing was supported by a system of struts, while the numerous bracing wires enhanced the rigidity of the biplane cell. The engine was attached under the upper wing and was fitted with a pusher propeller. The double-redan hull of the airplane was made quite narrow with straight, almost vertical sides that made it easier to fit the undercarriage. The narrow width of the fuselage led to an insufficient stability of this aircraft on water. Two auxiliary floats were mounted on struts under the wing. The Viking had been manufactured solely from wood, and an outer skin was made of a Consuta planking sewn together with a fine copper wire. The wing and tailfin were covered in canvass imbibed with a lacquer.

The undercarriage consisted of two undercarriage legs with wheels and a tailskid. Before performing the water landing, the wheeled legs were retracted forwards; the semi-

A Viking IV amphibian in Petrograd, 1922.

An accident involving a Viking of the 1st Separate Torpedo Bombing Squadron, 22 July 1926, Sevastopol.

The Viking after it was dragged out of the water following the accident.

axes of the wheels moved along an arc-shaped guides on the fuselage sides. The undercarriage lowering and lifting was mechanical, via a hand-operated winch. It looks that this layout was later used as the template for the undercarriage lifting mechanism on the widely used Soviet Sh-2 amphibian designed by V.B. Shavrov. The non-retractable tailskid was above the waterline when the aircraft was on the water. These amphibians were in series production in Britain from the end of summer 1921.

The Vickers Type 64 Viking – military but unarmed version of the type was acquired via a Soviet trade representation in Revel (Tallinn). This aircraft was powered by a Lion engine, had an enclosed cockpit, and the hull was planked with SCT plywood. On 4 April the amphibian arrived in Petrograd, for some time remained in the warehouse, and then the work started on unpacking and assembling the airplane in one of the hangars at the Komendantskiy airfield. On 21 October the Head of the Air Fleet ordered that assembly of this amphibian be stopped and for it to be sent to Moscow, but the order came too late, as the airplane was almost ready. Therefore, testing was undertaken in Petrograd, at the Grebnoy Port.

Once the tests had been completed the airplane was listed for some time as serving in the 1st Separate Naval Hydroaviation Unit of the Baltic Sea Air Force. For some unknown reason it was considered advisable to operate an amphibian on the Black Sea, and in May 1923 pilot L.I. Giksa and mechanic Radev ferried the airplane to Sevastopol. There the Viking was incorporated into the 4th Separate Naval Reconnaissance Air Unit. According to the reports in December this aircraft was in an airworthy condition. In 1925 it was handed over to the 2nd Separate Naval Fighter Air Unit based in Odessa, and then returned to Sevastopol, having become part of the 1st Separate Torpedo Bombing Squadron.

An NT.2B flying boat of the 1st Reconnaissance Hydroaviation Unit on the slipway in Oranienbaum, 1922.

On 22 July 1926 the commander of this squadron P.P. Sorokin flew a training flight in Sevastopol with pilot Bolotov. On take-off Bolotov lifted off from the water too early, porpoising twice, and then ploughed into the water. The aircraft capsized; Sorokin was killed, Bolotov survived. The amphibian was later towed by a launch to Sevastopol harbour and was lifted out of the water but no attempt was made to repair it. The Viking subsequently disappeared from the inventories of the Air Force.

In that same year 1922 a single Norman-Thompson NT.2B flying boat trainer was acquired in Britain for familiarisation purposes. The basic type of the NT.2 biplane was produced in small series in early 1915. This was a small amphibian of a wooden construction with a pusher propeller, which was designed for a crew of two. These machines were used, for the most part, to search for enemy submarines in coastal waters. Then the NT.2A version emerged, which was also a military version, and produced in small numbers as well. The aforementioned NT.2B trainer, however, was series produced from the end of 1917 in large numbers, but initially the British Admiralty could not decide what engines to fit onto these flying boats, and then the First World War came to an end. The majority of the flying boats that had already been completed were conserved, and then the search began for someone to sell them to. For export they were usually fitted with 200hp Wolseley Viper engines.

A single airplane that had not found a buyer (serial number N3312) fitted with a 200hp Hispano-Suiza engine, was acquired by Soviet Russia via the ARCOS organisation. The airplane was delivered by sea to Petrograd at the beginning of May 1922 in a dismantled state. From there the British flying boat was transferred to Oranienbaum where it was assembled. Interestingly, on 22 June this aircraft was already listed as being in service with the 1st Reconnaissance Hydroaviation Unit and L.M. Portsel tested this aircraft in July–August of the same year. For the entire month of

An NT.2B flying boat placed on ski undercarriage in winter of 1922-1923.

July, the aircraft flying time amounted to just 41 minutes, and for August – 4 hours 32 minutes. In his report Portsel noted that the acquired flying boat was of no particular value. Nevertheless, due to a shortage of materiel, a decision was taken to leave the Norman-Thompson in this unit. The biplane was not used as a trainer but as a liaison aircraft. In the 1st Reconnaissance Hydroaviation Unit the NT.2B was used up until mid-August 1923. It was then conserved and handed over to the storage depot. The aircraft did not take to the skies again, and the design was never carefully studied – the flying boat had obviously become completely obsolete.

2.9 Handley Page Torpedo Bombers

The idea of dropping torpedoes from the air emerged and was realised during the First World War years, but Russia did not have any torpedo bombers nor any air-launched torpedoes up until the end of the Civil War. Russian designers had attempted to create torpedo-carrying aircraft and some of projects had even reached the prototype stage, such as the GASN (Special Purpose Hydroplane) biplane with floats. However, up until the end of the Civil War, there were no torpedo bombers at the disposal of the RKKVF.

The task on the air-launched torpedoes development was given to the Petrograd-based Special Technical Bureau (OTB, *Osoboye Tekhnicheskoye Byuro*) headed by V.I. Bekauri. The OTB needed torpedo bombers in order to perform experiments with the first Soviet air-launched torpedoes designed to be dropped from low altitudes. These torpedoes were created by modifying the torpedo type 1912 and the type 1910/15 (shortened version).

In response to this demand, at the beginning of 1922 two single-seat torpedo-carrying H.P.19 Hanley I biplanes were ordered from Handley Page company through the ARCOS. The British sold one Hanley that had been repaired and one new airplane. At the beginning of 1923 they were delivered in a dismantled condition to Petrograd, and the British pilot McRosty accompanied this delivery. He provided oversight of the airplanes' assembly, and also carried out training of the Soviet pilots. These aircraft were designated T-4 and T-5.

Since the OTB did not have their own pilots, an agreement was reached with the military. The aforementioned L.I. Giksa and I.P. Antoshin underwent conversion training (the latter at that time was the commander of the 1st Fighter Air Squadron). The T-4 aircraft took to the skies on 26 May, and the T-5 on 31 May. Since the airplanes were single-seat, the instructor would lie at the student's feet in flight.

The mechanics were also borrowed from the military: Gurskiy, Kuznetsov and Chernokozhin served in the 1st Separate Air Unit.

The first flight for a test drop of a mock torpedo using a parachute was performed by Giksa from the T-5 on 14 July. The mock up landed on the Komendantskiy airfield, where the OTB hangar stood. On 17 July Antoshin made a similar drop from the T-4. On 23 September Antoshin carried out the first torpedo drop onto water; this took place close to the Yelagin lightship. On 26 September he repeated this operation successfully.

In summer 1924 one of the Hanleys (the T-5) was involved in an accident but was repaired. In course of the repair which was performed at the Leningrad (Petrograd had been renamed Leningrad following the death of V.I. Lenin) *Krasniy Lyotchik* factory in October of the same year, the biplane was converted into a two-seater (with a second cockpit arranged for the test engineer). The shift in the centre of gravity position was balanced by lengthening the engine mounts. Subsequently the second torpedo bomber was similarly modified.

Comparative testing with drops onto water of the reinforced type 1912 and type 1910/15 torpedoes enabled a conclusion to be reached in favour of the former. The type 1910/1915 torpedoes (which had been shortened and lightened, and originally designed for submarines) demonstrated lower strength and reliability characteristics.

The Hanleys continued to be tested up until 1926. The further tests continued using the German three-engine YuG-1 aircraft, and later using the indigenous TB-1 bombers. The modified type 1912 air-launched torpedo was accepted into service in 1930 under the designation TAN-12, and it was these torpedoes that were carried by the first Soviet TB-1a and R-5T torpedo bombers.

One of two Handley Page H.P.19 Hanley torpedo bombers sold to Russia.

Colour section 1

Color views by Andrey Yurgenson

NOT TO SCALE

Curtiss D which was based on cruiser *Kagul,* Black Sea Fleet, beginning of 1914.

Curtiss K flying boat of the Naval Pilots School, 1916.

Royal Aircraft Factory BE.2e reconnaissance airplane which was in service of the RKKVF.

NOT TO SCALE

Vickers FB.19 fighter of the Moscow Pilots School, summer 1919.

Sopwith 1½ Strutter of the Kuban Cossack Air Unit of Denikin's army.

Sopwith 1½ Strutter on ski undercarriage from the 1st Squadron of the Slavo-British Air Corps. The airplane was flown by pilot A.A. Kozakov, December 1918.

NOT TO SCALE

Sopwith 1½ Strutter of the 3rd Siberian Air Unit, Vagay station, October 1919.

Sopwith 1½ Strutter of the 3rd Reconnaissance Unit of the 5th Army, Eastern Front, Innokentyevskaya station near Irkutsk, summer 1920. The inscription on the fuselage reads 'The 1st of May Labor'.

De Havilland DH.4 reconnaissance airplane of the RKKVF, 1918.

NOT TO SCALE

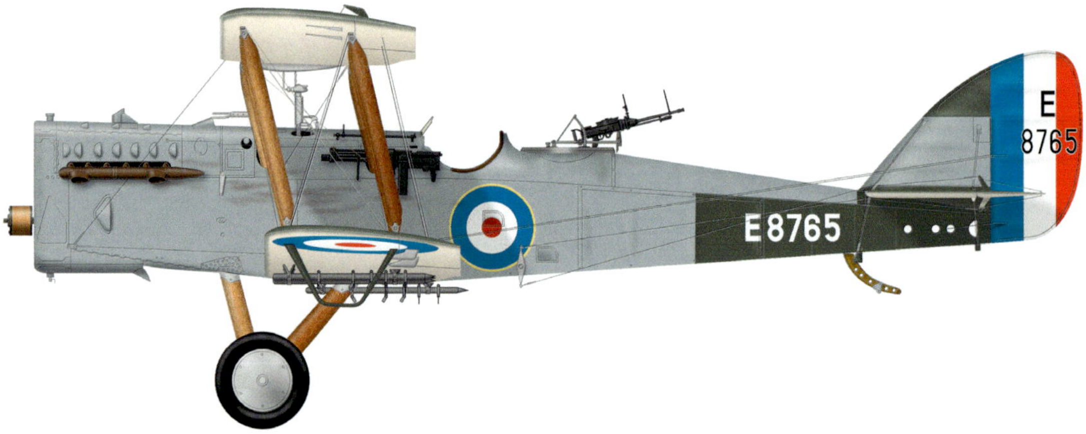

De Havilland DH.9A of the Slavo-British Air Corps, 1919.

A 'gift' DH.9A with the inscription 'The Poor Man of Odessa'. The aircraft belonged to the *Ilyich* Air Unit, summer 1924.

Martynside F.4 fighter during testing at the Scientific-Experimental Airfield (NOA) in Moscow, June 1924.

NOT TO SCALE

Martynside F.4 fighter which possibly belonged to the 7th Fighter Squadron, 1929.

One of Avro 504K trainers purchased in Britain. The inscription on the fuselage reads 'Chekist of Transportation System of Ukraine'.

A 'gift' U-1 trainer, Moscow Central airfield. The inscription on the fuselage reads 'The Woman Worker'. Caption:

NOT TO SCALE

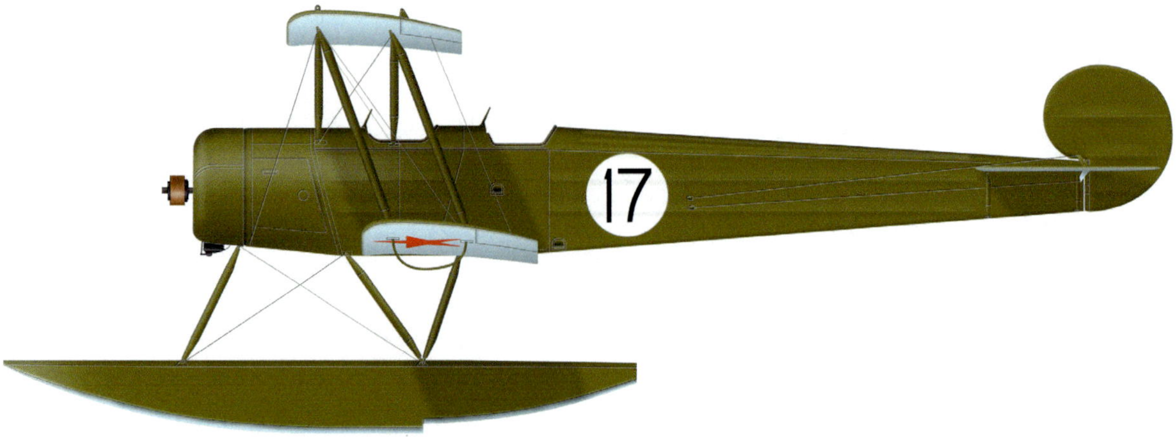

MU-1 training floatplane of the Naval Pilots School in Sevastopol.

One of R-1 airplanes (registration number R-RMPB, serial number 2733) which participated in the Great Eastern Long-range Flight on a route Moscow–Peking, 1925. The airplane was flown by pilot M.A. Volkovoynov and mechanic V.P. Kuznetsov.

R-1 airplane of the squadron 'Our Response to Chamberlain', Moscow, 1927.

NOT TO SCALE

The 'gift' R-1 of the 30th Squadron *Krasnaya Moskva* (Red Moscow) bearing the inscription 'The Red Khamovniki', May 1928.

R-1 of the 19th Separate Air Unit *Dalnevostochniy Ultimatum* (Far-Eastern Ultimatum) bearing the inscription 'The Working People of Amur', Grodekovo airfield, autumn 1929.

R-1 of the 2nd Unit of the 40th Squadron, with the inscription 'The Worker of the People's Commissariat of Food' and an order of the Red Banner, Far East, winter 1929-1930.

NOT TO SCALE

R-1 of the air brigade of the Air Force Academy, Moscow Central airfield, summer 1930. The inscription on the fuselage reads 'Moscow Textile. Union of Sewing Workers'.

R-1 of the 14th Military Pilots School, Engels, 1932.

MR-1 reconnaissance floatplane of the 64th Air Unit, Black Sea Fleet Air Force, Sevastopol, 1928.

NOT TO SCALE

MR-1 reconnaissance floatplane of the 68th Air Unit, Amur Military Flotilla. The airplane was based on barge *Amur*, October 1929.

MR-1 reconnaissance floatplane of the 68th Air Unit, Amur Military Flotilla, autumn 1929.

MR-1 reconnaissance floatplane of the 68th Air Unit, Amur Military Flotilla, autumn 1929.

NOT TO SCALE

MR-1 airplane (on ski undercarriage) of the 68th Air Unit, Amur Military Flotilla, December 1929.

The unarmed civil R-1 (P-1) trainer.

Fairey Firefly IIM fighter during testing at the NII VVS, 1933.

NOT TO SCALE

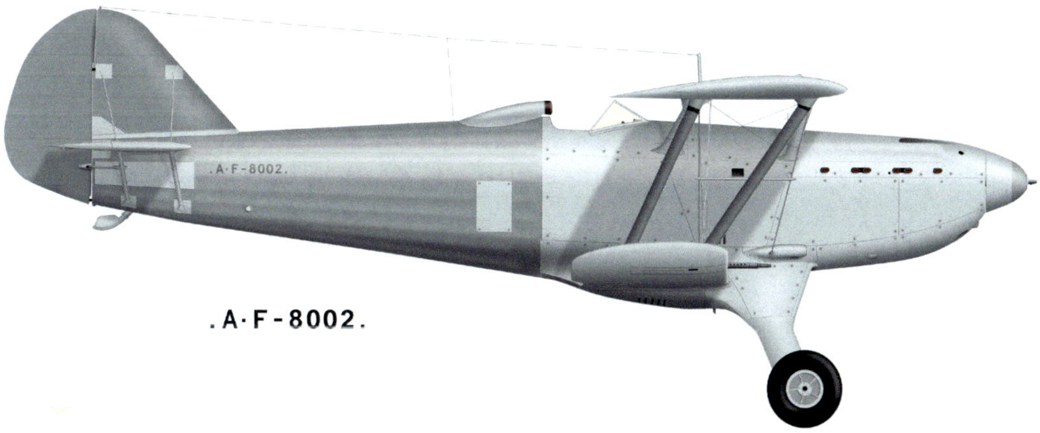

Fairey Fantôme fighter during testing at the NII VVS, spring 1936.

Fairey Fantôme fighter at the NII VVS, June 1938.

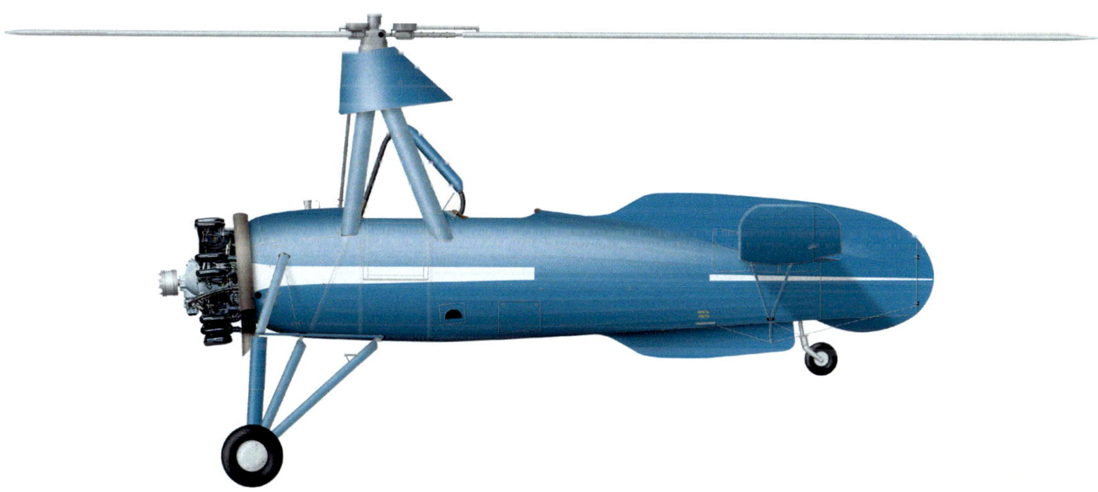

Avro C.30A autogyro during testing at the NII VVS, autumn 1935.

NOT TO SCALE

Miles Hawk Trainer during testing at the NII VVS, summer 1937.

One of two Consolidated 17AF Fleetster airplanes in colors of Pacific Alaska Airways purchased by Soviet Union, Nome, February 1934. S.A. Levanevskiy flew this airplane to Chukotka.

3

British Aircraft in Russia in the 1930s

In the 1930s British aircraft found their way into the Soviet Union only as examples intended for study. The interest was in aircraft that had been seen at various shows and exhibitions. In August 1930 the Chairman of the Scientific Technical Committee of the UVVS N.P. Dubenskiy made a trip to Great Britain. He visited the Hawker, Westland and Fairey factories, and at the latter he was given a demonstration of the Firefly fighter, the pilot of which performed an impressive display of aerobatics. Dubenskiy was also given a ride in the Fairey IIIF reconnaissance biplane.

In early 1932 the leadership of the GVF put forward a proposal to acquire examples of foreign passenger aircraft. A list was drawn up that included airplanes from the USA, Britain, France, and Czechoslovakia. In Britain it was planned to acquire a Blackburn Nile flying boat as well as a de Havilland Moth biplane. In the interests of saving money, however, this entire list was rejected.

A good deal more attention was paid to military interests, and the Soviet leadership came to the conclusion that in order to accelerate the modernisation of fighter aviation it would be necessary to purchase licences for contemporary power plants, along with examples of the fastest fighters. Purchases were to be made in the USA, Britain, and France. Some half a million roubles in hard currency were allocated from the budget for this purpose. It was given a task to perform comprehensive testing for these aircraft and to introduce all the useful innovations discovered in these airplanes into the design of new Soviet fighters.

On 22 April 1932 a meeting was held at the office of the Deputy Head of UVVS S.A. Mezheninov, as a result of which there was prepared a list of airplanes that were recommended for purchasing. Top of this list were biplanes manufactured by the British Hawker company – the single-seat Fury and the two-seat Hart (in the heavy fighter version); and two of each were proposed to be acquired. In addition, the UVVS wanted to purchase one Vickers Jockey fighter monoplane. If the Hawker refuse to sell their aircraft, or if the British government ban this deal, the meeting recommended ordering the airplanes from the competitor – the Fairey company. The intention was to acquire the single-seat Firefly and the two-seat Fox biplanes (also in the fighter version) from this company.

The draft of the decree to be issued by the Committee for Defence indicated a shorter list, which was reduced in the interests of saving money – the Firefly, Fox, and Hart remained, with two of each to be ordered. Finally, a commission led by Head of the Red Army Armament Department M.N. Tukhachevskiy, which was set up to examine this issue, decreed that only the Firefly and Hart were to be purchased.

Hawker refused to sell a single example of the Hart fighter over concerns that it would be copied in the Soviet Union and production would begin without a licence. The negotiations were more successful when it came to the Firefly – in 1932 one such fighter arrived in Moscow and underwent a complete program of testing.

Since the beginning of 1932 command of the VVS RKKA began to get interested in foreign autogyros. As a result, in 1935 an example of the wingless Avro C.30A autogyro was acquired, which was tested and studied at the Department of Operations, Flight Testing and Refinements of the Central Aero and Hydrodynamics Institute (OELID TsAGI – *Otdel Ekspluatatsii, Lyotnikh Ispytaniy i Dovodki Tsentralnogo Aerogidrodinamicheskogo Instituta*) and at the NII VVS.

In the 1930s another Fairey fighter found its way to the Soviet Union. This was the all-metal Fantôme biplane, which had been developed under an order from the Belgian Government but which was not accepted into service in that country. Soviet representatives ordered two of these biplanes in December 1935. The airplanes were delivered safely to Leningrad in the autumn of the following year and were carefully studied at the NII VVS.

British aircraft was also reviewed in course of a variety of long-range flights and visits. Different models of de Havilland Moths were seen in the skies over the USSR more than once. In August–September 1935 a group of British parliamentarians visited Moscow in a twin-engine DH.84 Dragon. In that same year an Airspeed Courier flown by Air Vice Marshal A. Borton landed at the Moscow Central airfield.

In 1936 Aeroflot opened their first independent international route Moscow–Prague but there were no contemporary passenger airplanes in the GVF fleet. The flagship of the Soviet civil aviation was the outdated PS-9 (the ANT-9, which had been modified to fit two M-17 engines). The management of Aeroflot turned to the government with a proposal to acquire aircraft in Britain. This idea, however, was subject to fierce criticism over issues of prestige. This, for example, was what the Head of the VVS Ya.I. Alksnis wrote: 'We have to fly our own aircraft, it would be a shame for us to purchase airplanes in Britain for this purpose, which our enemies would not hesitate to use against us'. At the end the same PS-9 was put into service on the route, and on 31 August 1936 it made the first and only flight to Prague. No further flights to the Czechoslovak capital were made that year at all. Operations began on this route in 1937 and a DC-2 purchased in the USA flew on this service.

In the course of the Civil War a twin-engine wooden de Havilland Dragon biplane was captured from the Nationalists, and along with trophy German and Italian aircraft it was taken to the USSR and studied at the NII VVS. The fate of this airplane will be described later, in a section dedicated to the same biplanes captured in the Baltic.

Soviet delegations would regularly come to Britain, visiting airshows at Hendon, and they also visited scientific research organisations, aircraft design offices, and factories. For example, in 1937 Soviet specialists attended a closed (not open to the public and intended for potential clients) demonstration of aircraft at Hatfield airfield.

The single-engine Battle bomber had been of interest since the beginning of 1936, when its prototype designated the P.27/32 had still been under construction. The purchase of such airplane was incorporated into the program that had been approved under a decree issued by the Council of Labour and Defence (STO, *Sovet Truda i Oborony*) on 21 March 1936. An amount of 438,000 roubles in gold was allocated for this purpose, and on 27 April the Head of the Main Directorate of the Aviation Industry (GUAP, *Glavnoe Upravlenie Aviatsionnoi Promyshlennosti)* M.M. Kaganovich sent I.V. Stalin a draft governmental decree in respect of this acquisition. The British, however, refused to sell this aircraft.

Among the airplanes demonstrated at Hatfield at the end of July 1937 was the new light bomber that had been created by Fairey under the specification P.4/34. Having inspected this aircraft, the Head of the NII VVS N.N. Bazhanov wrote in his report: 'The aircraft is being offered for sale. Evidently, they have something better'. The aerodynamic shapes of the airplane were particularly highly regarded but the firing armament was considered weak and ineffective.

In autumn of 1937 the Soviet delegation which included P.V. Rychagov, S.P. Suprun, and the military attaché in London Chyorniy attended a demonstration of the new P.4/34 light bomber which was carried out by Fairey representatives at the company's airfield. This aircraft was inspected both on the ground and in the air. The monoplane received a positive assessment and it was recommended to Moscow that a single example of this type be acquired for familiarisation. This possibility was explored via the trade representation but was rejected due to a ban put in place by the Air Ministry. In July 1938, however, Fairey themselves approached the Soviet Embassy with a proposal to sell a licence for 62,000 UK pounds. The Directorate of Material and Technical Supply of the VVS RKKA objected – 'we are only interested in the power plant of the P-4 ... we would like to purchase one or two airplanes, no more'. The British flatly refused to sell the 'full-size' P.4/34 as it was just a prototype example. In July 1939 the engineering department of the trade representation in London reported that the company had proposed three variants: a licence for 50,000 UK pounds, a single Battle for 13,500 UK pounds, or a licence plus a Battle for 62,000 UK pounds. The Soviet side did not accept any of these. *Voeninzhener* (Military Engineer) Strekalov from the Foreign Procurement Department of the People's Commissariat for Defence wrote in August 1939: 'The Fairey Battle monoplane does not represent any value for the VVS in terms of its flight-performance characteristics, any purchase should be rejected'. Thus, the bomber was not purchased, and this may have been for the best as in the air combats of the Second World War the Battle proved to be completely mediocre.

The Soviet Union expressed an interest in another British bomber – the fast, twin-engine Blenheim. It had initially been included in the draft procurement plan at the beginning of 1936 as the Bristol 142 (which back then was an unarmed high-speed passenger aircraft). In the aforementioned decree issued by the STO on 21 March it was listed as a 'twin-engine Bristol bomber', for which 438,000 roubles had been assigned. Interestingly, at the time it did not strictly speaking exist as a bomber, the British Air Ministry had just issued an order for a series of these aircraft. Soviet representatives wanted to acquire one of such airplanes but they were not successful.

In 1939 the Soviet trade representation in London again approached Bristol with a proposal to acquire a single 'type 1938' monoplane (evidently this was a Blenheim IV) but the company refused to sell the airplane. In a letter of 23 August, the company put forward a counter-offer: they were prepared to supply a batch of 20 aircraft for 30,000 UK pounds each. As the Soviet side only wanted to purchase an airplane for familiarisation, they just did not need this number of Blenheims, so the deal was not done.

Subsequently the VVS encountered these bombers in the course of the Winter War against Finland in 1939–1940 and did not rate them highly. Soviet fighter pilots nicknamed them 'Blin-heims' (*Blin* is an euphemism for a strong swear word in Russian). Nevertheless, they acknowledged that the British bomber can break away from the I-15bis and even the new I-153s biplane fighters, especially at low altitude. The Soviet side did not manage to capture any of these Finnish aircraft though. Later, in June 1941 the Romanians flew Blenheims in Moldova and in the area around Odessa.

As a result, up until the end of the 1930s only two Fairey fighters, an C.30A autogyro, and a Hawk Trainer monoplane found their way into the Soviet Union.

3.1 Fairey Fighters

In spring 1932 the Soviet leadership came to a conclusion to acquire an example of the Fairey Firefly biplane fighter for review. The deal was drawn up through the London-based company ARCOS that belonged to the Soviet Union.

Soviet specialists had first encountered the Firefly three years earlier. A delegation, which had come to the airshow at Hendon in 1929, received an invitation to visit the Fairey factory in Hayes. On 1 August the group of Soviet aviators and journalists arrived at the company's premises. The owner of the company personally met them and made a tour of the workshops and the airfield. Among the demonstrated aircraft was the Fairey Firefly. The well-known test pilot M.M. Gromov paid particular attention to this biplane, characterising it as an 'advanced machine'.

The impressions of the engineer Kvitko, who had attended the airshow in Hendon, are of interest: 'Much of the public attention was drawn to the flights performed by one aircraft, the Fairey Firefly. This biplane had arrived from Belgium, where it was in service, and the company's test pilot flew this machine'. Kvitko was also in touch with representatives of Fairey company, so he came to the conclusion that '... it is certain that the Fairey company ... is exceptionally interested in securing our order'.

Subsequently, this fighter was demonstrated to the Soviet representatives several times both in Britain and in Belgium. For example, in August 1932 a military delegation (which included the Deputy Head of the NII VVS A.K. Auzan) during a tour around Europe familiarised themselves with the Firefly at the factory in Britain, as well as at the Avions Fairey branch in Gosselies, Belgium, and at the airfield in Charlerois where two Belgian squadrons, equipped with these biplanes, were based. Auzan wrote: 'The Firefly and Fury airplanes appeared two years ago, and only now have we acquired a single example – the Firefly.' Negotiations with the company had in fact concluded successfully, the Soviet Union had managed to acquire one fighter as an example.

On 24 October 1932 a Firefly IIM biplane fitted with a Kestrel IIS engine (this was also being manufactured for the Belgian Air Force) arrived in Moscow. This airplane had the registration number F1876. The delivery was accompanied by a whole group of Fairey employees led by P. van de Velde (who was born in Russia). It was proposed that assembly of the airplane and the following testing would be conducted

A Firefly IIM fighter during testing at the NII VVS, 1933.

A Fantôme fighter during testing at the NII VVS, spring 1936.

at the Moscow Central airfield. Interestingly, the British described the airfield as 'large but dirty, unkempt, and with a very poorly prepared surface'.

Assembly of the fighter was completed on 30 October but an error had been found in the levelling of the biplane – the port side wing box was inclined lower than the right one. Then, deteriorating weather conditions interrupted the flying, and only on 2 November the British test pilot S. Trower did perform the first demonstration flight. After that the delivery tests began, and the last item in the test program – flying into a spin (with six rotations in each direction) was completed on 4 November. The following day I.F. Kozlov of the NII VVS flew the Firefly. On 7 November the British returned home.

The British airplane was tested at the NII VVS, then at the OELID TsAGI, and again at the NII VVS. Before the last series of tests, the biplane had spent some time at Factory No.39 where its design was carefully studied. The feedback on the airplane was benevolent: 'in terms of its structure and its manufacture the airplane is of great interest to us, and has a number of items that could be adopted into Soviet aircraft production'.

On 19 May 1933 Factory No.39 handed over the aircraft to the NII VVS, and on the same day pilot V.A. Stepanchyonok made the first flight. On 26 May, however, as it was taxiing the airplane hit the wheel tracks left by the TB-3 heavy bomber, and broke the propeller. It was being repaired till 22 June at Factory No.28, and flights then resumed. The reports mention that the Firefly was stable, easy to fly, and would recover benignly from a spin. The rate of climb of the British airplane exceeded the characteristic of all Soviet fighters. In terms of speed at low-level it conceded slightly to the I-5, but Soviet aircraft fell far short of the Firefly at all other altitudes. The fighter demonstrated excellent manoeuvrability and handling at altitude. The report stated: ' ... this is a formidable opponent'. Furthermore, according to the data both from the NII and from TsAGI the fighter's take-off weight turned out to be more than that claimed by the company, and correspondingly the performance characteristics were below than stated.

At the altitudes lower than 5,000m the turn time of the Fairey was greater than of the I-5 but above this altitude they did match up and the British fighter began to surpass the Soviet counterpart in manoeuvrability. All this

Testing of the Fantôme began in March 1936 on a ski undercarriage.

seems understandable taking into account the differences in the concepts for these two biplanes (a general-purpose manoeuvrable fighter and an interceptor), as well as the performances of the M-22 engine on the I-5 (a copy of the French Gnome-Rhone 9Aq Jupiter VI) and the Firefly's Kestrel (which was optimised for significantly greater altitudes and supplied with a supercharger).

Specialists of the NII VVS noted convenient maintenance arrangements on the British biplane. The engine cowlings ensured easy access to the power plant units, and a set of hatches enabled inspection, and where necessary, adjustment of the fighter's controls. Positioning of the instruments in the pilot's cockpit was rated highly, as was the comfort of the pilot's seat. High attention was paid to the cockpit heating system, which was absent on indigenous airplanes. The report stated: 'the cockpit heating system is so good that it enables flight at an altitude of 7,000m at ambient temperatures of -18 to -20 degrees wearing a summer flying suit. Such heating ... makes it possible to feel free when dressed in light flying gear, which does not restrict a pilot's movements'.

Mock air combats between the Firefly and the Soviet I-5 biplane were included in the NII VVS test program. The description of the first combat, which took place on 1 July 1935 stated: 'The manoeuvrability of the Firefly is worse than the I-5 but due to its speed it attacks from the vertical plane. With an altitude advantage over the I-5, it attacks at high vertical angles, which forces the I-5 to keep flying at a slow speed so it can not make use of its small turn radius. An attack from above caused the I-5 to stall and lose altitude in an attempt to confront the enemy's attack, which enables the enemy aircraft to carry out tail-on attacks several times. The Firefly's high speed in a dive enables it to regain altitude quickly and to repeat the attack as it exits a loop or a roll. At 4,000m altitude the I-5 was at a complete disadvantage. At 1,500m altitude the initiative was with the I-5 but the Firefly in a head-on attack developed a high speed, and departing in the climb, gained an altitude advantage. After this the combat again reverted to the vertical plane, and the Firefly took the initiative. The Firefly exits the combat in a dive while the I-5 immediately trails behind and is not able to open fire accurately.'

The outcome of this familiarisation with the Firefly was an additional argument in favour of developing indigenous high-speed fighters, for which the tactic of air combat in the verticals was the optimum consideration.

The information on the date when the only Soviet Firefly was written off has not yet been found in the records.

In early 1934 Fairey company suggested the Soviet Union to design and manufacture a single-seat fighter having a speed of 430km/h but with the proviso that no less than 30 examples would be purchased. A two-seat fighter with a speed of 350km/h and minimum quantity of six was also proposed. The negotiations started but a few days later the British announced that Air Ministry had banned any work on a single-seat airplane. The proposal for a two-seat airplane was repeated, having clarified the price of 3,965 UK pounds for each of the six examples. The speed of 350km/h was not guaranteed, however, and was dependent on the engine type chosen (with an output of no less than 860hp) – with a Kestrel engine the speed was set at 340km/h. This two-seat fighter was evidently a variant of the well-known Fairey Fox.

On 27 November 1934 this proposal was discussed at the UVVS and it was concluded that the aircraft would not meet the fighter requirements of the VVS. The main concern was that the speed was very low. The meeting protocol, however, contained the recommendation to acquire 10 examples of the type for study. The money for this though was not allocated by the Kremlin.

In the mid-1930s another Fairey fighter nevertheless ended up in the Soviet Union, the Fantôme. In July 1935 it was demonstrated to a Soviet aviation delegation in Britain. They were told that the biplane had been manufactured by the company's Belgian branch to the Belgian Air Force requirements and had an Hispano-Suiza engine (it later emerged that the Belgians had rejected this aircraft). In December of that same year Soviet representatives ordered two examples of this airplane. In total four Fantômes were produced, two of which were under the Soviet order.

Voeninzhener 1-go ranga (Military Engineer 1st rank) Grebenyov and Captain V.A. Stepanchyonok (who test flew the Firefly and who was at the time the military representative at Factory No.39) were directed from Moscow to accept these biplanes. They visited the Fairey factory in Hayes and also the factory of their sister company Avions Fairey in Gosselies (Belgium). It was the latter factory that was to assemble the biplanes from components supplied from Britain. The Fairey company changed the deadline for completing the order several times, setting 20 August as the final date. The state of the work was such, however, that Grebenyov and Stepanchyonok did not believe this, suggesting that the factory would not manage this before 1 September, and as it turned out they were right. Only at the beginning of November was Chris Staniland able to test fly both biplanes in Gosselies. The records have not been found whether Stepanchyonok was able to take part in these test flights.

According to the documents of Fairey company, the acquired Fantômes carried the designations F2264 and F2265. Photographs, however, show that the codes AF8001 and AF8002 were applied to the tail section of the airplanes. It is possible that Avions Fairey considered these fighters their own production and gave them its designations.

Following their official acceptance, the aircraft were dismantled once again, packed in crates and sent to the port. The steamer *Tovarishch Stalin* delivered them to Leningrad from where a train took the crates to Moscow. By the end of 1936 both fighters had arrived at the NII VVS.

The Fantômes produced for the Soviet Union differed in terms of their unusual armament, which was actually a combination of both Belgian versions – a 20mm Oerlikon S9 cannon, which had been manufactured under licence by Hispano company in France (with an ammunition load of 60 rounds), and four FN-Browning machine guns (two in the lower wing with an ammunition load of 300 rounds per gun and two in the fuselage with a load of 500 rounds each). This made the biplane much heavier and reduced its flight-performance characteristics. State testing was only carried out with one fighter – AF8002. The biplane was assembled and was put on a ski undercarriage, but it is not known whether this undercarriage was ordered in Britain or Belgium specially, or it was a unit borrowed from one of the Soviet fighters and modified to fit the Fantôme.

Whatever happened, the Fantôme made its first flights on a ski undercarriage. By 10 March seven flights had already been made. The leading pilot was Senior Lieutenant V. Yevseev, but P. Stefanovskiy, I. Petrov, P. Fedrovi, Altynov, A. Nikashin, and A. Nikolaev also participated in the test flights. In total 59 flights were undertaken (of which 35 were on ski undercarriage) with a total duration of 26 hours 25 minutes. Testing had been completed by June 1937.

The flight-performance characteristics turned out to be much lower than those obtained on tests with the first prototype in Britain. The maximum speed, even on wheeled undercarriage, reduced by approximately 60km/h, and the service ceiling was lower by 2,000m. This can be attributed partly to the increased flight weight (by approximately 200kg) as well as removing the cowlings from the wheels.

The view from below on the engine mount of the Fantôme with the cowlings removed.

The overall conclusion of the NII VVS report was as follows: 'The Fairey Fantôme airplane, in terms of its flight-performance characteristics, is already an obsolete fighter compared to contemporary fighters of the same class in service with foreign air forces.' At the same time Soviet pilots rated the landing and take-off characteristics and the piloting qualities of the Fantôme highly – this biplane was accessible to pilots with an average level of qualification. In contrast to its predecessor the Firefly, this fighter did not have a tendency to inadvertently enter a spin when the control stick was pulled too much in a turn.

Pilots remarked on the excellent field of view from the cockpit, and the comfortable and reliable pneumatic brakes. In general, the design of the fighter and its equipment were of greater interest to Soviet specialists than the flight-performance characteristics of the Fantôme. The report stated: 'the design of all the parts of the biplane and its power plant ensures their long and trouble-free operation'. The

The Fantôme with removed metal panels which covered the engine and the cockpit.

biplane's convenient layout, positioning of the equipment and armament, easy detachable cowlings, and the design of the wing load bearing structure were especially highlighted. It was proposed to use on the Soviet airplanes the design of the inter-wing struts and wires attachment, of the undercarriage legs, of the rudder and aileron control mechanism, of the wheel brakes, and the way the canvass was attached to the fuselage.

In contrast to Soviet fighters, the engine units were attached to the engine and to the engine frame, ensuring that the entire unit could be quickly removed when necessary. The positioning of the radiator inside the duct was of interest. The experiments were carried out with the Fantôme's cooling system, attempting to get it to operate on water instead of ethylene-glycol, but it turned out that this change can only take place at ambient temperatures at ground level of no higher than +10 degrees Celsius. After that the engine would overheat.

The specialists liked the British Superflex flexible fuel-feed hoses, the oxygen system with electric heating, and the convenient backlighting of the instruments.

It should be noted that the composition of the equipment in the Fantômes supplied to the USSR did not correspond to the originally agreed one. It was established that the fighter should have been fitted with coded three-coloured lights, heating system for the machine guns and pitot tube but all this was missing. The armament was of high interest, but the machine guns had not been tested. They were made not for the Soviet 7.62mm or the British 7.69mm cartridge, but for the 7.65mm one accepted in Belgium. No cartridges of this calibre were available at the NII VVS, and evidently nobody had thought of ordering them along with the biplane. The cannon, however, was fired at the firing range. On the ninth shot the Oerlikon shell exploded in the breach, so the breach, magazine, and the biplane itself were damaged. The cannon was not repaired, and the armament specialists noted that its operation was complicated and inconvenient.

The process of the machine guns setting to armed position and their firing was achieved using a pneumatic system, and the pilot was able to pull back on all the bolts and release them simply and easily. On the Soviet fighters of that time the cable mechanisms were used, so firing four machine guns required significant efforts, not to mention pulling back on the bolts and releasing them. Even the synchroniser drive on the Fantôme was not mechanical but pneumatic.

Testing concluded with mock combats against Soviet aircraft, and the adversaries included the I-16 fighter with M-25 engine, prototype of R-9 reconnaissance airplane, and the TsKB-30 bomber (which was put into series production under the DB-3 designation). It was tough for the Fantôme in combat with them as all these new aircraft surpassed it in terms of speed. It was unable to enforce combat neither to the I-16 nor to the R-9. The I-16 had the initiative and could choose to either attack or break away and could freely do one or the other. The Fantôme won over this type somewhat in the horizontal plane due to its tighter turning radius but it was completely helpless in a vertical manoeuvre.

The British fighter tried to combat the R-9 in the turns but after opening the throttle it would simply move away. Even the DB-3 could evade the Fantôme. The only way to engage it in combat was by adopting an advantageous position. At that, the Fantôme could make head-on attack on the Ilyushin bomber, but it could only be done in a single pass, as the British fighter was not able to catch up the adversary after the attack. The Fantôme's pilot just had to hope that the powerful cannon and machine-gun armament would enable him to shoot the enemy down in a single attack.

Following the conclusion of testing a demonstration was carried out of the British fighter at a number of factories so as to familiarise designers and production managers with the Fantôme's most interesting units and components. Study of the biplane's armament and equipment was continued as well.

As of 1 April 1938, NII VVS documents list single Fairey fighter in an unserviceable condition. No further details are known about these two biplanes.

3.2 Testing an Autogyro

During the mid-1930s one C.30A autogyro was acquired by the Soviet Union and underwent testing in the country. It all started with a letter that was written in January 1932 by the Head of the IV (Reconnaissance) Department of the RKKA command Ya.K. Berzin and addressed to the Head of the VVS Ya.I. Alksnis. This letter contained an extract from a report received from military intelligence agent in the USA stating that he had observed a landing of an 'auto-gyro' on the site of a railway goods yard. Alksnis became interested in this unusual flying machine and suggested attempting to purchase an example of one.

The corresponding task was given to the Amtorg Trading Corporation (*Amtorg* is short for *Amerikanskaya Torgovlya*, or American Trade) which was the first trade representation of the Soviet Union in the United States, registered as an American company with Soviet capital. Amtorg found a company that was selling an autogyro. Most likely, this was Kellett or Pitcairn companies – they both produced such flying machines under licence from the British Cierva Autogiro Company. The Americans, however, did not have the rights to export autogyros and recommended approaching the manufacturer in Britain. On 1 February 1932 the Deputy People's Commissar for Defence M.N. Tukhachevskiy tasked the Foreign Department of the Commissariat with making enquiries in Britain. Through the staff of the Soviet military attaché in London, there was made an approach to the Avro company, which was manufacturing the autogyro created by the Spanish designer Juan de la Cierva.

A C.30A autogyro during testing at the NII VVS, autumn 1935.

Protracted negotiations began, of which the author was not able to find any documentary evidence. Evidently, initially the talks were aimed at purchasing a C.19 autogyro but a short while later the more advanced C.30A type emerged, being a so-called 'jumping' autogyro. This aircraft had a drive for spinning the rotor blades, allowing it to make a vertical 'jump' on about six meters. In August 1934 Soviet specialists reviewed this autogyro at an aviation exhibition in Copenhagen. The report of Soviet delegation stated: 'The exhibited C.30 autogyro is of high interest in terms of its design – an autogyro without wings or control surfaces, offering a series of advantages in terms of simplicity of control and operation.' The decision was taken to acquire a single example of the C.30A.

This example was not purchased for the VVS but for study at TsAGI. A commission was sent to Britain which included Professor A.M. Cheryomukhin, engineer A.M. Izakson, and test pilot S.A. Korzinshchikov. In the USSR they were all involved with helicopters and autogyros development.

The British autogyro was accepted at the Avro factory and was then dismantled, crated up, and sent by sea to Leningrad. This was a civil C.30A version fitted with a Genet Major radial engine. Cheryomukhin and Korzinshchikov took a course in Britain on how to fly a rotary-winged aircraft. At the beginning of 1935 the autogyro arrived at the OELID TsAGI. There it was subjected to careful study, and a cycle of flight tests was carried out.

Following this, in September of that same year the type was handed over to the NII VVS, and there the C.30A underwent the full program of state testing. The aim of this was to define the actual flight-performance characteristics and to assess the potential for a military application. *Voeninzhener 2-go ranga* (Military Engineer 2nd rank) A.A. Ivanovskiy flew the autogyro accompanied by different pilot-observers – Shaurov, Nikitin, and Shishkin. In total from 25 September till 4 October there were completed some 38 flights at the NII VVS with a total duration of 14 hrs and 10 mins.

The flight-performance characteristics of the aircraft in general corresponded to those claimed by the company.

Given a take-off weight of 860kg, the C.30A had a maximum speed at the ground level of 164.5km/h, and it took 62.5 mins to climb to an altitude of 3,000m. The service ceiling was set at 3,050m, and the take-off run took 11 seconds (95m distance), while the landing roll lasted up to two seconds (up to 3m distance). The report stated: 'it allows to perform steep descents and landing almost without a landing roll'. The autogyro was able to land on a spot 100x100m in size.

The pilot reported that piloting the autogyro had its own specifics but overall it did not present any difficulties. The majority of the testing was aimed at studying the autogyro capabilities as a short-range reconnaissance, artillery-spotting, and liaison aircraft. Furthermore, it was being constantly compared with light airplanes, and in the end the conclusion was reached that an airplane was more capable of performing these missions. Any military application of the autogyro was considered as very limited. They could be tasked with reconnaissance of routes to be used by transport columns, checking the camouflage of the objects in the rear, as well as liaison flights.

The flight-performance characteristics of the autogyro were also compared with those of a Soviet A-7 winged autogyro. This aircraft had been designed specially for the military application and was considered to be superior to the C.30A.

The C.30A was returned to OELID TsAGI where different aspects of the behaviour of a wingless autogyro in flight were studied. The results of this research were subsequently used in the development of the similar Soviet A-12 autogyro.

On two occasions the C.30A was involved in serious accidents. In one case the autogyro unexpectedly turned over and rolled in flight. As a result, it lost altitude and hit the ground. Both crewmembers survived but the C.30A was seriously damaged. Flights resumed following repairs, and the autogyro turned over a second time being flown by the pilot Ivanovskiy at an altitude of 30m. The pilot, who was not strapped in, fell out. He was lucky, he missed the rotor blades and fell into a deep snowdrift on the edge of the airfield. The autogyro, however, was severely damaged and the question was raised over it being written off. It was decided though that it would be repaired, and after that the aircraft flew once again.

Soviet helicopter designer Mikhail Mil studied this incident carefully and came to the conclusion that the autogyro had insufficient lateral stability. Given a strong sideslip the pilot had not been able to correct the banking, which led to the accident.

In July 1939 it was planned to test a new rotor on the C.30A, which was designed for the A-10 autogyro. In December of that year a proposal was examined to modify the autogyro in order to shorten the take-off run. In the autumn of 1941, as German forces were approaching Moscow, the British autogyro along with other equipment from the Flight Testing Institute (LII, *Lyotno-Ispytatelniy Institut*), which had replaced OELID, was moved to the east. It is not known when this example of the C.30A was written off.

3.3 The Hawk for the Head of the VVS RKKA

In February 1937 an example of the Miles Hawk Trainer two-seat training airplane was acquired in Britain. This was a small cantilever wing monoplane with fixed undercarriage. In the summer of that year the Hawk Trainer serial number 480 underwent testing at the NII VVS. The leading test pilot was K.A. Kalilets, and the flight-observer was P.I. Nikitin. The test flying was also performed by other pilots – I.F. Petrov, P.M. Stefanovskiy, M.A. Lipkin, M.A. Nyukhtikov, and the Head of the NII VVS Division Commander N.N. Bazhanov.

In total 76 flights were performed with a total duration of 17 hrs 2 mins, including 45 mins in the inverted position. The point being that the airplane had special equipment to allow this, which was considered simple and original by the Soviet specialists. Senior Lieutenant V.N. Yevseev was entrusted with inverted flying the airplane.

The results recorded in course of testing conceded slightly to those claimed by the company. For example, the speed did not exceed 206 km/h; the airplane took 6 mins to reach an altitude of 1,000m, and 21 mins to reach 3,000m. The take-off run was 265m and the landing run 330m. In fact, use of the flaps reduced the latter to 200m and applying the brakes took it down to 130m.

The test pilots remarked on a series of advantages with this British airplane. The NII VVS report stated: 'The airplane has excellent stability (lateral, longitudinal, and directional) and is easy and simple to fly. It enables flight with the pilot's hands off the control stick'. The pilots liked the reliable and effective brakes, the wing-folding system, the flaps with hydraulic actuator, and a special hood for training the instrument flying.

The two-seat Hawk could be converted into a single-seat version just in 10 minutes – the windscreen in the front cockpit was removed and it was enclosed with a metal cover.

However, in general, the results of this aircraft assessment were quite low. 'In terms of its flight-performance characteristics the Miles Hawk does not hold any interest, as it concedes to airplane No.10 designed by engineer Yakovlev in this respect [*In series production it was manufactured under UT2 designation – Author's note*]. The flight-performance characteristics, particularly with respect to the maximum speeds at the ground level, differ from those provided by the company'.

The only useful thing that was derived from the testing of the Hawk was the study of the equipment for inverted flight. It differed advantageously from an analogous system mounted on a Czech Avia BH-122 airplane, which had also been studied at the NII VVS. The Czech system was more complicated but enabled the airplane to fly inverted for up to half an hour (for the Hawk this figure was 12 minutes). This

A Miles Hawk Trainer at the NII VVS, summer 1937.

Following testing at the NII VVS, the Hawk was handed over to the special-purpose squadron, to the personal flight of the Head of the VVS. This flight was deployed at the Moscow Central airfield, and several different types of aircraft – fighters, reconnaissance airplanes and trainers – both indigenous and foreign, were kept in a special hangar. The planes were intended to support the piloting skills of the Head of the VVS. On some of these aircraft he would fly off to inspect VVS units or to attend manoeuvres. The Head of the VVS did not always fly these airplanes himself, as seconded military pilots would occasionally perform this duty. It is not known whether Army Commander 2nd rank Ya.I. Alksnis managed to fly the Hawk, but he was always keen to try a new aircraft. In November 1937 Alksnis was arrested as a 'people's enemy', while Corps Commander A.D. Loktionov who replaced him did not demonstrate this same passion for flying. When the Hawk was written off is not known.

fact, however, was explained by the difference in purpose of these two aircraft – if the Hawk was mostly a training aircraft capable of aerobatics, then the BH-122 was originally designed as a highly specialised aircraft for demonstrating aerobatic skills.

A small number of production UT-1 airplanes were subsequently converted for inverted flight using the Hawk system as the template, and they were used during aviation parades and events.

The hood for the rear cockpit, which was intended to train pilots in instrument flying, was also borrowed from the British aircraft for the UT-2 two-seat trainer. There was an attempt to copy the wheels with their successful design of mechanical brakes. Samples of them were produced at Factory No.120 but during testing they proved not to be strong enough.

4

American Aircraft in Russia in the 1930s

The United States did not recognise Soviet Russia for a long time and formally the reason was the Soviet Government's refusal to repay loans from the pre-October revolution period. The Americans did trade though – the country was a huge market and they did not want to lose it.

In May 1924 the Amtorg Corporation was registered in the USA, which performed the functions of a trade mission. Soviet raw materials were sold through Amtorg, whilst machines and equipment were acquired in return, including those intended for the aviation industry.

In terms of the level of its development, in the 1920s the American aviation still lagged behind that of the leading European countries. As a result, aviation equipment purchased in the USA was limited to Liberty engines (both new and used ones), parts and units for them (which were used in the production of the M-5 engine – the Soviet copy of the Liberty), as well as components for the oil and fuel systems, and samples of instruments and other equipment. At the end of the decade orders were also placed in the USA for undercarriage semi-axles, manufactured from a compound steel, for the TB-1 bombers, I-4 fighters and R-5 reconnaissance aircraft.

By the end of the 1920s interest began to grow in the Soviet Union towards the original American aircraft and engine designs, as well as the organisation of the aviation industry, the new technologies, and the methods of operating aircraft in military and civil aviation. In response various companies in the USA began to offer their own products, both for civil and military purposes.

These mutually beneficial contacts gave rise to a powerful backlash from the US State Department and the entire administration under President H. Hoover. The latter objected categorically to any links with the 'godless Bolsheviks', even more so in such an important field as aviation. Attempts to acquire materiel for a military purpose provoked an especially coarse reaction. The Soviet side usually made these acquisitions through intermediaries, often under the cover of purchasing companies that had been set up fictitiously.

For example, in June 1929 the People's Commissariat for Military and Naval Affairs through the People's Commissariat for Trade held talks with the Curtiss company about acquiring examples of Condor aircraft in the bomber version fitted with Conqueror engines, several types of Hawk fighters fitted with a variety of engines (including one naval version), and the Curtiss Falcon reconnaissance and training airplane with a Challenger engine. All the initial attempts at purchasing military aircraft in the USA, however, were unsuccessful. The dealings with the Glenn Martin company ended in a furious row. In winter 1929 this company had proposed supplying the VVS RKKA with a batch of twin-engine flying boats – the short-range naval reconnaissance aircraft. The project that had been prepared by Martin designers was modified taking into account the technical requirements that had been forwarded from Moscow. In terms of its flight-performance characteristics this all-metal flying boat surpassed somewhat the wooden Savoia-Marchetti S.62bis biplane, which the Italian competitors were offering. It should have had a greater payload and better seaworthiness characteristics. An outline agreement was drawn up for the acquisition of 20 flying boats (at 50,000 US Dollars each) and a licence for their production in the USSR. However, when in July 1930 the company enquired unofficially at the State Department about the possibility of draft permission to export these hydroplanes it provoked a coarse reaction: 'Military aircraft, to Soviet Russia? Never!'. Afraid of a public disclosure both Martin and Amtorg began to completely deny the fact of these negotiations. In the Russian archives an entire file has survived of the plans to 'cover up this deal'. The story, however, did find its way to the papers and the affair reached President Hoover, who was a fierce anti-communist. He immediately banned any fulfilment of this order. The Italians were the winners in all this as they sold 52 flying boats to the VVS RKKA as well as a licence for their production, and a large batch of Isotta Fraschini Asso 500 engines.

A little later, in December 1929 a Soviet aviation delegation arrived in the USA led by the Head of the UVVS P.I. Baranov. The group included the Head of the Foreign Department of the UVVS M.A. Feldman, the Chairman of the Scientific-Technical Committee of the UVVS N.M. Kharlamov, and the well-known aircraft designer A.N. Tupolev, as well as engine designers B.S. Stechkin and B.V.

The Soviet aviation delegation led by A.N. Tupolev (on the right) in the USA.

Urmin, and other specialists. Baranov tried to reach an agreement on setting up a holding company in the USSR using joint capital to produce Curtiss-Wright aircraft and engines. Prior to this, in mid-October the Vice-President of Curtiss-Wright, Morgan, had visited Moscow and negotiations got underway with him on setting up a joint enterprise. Morgan, however, did not make any firm promises at the time, and in America Baranov touched on this topic once again. Aside from holding these talks the delegation visited several aircraft manufacturing enterprises. Baranov also spoke to a number of American specialists, discussing the question of the possibility of establishing an air service between Russia and America via the Bering Strait.

Apart from that, during the course of their stay in America the delegation selected an aircraft type with which to equip so-called 'special units' of *Dobrolyot* society in Kamchatka, which were semi-civil and semi-military formations. The aircraft and the personnel were the part of the *Dobrolyot* but took their orders from Joint State Political Directorate units. The functions of these special units were to encompass coastal patrols, searching for Japanese ships that were poaching for fish in Soviet waters, supplying remote border posts and ensuring links between border guard units, so to perform the functions of the coastal and border aviation.

Baranov chose the Keystone-Loening K-84 Commuter amphibian for these special units – it was comparatively small biplane flying boats of mixed construction with a Wright J6 engine. On 13 January 1930 he wrote to Moscow: 'During a visit to the Loening-Keystone factory in Bristol I familiarised myself with the designs and the production of amphibious aircraft and came to the conclusion that these very amphibians would be the most desirable aircraft type for our purposes, both for passenger services in the Far East, and especially for costal protection'. Baranov based his choice on the possibility of operating these aircraft from the shore and from water on a wheeled and a ski undercarriage, and the experience of using similar amphibians in Alaska and northern Canada, as well as the possibility of weapons installation on the aircraft. The civil air fleet in the USSR at the time was almost completely controlled by the military and their opinion, naturally, was decisive.

Each of the three planned special units was to receive four Commuters. Following Baranov's departure negotiations were undertaken with the company, and the agreement was reached on the purchase of 16 amphibians (extra four were ordered as a reserve) at 30,650 roubles in gold each. In total, including the spare parts, packaging and other items the cost was 518,298 roubles. The aircraft were to be handed over in three batches (of eight, four, and further four airplanes) in 1931. The acquisition of the Commuters was included in the draft procurement plan of imported aircraft drawn up by *Dobrolyot* for the 1929–1930 financial year (as an advance had to be paid), and this was then transferred into the plan for the 1930–1931 financial year.

After the detailed information on the design and characteristics of the amphibians had been received, however, doubts began to arise among *Dobrolyot* specialists regarding the aircraft suitability to perform the roles that had been

Members of the Soviet delegation inspect one of the Northrop airplanes.

assigned to it. On 20 July 1930 the STO declined the request to assign currency to purchase these aircraft from Keystone–Loening. Some time later the funds for the purchase in America were allocated nevertheless but they were spent on purchasing Wright engines for the ANT-9 passenger aircraft.

For civil aviation Baranov also suggested acquiring 30 Travel Air 6000B aircraft, and five Curtiss Robins. In this period, it was proposed that examples of several different types of aircraft be purchased in the USA for study – a fighter from Boeing, a reconnaissance aircraft from Douglas, and a training aircraft from Fleet. Initially, however, the Soviets encountered a problem with a shortage of hard currency, and then resistance from the state apparatus in the USA. Therefore, nothing was actually purchased.

The constant friction with the US State Department led to a significant drop in trade between the Soviet Union and the USA. As a result, on 7 September 1931, the Soviet Government issued a decree to stop placing orders in America. In reality this probably did not last long but it certainly did have an influence on contacts in every sphere, including aviation.

In this period the Soviet side was applying its efforts mainly in the field of civil aviation. At the end of 1931 and the start of 1932, an overseas voyage was undertaken by a delegation from the All-Union Association of the GVF, which was led by Chief Inspector I.S. Silin. Members of the delegation visited airfields and factories and made several flights on regular air routes. They familiarised themselves with aircraft, engines, airfield equipment, and organisation of the passenger services. Silin also attempted to purchase at auction a batch of used aircraft produced by Lockheed (five Orions and two Vegas). The Moscow office though refused

Soviet aviation engineers at an airfield in the USA.

to allocate the money he was asking (50,000 roubles in hard currency).

Silin also tried to find an airline in America that was ready to take a concession on the air route Kharkov–Sochi–Tiflis (now Tbilisi). The total cost of this project was estimated to be five million roubles. It was proposed that Soviet ANT-9 aircraft (with American engines) would be operating on this route, and various equipment for supporting the operation would be imported from the USA. Personnel were to have comprised of half Russians and half Americans. Silin, however, did not find a company that wanted to take this on.

After returning to Moscow the delegation made the proposals to acquire licences and technical support in America for Wright engines, Hamilton propellers, and Bendix brake wheels. The two first points were subsequently brought to fruition.

In June 1932 the Americans, in their turn, proposed establishing an airline on Soviet territory. These discussions concerned a sector of the projected route New York–Peking–Manila. The Curtiss-Wright Corporation wanted to establish

The airplane flown by pilot James Mattern that crashed in Chukotka.

this route to bypass Japan, running through Anadyr and Khabarovsk. In connection with the strategic importance of this route the American Government supported this project and were ready to allocate a financial subsidy. The aforementioned Vice-President Morgan was conducting the negotiations through Amtorg. The Soviet Union just had to allocate sites for intermediate airfields and the Americans took responsibility for everything else. It was planned that the American aircraft would make two or three flights a week. The negotiations were not successful, the Soviet side insisted on joint operation of the route and Curtiss-Wright did not go for it.

At the beginning of 1932 the Main Directorate of the Civil Air Fleet (GU GVF, *Glavnoe Upravlenie Grazhdanskogo Vozdushnogo Flota*) attempted to secure an allocation of funds to purchase examples of contemporary passenger aircraft abroad. It was planned to purchase the 10-seat Fairchild 100 Pilgrim and the high-speed Lockheed Orion monoplane in the USA. The government, however, did not offered any funds for this.

The Soviet military were no more successful. The aforementioned commission under Chairman M.N. Tukhachevskiy in April 1932 suggested purchasing examples of Boeing P-12F and Lockheed YP-24 fighters (two of each) in America for study. The commission received a letter from Boeing with the proposal for the first type. Despite the fact that the purchase has been approved by a decree from the Committee for Defence, in reality the American fighters were not purchased at that time.

Up until 1934 the American aircraft would only appear in the skies over Russia in passing, but this was happening relatively often. The point being that the most convenient route for round the world long-range flights passed through Russia. American actor J. Mears made the first round-the-world trip by plane. He crossed the oceans and seas on steamboats but was carried overland by a Fairchild monoplane flown by Captain Collyer. The aircraft flew via Konigsberg, Moscow, Kazan, Chita, Krasnoyarsk, and then flew on via Mukden in Manchuria.

American aviator Carl Eielson and mechanic Earl Borland died in an accident in Chukotka while attempting to evacuate furs and personnel from the *Nanuk*, a US cargo vessel trapped in the ice at North Cape. Their bodies and remains of Hamilton H-45 airplane were discovered on 18 February 1930 by Soviet rescue mission.

In June 1931 the one-eyed pilot Wiley Post and his navigator Harold Gatty, who had completed a round the world flight in their Lockheed Vega monoplane, flew via the Soviet Union and returned home via Alaska.

In 1932 the famous pilot James Mattern with his co-pilot Bennett Griffin attempted to fly around the world in a Lockheed Vega monoplane called 'The Century of Progress'. On 7 July, however, this flight ended in an accident during an emergency landing one kilometre away from Borisov in Belorussia. The pilot mistook a peat bog for a meadow and the aircraft ground-looped and was destroyed, Griffin was slightly injured and Mattern escaped with bruises. A commission arrived at the accident site led by the Senior Inspector of the GVF P.I. Machkov. The GU GVF tried to purchase the wreckage of the Vega for study purposes but they could not reach agreement with the Americans on a price. On 8 July the aircraft began to be dismantled and the following day it was sent to Moscow. From there it returned to the USA in crates.

Mattern, however, did not abandon his undertaking and the second time he flew alone. In June 1933 his new Vega made a stop in Moscow and was in need of light repairs, which were undertaken by NII VVS mechanics at the Central airfield. In the meantime, the aircraft was subjected to detailed study. When continuing the flight, despite an emergency landing in Prokopyevsk in Siberia, Mattern almost had reached Anadyr safely when his engine began to overheat. The undercarriage legs failed in a landing on a marsh. Only on a twelfth day the local Chukchi had found the monoplane and its pilot on the banks of the Anadyr River. A flying boat piloted by S.A. Levanevskiy delivered Mattern and the most valuable parts of his aircraft to Nome in Alaska.

In the same year Wiley Post flew another long-range flight via Soviet territory, also flying alone, but he had fitted Sperry autopilot in his aircraft. His flight was less rich in misfortune as the Mattern's and they, for the most part, were light-hearted in nature: in the village of Rykhlovo just outside Irkutsk, where he had asked for a drink following an emergency landing, the locals brought him a glass of vodka; in Khabarovsk a Red Army soldier, who was guarding the aircraft at the airfield, wrote on the side: 'Hello to the American People from the members of the Khabarovsk Komsomol'. Post set the record for a round the world flight of seven days, 18 hours and 50 mins.

In September–October 1933 the famous pilot Charles Lindberg visited Leningrad and Moscow in his Lockheed

Model 8 Sirius floatplane. At the time he was on a tour around Europe and had taken his wife along with him as a passenger.

Following the victory of Franklin Roosevelt in the presidential elections of 1933 the situation changed for the better. The Americans established diplomatic relations with the USSR, and the obstacles to export gradually began to be lifted. The only restriction was that purchasing materiel that was being supplied to the US armed forces was banned.

The acquisition of licences for American engines in 1934 was an important step, and according to the agreements the Soviet factories received examples of these engines, as well as the full set of documentation, and the description of the technological processes for manufacturing the Wright R-1820 Cyclone and Curtiss V-1800. Purchases of equipment sets were carried out for the factory in Perm. In reality, however, only the Cyclone was introduced into production under the designation M-25. These engines were subsequently fitted to I-15, I-15bis and I-16 fighters, and R-10 reconnaissance aircraft. It took a long time to set up production of the M-25, therefore a batch of R-1820-F3 engines, known in the USSR as RTsF-3, was purchased in the USA for the series I-16 and I-14 fighters. The agreements envisaged not only assistance in arranging the production but in providing information on the further refinements of the engine design and on its future developments. This information was used during creation of the Soviet M-62 and M-63 engines – the descendants of the Cyclone, while some of its design solutions can be found even in the M-82 engine which was built much later.

In this period the nomenclature of items purchased in the USA increased significantly – instruments, lifejackets, and inflatable life rafts, fuel bowsers, hydraulic jacks, oxygen units, and parachutes. As mentioned above, in 1934 a turbocharger was acquired from General Electric company, which was fitted onto an M-5 engine and tested in the R-1 biplane. The results of this experiment proved to be useful for the creation of the first Soviet turbochargers.

In 1934 examples of aviation lubrication oils were brought to Moscow from USA. The samples were analysed and the results were used to compile the technical specifications for new indigenously manufactured oils.

A short time later American aircraft appeared again in the skies over Russia. The first of these had evidently been brought into the country by the American Embassy. It was even listed in the Soviet civil register using a very rare designation starting with the letter Ч – Ч-2, where *Ч* denoted *chastniy* (private). This was a disarmed Douglas O-38 reconnaissance airplane, the owner of which was the assistant US military attaché for air Thomas White. On 24 June 1934 during a flight from Moscow to Leningrad the engine on this biplane failed. White landed on a waterlogged landing site and as a result of sharp braking in front of a drainage ditch the aircraft fell onto its nose but the pilot was uninjured.

Two Consolidated Fleetster airplanes became the first American aircraft to actually become the Soviet property. They were not purchased in accordance with any plan but as a result of extraordinary circumstances. The steamer *Chelyuskin* had sunk off the coast of Chukotka after it had been crushed by ice during a voyage along the Northern Sea Route with a scientific expedition on board. Aircraft were sent to save those on board who had ended up on the drifting ice. For extra backup, aside from indigenous airplanes, a decision was taken to purchase airplanes in Alaska and to ferry them across the Bering Strait, so the Fleetsters played their role in the rescue operations.

Delegations of Soviet aircraft manufacturers became frequent visitors to America and following the visit of a group led by the designer A.N. Tupolev in 1935 examples were ordered of the ground attack Northrop 2E monoplane, and the Douglas DC-2 passenger airplane. Soviet specialists familiarised themselves for the first time with welded fuel tanks, as well as machine riveting and many other technical innovations.

In spring 1936 a V-1A airplane was purchased from Vultee for the famous Soviet pilot S.A. Levanevskiy. It was on this monoplane that he flew a long-range flight from Los Angeles to Moscow. A year later three contemporary hydroplanes were brought in from the USA to service the routes along the large Siberian rivers – two Douglas DF flying boats and a Sikorsky S-43A amphibian.

In May–September 1936 a group of VVS officials led by the Head of the Directorate of Material and Technical Supply, Brigade Commander B.I. Bazenkov, visited America. This group reviewed factories and airfields and spent time with their American colleagues at the Wright Field airbase. There the Americans showed them round laboratories, test installations, and some aircraft being tested – Martin B-12 and Douglas B-18 bombers, a Seversky P-35 fighter, and passenger aircraft produced by Douglas and Lockheed. On their return to Moscow Bazenkov proposed introducing many of the innovations he had seen in America into the indigenous aviation industry. Specifically, he recommended purchasing licences and technical assistance for instruments, and special lacquers and paints.

The next step forward was arranging licences in 1936 1937 for a range of American military and civil aircraft. Prior to this arrangement, two opinions had clashed on the issue. The leadership of the Main Directorate of the Aviation Industry under the People's Commissariat for Heavy Industry headed by M.M. Kaganovich, had initially supported acquiring examples of these aircraft and then copying them. The Air Force command, including the Head of the VVS RKKA Ya.I. Alksnis, thought that the acquisition of technical assistance would significantly accelerate the process of series production arrangement, while the excessive economy could lead to the introduction of already obsolete types. In accordance with a decree issued by the STO on 9 January 1936, the GUAP was tasked with the responsibility for compiling a preliminary list of types to be acquired. There was all manner of airplanes on this list! Even the record-breaking Howard Hughes' aircraft was included, and in the second draft of the list the Wedell-Williams XP-34 fighter appeared (even in two examples) which was only at the project stage at that time. In fact, a letter arrived in Moscow from this company which had proposed to produce by mid-1937 two aircraft for 54,000 US Dollars.

In reality, by autumn the discussions were being held on the possibility of acquiring a Vultee V-11 light bomber/ground attack aircraft, Martin 139, Douglas DB-1 (the B-18) and the Boeing 299 (the B-17) bombers, as well as the Douglas DC-2 transport airplane. On the initiative of Kaganovich, a Consolidated 28 (PBY-1) flying boat was added to the list, and later on there were added Seversky 2PA fighter and the large four-engine Martin 156 flying boat which was inspected at the factory by the Head of TsAGI N.M. Kharlamov. The purchase of the licences was conducted under a decree issued by the STO on 11 April 1936.

Five licences were acquired: for the V-11, Consolidated 28, Seversky 2PA, Martin 156, and the DC-3 (which was a development of the DC-2). Of these types, three entered production – the V-11 (which in the USSR was designated as BSh-1 in the military version, and PS-43 in the civil version), the Consolidated 28 (designated GST and MP-7), and the DC-3 (PS-84 designation was used which was later changed to the Li-2). Only the latter really became a widespread aircraft type. Production of all three types has been set up only in 1939. Only one example of the Martin 139 bomber was purchased for study.

American companies offered other aircraft types to the USSR as well – Boeing suggested the Boeing 307 four-engine passenger aircraft. In accordance with a draft agreement a single example was quoted at 650,000 US Dollars (with a lead time of 14 months), and for the documentation (in the metric system), licensing, and the provision of technical support a further 710,000 US Dollars was requested.

All the American aircraft were characterised by the forethought that had gone into their technology, suitability for mass production, and the attention that had been paid to ease of operation. In preparing them for production the Soviet factories mastered the advanced loft-template production technology. The introduction of the American types required the significant step-up of related sectors of the industry – almost all licensing agreements envisaged the package procurement of the equipment and the introduction of technology processes unfamiliar to the Soviet industry. Furthermore, the agreements incorporated clauses on training specialists, on the supply of information not only for the specific designs but also on methods of calculation and testing, on the prospective versions, and even on the new aircraft designs. Thus, Vultee supplied preliminary projects of several ground attack aircraft and light bombers (including one carrier-based airplane). For example, in December 1939 materials were provided on the V-12 ground attack aircraft with an R-2600 engine.

In 1937 a further two airplanes were purchased in the USA in extraordinary circumstances. To search for S.A. Levanevskiy's crew, who had gone missing during a long-range flight from Moscow to America, an unarmed Consolidated PBY-1 flying boat was urgently acquired, and then a twin-engine Lockheed L-10E passenger airplane. The crew of the famous polar explorer Hubert Wilkins had been using these airplanes for flights in northern Canada. The aircraft were taken to the USSR where they later served for several years in Polar aviation.

Without waiting for the delayed mass production of the PS-84, batches of the DC-3 began to be acquired in America. These aircraft were used in civil and military aviation and it became the only American type that was acquired in the 1930s in significant quantities.

In parallel, there were obtained licences and samples of advanced aviation equipment. The first variable pitch propellers in the Soviet Union – the VISh-2, VISh-3, and VISh-5 were manufactured under licence from Hamilton Standard. These were fitted to the SB and DB-3 bombers, and the R-10 reconnaissance airplanes. The hydraulic AVP-12 autopilot, which was introduced into service of the VVS RKKA in 1939, was a copy of the American Sperry model of 1934. The TsKB-30 *Moskva*, on which V.K. Kokkinaki and M.Kh. Gordienko crossed the Atlantic Ocean, was fitted with the Fairchild radio compass.

A batch of MN-12 radio compasses was purchased from Bendix, and they were accepted in March 1939 in the USA by a Soviet commission led by I.S. Mitsner. Counting on new orders the Americans demonstrated their new, much more refined design – the MN-26 radio compass. Subsequently, these found their way into the Soviet Union under lend-lease program. The purchased instruments were loaded onto the *Chelyuskinets* steamer, but unfortunately, they were damaged in transit.

In the second half of the 1930s the USSR began to order from American companies ever-larger scientific-research and design work in the aviation field. The Radio Corporation of America received an order to develop a special television system for installation on board an aircraft. According to the ideas of Soviet strategists, such television reconnaissance aircraft would be transmitting a picture of a battle or troops on the march directly to the headquarters. This system was developed and manufactured; it weighed 270kg and could send an image at a distance of up to 25km. In October 1937 this innovation was tested on a TB-3 airplane. By that time the NII-8 Scientific Research Institute under the People's Commissariat for the Defence Industry had already copied the American example and had begun to prepare its more compact variant for the DB-3 bomber. Testing, however, demonstrated that tele-visual monitoring was not sufficiently effective as the screen was just 12x17cm in size and the cumbersome TB-3 was very vulnerable target flying at low level over the battlefield.

In May 1937 an agreement was drawn up on the development of a 'sub-stratospheric bomber' for the VVS RKKA. The subcontractor was the little-known Jackson and Moreland company, but it was not really any more than an intermediary acting as a front company for a much larger aircraft manufacturing firm. The heavy four-engine bomber (fitted with Wright Cyclone G100 or G102A engines) should have had a take-off weight of 27,000kg and a maximum speed at altitude of 600 km/h. The flight range according to the specification was 4,800km, and a pressurised cabin made it possible for the crew to work for long periods of time at high altitude.

The preliminary development was successfully completed, and in October 1936 a model of the aircraft was tested in a wind tunnel at the Massachusetts Institute of Technology. The set of documents that included 55 pages of drawings, consolidated data, calculations, description note with attachments, as well as the model of the fuselage were handed over to the Amtorg in February 1939, and on 4 March this cargo arrived in Moscow. In April the documentation began to be translated into Russian and at the same time an acceptance commission began to be set up that comprised representatives of the UVVS, NII VVS, and People's Commissariat for Aviation Industry (NKAP, *Narodniy Komissariat Aviatsionnoy Promyshlennosti*). Unfortunately, the further fate of this project is not known.

The culmination of Soviet-American cooperation in the aviation field was to have been the joint project conducted with Douglas company. Preparations were made for a development of new twin-engine dive bomber by a design group in which the Soviet specialists would participate. On 10 September 1939 the Committee for Defence approved the decision on the corresponding agreement with Douglas. According to the technical specification prepared in Moscow, this should have been an ultra-modern aircraft, with pressurised cockpits, tricycle undercarriage, internal storage for the bombs, and maximum automation of the aircraft and power plant controls.

In addition to the above, various technical literature and documentation were delivered to the USSR in a constant stream. The manuals and handbooks for the aircraft designers, study materials for the personnel of the US Army Air Corps, technical requirements for acceptance of the aircraft, engines, equipment, fuel and lubricants, and descriptions of the instruments and mechanisms were all delivered and translated. All this was obtained through official and unofficial channels.

In July 1938, the last long-range flight of an American crew via the territory of the Soviet Union was performed – Howard Hughes flew his specially converted Lockheed L-14 passenger airplane, performing intermediate landings in Moscow, Omsk, and Yakutsk. Hughes improved significantly on Post's results, taking a little over three days for his trip.

In 1938–1939 negotiations resumed concerning the acquisition of examples of contemporary American military aircraft in order to arrange their production in the USSR. The B-18 was again considered but was rejected as an obsolete type. Another American twin-engine bomber – Martin 167 (which was subsequently delivered to Britain and France), according to the feedback from NII VVS specialists 'did not hold any future potential'. On the other hand, a great deal of effort was expended on wangling a dozen of the newest A-20 bomber/ground attack aircraft, which were later used widely by the Soviet VVS during the course of the war with Germany and Japan.

The Soviet side did reject some aircraft that were proposed – in December 1939 Beechcraft company sent a letter with a proposal to sell a batch (from five to 50 examples) of the AT-18 or BT-18D twin-engine training aircraft. Negotiations took almost a year and the opinions of the Soviet specialists differed. The Head of the Foreign Procurement Department Colonel Albokrinov thought that the 'monoplane would be of interest to the VVS RKKA', and proposed purchasing a single AT-18 and a single BT-18D. In the end, however, the completely opposite opinion held by Senior Military Representative Strekalov won through, who wrote: ' ... the aircraft ... of AT-18 and BT-18D types are not of interest to the VVS RKKA at all'. Even the purchase of examples of these aircraft was rejected as the proposed price of between 56,650–59,695 US Dollars for each aircraft was thought to be too high.

Then the war with Finland began, and on 2 December 1939 the president of the United States announced a 'moral embargo' on supplying aviation materiel to the Soviet Union. American companies, one after another, began to break agreements with the USSR. All official channels were paralysed.

The unofficial channels remained – the intelligence services continued to 'purloin' technical documentation as they had done previously. Thus, back in September 1938 a project documentation was delivered to Moscow for the new Lockheed model 22 interceptor, the future P-38 Lightning. These were thick files of photocopies with 'secret' clearly stamped on them. The type was of interest and in July 1939 the NKAP asked permission of the government to enter into negotiations with Lockheed on the licensing and provision of technical assistance for arranging production of this twin-engine fighter at Factory No.1 in Moscow, although nothing further came of this.

On 21 September 1938 the NII VVS received documentation from the Intelligence Directorate of the General Headquarters on the Lockheed Hudson bomber, which included secret drawings from the British Air Ministry. In April 1939 from China, where Soviet pilots were at the time, materials were sent to Moscow on the Curtiss Hawk

75 fighter (the export version of the P-36). In a report written by Major G.I. Tkhor comparative tests were described of the Hawk 75, I-15bis and I-16 fighters, which included mock air combats. This documentation also included technical and service manuals, and 33 photos of the fighter's parts and components.

In April 1940 in the Soviet Union appeared detailed drawings of the Allison V-1710 and Wright R-2600 engines (the Soviet side had tried for a long time to obtain a licence for the latter engine), and of the Curtiss Electric propellers. These were immediately sent out to the factories and design bureaux for study. This, of course, could not replace full-scale contacts with American aircraft manufacturers.

From March 1940 onwards these contacts gradually began to return, and the Soviet Union under an agreement with Curtiss-Wright received the documentation they had already paid for on the R-1820-G100 engine, which was subsequently used to refine the M-62 and M-63 engines. The VVS Main Directorate of Aviation Supply again raised the question of purchasing examples of contemporary military aircraft in the USA to study. On 14 March, the list of the most interesting machines was approved, which included the Lockheed XP-38 and Curtiss XP-40 fighter, and the Stearman X-100 bomber. The latter, which remained the only prototype example, did not find its way to the USSR, while the Soviet specialists were able to familiarise themselves with two fighter types in the course of the war with Germany.

Overall, the volume of Soviet-American cooperation in 1940 reduced, however in 1941 it not only rebound again but increased many times over.

4.1 To Rescue the *Chelyuskintsy*

The first American aircraft to enter the Soviet Union following the end of the Civil War were to a great extent purchased by chance. A scientific expedition led by the Academician O.Yu. Schmidt had been attempting to traverse the Northern Sea Route on board the ice-breaking steamer *Chelyuskin* and had been crushed by drifting ice off the coast of Chukotka. The crew and members of the expedition had disembarked from the ship onto the ice, and aircraft and ships were sent to rescue them. In addition to the deployment of different types of indigenous aircraft to the location of the crushed ship, it was decided that some airplanes would be purchased in the USA. A group was sent to America that was led by the well-known polar explorer G.A. Ushakov and included two pilots – S.A. Levanevskiy and M.T. Slepnyov.

After arriving in Alaska, Ushakov reached agreement with Pacific Alaska Airways on the purchase of two all-metal Consolidated 17AF Fleetster monoplanes. These were single-engine airplanes that operated on local routes, which were designed for a crew of two and six passengers.

The Fleetster had long been of interest to Soviet aviation specialists, and a delegation led by P.I. Baranov had encountered this aircraft for the first time early in 1930. The delegation visited the Consolidated factory and had reviewed a range of aircraft, including the Fleetster. The Head of the Foreign Procurement Department of the UVVS I.A. Feldman wrote to Moscow about his impressions: 'The eight-seat Fleetster passenger aircraft is interesting; it develops a speed of 160mph with a Wasp engine and 180mph (250–270km/h) with a Hornet engine. It is a cigar-shaped monoplane.'

The Fleetster 17AF version was equipped with more powerful 575hp Pratt & Whitney Hornet engine. The aircraft purchased by Ushakov were not new but modified for operations in the north: they had enclosed heated cabins, ski undercarriage, and a decent, for its time, set of instruments. The deal was drawn up through Amtorg company.

Mechanics were temporarily hired from that same Pacific Alaska Airways – they knew the Fleetster well and had experience of winter operations. The acceptance of the aircraft took place in Fairbanks, and from there both

Two Fleetsters which were acquired by the Soviet commission in Alaska.

One of the two Fleetsters in Fairbanks still with its original American markings.

Fleetsters prior to departure from Alaska.

M.T. Slepnyov's airplane with its ski undercarriage damaged following an unfortunate landing.

Slepnyov's Fleetster at the *Chelyuskin* camp.

The Fleetster with the registration number I 155 during its service at the Krasnoyarsk route of the GUSMP.

airplanes were flown to Nome but due to bad weather they made a forced landing close to the Indian village of Nulato. When visibility improved, they again took off and got in a snowstorm. The aircraft were approaching Nome at low-level but landed safely. This took place on 22 February 1934.

Immediately after receiving a more or less favourable weather forecast Levanevskiy took off from Nome, having taken Ushakov on board with him. On the Soviet side of the Bering Strait, in Uelen, a Popham panel had been laid out on the ground, requiring them to land. Levanevskiy, however, ignored these, hoping nevertheless on being able to get through to the campsite of Vankarem, where the rescuers camp was situated. This was not the best decision, as the

Standing alongside the Fleetster (from left to right): the American pilot Joe Crosson, M.T. Slepnyov, representative of the Soviet Government Commission G.A. Ushakov, S.A. Levanevskiy, and radio operator of Fairbanks airfield.

instructions from the ground had not been set out by chance – meteorologists had informed about a rapid deterioration in the weather.

Levanevskiy soon encountered a powerful squall of snow. The ice started to cover the aircraft, there was almost zero visibility so the pilot was navigating using the instruments. The engine cut out, then again restarted. When, according to their calculations, Vankarem should have been under them, Levanevskiy broke one of the windows in the windscreen with a gloved hand, and finding his way somehow in the driving snow, he made an approach to land. The impact shook the airplane, and one ski flew off from the unforeseen impact with a ridge of ice. Levanevskiy tore the other one off deliberately on another ridge of ice. He performed a belly landing and was not able to see where he was moving. After hitting a block of ice, the aircraft came to a stop. The pilot was knocked senseless.

The Fleetster was damaged beyond repair, while Levanevskiy, once he had come his senses, sent a radiogram from the camp to Stalin stating his readiness to work on. However, he did not make any more flights at all because he had nothing to fly there, as the airplane was written off.

Slepnyov remained in Nome until he received an order to fly. He reached Vankarem without incident and his aircraft was the second to arrive at the *Chelyuskin* camp (after A.V. Lyapidevskiy's twin-engine TB-1). Slepnyov transported Ushakov and eight sled dogs, which later become the main means of local transport, to the camp. During landing on the uneven ice, the Fleetster had damaged its undercarriage but this was repaired. On his return flight Slepnyov rescued five people. In Vankarem he was given a new mission – to take Schmidt, who was unwell, to Alaska (Schmidt had been rescued from the camp and taken to Vankarem by the pilot Molokov). This mission was completed.

Interestingly, the award of the Gold Star of a Hero of the Soviet Union was given to M.T. Slepnyov, who actually did rescue people, but also to S.A. Levanevskiy, whose entire contribution was that, due to his own overconfidence, he destroyed an aircraft purchased in America and almost killed the chairman of a government commission. This is what he had achieved by sending his telegram in good time!

Subsequently, the single remaining Fleetster served in Polar Aviation. Following the completion of the rescue operation in 1934 it was taken to Moscow, where it was handed over to repair Factory No.89. There the aircraft was carefully studied, and the elaborate design and the ease of repair were noted.

A Fleetster in Vankarem.

In the second half of the 1930s the Fleetster operated in Siberia as part of the various aviation formations of the Main Directorate of the Northern Sea Route (GUSMP, *Glavnoe Upravlenie Severnogo Morskogo Puti*). The aircraft carried the registration number H55. Thus, in early 1935 it was based in Tyumen where it was nicknamed *Mister Fleetster*, and on 8 February pilot S.I. Antyushev and mechanic N.L. Kekushev opened an air service with this airplane on a route Tyumen–Salekhard. Following the formation of the Ob group, which provided flights in the basin of the Ob River, the H55 was transferred to this group. In 1936 the Fleetster had flown 21.5 hours in a relatively short period of time. In that same year the aircraft again underwent some light repairs at Factory No.89.

From the beginning of 1937 this monoplane was handed over to the Moscow Air Unit of the GUSMP, which was based at Zakharkovo (now this is Khimki district). The aircraft was already quite badly worn out and the intention was to use it as a trainer. Then the plans changed, and the Fleetster was ferried to Krasnoyarsk. There the Factory named after Pobezhimov, which specialised in Polar Aviation aircraft, set about performing a major overhaul of this airplane. An amount of 46,246 roubles were spent on this work, and the airplane was fitted with an RSRI Soviet radio set. Fleetster left the workshop in August 1937 and was attached to the Yenisey air group.

In December 1937 pilot V.N. Makhotkin performed a long-range flight in the Fleetster on a route Krasnoyarsk–Ust-Port–Dickson–Cape Sterligov–Russkiy Island–Ust-Taimyr–Cape Chelyuskin–Kamenev Island, and back again.

The records show that in July 1938 the aircraft was still operational, but what happened to it after that is not known.

A Fleetster is towed on a sled by a tractor.

4.2 The Northrop

During the mid-1930s, the American aircraft designer John Northrop designed a whole family of ground attack aircraft on the basis of the multi-role (mail, passenger, and sports) single-engine Gamma monoplane.

In early 1933 the design bureau of Northrop Corporation started development of the military version of the Gamma, as the type had certain potential for modification into an airplane of close support. This all-metal monoplane had quite a good lifting capability and high survivability (primarily due to the multi-spar wing), while in terms of speed it was not much inferior to the contemporary American fighters.

A prototype of the military Gamma 2C was completed in May 1933 and in July, in accordance with an agreement with Northrop, the aircraft was accepted for evaluation at the Wright Field, where the Materiel Division of US Army Air Corps was located. The military reacted favourably to the new type of ground attack aircraft, as its flight characteristics surpassed the Curtiss A-12 Shrike that was in service at the time, but they did not purchase this machine and made a series of remarks. The Chinese turned out to be less fastidious and they ordered 24 examples of the 2E version, which was actually a copy of the 2C with minor changes. The main external difference was the semi-retractable ventral fairing for the gunner/radio-operator, who also performed the responsibilities of a bomb-aimer. This fairing provided downward and forward visibility the during aiming.

The 2E, 2EC, and 2ED versions were delivered to China, and the assembly of the Chinese ground attack aircraft was actually demonstrated to a Soviet delegation led by A.N. Tupolev in 1935. A short time after that a single example of the 2ED version of the ground attack aircraft was

Manufacturing of Soviet Northrop 2ED at the factory in the USA.

A Northrop 2ED ground attack airplane prior to the delivery to the Soviet Union, November 1935.

A Northrop 2ED during factory tests in USA.

A Northrop 2ED during testing at the NII VVS, August 1936.

purchased, using Amtorg as an intermediary, for study in the Soviet Union. The Americans undertook to fulfil the order in three months, and in November of that year the aircraft was shipped to the USSR. The Northrop was delivered to Moscow at the beginning of 1936. This ground attack aircraft had a 735hp R-1820-F53 engine and a three-bladed propeller, and it differed slightly from the airplanes of the Chinese order.

As the aircraft was purchased for the GUAP, it was initially tested at the OELID TsAGI and for the most part was flown by M.M. Gromov. The feedback from TsAGI, which was presented to the VVS in June, was very favourable: 'TsAGI pilots think that this airplane has exceptionally good flight-performance characteristics, which make piloting the aircraft much easier, and improving its flight safety. In the opinion of comrade Gromov the numerous design and production specifics of this aircraft, the layout of the instruments and equipment, should be immediately introduced into mass production, and into the design of our series and prototype airplanes.'

This though is what Gromov himself wrote: 'The combination of dynamic stability, the responsiveness and simplicity of control, the lack of drafts, the warm cockpit, and the excellent quality of manufacturing of the airplane, engine, instruments, and equipment, makes piloting this machine a very pleasant task'.

TsAGI specialists remarked on the light and rigid wing, the spacious and comfortable cockpits, the elaborate engine cowling, the efficiency of the brakes, and the cockpits heating. The technologists spoke of such advantages in the design of the American ground attack aircraft, as the limited selection of metal profiles used, the absence of complex hand stamped components, and the widespread use of machine riveting, which made mass production much easier. Two points were of particular interest: the availability of cabin heating using warm air, which was heated up by the exhaust

A Northrop 2ED in Soviet Union, September 1937.

Pilot M.L. Gallay in the cockpit of a Northrop 2ED ground attack aircraft at the LII.

A group of LII pilots standing next to a Northrop 2ED.

gases, and the welded fuel tanks made from an aluminium alloy. It was planned to copy the Northrop type heating system for the SB bomber: this task was entrusted to TsAGI collective, with a deadline set for 15 September 1936. In reality, however, heating system for the SB cockpits was never actually produced. Welding of the aluminium fuel tanks began to be introduced at Soviet factories from the second half of 1936, in many ways this was influenced by the studied American designs.

In mid-1936 the military requested the Northrop 2ED be handed over for evaluation at the NII VVS. By July the aircraft was transferred there and underwent testing with a total flying time of 18.5 hours.

Pilot *Voeninzhener 2-go ranga* K.A. Kalilets flew this airplane at the NII VVS and in his report he wrote that the aircraft was stable, simple and easy to fly. Take-off and landing did not present any difficulty. In the opinion of the test pilot the aircraft '... fully allows piloting by pilots of average and below average qualifications'. The armament, however, was considered weak for a ground attack airplane, and even more so for a light bomber. The rear turret at speeds close to the maximum became almost unsuitable for firing. 'An aircraft that is pleasant to fly is not the main consideration for a military airplane.' The flight-performance characteristics of the 2ED turned out to be significantly less than those required by the VVS RKKA in 1936 – the maximum speed was just 360km/h.

The Northrop was returned to the OELID TsAGI and, as the famous test pilot M.L. Gallay commented, every young pilot had to fly this machine 'so as to understand what balanced controls were'. The pilot did not have to battle the airplane, imposing his will on it, or tensely wait for the aircraft to play a trick on him – he would just gain pleasure from the flight. As this airplane was considered a kind of standard in terms of an excellent combination of stability and controllability, in 1938 an expanded test program was conducted in this aircraft, the results of which assisted in the development of norms in this field for Soviet designers.

The American ground attack aircraft 'passed by inheritance' to the LII NKAP, and in the autumn of 1941 it was ferried to Kazan, where the institute was evacuated to. Whether the airplane was used during the war is not known. It was not brought back to Zhukovskiy though, so it must have just rotted away in the corner of an airfield somewhere.

4.3 The Martin

In the mid-1930s another American military aircraft – a twin-engine Martin 139 bomber, was purchased by the Soviet Union for evaluation. This all-metal monoplane was able to overtake the biplane fighters of the time. Following refinements in 1934 the machine entered series production as the Martin 139, and the US Army Air Corps designated different versions of this bomber the B-10 and the B-12.

The creation of this airplane did not go unnoticed in Soviet Russia either. Back in 1933 the Head of the Intelligence Department at RKKA Headquarters Ya.K. Berzin provided GUAP with a large set of materials on the B-10, which the agents had collected: drawings of the main assemblies, as well as aerodynamic and strength calculations.

High flight-performance characteristics of the airplane gave rise to a desire to create something similar in the USSR. The explanatory note to the plan for experimental aircraft manufacturing for 1934 with respect to the specifications for the future SB bomber stated the following: 'The aircraft for the most part should follow the layout of the high-speed American bombers (produced by Glenn-Martin)'. However,

A Martin 139WR bomber from a Soviet order during tests in the USA.

Nose section of a Martin 139WR; the photo taken during testing in the USSR, February 1937, Leningrad, Komendantskiy airfield.

The rear gunner's position with an enclosed canopy.

the Tupolev SB in the end did not resemble the Martin 139 at all. Tupolev had gone much further than his American predecessors and the SB with its smooth skin and narrow fuselage had significantly better aerodynamics and surpassed the Martin significantly in terms of speed. Nevertheless, it is impossible to deny the influence of the concept of a high-speed bomber monoplane that had been proposed by the Americans, on the creation of the SB.

In parallel to the development of indigenous high-speed bombers the Soviets were also interested in the possibility of acquiring Martin 139 in the USA. The management of Amtorg reported to Moscow on 4 April 1934: 'Martin is prepared to sell us a batch of no less than 40 airplanes and has agreed to send one or two examples for testing in the USSR. If all the flight-performance characteristics meet the requirements, the USSR will have to purchase the entire batch'. On 22 April M.N. Tukhachevskiy, who was in charge of new armament for the RKKA, sent I.V. Stalin a letter, in which he stated in particular: 'I am sending you a copy of the letter from the Head of Amtorg comrade Bogdanov on the readiness of American companies to sell us airplanes, which in comparison to our bombers surpass them in terms of speed and flight range. It is imperative that we acquire these airplanes'.

In October 1934, having visited Glenn Martin factory in Baltimore, the Soviet engineer Zharov was given the opportunity to review the aircraft in the workshop. Zharov was an engine designer so he paid particular attention to the power plant. The oil radiators sparked his interest, and he recommended they be copied in the USSR.

In November of the same year, the UVVS documents mention the intention to purchase two examples of the B-10 version. The ban on sales of such aircraft type in the USA, however, became a stumbling block to this purchase.

Two years went by: having saturated American military aviation with medium bombers Martin switched to export orders. The export of the 'Model 139' was approved by the US State Department in 1936. Amtorg representatives then drew up a purchasing agreement that was to be realised in July of that year. Only one aircraft was actually purchased, evidently this was in the interests of saving hard currency. In September of the same year the dismantled Martin 139WR was delivered by sea to Leningrad. This airplane was fitted with the GR-1820-F53 engines and Hamilton Standard

The canopy of the rear gun mount is open; the machine gun is in the deployed position.

The lower gun mount: the hatch is open; the machine gun is in the deployed position.

propellers. Three Colt-Browning machine guns arrived along with the airplane.

This aircraft underwent testing from the end of 1936 till the beginning of 1937. The leading pilot was A.P. Chernavskiy but other pilots did participate in the testing as well. Flights were undertaken at a weight of 5,950kg.

The flight-performance characteristics of the American aircraft did not arise much interest. The maximum speed did not exceed 342km/h at an altitude of 3,600m. The airplane, which was developed in 1931, clearly became obsolete by

The external bomb rack under the wing.

1937. In terms of its flight-performance characteristics the Martin was inferior to the new Soviet bombers such as the SB with M-100A engines, and the DB-3 with M-85 engines. As to the advantages of the Martin 139WR, good visibility from the cockpit was noted, as was excellent operation of the wheel brakes, and manoeuvrability on the ground.

On the other hand, the piloting characteristics of the American bomber were highly rated. The aircraft was stable and responded well to the controls. The test pilots wrote in their reports: 'The aircraft takes off well, and there is no tendency to turn off the runway ... It is piloted easily and well; it perfectly reacts to the movement of controls ... it is responsive and not inert ... it sits 'firmly' in the air ... Flying this aircraft does not cause fatigue ... Landing is simple and standard'. The test pilots remarked on how easy it could perform turns, and on the high efficiency of the ailerons. Some considerable time was spent trying to understand how the American designers had achieved a harmonious combination of stability and controllability. One of the test pilots wrote: 'of all the twin-engine aircraft I consider the Glenn Martin one of the simplest and most pleasant to fly'.

Two main shortcomings were identified. During a glide at a speed of 150km/h strong tail buffeting was detected, and the aircraft would vibrate a fair amount when making a turn to port at a speed of less than 230km/h. The second significant defect was identified as the insufficient level of the rudder efficiency when flying on a single engine. Apart from that, the tendency to pancake on landing with a stall onto the starboard wing was criticised. On the landing roll the aircraft would always drift significantly to starboard.

Testing included aerial gunnery and bombing (with dummy bombs) at a test range near Noginsk.

Overall, the aircraft armament was not rated highly. The gun sights were not sufficiently rigid and the same was said of the machine gun mounts – which caused a wide spread of the bullets. The cartridge cases and link ejection chutes were absent: from the nose machine gun mount the cartridge cases flew into the port propeller, and in the rear machine gun mount the scattered cartridge cases and links ended up in the groove and jammed the turret carriage. In the nose turret, it was blowing heavily into the slot for the machine gun. Another curious detail was noted: 'there is no machine gun fixation in the stowed position, so when taxiing and on landing the machine gun needs to be held down by hand to avoid the rear part of the machine gun hitting the gunner in the head'. The Estoppey D-4A bombsight, which had been mounted in place of the secret Norden sight, did not work at all during testing as its lubrication froze.

In the end an unsurprising conclusion was reached: 'If we take a closer look at the gun mounts installed on the aircraft, it becomes abundantly clear that that they do not represent examples of the achievements of American technology in the armament industry, even for the period of 1932–1934 to which the development of the airplane belongs'.

On the other hand, Soviet technologists found many positive aspects – a high degree of standardisation, the use of the most modern materials and methods of their processing, and a well-thought-out design from the point of view of mass production. 'The exceptional simplicity in the structural shapes is especially striking, and it is very rare to find a relatively complex detail. Stamping, various types of welding, the very precise and clean casting, the standard – these are the cornerstones of American designs ... The excellent quality of materials and the skilful way in which they are used make it possible to create very light and at the same time reliable structures'.

After the Martin was damaged on landing in the middle of 1937, it was transferred for study to Factory No.156 in Moscow (the former Factory of Experimental Designs of TsAGI). There it was studied at least up until mid-1939 and the aircraft was not returned to an airworthy condition again.

4.4 Flying Boats for the GUSMP

In the closing scenes of the pre-war film 'Volga-Volga', widely known in Russia, pictures unfold in front of the passengers of the ship on its way to Moscow, demonstrating the beauty of the new, socialist, way of life. As part of this they observe a wonderful silver monoplane as it takes off from water. What the viewers did not know that this monoplane was not built in the Soviet Union. It was an American S-43 amphibian, created by the Russian designer I.I. Sikorsky.

The airplane belonged to the GUSMP and it actually came to the attention of the film crew by chance. The film was made at the Kama River close to Sarapul and the

The S-43A amphibian at the GUSMP aviation base in Zakharkovo.

An S-43A aircraft on the water.

An S-43A on the reservoir adjacent to the Northern riverboat station in Moscow.

The H207 amphibian that had been sent to search for the missing crew of S.A. Levanevskiy, close to Cape Barrow, 1937.

Sikorsky and two Douglas DF flying boats. The history of their acquisition began in 1935.

In the mid-1930s Soviet Polar aviation operated two main types of flying boats – the all-metal Dornier Wal (of both Italian and German manufacture) and the indigenous MBR-2 with its wooden hull. The first type was already obsolete, and the second was poorly suited to operations in the Arctic, since the insufficiently strong bottom of the hull was quickly damaged even by small pieces of ice floating in the water. First and foremost, contemporary passenger aircraft were required for the regular routes along Lena and Yenisey rivers, and operating these routed were under the responsibility of the GUSMP at that time.

In January 1935 a representative delegation of Soviet aircraft designers headed by A.N. Tupolev was preparing for departure to the USA. In his letter to Tupolev the Head of the VVS Ya.I. Alksnis recommended paying attention to the flying boats manufactured by Sikorsky and Douglas companies. For new Sikorsky amphibian, the S-43A, the decision was made earlier – the purchase of an example of this aircraft had been approved by the Political Bureau of the Central Committee of the All-Union Communist Party (Bolsheviks) back on 23 October 1934.

At the Sikorsky factory in Bridgeport, the delegation was shown the first stage of assembly of the S-43. This was an elegant all-metal monoplane with a wing elevated above the boat-fuselage and with a teardrop-shaped pylon and a system of struts. The boat hull had a well-streamlined shape, which ensured excellent aerodynamic and hydrodynamic properties. Soviet specialists had a high opinion of this aircraft, and they immediately realised the potential to convert it into a military version with an armament of four machine guns and a bomb load

amphibian made an emergency landing there after a failure in one engine. Nevertheless, the footage featuring this airplane was successfully written into the epilogue to the film.

At that time the GUSMP had three American hydroplanes in service – the aforementioned amphibian of

An S-43A lands on wheels in Fairbanks, October 1937.

The crew of the H207, photographed on 30 October 1937 in Fairbanks. From left to right: Smirnov, Shtepenko, Pisarev, Krasnov, Gratsianskiy, Kozin, and Belyakov.

Shtepenko and Kozin next to the H207, which was parked in the lagoon close to Cape Barrow, autumn 1937.

Preparing the S-43A amphibian for flight, 1937.

An S-43A airplane in Nikolaev, at the base of Polar Pilots School, 1937.

of up to 900kg. The amphibian was of interest and on their return the delegation wrote favourably about this aircraft in their report.

As a result, in Moscow the final decision was taken to purchase the hydroplane for experimental operations in the North. The agreement was drawn up through Amtorg in 1936. The flying boat was to have been fitted with two 550hp Pratt & Whitney Wasp S3H1 engines and equipped with seats to accommodate 15 passengers.

Although all foreign sources mention that the Soviet Union did purchase two S-43s, the author has not been able to find any trace of this second flying boat. One aircraft of the S-43A version (with a single-fin tail) arrived in Murmansk in spring 1937. On 20 April the famous pilot S.A. Levanevskiy left for Murmansk to supervise the assembly of this airplane. As his contemporaries testified, he considered the American amphibian as a possible contender for the long-range flight to the USA that had been planned for some time. Levanevskiy considered the possibility of landing both on land and on water a big advantage. The aircraft was successfully assembled and test-flown, and it was from there that Levanevskiy took the flying boat south. In Murmansk, he took off from water (in a strong wind) and water landed in Leningrad on the Neva River, and on next leg he landed on wheels at Shchelkovo airfield just outside Moscow. The flying boat was taken to

The H207 amphibian accelerates along the water prior to take-off.

Mechanics standing next to an S-43A.

M.N. Kaminskiy's crew, standing next to the H207 amphibian.

One of the DF flying boats at the Grebnoy Port in Leningrad, May 1937

An underwing float of the DF, which was damaged during testing in Sevastopol, summer 1937.

the Crimea, to Sevastopol in May, and at around this time two Douglas DF-195 flying boats were delivered from the USA by sea (in the Soviet Union they were designated simply DF). They were larger than the S-43A and could carry up to 32 passengers. These flying boats were ordered in America in autumn 1936. The DF was also twin-engine all-metal airplane, but its wing was not mounted on a pylon, but lay on top of a high fuselage. These airplanes were fitted with Wright Cyclone engines.

All three aircraft received Soviet registration numbers beginning with the letter 'H', typical for Polar aviation. On the sides and on wing of both DF flying boats were, the designations H205 and H206 were applied, and on the S-43A – H207.

The H206 at an intermediate point in the ferry route to Yakutia.

On 17 May S.A. Levanevskiy ferried the first DF, H205, for testing in Sevastopol. Two types of American hydroplanes were being evaluated in Sevastopol almost in parallel – the DF and the S-43A. Testing was undertaken under the aegis of the Scientific-Research Institute of Civil Air Fleet (NII GVF, *Nauchno-Isseldovatelskiy Institut Grazhdanskogo Vozdushnogo Flota),* but the crews were provided by Polar Aviation. The famous pilots S.A. Levanevskiy and A.N. Gratsianskiy, as well as pilot S.A. Antyushev, who had been seconded from Siberia, flew the airplanes. The flying boats quickly passed the entire test program, which included recording the flight-performance characteristics, long-range flights, testing of the on-board equipment and the seaworthiness of the flying boat. The seaworthiness tests were performed by water landing on waves of different heights, and also there were measured the take-off distance and the service ceiling with various flight weights. The water landing run was measured in both windy and calm conditions. The airplanes were tested for range by flying around the Crimean Peninsula. The tests were concluded in July 1937. During the tests, one of the underwing floats was damaged on the DF. Gratsianskiy flew the last few flights as Levanevskiy had been recalled to Moscow to prepare for the long-range flight over the North Pole.

Gratsianskiy later wrote: 'The aircraft attracted with its beautiful streamlined shape, elegance, smooth lines'. In the hull of the amphibian were soft sofas, as well as a toilet and a small galley. Naturally, after the MBR-2 this aircraft seemed to Gratsianskiy a technical marvel.

In general, both the flying boat and the amphibian were rated highly by the test pilots. In comparison with the obsolete Dornier Wal airplanes then being operated by Polar Aviation, they represented a completely new stage in the development of hydroaviation, not only significantly surpassing their predecessors in terms of their flight-performance characteristics, but also providing the crew with comfort and safety. Suffice it to say that on the Wal the cockpits were open and there was no heating (even during operations in the Arctic). The airplanes were not comparable in terms of payload either. The Wals were, for the most part, converted military aircraft – in view of their obsolescence

The H205 flying boat has been pulled up onto the shore.

One of the two DF flying boats on the water.

they were no longer required by the VVS, and they were not capable of operating fully as passenger carrying aircraft. Polar Aviation was actually developing regular air routes in Siberia, and the DF and S-43A were intended for them.

The difficulties in piloting the DF flying boat was a certain disadvantage. Their test report indicated: ' ... this aircraft needs to be flown ... by a highly qualified pilot'. The Directorate of Polar Aviation did not have any problems with the latter – there was nothing to suggest a shortage of highly qualified pilots there.

Subsequently, the design of the hydroplanes was also subject to study by specialists at Factory No.156 (the former Factory of Experimental Designs of TsAGI), which had reviewed all the foreign aviation equipment that arrived in the country. For Soviet specialists the modern technologies and materials used in aircraft production in the USA were of great interest. From this perspective both aircraft were characteristic examples of the advanced level of the American aviation industry. A report on the DF issued by Factory No.156 stated: 'The entire design is characterised by simplicity, lightness, and convenience in a technological sense'. An attention was paid to the way individual assemblies were made as well as the well-thought-out unsinkability system of the hull and underwing floats, as well as the use of highly-effective anticorrosion coatings.

The airplanes were then ferried back from Crimea to the Moscow region, to the Polar Aviation base at Zakharkovo, and preparations were started for entering them into service on the air routes. The amphibian was fitted out for operations

The H206 flying boat afloat.

This DF has been moored at the shore.

A DF flying boat prior to flight.

in the North, and an auxiliary electrical generator with small petrol engine was fitted in order to feed the equipment whilst the airplane was parked.

All three American airplanes were intended for the marine unit of the Yenisey Air Group under the GUSMP, which at the time was commanded by A.G. Alekseev. The plan was to use the S-43A on the route Krasnoyarsk–Igarka. The crew remained the same as during the tests: pilot Gratsianskiy, radio-operator Kozin, and mechanics Krasnov and Pisarev. On the very first flight on 14 August 1937 a radiogram was received with an order to return to Krasnoyarsk to prepare to search for the missing Levanevskiy's aircraft. His four-engine DB-A with the registration number H209 had disappeared somewhere in the Arctic during the long-range flight to America, along with his entire crew.

One DF flying boat, H206, and S-43A H207 were drafted in to the search for the missing airplane. The amphibian re-deployed to Krasnoyarsk where, at the factory named after Pobezhimov, it was fitted with a radio compass and additional fuel tanks, having removed some of the seats from the cabin. After taking on board a range of supplies and a barrel of tetraethyl lead (the American engines refused to work on the standard Soviet fuel), Gratsianskiy departed for Tiksi. Having made a few flights in the Soviet part of the Arctic the crew flew to the American Cape Barrow and operated from there for some considerable time.

Sortie after sortie ended without success, and no trace of H209 was found. The sea had frozen over close to the coast, attempts were made to operate the aircraft using a wheeled undercarriage but the ice was very thin. This culminated in the tail wheel falling through the ice and breaking, and a scratch-built ski was fitted in its place. The last flight took place on 26 October. After the search had been called off the S-43A was flown to Fairbanks where the tail wheel was replaced. As the service life of the engines was almost totally used up by these intensive operations, the crew were ordered to fly only to Providence Bay, where the steamer *Okhotsk* picked up the amphibian.

From there, Gratsianskiy informed that the frames in the nose-section of the hull were crumpled, some of the glazing had been broken, the wing centerplane struts on the starboard were bent, a flap was damaged, as was one of the blades of the starboard propeller. Initially, the intention was to conserve the aircraft till the next season in Chukotka, but there were concerns over storing the airplane out in the open. Then the idea emerged of placing the aircraft into one of the warehouses in the Port of Vladivostok for the winter. In the end, however, in January 1938 the amphibian was dismantled and was brought by train initially to Moscow, and then to Sevastopol, to Repair Factory No.45. Some time later there were delivered new engines and struts that had been purchased in the USA, as well as seats and mats for the cabin which had been left behind in Krasnoyarsk.

The Douglas was somewhat delayed with the departure to Chukotka. On 22 August 1937 the flying boat made an emergency water landing close to the village of Korynkar (not far from Beryozov). The reason for this was the low-quality fuel that had been put on board in Tyumen. The aircraft had to be ferried to Samarovo, where a brigade from Factory No.19 (which manufactured under licence the Cyclone engines, similar to those fitted to the DF) began to repair the engines. Only on 4 September did H206 depart for the east, to Dudinka. The crew was comprised of pilots P.G. Golovin and M.T. Slepnyov and mechanic Chechin. The search for Levanevskiy's airplane continued until late autumn, and then the DF returned home 'under its own power'.

The intensive flights during the course of this rescue operation enabled an objective assessment of the capabilities of American aircraft. The S-43A amphibian was considered

A DF flying boat close to the shore at Zakharkovo.

One of the DF flying boats is moored at the shore.

A parked DF.

A poster advertising flights in the DF airplanes on the Lena air route.

very suitable for expedition work in the Arctic and this is how it began to be used moving forward. The DF received the following positive assessment: 'according to the testimony of crews this is an excellent passenger aircraft but not such a good expedition airplane ... '

During the 1938 summer season both DFs were used on regular routes (Gorskiy's crew flew the H205) and the S-43A was assigned to the Moscow Special Purpose Air Group (MAGON, *Moskovskaya Aviagruppa Osobogo Naznacheniya*) under the GUSMP. There the amphibian served for some time as a trainer and was then flown to Igarka where it carried out the ice reconnaissance and delivered cargoes around winter locations of various expeditions. When the record-breaking *Rodina* aircraft went missing during a long-range flight to the Far East with its female crew led by V. Grizodubova, some 50 aircraft were sent to search for it. The intention was to send H207 as well from Moscow and departure was set for 4 October. The previous day, however, pilot Sakharov on MP-1 flying boat discovered the site of the emergency landing. They coped therefore without Sikorsky's amphibian.

In July 1939 the GU GVF requested that these three American hydroplanes be transferred to them to set up their own air route Krasnoyarsk–Norilsk, but the GUSMP refused.

The commanders of H207 were changed several times – after Gratsianskiy the amphibian was flown by A.N. Tyagunin, Alekseev, P.G. Golovin, M.N. Kaminskiy and V.N. Zadkov. On 16 May 1939 Tyagunin water landed the airplane on the Ivankovskoye Reservoir (informally known as the Moscow Sea) following a training flight. As a result of the hard impact with the water the wing strut on the starboard side was bent, and the bracing wire of the port side float was torn. The aircraft was repaired and ferried to the North by Alekseev. On 19 June, shortly after take-off in Arkhangelsk, oil began to leak from the port engine. The pilot water landed on the Severnaya Dvina River some 115km from the city. From there the aircraft was taken to Arkhangelsk by a tugboat. The conclusion was reached that this was the fault of the pilot, who had overheated the engine.

In August–September 1939 Hero of the Soviet Union P.G. Golovin performed a long-range flight of over 27,000km in this amphibian. He flew from Moscow via Krasnoyarsk, Kirensk and Yakutsk, and reached Tiksi. From there the crew made a series of flights along the coastline of the eastern part of the Northern Sea Route. The airplane visited Kotelniy Island, Russkoye Ustye, Khatykhtakh on

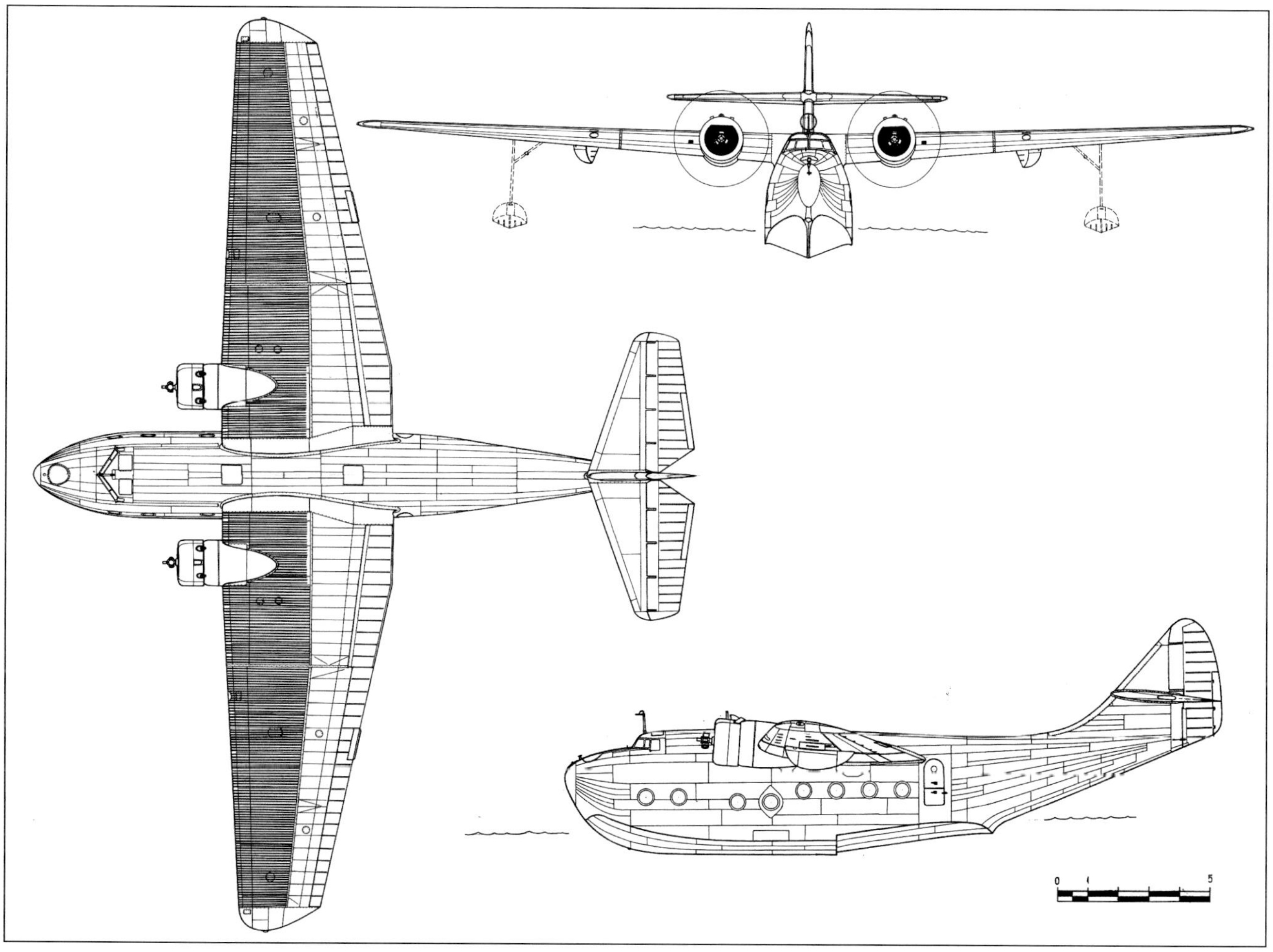

Three-view drawings of a DF flying boat.

the Indigirka River, as well as Pevek and Nizhnekolymsk. Close to Wrangel Island the pilots flew into a dense fog and made an emergency landing on Cape Schmidt, which ended quite safely. Golovin's main task was to search for bays that were suitable for anchoring vessels, and for the construction of ports. Occasionally the S-43A carried passengers and cargoes to and from the winter locations of the expeditions. Having reached Uelen in Chukotka, Golovin turned back and returned to Moscow via Pevek, Tiksi, Ust-Olyenyok, Dudinka, Igarka, and Krasnoyarsk.

In the 1940 season, G.K. Orlov's crew flew the amphibian, and he ferried it from Moscow to Pevek, covering 10,780km. From 1 July Orlov was engaged in ice reconnaissance in the western part of the Kara Sea. Having amassed some 23 hrs flying time the flights had to be stopped for the engines repair. On 15 July the aircraft arrived in Ust-Kara and resumed operations. On 16 August Orlov was returning from his next flight and, as he was water landing close to Oleniy Island, the amphibian hit a sunken log at high-speed and was thrown round 180 degrees from the impact. On the port side the fuselage frames were bent and the centerplane struts had broken, the starboard float had been torn off completely, and the propeller had cut through the side of the airplane. Water was gushing in through a hole in the bottom of the airplane and it was half sunk. The aircraft delivery from Dikson to Krasnoyarsk for repair cost 139,000 roubles. It was expected that the amphibian would be ready for use in the spring of 1941 but the deadline was not maintained, and then the war broke out. Up until mid-1942 the S-43A was still listed in the Polar Aviation as unserviceable, and then it was written off.

The Douglas flying boats went on to serve for longer. In May 1939 H206 was transferred to the Lena Air Group, and at that time V.N. Zadkov was head of the crew on this airplane. His flight crew also included co-pilot Streltsov, mechanic Pyatin and radio-operator Abramchuk.

A second flying boat – H205, soon followed the H206. Pilot B.N. Agrov was flying this airplane, and on 25 July 1939 during a take off in Kazachiy he ran aground. The aircraft spun round at high speed and the strut of one of the floats was bent. It was quickly repaired, however, and was also operational the following year.

In 1940 the H206 stood idle for almost the entire summer, as the engines had been badly repaired in Krasnoyarsk. On top of that the flying boat had been filled with a bad batch of oil on 13 July.

S.A. Asyamov took up the captain's seat of H205, and on 14 July he water-landed badly on the Lena River in Yakutsk after sundown. Furthermore, the pilot had ignored a warning that had been sent from Sangar that he would not get to his destination whilst it was still light; the head of the port in Sangar had suggested landing there and departing for Yakutsk in the morning. As a result of this accident, the hull, one propeller, a float, and the aileron on the port side were damaged. The aircraft again had to be repaired.

An engine was removed from the parked H205 and it was fitted to the H206. This enabled I.D. Cherepkov's crew to fly this aircraft and make the best of the end of the season prior to the area completely freezing over.

In April 1941 the Lena air route was transferred from Polar Aviation to come under Aeroflot, and in May the Yakutsk Air Group of the GVF accepted some of the aircraft that were operating under Polar Aviation, including both DFs. Their crew commanders at the time were S.A. Asyamov and I.D. Cherepkov. In June 1941 the H205 was destroyed on landing in Yakutsk. The second flying boat was used on the Lena route for much longer and met the war there. The American airplane continued to fly in this area but with an ever-increasing intensity because of other aircraft being sent to the front line. In particular, a brigade which was building the reserve airfield for the ALSIB route (the Soviet Union portion of the Alaska-Siberian air route receiving Lend-Lease aircraft) at Omolon was re-deployed to Shcherbakovo Lake by the Douglas. In total, over that year the aircraft performed 36 flights for the needs of the ALSIB route. The airplane was known for its excellent reliability. Only in August 1942 with pilot I.I. Serebryannikov at the controls did one engine fail on take-off from Kirensk but he managed to land without breaking anything. In the following year 1943 the DF fulfilled 209 percent of the plan for air transportation.

The H206 survived the war and continued to fly with A.P. Fisher's crew. The airplane was based in Yakutsk at Zhatayskiy hydroplane port. In March–April 1946 it was being repaired, but in August of the following year the aircraft became unserviceable. In the first half of 1948, after standing idle for almost a year, the Douglas was written off in view of the fact that it was 'worn out and would be inexpedient to repair'.

4.5 Levanevskiy's Vultee

Following the unsuccessful attempt of a long-range flight to the USA over the North Pole in August 1935, the famous pilot S.A. Levanevskiy changed his mind about the possibility of performing such flight in an indigenous aircraft. At that same time the idea of opening air routes with America continued to look very attractive, and Levanevskiy succeeded in convincing the Soviet leadership of this. He was allowed to go abroad and select a suitable aircraft.

In July 1936 Levanevskiy arrived in the USA. After having looked around various enterprises he settled on the V-1A. 'This is a wonderful high-speed monoplane' – wrote Levanevskiy. The V-1A was the first aircraft that was created by a young company headed by Gerard Vultee, and it belonged to the category of high-speed passenger airplanes that was very popular in the mid-1930s. The V-1 was a single-

S.A. Levanevskiy (on the right) observes the modification of his V-1AS at the Vultee factory in San Francisco, summer 1936.

Preparing the V-1AS for flight; standing on the wing (on the right) is S.A. Levanevskiy.

engine, all-metal monoplane with retractable undercarriage and a comfortable cabin for its time that was capable of accommodating eight passengers and two crew members. Small batches of this aircraft were built from 1934 onwards.

TsAGI documents recorded that Levanevskiy had been offered a completed aircraft, which was later modified and fitted out in accordance with the customer's requirements. This was the 24th airplane, the last in the series of the V-1A. Modifications of the aircraft took one and half months, and a number of changes had been introduced so its designation was changed to a V-1AS.

Firstly, the airplane was fitted with two all-metal floats manufactured by the EDO Aircraft Corporation. The wheeled undercarriage was not removed – it was simply retracted into the landing gear bays and enclosed by easily removable doors. As the floats had an effect on the directional stability, the area of the vertical tail was enlarged by adding an additional section. The weight and the drag of the floats reduced the maximum speed by more than 50km/h. Even fitting a more powerful 890hp R-1820-F52 engine in place of the standard 735hp F2 with a three-bladed (instead of a

The V-1AS airplane shortly before its departure from San Francisco.

from icing. Goodrich pneumatic de-icers were fitted on the leading edges of the wings and tail. The propeller blades could be squirted with an alcoholic mixture where necessary. A panel with adjustable shutters was installed in the cowling in front of the engine.

Most of the V-1A airplanes was equipped with Fairchild radio compasses, the antenna for which was located in a teardrop shaped cowling above the pilot's cockpit. On the V-1AS, a more contemporary Lear radio compass was installed with a large loop antenna that was fitted atop of the fuselage tail part.

The aircraft was completed in July. Then the wheeled undercarriage was removed and shipped to the USSR, and the floats were installed in its place. They did not stop there, however, and the V-1AS was again placed on wheels and was test-flown. Floats again replaced the wheeled undercarriage and the airplane was tested again.

two-bladed) propeller did not help. Series V-1As had two fuel tanks in the wing centerplane with an overall capacity of 764l. The V-1AS had nine fuel tanks, which could hold 1,536l of fuel – two additional tanks were located close to the wing joint, and another four were in the wing sections. One more fuel tank was fitted in place of one of the seats in the passenger cabin. An additional oil tank was also installed, which could be topped up in flight.

As part of the route passed along the areas of the Far North, considerable attention was paid to the protection

Levanevskiy monitored the process of the airplane modification on the daily basis, and soon he was joined by a second member of the crew, navigator V.I. Levchenko. He was a Captain of the VVS who had flown previously with Levanevskiy on the Dornier Wal flying boat, when they were entrusted with recovering the American pilot Mattern who had crashed in Chukotka, and also accompanied Levanevskiy on the ANT-25 during an unsuccessful attempt to reach America via the North Pole.

The acquisition of the aircraft was administered through the Vimalert company, and the V-1AS was registered with Polar Aviation with the registration number CCCP H208.

Pilot S.A. Levanevskiy.

The pilot's cockpit of the V-1AS airplane.

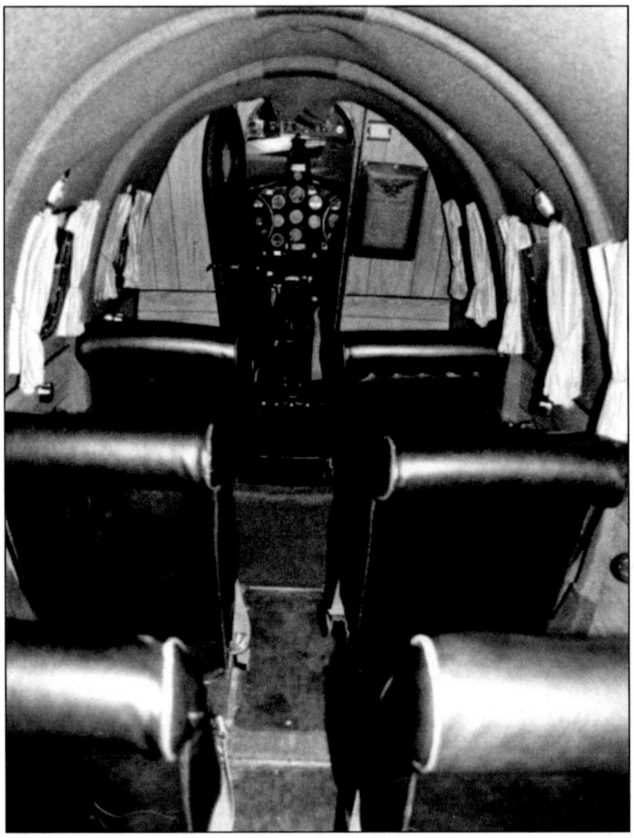

The passenger cabin of the V-1AS (viewed from the tail of the airplane).

The passenger cabin of the V-1AS (viewed from the pilot's cockpit).

The V-1AS takes off from San Francisco.

The V-1AS parked at an intermediate point of the ferry route.

Pilot S.A. Levanevskiy, navigator V.I. Levchenko (in the centre) and two Americans standing next to the Vultee in Fairbanks.

The registration number was applied to the fuselage and the red wings of the airplane. The Soviet crew performed several training flights from Los Angeles to Phoenix and San Diego, familiarising themselves with the aircraft equipment. They flew on wheels and on floats, measuring the fuel and oil consumption. The water landings were performed in the ocean on waves of up to two metres in height.

The American aircraft did not have the range of the ANT-25 but on the other hand it was more suitable for commercial flights on the norther coastline route Levanevskiy had set out.

On the morning of 5 August 1936, the V-1AS took off from Los Angeles and flew to San Francisco. This portion of the route was in heavy forecast, so the flight was done above the clouds using radio compass. The further flight up to the Canadian border was flown in good weather and passed without incident. The difficulties set in on the section Seattle–Juno when the crew flew into rain and fog. One moment they were flying above the clouds, and the other they were getting

A V-1AS airplane on the water.

A Vultee on the Yenisey River in Krasnoyarsk prior to having its floats changed for a wheeled undercarriage

A V-1AS after Levanevskiy's crew landing at Shchelkovo airfield, 13 September 1936.

close to the water itself. When the visibility deteriorated to a really low level the coastline would come into view. This turned out to be the uninhabited Goose Island and the pilots landed on the water, brought the aircraft in between two cliffs, and began to ride out the storm. They found they had nothing to eat as no provisions had been envisaged for that portion of the route. Levanevskiy and Levchenko spent the whole night sitting on the wing, watching how the waves were taking the hydroplane away. When the airplane began floating towards rocks, they both jumped into the water fully clothed and held the aircraft at a safe distance away from the rocks. In the morning the storm had passed but the tide was beginning to go out. The Vultee ended up on the shore and they had to wait another day for a high tide, after which the aircraft could again be put to sea.

The next stop was made in Swansea Bay. Levanevskiy saw stone-built houses, a factory chimney and a quay and thought that this was a large settlement. This, however, turned out to be an abandoned mining camp, where only two people now lived. Then the V-1AS landed in Ketchikan, Juneau, Fairbanks, and Nome. In Nome, such a thick fog descended on the bay that Levchenko, who had gone into town, could not find his aircraft when he came back. He wandered around for several hours before he was shown where the aircraft was anchored.

Uelen, which is situated on the Soviet side of the Bering Strait, was in the thick overcast. Suddenly and miraculously a gap opened in the clouds and Levanevskiy was able to land safely. From Chukotka the aircraft flew along the Northern Sea Route for some time. They made intermediate stops in Vankarem and then in Kolyuchinskaya Bay. In Ambarchik Bay the aircraft stayed for a few days along with the Molokov's crew, who had flown the Wal. They were waiting for the fog to clear, but at the end, fearing the onset of a polar autumn, they took off with almost zero visibility. From Tiksi Levanevskiy turned towards the continent, crossed the mountains and

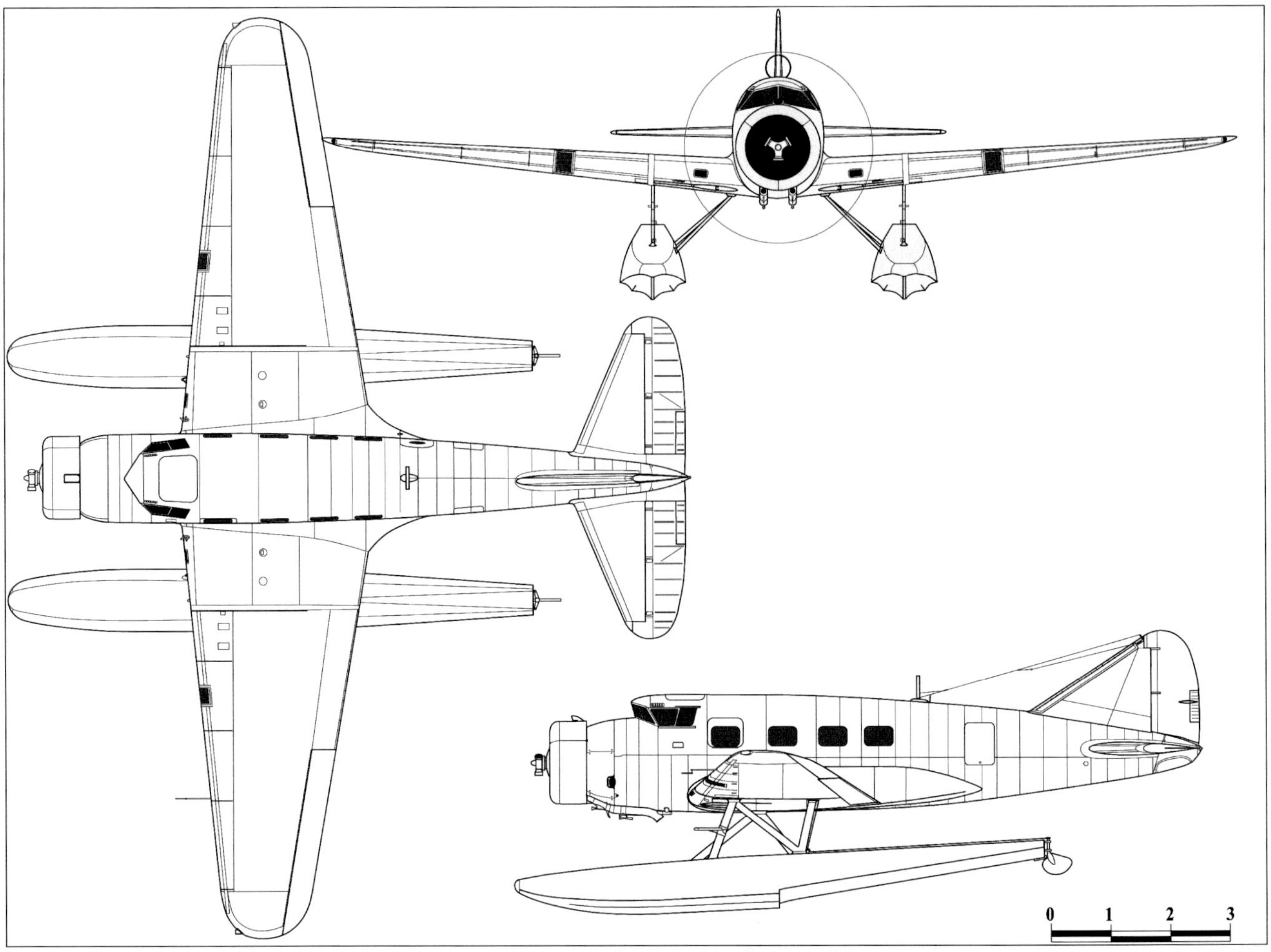

Three-view drawings of a V-1AS airplane on floats.

landed on the Lena River. The Vultee had covered 11,000km by the time it had reached Yakutsk, and a further 6,000km remained ahead until they reached Moscow.

From Yakutsk the route was laid to Krasnoyarsk and on 9 September the Vultee was towed up onto the shore at the aircraft repair factory of the GUSMP. The floats were removed and the undercarriage was put to its operational condition. The additional section of the vertical tail was not removed, possibly because they were afraid of damaging the anti-icing device that had been installed on it. The V-1AS spent the remaining part of the journey operating on a wheeled undercarriage.

On 13 September the H208 landed at Shchelkovo airfield. In total it had covered 17,166km. The reception was very ceremonial, among attendees were V.M. Molotov, L.M. Kaganovich (a member of the Political Bureau) N.S. Khrushchyov (who was the then secretary of the Moscow city committee of the All-Union Communist Party of Bolsheviks) and for some reason the Head of the Joint State Political Directorate G.G. Yagoda. Kaganovich handed Levanevskiy a congratulatory letter from Stalin and there was a large gathering. The crew stood on a podium, towards which the aircraft itself was towed. In his speech Molotov said: 'The long-range flight by Levanevskiy and Levchenko demonstrates how well Soviet pilots fulfil Stalin's order: combining courage and bravery with skills and knowledge of technical achievements'. In the evening a banquet was held in honour of the entire crew in the building of the Moscow City Council. The following day Levanevskiy was awarded the Order of the Red Banner of Labour, as well as 25,000 roubles, Levchenko received the Order of Lenin and 15,000 roubles.

The Vultee joined the Moscow Air Unit of Polar Aviation but was soon handed over for study to Factory No.156. By 20 October the aircraft had already been dismantled into separate assemblies, measured, and photographed. Although the V-1A never became mass-produced, its design was well suited to large-scale production. The airplane was characterised by an almost complete absence of welded joints and the widespread use of stamped parts. Soviet engineers were surprised not to find a part which was done by manual stamping process, which was widespread at the time in Russia. The Americans had used machine riveting and a wide selection of open-section profiles that were well suited to series production.

The American designers had paid a great deal of attention to the ease of maintenance and repair of the aircraft. 'The design of the engine mount and the cowling is very convenient from the standpoint of ease approach and quick removal of the engine cowling ... the design of the undercarriage is well-thought-out with respect to installation and removal. Access to all the bolts and attachment parts is very easy and does not require any specialist tools. The access to the undercarriage maintenance parts is likewise very convenient ... '.

The comfortable cabin was highly marked: 'The well-adjusted parts attract attention; the cabin looks very neat from inside and from the outside'.

Naturally, there were some things that came under criticism. The forward-slanted windscreen, which was fashionable at that time in America, was not liked. 'The canopy is not very convenient, as the field of view is very restricted in its upper part'. Other shortcomings were also found: ' ... the stabiliser and the elevator are difficult to remove'.

The VVS representatives also studied the V-1AS, while the aircraft did not interest them as a potential military airplane – they just wanted to search for anything useful for improving the indigenous designs. They found quite a few. According to the report written by *Voeninzhener* Rumyantsev, who reviewed Vultee in November 1936, approximately one and a half dozen design elements were found which could be introduced into Soviet aircraft manufacturing. In particular, illumination of the instrument panel by reflected light, electric actuators of the undercarriage and flaps, heating of the venturi tube using exhaust gases, remote control for the radio set and radio compass, the convenient and reliable locks on the cowling and hatches, plastic rollers of the control cables support, and much more.

In August 1937 the V-1AS was returned to Polar Aviation. The intention was to use this airplane for searching Levanevskiy's crew, which had vanished without trace in the Arctic on his long-range flight to America. Two circumstances, however, prevented this: a ski undercarriage was not available for this aircraft, and a sufficiently experienced pilot who was familiar with the American aircraft could not be found either.

In December 1937 the Vultee was listed in the Moscow Air Group but it was in need of repair. The repair works were completed, and in 1938 the airplane was used in the Moscow Air Group as a trainer for pilots, which were to fly American aircraft purchased for the Polar Aviation. Among them were some well-known pilots, such as Gratsianskiy, Zadkov, Kotov, Mazuruk, and Tyagunin. The overall flying hours of the airplane were not so high though just eight hours in a year. In that same year the Bureau of Special Designs developed ski undercarriage for this airplane.

In 1940 the V-1As underwent an overhaul in the workshops of the Moscow Air Group, to it was again able to fly on both ski and wheeled undercarriage. This work was supervised G.G. Sokolov.

The airplane was based at Zakharovo airfield just outside Moscow right up until the outbreak of war with Germany. As the Germans approached Moscow the aircraft was ferried to Siberia, and the decision was taken to use it for transportation carried out by the Igarka Air Group. As the Polar Aviation had transferred some of its aircraft to the VVS and naval aviation after the outbreak of war, it was decided to put whatever was left to use. In Igarka the aircraft was fitted with a non-retractable ski undercarriage, and it was operated at this location for approximately a month.

In summer 1941 pilot V.V. Malkov was to have ferried the V-1AS from Igarka to Gorkiy but on take-off the propeller failed, as it refused to move from a fine pitch to a coarse pitch. The aircraft descended and hit the riverbank.

On 2 December, following repairs, a test flight was undertaken. The Vultee was flown by pilot A.V. Kiselyov and the engineer of the air group N.F. Potapov. Whilst taxiing in deep snow the pilot overheated the engine. After lift-off he got confused and tried to land immediately. This is how the events were described in a report written by the commander of the air group: 'Having turned the aircraft 300 degrees in the direction of Staraya Igarka, at an altitude of just two to four metres, and afraid of crashing into the high bank of the Yenisey River, comrade Kiselyov began to turn the aircraft to the right. In doing so, he caught the snow by the starboard wing, the undercarriage was torn off, after which the aircraft turned over onto its port side and buried itself in the snow. The aircraft was crashed and became 100 percent out of action'.

In the first half of 1942 the airplane was still listed with the Igarka Air Group (a plan for future flights was even written for it) until it was officially written off.

4.6 The Ill-Fated 'Convoy Fighter'

A.N. Prokofiev-Seversky, the Russian naval pilot and First World War ace, emigrated abroad after the revolution, settled in the USA and changed his surname to simply Seversky. In 1931 he founded his own company, the Seversky Aircraft Corporation. The chief designer of the company was Seversky's fellow countryman, a native of Tiflis, A.M. Kartveli, was also a former officer in the Russian Army. At the beginning of the 1930s Seversky and Kartveli created a range of aircraft, the most successful of which was the SEV-1XP fighter, which was accepted into service of US Army Air Corps in 1937 under the P-35 designation.

One of the versions of this basic design was the two-seat SEV-2PA dubbed 'Convoy Fighter'. As the name suggests this airplane was designed as a two-seat long-range escort fighter. In fact, it was the same P-35, in the fuselage fairing of which a cockpit was arranged for a second crewmember. There was more than enough space in the fuselage for this since the P-35 itself was a product of the evolution of the prototype two-seat SEV-2XP fighter, which was manufactured in spring 1935. Several variants of the power plants of the R-1820 and R-1830 engine families were tried for the fighter. Aside from the retractable undercarriage, an original amphibious undercarriage was proposed, which was initially created for the SEV-3M amphibian, the first aircraft to be manufactured by Seversky company. It consisted of two floats, into which the main wheels retracted. In case of take-off from and

A two-seat 2PA-L fighter from a Soviet order at the factory airfield in the USA.

Flight testing of a 2PA-L in the USA; the airplane carries a black letter R (Russia) on the starboard wing.

landing on water, the wheels remained inside the floats, while there was sufficient height for the aircraft tail. On landing, the wheels extended from the bays in the base of the floats, the rear support struts of the floats shortened and the airplane 'squatted down', allowing the tail wheel to touch down. The SEV-3M had been demonstrated to a Soviet delegation led by I.I. Pogosskiy back in 1934.

The purely wheeled version was designated the 2PA-L, and the amphibian the 2PA-A. The fixed armament of the 2PA corresponded to that of the P-35 and comprised a single 12.7mm machine gun (with an ammunition load of 200 cartridges), and a single 7.62mm machine gun (with an ammunition load of 500 cartridges) above the engine. To protect the fighter from the rear hemisphere a 7.62mm Colt MG40 machine gun was fitted on a movable gun mount in the observer's cockpit (for which there was an ammunition load of five magazines with 100 cartridges each). The monoplane layout ensured a high speed for the aircraft that significantly exceeded the speed of other two-seat fighters of the time, which for the most part were biplanes. The 2PA attracted interest from abroad. At the beginning of 1939, the version fitted with the 1,100hp R-1830-S3C made a long-range flight to Britain, where in the March it underwent a series of testing at the research centre at Martlesham Heath. However, the British specialists decided against purchasing the Seversky fighter, evidently relying on their indigenous Hawker Hotspur and Bolton-Paul Defiant.

Seversky Aircraft Corporation did not have any large-scale contracts for some

The rear machine-gun mount of the 2PA-L.

Open canopy and rear machine gun of the 2PA-L.

The GR 1820 G2 engine, the propeller has been removed, February 1939.

time, and as a consequence of this, they were actively seeking for new customers. One evening in October 1936 Seversky unexpectedly appeared at the Washington apartment of Brigade Commander V.A. Kreyn-Burzin, the Soviet military attaché, whom he had once known from his service in naval aviation of the Baltic Fleet. In his conversation with Kreyn-Burzin he unofficially offered the USSR training aircraft and fighters, as well as transfer of the contemporary American technology of aircraft manufacturing, and the training of engineering and technical personnel.

Kreyn-Burzin immediately sent a message to Moscow, and this message was certainly of interest. On 5 January 1937 the Head of the VVS Ya.I. Alksnis wrote to Marshal M.N. Tukhachevskiy who was in charge of the re-arming of the Red Army: '... I consider it necessary to accept Seversky's proposal, and to establish a practical business relationship with him'.

The initiative to purchase the 'Convoy Fighter' was made by the Director of the Engineering Department of Amtorg, N.A. Sokolov. The Head of TsAGI N.M. Kharlamov, the Head of the GUAP M.M. Kaganovich, and the Head of the VVS RKKA Ya.I. Alksnis supported Sokolov. The Soviet Union took the risk of immediately acquiring a license for the production of the 2PA in both (wheeled and amphibious) versions.

On 28 April 1937 representatives of Amtorg and Seversky Aircraft Corporation signed a licensing agreement on production of the 2PA fighter in the USSR. The company provided drawings, a variety of engineering and technological documentation which had already been translated into the metric system and ensured that specialists would be trained at their own factory in Farmingdale. The agreement also included delivery of one example of the 2PA-A (in the USSR this was designated just the 2PA) and a single 2PA-L. Both aircraft, without the engines, equipment and armament, which were purchased separately, cost together 90,000 US Dollars. The airplanes were fitted with different engines: the 2PA-A had 850hp GR-1820-G2 and the 2PA-L was equipped with 745hp GR-1820-G7. This land-based fighter was to have been ready by the end of September 1937, while the amphibian by the end of November. The agreement envisaged the arrangement of series production at Soviet factories by April

1940. Not only could the Soviet Union produce the 2PA for its own use but could also export them to Afghanistan, Iran, and Mongolia, while exporting to any other countries was banned. The company fulfilled its obligations and delivered all the documentation to Moscow. The 2PA-L was built on time, passed the prescribed program of delivery tests, dismantled and shipped by sea to the USSR in the steamer *City of Fairburn* on 19 November. The amphibian was completed later, and Soviet pilots V.A. Stepanchyonok and S.N. Chasovikov participated in the delivery test flying in America. The official handover of this aircraft took place only on 15 March 1938, and a week later it was shipped to the Soviet Union.

At the end of 1937 all the documentation and the first aircraft arrived at TsAGI, where the work began with manufacturing a ski undercarriage for the American fighter (at that time at TsAGI all the VVS RKKA airplanes were fitted with ski undercarriage in winter). For the 2PA-L, the rectangular wooden skis with metal edging were designed. The skis retracted in flight: the landing gear leg, strut, and ski formed a parallelogram, which retracted rearwards. The small tail ski was retractable as well, in the same manner as the removed tail wheel. In order for the main ski lay flush on the undercarriage fairing in the retracted position, the shape of the fairing was changed. For the tail-mounted ski, the tail wheel bay doors were simply removed. The modification of the aircraft onto a ski undercarriage was carried out by Factory No.156 in Moscow. After a relatively short program of testing at OELID TsAGI which comprised just eight flights (the airplane was flown by Yu.K. Stankevich), on 14 March 1938 the fighter was handed over to the NII VVS.

The Soviet markings were not applied to this aircraft and it just remained silver, with the Seversky emblem on the side. In those locations where the American markings were usually applied (on top of the starboard wing, and underneath the port wing), there have been painted the

A 2PA-L fighter during testing at the OELID TsAGI; Soviet markings were not applied to this airplane.

The 'Convoy Fighter' during testing at the NII VVS, spring, 1938.

The fuselage of a dismantled 2PA-L airplane at Factory No.156 in Moscow, March 1938.

The rear cockpit and machine-gun mount of a 2PA-A amphibian.

large black letters R. These were repeated (in a smaller size) on both sides of the tail fin.

At the NII VVS the 2PA-L was flown by the famous test pilot Major S.P. Suprun, with different flight observers (Pistolkors, Shcherbakov, and Shaurov). In the course of the eighth flight the engine piston burned through. The 2PA-L was returned to testing only in May, now on a wheeled undercarriage. This time the program was almost brought to a conclusion. On 31 May–10 July some 48 flights were performed before another piston burned through again. According to the pilots' report, piloting characteristics of the 2PA-L were similar to the ones of the I-16 fighter but it was more stable in the air.

Overall, a lot of advantages were found with this American airplane. The aircraft turned out to be very manoeuvrable on the ground due to the controllable tail wheel and effective brakes. The pilot's cockpit was spacious and comfortable, with excellent field of view. There also turned out to be a number of drawbacks, however. The strength of the airplane did not correspond to the norms for 1937 that were valid in the USSR at the time. The cockpit ventilation was found to be unsatisfactory, while the tail wheel shook on the landing roll. The flight observer's cockpit was severely criticised: it was cramped and uncomfortable. The rear machine gun could only fire across a narrow sector behind the airplane's tail as the canopy got in the gunner's way. At high flight speeds moving the machine gun along the horizontal plane required considerable efforts – the gun mount did not have a wind compensator.

The machine guns were test fired only on the ground – their mounts turned out to be not rigid enough and there was a significant shot dispersion. Furthermore, it was noted that using the same sight for two machine guns of different calibres was clearly inconvenient.

The operation of the power plant was acknowledged as unsatisfactory – the high thermal stress of the engine often led to its overheating. In contrast, the cylinder heads overcooled in a dive. The cowling did not have the controllable flaps thus the control of the engine ventilation was not possible. Specialists of the NII VVS treated the integrated fuel tanks with distrust, considering this solution as reducing the airplane survivability in combat. Furthermore, the American designers did not envisage making the fuel tanks self-sealing and did not make arrangements for jettisoning fuel in an emergency.

The results of mock air combats with I-16 and DI-6 (two-seat biplane) fighters, and the R-10 reconnaissance aircraft turned out to be quite interesting. The only worthy opponent for the American airplane was the I-16. At low altitudes it surpassed the 2PA-L, but at higher altitudes all its advantages would fall away. At an altitude of 5,000m the I-16 was significantly inferior to the 2PA-L in terms of speed and manoeuvrability in the horizontal plane. The I-16 could get away from the American fighter only in a dive, while the

A 2PA-A amphibian at an airfield.

A 2PA-A amphibian during testing in the USA.

2PA-L easily left behind the R-10 and the DI-6.

TsAGI designers attempted at refining the power plant – a direct intake duct was made into the oil radiator, and the intake slits for the second (internal) cowling were enlarged. This however, did not give rise to any significant improvements. Thus, the assessment of the aircraft was two-fold. On the one hand, the airplane characteristics were attractive: 'The flight-performance characteristics of the Seversky airplane are at the level of single-seat high-speed fighters in service with VVS RKKA, and significantly surpass the characteristics of the two-seat airplanes (both fighters and reconnaissance aircraft) ... In terms of its range the airplane differs significantly from all the fighters and is closer to the long-range reconnaissance aircraft', the NII VVS report noted. This position was supported by TsAGI specialists, who had praised the airplane's technological perfection: 'The use of open profiles, stamping, forged and cast parts is widely applied in the aircraft structure. The airplane is not complex for manufacturing and can be mass-produced'.

The 2PA-L was also of interest to Soviet specialists as a potential long-range reconnaissance aircraft. The conclusion was unanimous on this point, however: 'To use this aircraft in a reconnaissance variant, some fundamental changes would be required, especially in the rear cockpit, which would completely change the design of the aircraft'. Therefore, only the long-range fighter version remained in question. At the end of 1938 this was given up as well. A decision followed: ' ... The VVS RKKA cannot accept the fighter into service in view of considerable vulnerability of its wings and fuel tanks, and due to the overall imperfection of its machine-gun armament and power plant'.

The 2PA-A amphibious version began its testing at TsAGI in August 1938 but was involved in an accident on the very first flight. The floats were removed in course of the repairs and were replaced by a wheeled undercarriage similar to the 2PA-L, which had been manufactured at Factory No.156. In this configuration it was test-flown by Yu.K. Stankevich. Testing came to an end in March 1939 as there were concerns over the lack of strength in the undercarriage; an attempt was made to acquire a new set of undercarriage in the USA. It is not known whether these were obtained or whether the airplane continued to fly on the Soviet set. Another accident happened on 22 July 1939. When landing on a concrete runway, a fork of the starboard landing gear leg broke down, the airplane turned and the wheels came off. According to the conclusion of the commission, the reason of this failure was a manufacturing defect – poor welding and warping of the rib. No further information is available regarding the flights of the 2PA-A.

From August 1938 the relations with Seversky company deteriorated significantly. The Soviet engineers had to return home, and in response Amtorg withheld the payment under the agreement. Only after Seversky was forced out of the company board of directors in July 1939, the leadership of the company, which had been renamed Republic Aviation Corporation, agreed to supply the R-1820-G105B engine to replace the old one in the 2PA-L. In autumn, however, the war with Finland broke out and the USA announced a 'moral embargo' in respect of the USSR, and the engine never arrived.

In April 1940 the agreement with the American company expired and it was never prolonged. The 2PA-L was equipped with an M-25 engine at TsAGI and up until mid-1940 this airplane was used for different kinds of research in the field of aerodynamics. Subsequently, both purchased fighters were laid up. During the evacuation of the LII in autumn 1941 they were destroyed.

4.7 From Martin M-156 to the PS-30 (or how the Soviet Union did not get the 'Ocean Bomber')

At the beginning of 1936 *Voeninzhener 1-go ranga* Goroshchenko, who had visited the USA with a Soviet aviation delegation, wrote a report in which he specifically mentioned that Martin company was working on a new M-156A flying boat with a flight weight of 26,000kg and a range of 4,000km.

As mentioned above, on 11 April 1936 STO made a decision to acquire licences and technical assistance in the USA for a range of aircraft types. In connection with the fact that the country was lagging behind in the field of hydroaviation, two large flying boats were included on this list – Consolidated 28 and Martin M-156.

The latter aircraft did not yet exist at the time as the designers of Glenn Martin was in process of developing this flying boat, which was a further evolution of the successful Martin M-130, built in 1935. Three such flying boats, also dubbed Clippers, have been serving the route San Francisco–Manila, which was later extended to Hong Kong. The maximum flight range of these airplanes exceeded 5,000km.

The M-156 differed from the Clippers by the larger wingspan (with shorter wing profile), new 1,000hp Wright GR-1820-G2 engines, twin vertical fins, and a number of minor structural and technological changes related to the experience gained in course of operating the previous airplane types. Like the M-130, the new type was a large, four-engine flying boat monoplane. The lateral stability on water was provided by the short sponsons at the waterline level, so the aircraft did not require supportive under-wing floats. These sponsons also contained additional fuel tanks. The aircraft wing laid on the hull and was connected to the sponsons by a system of struts.

The aircraft cabin could accommodate 46 passengers (in seated configuration), but it was also possible to install folding beds or sofas for the higher comfort, or to arrange denser seating so to carry 53 passengers. A crew of eight operated the flying boat and comprised commander of the

A Martin M-156 flying boat in the USA.

aircraft (who was actually the navigator), three pilots (the third was listed as a 'junior pilot'), the flight engineer and his assistant, the radio-operator, and the steward. There were two pilots' seats in the flight deck, each was fitted with a full set of controls. The flying boat was equipped with the most contemporary navigational aids of that era and was capable of day and night flying, and of flying in cloud.

A Martin M-156 airplane on a beaching trolley.

Loading the fuselage of the purchased M-156 onto the steamer *Southlure*.

There was nothing like this in the USSR at the time. Civil Aviation in the Far East operated the worn-out twin-engine Italian Savoia S.55 flying boats, while the most powerful hydroplane in the military service was Tupolev three-engine MTB-1, which had already become obsolete by the time it entered production. Even then, only a few of these were built.

Therefore, it would have seemed attractive to make a leap from the technology of yesterday's aircraft to the contemporary flying boats. In September 1936 an agreement was signed by Amtorg with Glenn Martin for assistance in arranging production of the M-156 in the Soviet Union.

According to this document, the company committed to hand over a set of engineering drawings and calculations on the Martin M-130 flying boat, and then a full set of documentation on the M-156 – drawings, calculations, photographs of the parts and joints, descriptions of the production processes, manufacturing instructions, drawings of the fixtures and special tools. All the documentation was originally provided in English and in the imperial system and was then translated into Russian and into the metric system. The drawings were provided on tracing paper (two sets) plus 10 sets of blueprints.

An example aircraft was ordered from the company, which the Americans dubbed the 'Soviet Clipper'. It should have been ready for delivery to the customer on 12 October 1937, so to be shipped to the Soviet Union in November. The licence along with the aircraft example amounted to 1,050,000 US Dollars, which for the time was a crazy amount of money.

Almost immediately after the agreement signing, the selection began of the factory where the American flying boats were to be produced. In October 1936 the Head of the VVS Directorate of Material and Technical Supply *Kombrig* (Brigade Commander) B.I. Bazenkov proposed that the Martin M-156 be manufactured at two factories simultaneously, Factory No.31 in Taganrog, and Factory No.126 in Komsomolsk-on-Amur. The former was mass-producing MBR-2 flying boats at that time, and the latter had yet to be erected. Bazenkov at the same time suggested to change the Soviet range of rolled products, which included the necessary profiles for the American airplanes (so not to waste any time on a complete recalculation of the strength parameters) and to purchase licences for instruments, special paints and lacquers in the USA.

In the end, the arrangement of series production of the aircraft, which in Soviet documents was designated the M-156, GM-156 or simply 'Glen-Martin', was entrusted to the new Factory No.30 in the city of Savyolovo in the Kalinin region, on the banks of the Rybinsk Reservoir. Building of this enterprise has been started back in 1931, while the plans for its use were constantly changing. According to the previous variant, the plan was to manufacture MTB-1 (ANT-27bis) hydroplanes there, doubling the efforts of Factory No.31. To

A Martin M-156 in Leningrad, spring 1938.

assist in arranging the American aircraft production there, a group of designers led by A.P. Golubkov was transferred from TsAGI to Savyolovo.

It was this group that began to accept the documentation from the USA, and by October 1937 around 80 percent of the drawings had arrived. The factory, however, mentioned that the metric drawings had been 'incorrect'.

The erection of the workshops was protracted, and it was undertaken around the preceding plan, which relied on the MTB-1 with a completely different production technology. The First Main Directorate of the People's Commissariat for the Defence Industry, headed by M.M. Kaganovich, firmly decided that the factory was to be re-orientated towards production of the American flying boats. In February 1937 Soviet side purchased from Glenn Martin and other American suppliers stock of the most complex parts, special tools, fixtures and equipment for a total amount of 800,000 US Dollars. All this began to arrive at Savyolovo.

The production of a prototype in America was delayed, and only in November did the handover tests begin in Baltimore. The flying boat was given the American registration number X19167, and the first flight took place on 27 November. The airplane was flown by the company's crew, under supervision of representatives of Amtorg engineering department. A group was sent from the Soviet Union led by engineer S. Borisenko especially for this testing. This group also comprised pilot Yershov and engineer Kozlov. They arrived in Baltimore on 14 December, when the tests were already in full swing. Nevertheless, Yershov did fly the American flying boat a few times.

The flight-performance characteristics of the M-156 corresponded to those claimed by the company and satisfied the acceptance commission. On 20 January the aircraft was officially handed over to the Soviet representatives. The airplane was ferried to New York, where its dismantling and crating were started. Borisenko and Kozlov supervised this process, while Yershov was transferred to a group of pilots who were test-flying the S-43A amphibian, which had been purchased from Sikorsky company for Soviet Polar Aviation.

On 27 January 1938 Amtorg drew up a delivery note for the purchase of the Martin flying boat prototype. The aircraft was loaded onto the steamer *Southlure* and set off for Leningrad. By no means everything was crated up because the aircraft dimensions were so large. The fuselage was simply placed onto the deck and secured.

At that time a question was raised regarding the purchase of a second example of the flying boat in the form of a set of parts for the further assembly in the USSR. Many were against this, but the Chairman of the Board of Amtorg Rozov asked Kaganovich for his opinion and a month later he received instructions from Moscow to conclude another agreement. This was signed on 17 December 1937.

Doubts about the expediency of acquiring the Martin flying boat came from the fact that it was planned to use it not for the role for which it had been designed. The M-156 was a transoceanic airliner, while the military leadership of the Soviet Union was eager to turn it into a long-range naval aircraft, an 'Ocean Bomber' as the documents of the time described it. The prerequisites for this transformation could be considered a significant range, large load-carrying capacity, and excellent seaworthiness of the flying boat.

In fact, almost 50 passengers and cabin equipment could be replaced with significant quantity of bombs and a powerful firing armament. Where though were the bombs to be placed? According to Borisenko's assessment, the wing structure could 'more or less satisfactory' allow for carrying two tonnes of bombs under the wing – a tonne under each side. For such a large aircraft this was not so much at all. Apart from that, the external carrying of the bombs could adversely affect the flight-performance characteristics which already have been low for the military aircraft. In the end, passenger airliner needed to have significant flight range and reliability, and not a high speed, service ceiling and manoeuvrability of the military airplane.

While the first prototype of the Martin 156 was being manufactured in America, the Soviet side was already thinking about how it could be fit for military purposes. P.D. Samsonov proposed carrying the bombs inside the fuselage and dropping them through hatches to be arranged on the underside of the hull. Obviously, the hatches should have to be hermetically sealed. In fact, nobody in the world had attempted such solution at that time. In 1937 a full-scale mock-up of the fuselage part 'in the heavy bomber version' was built. This structure was presented to the mock-up commission, and the commission came to the conclusion that the modification would require significant design changes and a recalculation of the fuselage strength.

A model of the GM-156 military version project in the Museum of the A.N. Tupolev Design Bureau.

There was preserved a model of the GM-156 military version, which corresponded to a project developed by Golubkov's group. It was planned to fit turrets in the forward and rear part of the fuselage, as well as an upper turret behind the trailing edge of the wing. In addition to these positions, the machine guns posts were arranged in the windows on the sides underneath the upper turret. Interestingly, Golubkov was planning to return to a single tail fin, contrary to the layout of the M-130. The proposed tail surfaces had typically angular outlines, which were characteristic of Tupolev heavy aircraft of the first half of the 1930s, resembling the ones on the TB-4.

The front part of the model of the GM-156 military version.

Another argument against the acceptance of the GM-156 into the naval aviation service was that Soviet coastal waters froze over in winter. The only place where it could be possible to operate all year round was the Black Sea and even then not everywhere, but for other fleets the available period constituted five to seven months. All the rest of the time the flying boats would be standing idle or they would have to be put on skis like the Soviet MBR-2s. Apart from that, the enormous Martin would have required significant investments in infrastructure of the coastal bases. Mechanised slipways would be needed since the flying boat could not be dragged out of the water manually, as well as large hangars for storage in the winter and for repair in the summer and fuelling stations – refuelling the flying boat of such size with buckets could take all day long. The aircraft could only be re-deployed from one sea to another by ship or by air because its subassemblies would not meet the railway loading gauges. As the result, the naval leadership began to actively speak out against the introduction of the GM-156 into series.

This position was also supported by the Directorate of Material and Technical Supply of the VVS, where almost the entire leadership had been replaced after the recent wave of repressions. In November 1937 a report was written from the directorate to the Military Council of the Air Force: 'The purchased Glenn-Martin is an obsolete design'. The military also noted that the choice of Factory No.30 was not expedient: the Rybinsk Reservoir is covered in ice for up to six months a year, and it would be impossible to transport these aircraft to Taganrog or Sevastopol for final assembly – the fuselage and wings could not be disassembled to fit the railway flatcars.

The leadership of Factory No.30 were not in favour of arranging the production of the bulky and complex Martin either. Back in November 1937 they raised a question of the expediency of the aircraft manufacturing.

In fact, the only support for the Martin came from the leadership of the First Main Directorate headed by M.M. Kaganovich. The directorate documents explain this first and foremost as a desire to bring one more factory up to a new technological level. They wanted to acquire the most up to date equipment, to master new processes and materials so then to use all this to produce indigenous aircraft, which would be better suited to conditions of the Soviet Union.

Events, however, moved onto a political plane – at the end of 1937 the wave of repressions engulfed the VVS and the aviation industry. Many of the Martin supporters ended up in prison. The situation at that time is illustrated well by a quote from a letter written on 11 April 1938 by the Director of Factory No.30 A.P. Sverdlov to Stalin: 'This flying boat, as it has subsequently emerged, was purchased by the enemies of the people – Tupolev, Kharlamov, Chernyshev and others ... Today it is clear that the GM-156 flying boat does not contain any original American technology, and there is no sense in equipping the navy with this aircraft'. People's Commissar for the Navy P.A. Smirnov echoed Sverdlov and, at a commissariat meeting in March 1938, he approved a decision stating that the navy did not need the Martin flying boats. Stalin wrote the following resolution on the Sverdlov's letter: 'It is worth raising this issue at the next meeting of the Committee for Defence ... '

The 'organisational conclusions' followed immediately: the work on the aircraft military version was ceased, the purchased parts and fixtures were sent for scrap, and the losses were written off. Whether or not a second example of Martin M-156 arrived in the Soviet Union is not known. There is a probability that it actually showed up there, as on 13 August 1938 Glenn Martin received an export licence for this flying boat. American sources mention a 'set of parts' that was delivered to the Soviet Union. It is possible that it met its fate on a scrapheap somewhere near Savyolovo.

As for the first aircraft, it arrived in Leningrad where it was assembled. In 1938 the flying boat was ferried to the Moscow region, to the Khimkinskoe Reservoir. As neither the military nor the aviation industry had any interest in the airplane, the GM-156 was handed over to the civil aviation. The GVF, in accordance with the existing practice, first of all arranged the aircraft testing. This was performed at the NII GVF, and the leading pilot was A.V. Krzhizhevskiy. E.I. Schwartz and V. Matveev also flew the airplane. The leading engineer initially was L.I. Izraetskiy, and from the beginning of 1939 he was replaced by B.A. Andreev.

Although the testing began in Khimki, another location soon had to be found as there was not enough room for the take off run of enormous Martin – the passing ships were always getting in the way. Therefore, one of the bays in the Pirogovskoe Reservoir was selected, where a base for this flying boat was arranged by the forces of the GVF Special Purpose Squadron (EON, *Eskadrilya Osobogo Naznacheniya*). The airplane maintenance during the testing was also entrusted to the mechanics of the EON. The flying boat, which had been designated the PS-30 in the GVF, passed the complete program of state testing –17 flights were undertaken in 1939, and in the following year a further 39 were completed. 'Testing ... confirmed the hydroplane's suitability for operations on the air routes of the USSR', – wrote Izraetskiy.

Following the conclusion of testing, the flying boat was handed over to the EON but it was not operated by this unit. Evidently, the GVF leadership was deciding what to do with this airplane. Finally, in May 1940 'with the aim of establishing an episodical connection between Khabarovsk and Petropavlovsk-Kamchatsky' the PS-30 was handed over to the Far Eastern Directorate of the GVF. The airplane received registration number Λ2940 and was ferried to Khabarovsk by a crew trained at the NII GVF, which comprised commander A.N. Ovechkin, co-pilot N.M. Derkunskiy, mechanic M.V. Tulikov, and radio-operator A. Tulvinskiy.

At the Far Eastern Directorate, the initial intention was to put the aircraft into operation on the route to Aleksandrovsk at Sakhalin Island, but then they returned to the original idea of making maximum use of the flying boat range on flights to Kamchatka. The PS-30 became part of the 13th Transport Unit comprised of a variety of hydroplanes. In June 1940 a crew headed by Ovechkin made the first flight from Khabarovsk to Petropavlovsk. In total in 1940 the PS-30 amassed 223 flying hours in the Far East. This figure could have been greater, but a passing steamer struck the aircraft when it was anchored on the Amur River in Khabarovsk.

The damages turned out to be minor, and the airplane was repaired at the local workshops. The service life on the imported G2 engines, however, had been used up and before new engines arrived the PS-30 stood idle for almost the entire first half of 1941. The airplane only managed to amass 168 flying hours up until the end of the season.

Even after the outbreak of the war with Germany the military still did not express any interest in this flying boat. It was periodically drafted in for transport flights in the interests of the army and the navy but the airplane remained in civil register.

The engine problems continued to plague the Martin for the whole of 1942. Moreover, production of this engine type was ceased in the USA, so the new engines could not even be acquired there. As a result, the airplane flew just 82 hours that year.

At the beginning of 1943 the Wright engines began to be replaced by very similar indigenous ASh-621R power plants. Both types had a mutual 'predecessor' – the Wright SR-1820-F3. This engine was built in series under a licence at the factory in Perm under the M-25 designation, while A.D. Shvetsov design bureau continued to improve the engine by partly borrowing successful solutions from their American colleagues. Specifically, the M-62IR (ASh-62IR) copied the G2 version, also using some solutions from more contemporary G100.

By the start of the 1943 season the aircraft was ready, and it again began to fly to Petropavlovsk. In October the PS-30 performed a special flight transporting to Khabarovsk the

American bomber crews who had made emergency landings in Kamchatka. In accordance with a Soviet-Japanese agreement they were considered internees. These pilots were then directed to Tashkent where a collection camp had been set up. From there the Americans, secretly from the Japanese Embassy, were transferred to bases in Iran, declaring them to have escaped. The intensity of the PS-30 flights was limited by the shortage of aviation fuel at Petropavlovsk, but nevertheless the flying boat amassed 115 flying hours over the course of 1943.

The Martin flew a further 76 hours the following year, after which in August 1944 it was laid up because of numerous failures. No spares were on hand for this aircraft and many of its units were worn out. The flying boat was put into long-term storage, and a proposal was sent to Moscow for it to be written off. On 29 April 1945 the Central Inventory Commission of the GVF Main Directorate issued protocol of the PS-30 write-off.

But in fact, the flying boat remained in Khabarovsk for quite a long time, and the Far Eastern Directorate kept the aircraft in its list as unserviceable. Only in July 1946 was the Martin sent for scrap.

Occasionally, foreign and Russian publications mention about three PS-30s operated in Russia. The records of the GVF Main Directorate indeed indicate that on 1 January 1940 one 'Glenn-Martin' was listed as serving in the EON, while there were two PS-30s in the NII GVF. Most likely, however, this is simply a typo, as two enormous airplanes cannot simply disappear without leaving a trace!

4.8 The Unlucky Vultee V-11

At the close of 1935 information began to arrive in Moscow concerning a new American light bomber and ground attack aircraft, the Vultee V-11. A delegation that comprised I.G. Neman, A.V. Kvitko, and the Chief Engineer of the VVS A.K. Auzan, which had visited the USA, reported back about this airplane. This was a single-engine all-metal monoplane with retractable undercarriage and an enclosed cockpit, which looked much more contemporary than the wooden R-5Sh biplane that was in service with the VVS RKKA, and its more refined version the SSS (3S). Reporting back to K.E. Voroshilov on the prospects for acquiring a licence in the USA, the Head of the VVS Headquarters V.K. Lavrov underlined that the Vultee ground attack aircraft ' ... has exceptionally good flight-performance characteristics in terms of speed and range ... '. In comparison with the obsolete Soviet R-5Sh and SSS ground attack biplanes this was certainly the case. As a result, the Vultee V-11 was included in a list of aircraft for which licences were to be acquired in the USA. The list was approved by the STO on 11 April 1935, and negotiations with the company began. In the meantime, A.N. Tupolev, who at the time was the Chief Engineer of the GUAP, came out against this. In his report to the government, he did not even mention the Vultee ground attack aircraft as a prospective type.

In 1936 a group of specialists led by the Director of TsAGI N.M. Kharlamov travelled to America and the V-11GB light bomber was demonstrated to them. On 7 September 1936 Amtorg signed an agreement with the Aviation Manufacturing Corporation, of which Vultee were a part. Under this agreement, the GUAP NKTP acquired a licence to produce the V-11 in the ground attack (V-11G), and light-bomber (V-11GB) versions. For the latter a third crewmember was added – a gunner-bombardier. The American side provided engineering drawings, specifications, various instructions and descriptions, schedules of materials, bought-in items, documentation on lathes and production processes, data from the aircraft flight and ground tests, wind tunnel tests, materials on the strength calculations, and more than 300 photographs of components, units and sub-assemblies at different stages of manufacture. Various appendices of the agreement define the acquisition of examples of the aircraft, components, units and sub-assemblies for series production, and the use of Vultee engineers for arranging the production in the USSR. The agreement was subsequently augmented

The V-11G ground attack aircraft, which was demonstrated to a Soviet delegation in the USA. This airplane only differed from examples subsequently purchased by the presence of a radio-compass, a loop antenna of which was located in a teardrop shaped fairing atop the rear part of the airplane.

Flight testing of one of the V-11Gs in America.

The tail part of a V-11G.

with a clause on the transition of all the drawings into the metric system.

Kharlamov suggested the designer Gerard Vultee to visit the Soviet Union personally and to lead the modification of the type in order to meet the Soviet requirements but the company's main shareholders spoke out against this.

It was planned to purchase two fully assembled airplanes. The first one, serial number 32, left the assembly workshops on 22 December 1936. Initially, it was proposed that in January 1937 it would be shipped to the USSR, however, the process of eliminating minor shortcomings moved the schedule, and the airplane took to the skies only on 31 January.

The famous pilot S.A. Levanevskiy, who had just ferried Vultee V-1AS airplane to Russia in August 1936, took part in the acceptance tests of the V-11. He made the first flight in this aircraft on 2 February 1937. A report written by the Soviet Acceptance Commission stated: 'The flight by Hero of the Soviet Union comrade Levanevskiy and flight engineer Chechin in the Vultee V-11 ... was undertaken under the task of the commission led by comrade Yurgens. The aim of this flight – familiarisation with the ground attack version of airplane and testing its manoeuvrability'. Among those present at the airfield was the Head of the Directorate of Material-Technical Supply of the VVS B.I. Bazenkov and the Director of TsAGI N.M. Kharlamov. Levanevskiy was happy with the airplane, remarking on its good controllability, manoeuvrability, and stability.

The tests lasted till mid-February 1937 and the aircraft was flown both from the factory airfield in Downey and from the military base at Long Beach. The airplane's machine-gun and bomb armament were tested over the ocean, and this aircraft was assessed both in ground attack and bomber versions. The recorded characteristics turned out to be lower than those claimed by the company but not by much. The second purchased example (serial number 33) took to the skies on 26 February 1937. The Soviet representatives accepted the first airplane in March, and the second – in April. At the end of April both airplanes were sent by sea to the USSR.

Both Vultees were fitted with the SR-1820-G2 engines and had a full set of bomb and machine-gun armament, with the exception of machine guns in the retractable ventral mount. The aircraft did not have radio compasses either. Further two aircraft (serial numbers 34 and 35) were acquired in a dismantled condition, without engines.

On their arrival in the Soviet Union, the airplanes were

A V-11G airplane during state testing at the NII VVS.

An SR-1820-G2 engine with its cowling removed.

The instrument panel in the pilot's cockpit of a V-11G.

subjected to thorough study. The serial number 33, with the original set of American equipment and armament, was directed for state testing at the NII VVS. In the first half of 1937 the V-11GB was extensively studied at TsAGI and at the NII VVS. The leading test pilot of the Vultee was Captain A.K. Dolgov, but number of other pilots tried their hands at flying this airplane, starting with the then Head of the NII VVS *Komdiv* (Division Commander) N.N. Bazhanov and also well-known pilots such as Stefanovskiy, Fedrovi, and Nyukhtikov. The aircraft completed the test program,

A KD-1-8 bomb cassette with eight ZAB-10TG incendiary bombs, which was tested on airplane serial number 32.

comprising more than 70 hours of testing, including mock

A KD-1-8 bomb cassette with eight AO-8M6 fragmentation bombs.

air combats.

The conclusions were mixed. On the one hand the NII VVS stated that 'The Voltee airplane [at that time they would render the name as Voltee, Vultee or Vul'tee] given its existing bomb armament and equipment is capable of performing the

A Soviet BSh-1 ground attack aircraft during state testing at the NII VVS, 1939.

An M-62IR engine without cowling and a VISh-2PA propeller on a BSh-1 airplane.

The engine cowling on a BSh-1 differed by additional ventilation gills that were absent on the original.

The pilot's instrument panel and the control column on the BSh-1.

roles of ground attack aircraft and bomber. On the other hand, in terms of its flight-performance characteristics (insufficient flight speed and long time of the turn) and poor defensive capabilities, as a combat aircraft it is, by this time, obsolete'. In fact, the V-11G, in the ground attack version (carrying fuel in the fuselage tanks only and small-calibre bombs in the internal bomb rack), weighed 4,015kg – almost twice the weight of the new Soviet R-10 reconnaissance aircraft. Even with the less powerful M-25 engine (based on the licence-built SR-1820 series F engine) the R-10 had a maximum flight speed almost 30km/h greater, possessed a significant advantage in the rate of climb (it would take 12.4 mins to reach 5,000m compared to 18 mins for the V-11G), and had an even greater margin in a horizontal manoeuvre. The take-off and landing characteristics of the R-10 were also better. The American aircraft turned out to be more difficult to fly than the Soviet R-5 and R-10, and its stability was acknowledged as unsatisfactory as the pilot was not able to drop the stick in flight.

As for the armament, the Soviet specialists considered the American aircraft obsolete. The rear machine-gun mount had a narrow arc of fire and did not provide the necessary protection from fighters; given the absence of a ventral

The series BSh-1 ground attack aircraft during testing.

The BSh-1 aircraft on the non-retractable ski undercarriage; the undercarriage legs are enclosed in fairings.

The prototype BSh-1m during testing at the Scientific Testing Range of Aircraft Armament.

A glazed MV-3 turret on a BSh-1m aircraft.

ShKAS machine guns in the wing of the BSh-1m.

The ventral machine-gun mount with a ShKAS machine gun in the deployed position.

mount, the lower hemisphere remained all but undefended from enemy attack. Mock air combat against an I-16 Type 4 demonstrated that the V-11G was unable to get away from a fighter or evade an attack. In combination with the low effectiveness in the defensive armament this meant that the aircraft was doomed the moment it was intercepted. The internal bomb rack for small-calibre bombs was considered unsuccessful and unreliable, while the bombs were loaded inside this carrier only by touch. The V-11G was not designed for carrying chemical weapons (which at that time was a subject of additional attention by the VVS RKKA), while positioning of the external bomb racks did not allow them to be used for carrying the Soviet chemical spraying equipment. The American aircraft was also not designed to operate at very low temperatures.

In many respects, however, Gerard Vultee was far ahead of the Soviet aircraft manufacturers. The act which approved the NII VVS report indicates: 'In terms of its design, and the used parts (open metal profiles), materials (anti-corrosion alloy, plastics), and production technology (casing and stamping), the 'Voltee' airplane represents a good example for introduction of new types of technological processes, as well as new types of parts and materials into our aviation industry which makes it easier to achieve mass production of aircraft'.

Both TsAGI and NI VVS specialists remarked many new innovations used by American designers. The comfortable and ergonomic cockpit with its excellent visibility, the reliable undercarriage shock absorbers, and the efficient brakes provided for a positive evaluation of this airplane. The mechanism of retracting the main landing gear with a self-locking worm gear gave rise to a great deal of interest; an undercarriage leg designed that way could not collapse inadvertently on landing. The clever way the Americans had combated vibrations also came as a surprise. The dampers of the engine mount completely absorbed the vibrations, preventing them from being transferred to the fuselage.

The aircraft could be assembled and disassembled quickly, and the designers had foreseen easy access to all the main assemblies and units. Test pilots highly rated the aircraft stability in flight, the excellent operation of all the

A view inside the ventral machine-gun mount on a BSh-1m.

A KD-1-10 bomb cassette with 10 AO-M6 fragmentation bombs, which were installed inside the bomb bay of the BSh-1m.

mechanisms, and the reliability of the engine. During the whole period of the tests, only three failures were revealed. First, the starboard leg began to shake badly at the start of the undercarriage retraction. The reason for this turned out to be a defect in the worm gear, which had been replaced by the brigade from Factory No.1 under the direction of the American specialists (their assistance in mastering the aircraft was envisaged under the agreement). The second failure was the burnt-through cowling, which had happened because of a defective connection of the exhaust manifold. No attempt was made to repair the cowling, but the connecting clamps were replaced. As for the third failure, the plunger in the tail wheel shock absorber failed on landing, resulting in the wheel skewing and damage of the wheel, its fairing, and the tail fin (albeit slightly).

Having objectively examined the advantages and shortcomings of the V-11G the decision was nevertheless taken to put this aircraft into series production. Nevertheless, the airplane's combat capabilities were not overestimated. 'Manufacture of the 'Voltee' aircraft pursues the objective of mastering new, for our aviation industry, technologies of aircraft manufacturing which have been implemented in this machine', – the NII VVS specialists concluded. On 13 October 1936 a meeting took place at the GUAP, at which it was decided that the small Factory No.81 (which had previously belonged to the Main Directorate of the GVF) in the Moscow region was to be tasked with arranging production of the Vultee. Then, considering the acute need for aircraft of this type in the VVS, the order was re-assigned to Factory No.1 in Moscow, which was one of the largest in the country at that time.

Arranging the V-11G production (which in the USSR was given a designation the BSh-1) was to become just the first step towards creating a contemporary Soviet ground attack aircraft and light bomber. But even the V-11G was to undergo certain changes before it could be put on the factory conveyor. It was planned that the American engine be replaced with an indigenous M 62 and that the Soviet types of armament and equipment be fitted. This engineering work was assigned to a brigade of designers from OKB-1 under the leadership of S.A. Kocherigin. The latter was not happy with the additional responsibility that had been placed on him, as it got in the way of the refinement work on the R-9 high-speed reconnaissance aircraft that he had designed.

Replacement of the SR-1820-G2 with the M-62IR did not present any significant problems, since both belonged to one and the same family of Cyclone engines. The M-62 only differed slightly from its ancestor in terms of dimensions and weight and had the same fitting points. The VISh-2PA propeller, which had been selected to fit the BSh-1, was itself similar to the Hamilton one, as it too was based on a licence-built American propeller.

Development of the Soviet version of the V-11 began even prior to the arrival of aircraft examples from the USA. On the meeting of 22 March 1937, Kocherigin presented his variant of the aircraft armament. Instead of the Brownings, he proposed to fit four ShKAS machine guns, which had higher rate of fire, in the wings. Each pair of machine guns had ammunition load of 1,600 cartridges. The used cartridge cases would be ejected under the wing, and the links would be collected in boxes, one for each pair of machine guns. The firing would be performed using an electrical system with mechanical back-up.

The designers suggested to replace the American machine-gun swivelling mount in the rear cabin with a turret from a prototype of SR reconnaissance aircraft. Its dimensions enabled the shape of the fuselage to be retained, together with the original glazing of the cockpit canopy. The variant of the Tur-10 turret installation was rejected, as it did not meet to the latter condition – the glazing of the rear canopy would have to be changed. The ventral mount was combined of a LU DB-3 mount and the mechanism of transferring the machine gun into a stowed position taken from a V-11GB. The ammunition load of the ventral machine gun was 500 cartridges.

Two FAB-100 high-explosive bombs, and two FAB-50 bombs on external racks under the BSh-1m centerplane.

The first PS-43 postal airplane to be accepted by civil aviation.

The bomb armament was also considerably re-designed. Two KD-1-8 bomb cassettes, with eight bomb locks in each, were positioned inside the fuselage. They enabled carrying bombs of calibre from five to 25kg. In contrast to the American bomb cassettes, which were fixed, the KD-1-8 was loaded in lowered position outside the bomb bay, and then lifted inside using a winch. For external carrying of the bombs, 10 Der-31 bomb racks were installed in two rows under the wing centerplane. These could carry bombs of up to 100kg calibre, while in case of using the bomb attachment from the R-Zet bomber, a bomb up to 250kg could be carried. The bombs were dropped using an ESBR-2 electric bomb release mechanism or a mechanism taken from the DI-6 fighter.

Kocherigin and weapons engineer Mikheev of his design group could not solve the issue of how to fit chemical spray units. The minutes of the meeting noted: 'The issue of the aircraft chemical weapons is to be left open'.

Two trends were competing with one another in the Air Force leadership: one was to make a radical change to the armament and equipment of the American ground attack aircraft, but this will slow down its production and introduction into service, or to make minimal changes but allow the type to enter service quickly. In the end, on 15 April the UVVS took a contradictory decision. On the one hand, they agreed to retain the original American machine-gun mount in the rear cabin, adapting it around a DA machine gun with ammunition load of 750 cartridges, and to reduce the number of Der-31 bomb racks under the fuselage to eight (as it is in the American configuration). On the other hand – they insisted on fitting the airplane with chemical armament: two DAP-100 smoke generators under the fuselage, or six VAP-4 chemical spray devices (four under the fuselage, and two under the wing outer panels). Since bomb racks would need to be fitted under the wing to allow chemical VAP units to be installed, the issue immediately arose: could bombs be carried on them instead?

The proponents of the deep modernisation of the V-11G went further. They required that aircraft of the first series would have the movable gun mount adapted not for DA machine gun but for the more modern ShKAS unit, and with a continuous (belt) feed (in the DA the cartridges were fed from disk magazines that had to be changed). In future, a glazed turret would have to be fitted. It was planned to include a radio compass in the set of on-board equipment, which was a rarity at that time even for a larger aircraft in service of the VVS RKKA.

Production of three versions of the aircraft was planned: ground attack, light bomber, and reconnaissance airplane. The first would have a crew of two, while the two others would have a crew of three. The ground attack version carried four machine guns in the wings, while the bomber and reconnaissance versions – had two each.

The Soviet aviation industry was, however, actively objecting to the deep modernisation. The leadership of the State Directorate of the Aviation Industry, under the People's Commissariat for Heavy Industry, and of its successor – the First Main Directorate of the People's Commissariat for the Defence industry, was looking to introduce the aircraft into production more quickly so to report on the fulfilment of the set tasks. Any modifications inevitably delayed this process. It was suggested to build the first series with minimal divergence from the American original, and the modernisation was to be left 'for later'. The Air Force command was eager to replace the obsolete R-5Sh and SSS aircraft, and therefore in agreement with this. In April 1937 the Head of the VVS Headquarters V.K. Lavrov wrote to the Head of the VVS Ya.I. Alksnis: 'The main policy that we have agreed on now is to make as few major changes as we can in production of the first series aircraft.'

As a result of discussions, on 11 November 1937 the Committee for Defence issued a decree which supported this point of view. In accordance with this document, all aircraft up until the end of 1938 were to be delivered as ground attack versions, with the armament comprising four ShKAS machine guns in the wings (total ammunition load of 2,400 cartridges), a DA machine gun on the American movable mount in the rear cabin, and without a ventral machine gun. Bomb armament consisted of two KD-1-8 cassettes, and eight Der-31 bomb racks.

This version was tested on aircraft serial number 32. At Factory No.1, four ShKAS machine guns were fitted in the wings of the airplane, in place of the Brownings, which increased the aircraft firepower considerably due to the higher rate of fire. The ammunition load in the wing-mounted machine guns remained the same as in the American configuration – 600 cartridges per barrel. A DA machine gun was fitted in the rear cockpit with an ammunition load of 500 cartridges. Along with the machine guns, the very basic and ineffective gun sights were also replaced. The American light-bomb cassettes, which had been criticised by test pilots, were replaced with two KD-1-8s. To install these cassettes, the bomb bay had to be expanded by 350mm and its forward wall was covered in duralumin. Each bomb cassette held eight AO-8M3, AO-8M6, AO-10, AO-15, or ZAB-10TG bombs. After fitting of the KD-1-8, the aircraft internal bomb load reduced slightly – from 272kg to 260kg. The set of external American bomb racks was replaced with identical Der-31 bomb racks with the same number of attachment points on them. These could carry bombs ranging from AO-10s to FAB-100s. The replacement of the bomb release mechanisms completed the revision of the V-11G bomb armament. Following the fitting of the ESBR-2 electrical bomb release, and the ASBR emergency mechanical bomb release, one of the airplane's most significant shortcomings was eradicated – the bombs could now be dropped not only individually, and in a salvo, but also in a series.

In October 1937, the aircraft serial number 32 completed factory testing with its new armament, where a number of shortcomings had been revealed. The mounts for the ShKAS machine guns had been modified twice until the required rigidity was achieved. The cartridge casings jammed in the cartridge case sleeves. The rear row Der-31 racks could only carry the bombs of up to 25kg calibre, as the higher calibres would not fit – their tails caught the ground. When the aircraft was carrying bombs internally and externally, the ASBR emergency mechanical bomb release could not be used – it would release them all in a single salvo. At that, the bombs from the internal cassettes fell onto the closed bomb bay doors, while the doors could not be opened in advance, as the externally mounted bombs would get in the way. Nevertheless, the aircraft was sent for state testing to the Scientific Testing Range of Aircraft Armament.

There the aircraft flew 17 sorties, and practiced bombing and strafing. The same shortcomings were noted that had been revealed at the factory, and in addition the rear machine gun mount was criticised: the replacement of the Browning with the DA did not make it any more effective. Apart from that the KD-1-8 cassettes were found to be not sufficiently reliable – the bombs sometimes twisted and jammed between the cassette and the wall of the bomb bay.

The arrangement of series production of the BSh-1 was given a high priority. Initially, the plan was to manufacture two series of these airplanes in 1937 but these plans were in the end thwarted completely. Equipment and fixtures were delayed arriving from the USA. All the production templates were rendered useless in transit from America; the shipping containers arrived broken so the cardboard templates were soaked and misshapen. A decision was taken to limit assembly to two aircraft made of the American parts; this work was undertaken from October 1937 and to a considerable extent in a handicraft manner.

Some 200 aircraft in the light bomber version and 150 in the ground attack version were written into the plan for 1938. The first 10 airplanes, which used the American parts and components, were to be handed over in the first quarter. The sequence for re-equipping the air force units was planned in advance. In the second quarter, 20 BSh-1s were to be sent to the Leningrad Military District. The light-bomber regiments in the Leningrad, Belorussia, Kiev, and Moscow military districts were scheduled to receive these new aircraft first. In terms of numbers of aircraft, a fully equipped regiment was to consist of 63 airplanes.

There was considered a project of the 'tele-mechanical' (radio-controlled) version of the BSh-1, which, as it was envisaged, would be taken for testing in 1939. This project, however, never came to fruition.

Factory No.1 had previously mass-produced aircraft of a similar role – SSS and R-Zet, but both of which were of a mixed construction, and their production technology differed significantly from the one of the BSh-1. The loft-template technology, used in the production of the Vultee, was something completely new for Soviet aircraft manufacturers.

By December 1937, the factory prepared a full set of engineering drawings which took into consideration the changes in equipment and armament, the use of indigenous materials, and the correspondence to Soviet standards. Assembly work began on the first of these aircraft but using alternative technology, as the main workshops were busy with the I-15bis fighter production. By 15 January 1938 the tooling needed to be put in place to build between eight to 10 aircraft a month. In the first six months, the plan was to hand over 50 ground attack aircraft.

The introduction of the type into series production at Factory No.1, however, was moving forward at a pace that was far short of the plan. The unusual design and materials, the unfamiliar technology, and the abundance of electrical equipment that did not have any Soviet analogues, significantly delayed the manufacture of these aircraft. The first airplanes had a number of defects (in particular, there were problems with the landing gear operating mechanism) as a result of which the military acceptance committee rejected them. There were quite a number of American components in these aircraft: cast and stamped parts, and subassemblies had been acquired for 100 airplanes. Metal profiles, Alclad sheet metal, electrical equipment parts (lights, limit switches, relays, and even electric bulbs, which did not correspond to Soviet standards) had also been brought over from America. The first five aircraft were actually assembled in the USSR entirely from parts supplied by the Vultee company.

A PS-43 airplane in flight.

A PS-43 postal airplane during testing at the NII GVF.

Externally, the BSh-1 differed from the V-11G by the power plant, forward shutters of the engine cowling (which made winter operations easier), the additional gills on the cowling, the propeller spinner, the absence of a bracket for the bead of the gun sight, and by the radio antenna. The equipment inside the airplane became almost exclusively Soviet: the starter mechanism was replaced, as was the electrical generator, the sights, and the bomb release mechanisms. Although it was sufficiently quiet in the cockpit, an SPU-2 intercom system was fitted as well as an SL-36 color lights warning system. The American Fairchild F-14 camera was initially planned to be replaced with the AFA-21 (for the ground attack version), or the AFA-27 (for the bomber version), but at the end the preference was given to the unified AFA-13 camera. The observer was supplied with an indigenous RSB (*Dvina*) radio set, the antenna for which was attached to a 500mm mast fixed on the cockpit windscreen.

Introduction of the BSh-1 into service in ground attack aviation also had a number of opponents. The Deputy Head of the VVS Ya.V. Smushkevich, who flew a lot and willingly, personally carried out comparative tests of various ground attack aircraft, including the V-11G at the time when it was at the NII VVS. 'With your permission, I flight-tested the Volte airplane, which is proposed for the ground attack role', – he reported to Alksnis on 21 October 1937. Smushkevich did not like the American aircraft in view of its large size and heavy weight, insufficient manoeuvrability at low level, and low speed. Having tried also the DI-6, I-15, I-16, and R-10 types, he expressed a preference for the latter.

The Head of the VVS Ya.I. Alksnis did not have time to formulate his opinion on this subject, however. In the course of the mass Stalinist repressions he was arrested, named an 'enemy of the people,' and a 'Latvian spy.' At the same time a number of people from his inner circle fell victim to this. What they had defended began to be called 'sabotaged'. Now, things had to be done differently.

The new Head of the Directorate of Material and Technical Supply of the VVS *Voeninzhener 2-go ranga* Z.A. Ioffe, who had replaced Bazenkov after his arrest, wrote a report to the new Head of the VVS *Komkor* (Corps Commander) A.D. Loktionov. This report stated: 'The heads of the VVS, Material and Technical Supply of the VVS, and the First Main Directorate of the People's Commissariat for the Defence industry (Alksnis, Bazenkov, Lavrov, and Tupolev), who have now been exposed as enemies of the people, pushed through the unsatisfactory armament of this aircraft ... '. Ioffe proposed increasing the ammunition load for machine guns in the wing to 3,600 cartridges, fitting an MV-3 turret (with 300 cartridges) and a ULU ventral machine-gun mount (with 500 cartridges). Both the turret and the mount were to have been adapted for the ShKAS machine gun. He also suggested to remove the external bomb racks, and to increase the internal bomb load – the fuselage fuel tank should be removed thus giving the possibility to expand the bomb bay significantly, so to fit either four KD-1-10 cassettes (with 10 bomb locks each), or a box-type cassette designed by Onisko-Yefimov for small bombs (with a calibre of 2.5kg) along with eight Der-31 bomb racks. The Onisko-Yefimov cassette could be replaced by an AK-1 cassette

A PS-43 which was destroyed on the Moscow Central airfield. On 28 February 1941 a MiG-3 crashed into this aircraft after the pilot had run off the runway on landing. Note the TB-3 heavy bomber in the background, which was damaged in the same incident.

for spherical ampoules, containing either toxic agents or a self-igniting liquid. Ioffe proposed to increase armament capability by carrying four VAP-4 chemical spray tanks under the wings of the aircraft, or a pair of DAP-100 smoke units in the same location.

It was this version of the aircraft armament that the new leadership of the Air Force began to 'push' as a reference for the second half of 1938. Designers of the OKB-1 had undertaken development of this project since November 1937. The fitting of the ULU ventral machine-gun mount did not present any problems, and the MV-3 turret did not present any great difficulties either. On 13 November this turret was tried on the aircraft serial number 32. As a result, a conclusion was reached: 'The MV-3 turret can be fitted on the 'Volti' aircraft without affecting the aircraft load bearing structure'. The designers coped easily with increasing the ammunition load for the fixed machine guns. The new unit was manufactured and tested successfully at the Scientific Testing Range of Aircraft Armament. The fitting of the spray tanks and bombs under the wings, however, was considered a complex task, and the reason for this was linked to altering the structural framework of the wing outer sections. The designers could adapt a pair of VAP-4ms under the fuselage but getting airborne with them was risky – the ground clearance did not exceed 200mm.

When this installation of the VAP was tested at the firing range, it turned out that the airflow from the propeller was splitting up and scattering the droplets. The airplane's entire rear part ended up spattered with water. What would have happened if this had been a mustard gas solution? Apart from that, the small droplets evaporated before they reached the ground. This would not enable a build-up of a high concentration of a toxic substance on the battlefield.

While the UVVS was arguing with the OKB-1, factory and First Main Directorate, the industry was being questioned about the fulfilment of the production plan. On 2 January 1938 the Head of the First Main Directorate S.V. Ilyushin set out an ultimatum in a letter to the military: either they submit clearly defined and realistic specifications for the changes they want to get, which are underpinned by engineering documentation, or the factory will begin to manufacture this aircraft in accordance with the decree they had already received from the Committee for Defence. The military had not been able to produce anything by the deadline, and in the end they received 'the judgement of Solomon' – the aircraft was to be manufactured according to the original standard, and then they would see what would happen. By this time, proposals had already begun to appear to limit production to 100 BSh-1s, and then replace it with a new aircraft, or a product of the 'in-depth modernisation' of the Vultee.

On 28 March, A.D. Loktionov finally approved specifications for the 'modified BSh-1' (later it received designation the BSh-1m). They included some of Ioffe's proposals, and in some respects they went even further. An ammunition load of 3,600 cartridges was proposed for the machine guns in the wings, as well as an MV-3 turret (on the topside) and an MV-2 turret (on the underside), four KD-1-10 cassettes (or an alternative for carrying 400kg of bombs), and two DAP-100 or two VAP-4m (with ZAP ignition unit) devices mounted under the fuselage.

The ZAP units were intended for the 'fiery rain' system – the VAP-4m's were loaded with granulated phosphorous, while an incendiary mixture was supplied from ZAP ignition unit carried underneath them. The specifications were later augmented with the introduction of electric heating for the machine guns, as well as an armoured pilot's seat, and the replacement of the M 62 engine with the geared M-62R.

OKB-1 tried to realise these requirements and on 27 April 1938 the commission led by *Voeninzhener 1-go ranga* Kryzhanovskiy examined a mock-up of the BSh-1m. It was approved, but a number of minor corrections have been requested. Meanwhile, the modification of the aircraft serial number 33 had already been underway since 28 March. This airplane received enlarged ammunition boxes in the wings (the boxes for collecting the cartridge cases were also enlarged proportionally), four KD-1-10 cassettes, in place of which six box-type cassettes could be fitted, as well as an improved PAK-1 collimator gun sight (which replaced the old-fashioned long tube of the OP-1 Aldis sight), and a new mechanical ASBR-2 bomb release mechanism. Four Der-31 bomb racks were positioned under the fuselage, and two were mounted under the wings, which meant the design of the wing outer sections had to be strengthened. The engine that was fitted was a Soviet one, but this was an un-geared M-62. The pilot did not get the armoured seat, as it had only just been manufactured. The airplane was fitted with a non-standard MV-5 turret with a reduced glazing and firing from this turret was a cramped affair.

A PS-43 airplane, flown by pilot Muzelevskiy, takes off on a combat mission, a Special Liaison Air Group, Myachkovo airfield, 1942

Work on the modified BSh-1m continued at a slow pace. The OKB-1 designers were caught up with parallel work on the R-9 reconnaissance aircraft, and the leadership of the factory, which for the most part manufactured fighters, acknowledged the growing futility of modernising the Vultee. The lack of a number of equipment and armament components was slowing down the work. Everything can be written down on paper, but where can you get it? The KD-1-10 cassettes that were initially sent were defective. The prototype MV-2 turret was manufactured under an order placed at the Factory of the Air Force Academy. As of 13 July, electric triggers were available only for two wing-mounted machine guns out of the four – there was simply no more available. The M-62R engine was not delivered either, as Factory No.19 was still refining the test batch. Only by 27 September did the factory receive and install the geared engine, and a standard MV-5 turret was installed (as an alternative, the SU-32 turret created at Factory No.32 basing on the Tur-9 turret was offered).

Time, however, went by. The modified BSh-1m was being built almost under its own steam. In the best-case scenario this aircraft could be put into production only at the beginning of 1939. All this time, Factory No.1 was manufacturing aircraft according to the old layout. Moreover, in September the director of the factory informed the UVVS that the 'modified ground attack aircraft' would not be manufactured. As a result, the First Main Directorate issued an order just to complete the first of 50 airplanes without any changes, and that was it. At that, the Directorate had a 'cast iron' basis for this – a decree issued by the Committee for Defence, which had been accepted already in April 1938. It stated: 'The Vultee airplane manufactured by Factory No.1 does not meet the contemporary tactical-technical requirements, and on that basis any future development of this aircraft is futile. The People's Commissariat for the Defence Industry is tasked with fulfilling the order for the Vultee for 1938 in full extent, and at the same time to arrange withdrawal of the Vultee from series production in 1939, and to set up a production of a new aircraft at Factory No.1.' Admittedly, the leadership of the First Main Directorate had 'forgotten' that the order for 1938 was for the production not of 50 aircraft, but of 350 BSh-1s. The military, however, already did not insist on this. They were not keen to receive what were 'untested' and at the same time morally obsolete ground attack aircraft.

The authorities had to consider how the aircraft that had already been built were to be used. With this in mind, in 1939 one of the BSh-1s, fitted with an M-62IR engine (with a single-speed supercharger in place of a two-speed one) was taken for state testing. The crew consisted of Major B.N. Pokrovskiy (the pilot), and Captain I.D. Sokolov (the flight observer). The aircraft flew on non-retractable skis and also on wheeled undercarriage. During testing, the leading BSh-1 failed miserably. The conclusions of the NII VVS test report stated: 'The BSh-1 aircraft fitted with an M-62IR engine does not meet the contemporary requirements to the ground attack aircraft and light bomber neither in terms of the flight-technical characteristics, nor in terms of defensive capability, nor in terms of the visibility from the flight observer's cockpit when measuring the wind or bombing.' In reality, in 1937 the original V-11G was inferior in many ways to most indigenous and foreign aircraft of the same class, and in 1939 the further differences in the BSh-1 only made the situation worse. The Soviet version had become heavier (the flight weight in the ground attack version was 4,056kg as opposed to 4,015kg, and moreover this was with a decreased payload) while the engine output had reduced. The American SR-1820-G2 engine developed 850hp at an altitude of 1,676m, and the M-62IR developed 840hp at an altitude of 1,500m, and this was only on paper. The M-62IR at that time had yet to be refined, its operation was unreliable, and it almost never worked to its nominal output. The test pilots consciously reduced the boost, fearing an overheat. In the end, the maximum speed of the ground attack version did not exceed 339km/h (and the R-10 mentioned above produced 388km/h), the rate of climb deteriorated, as did the take-off and landing characteristics.

The manufacturing imperfections undermined the aircraft reputation further. The visibility for the pilot, which on the original aircraft was described as excellent, deteriorated considerably due to the use of the muddy Soviet plexiglass. The intercom system worked intermittently. The undercarriage retraction system operated badly: over the course of testing the undercarriage either failed to deploy at all or did not deploy fully on 10 occasions.

Thus, for 1939 the BSh-1 did not offer any combat value: 'After a reliable engine has been fitted and the defects with this aircraft have been eradicated ... it could be used as a transition and training aircraft' – the NII VVS specialists acknowledged. 'This, however, was not worth the effort', as the R-10 designed by I.G. Neman was in series production, and the BB-1 (the future Su-2) designed by P.O. Sukhoi was 'coming along.' The Air Force refused to accept the BSh-1 into service.

By that time manufacturing of this aircraft type had been ceased, and some 50 airplanes had been produced according to the factory data, while the famous historian of Russian aviation V.B. Shavrov makes reference to a total of 38 machines. It is possible, that some of these aircraft remained unfinished. As a result, the airplanes that had not been accepted by the customer were lined up on the so-called 'iron line' on the edge of the Moscow Central airfield.

As a further step, the type was offered to civil aviation as a postal aircraft. The GU GVF had made a claim for the Vultee back in 1937 and prepared a technical specification for its civil version. The GVF plan for 1937 included the acquisition of three airplanes costing 400,000 roubles each, but, of course, they received nothing.

The shift came in December 1938, when the Committee for Defence decided to hand over 30 unarmed BSh-1s to civil aviation. On 31 December the Council for Economy allocated 15,000,000 roubles to the GU GVF for this purpose. In civil aviation this type was designated PS-43.

The aircraft, however, remained in the 'iron line', as no engines were available for them – there was an acute shortage of M-62IRs, due to a small production run and low reliability which resulted in frequent replacements. Furthermore, the Air Force remained the priority in terms of engine deliveries, and the GVF had to wait longer and longer.

Civil pilots got a chance to test fly the first aircraft only in April 1939. This was considered a postal and cargo airplane, and carrying passengers was not envisaged. All the armament and military equipment was removed, and the crew consisted of a pilot and a radio-operator. Four cargo compartments had been arranged in the fuselage: the biggest was between the back of the seat in the rear cabin and the forward edge of the entrance door, while the smallest was under the radio-operator's seat.

As of 1 September 1939, civil aviation was operating two Vultees: one in a special duty squadron, the other in the directorate of Southern Kazakhstan. In the winter of 1939–1940, the aircraft serving in the special duty squadron came under the Special Air Group, which carried passengers and cargo for the army in the course of the Winter War with Finland.

In 1940, the PS-43 underwent testing at the NII GVF, and was flown by A.A. Kolosov. This aircraft attained a maximum speed of 342km/h and the service ceiling was 5,420m. The maximum range was assessed as being 2,550km. The airplane took 35 mins to reach an altitude of 5,000m. Problems emerged with taxiing the aircraft around the airfield – the nose part restricted the pilot's visibility, so he would move in a zigzag pattern, working the brakes intensively as the rudder was not very effective at low speeds. On take-off, when fully loaded, the Vultee stubbornly refused to lift the tail. In flight the aircraft was stable, enabling the pilot to let go of the stick for a short time. It was, however, sloppy in the turn, with a large turn radius, and moreover it would try to increase the angle of bank. On landing, when the flaps were deployed it would quickly 'nosedive,' which had to be corrected immediately.

By 15 June 1940, Aeroflot had accepted 23 aircraft. The first eight of them were of the 1st series, which included some of the American electrical equipment. Some of them also had imported engines and Hamilton 3E50 propellers, 3.37m in diameter. The rest were fitted with M-62IR engines and VISh-21 propellers, 3.4m in diameter.

At the aviation show on 18 August 1940 at Tushino airfield, three PS-43 aircraft flew together in a demonstration. Far from all the Vultees that had been received, however, were able to fly. Having stood for two years out in the open the aircraft were in need of repair. In view of this and due to the shortage of engines 16 PS-43s had to be put into storage in the end of 1940. Nevertheless, in the end of 1940 and beginning of 1941 the PS-43s began to arrive at various GVF directorates. Specifically, they operated on the routes Moscow–Kiev, Moscow–Tashkent, and Kiev–Odessa. By June 1941, 10 PS-43s served in the Ukrainian directorate. The civil pilots took to the PS-43 well, they fully approved of the comfortable cockpit with its well thought out instrument layout, and the reliable undercarriage deployment and retraction system. A proposal emerged to convert some of the PS-43s into a six-seat passenger aircraft. It was however noted that the aircraft would need large and level airfields.

With the outbreak of the Great Patriotic War the PS-43s, together with other airplanes of civil aviation, were drafted service as a military transport. From 25 June 1941,

Preparing a PS-43 for a flight; on the left is the commander of the 3rd Squadron OAGS Captain Gvozdev.

special air groups and units began to be formed, which were attached to the fronts and naval fleets. The first two PS-43s, which had previously belonged to the Ukrainian directorate of the GVF, came under the Kiev Air Group. By 1 July, it had already lost these aircraft, but had received a third machine. In total, at different times there were five PS-43s in service with this group.

A single PS-43 found its way into the 69th Fighter Air Regiment, which was active around Odessa. It became part of the supernumerary ground attack squadron of the regiment. The armament for this aircraft, and how it was configured, remains a mystery. It operated jointly with four Il-2s, a single R-5, and a former Yugoslavian three-engine S.79 bomber of Italian origin. During the evacuation of Odessa in October 1941 the aircraft was ferried to Crimea but there was an accident on landing. The pilot Major Rykachyov and the passengers were unhurt, but the aircraft had to be written off.

Five PS-43s joined the MAGON, which had been deployed to Vnukovo airfield in the Moscow region that was still under construction.

At the start of the war quite a few Vultees continued to stand at the edge of the Moscow Central airfield. Some of their parts were pulled off, some parts deteriorated with time and the negligent way in which they were stored. No engines, dented outer skin, deflated tyres, and the electrics that no longer worked ... Several aircraft were damaged when a MiG-3 fighter crashed into the 'iron line' on landing after it had overshot the runway. As all available aircraft were being mobilised, the decision was taken to use these PS-43s as well.

Engineer of the NII GVF I.A. Ivanov, who knew the Vultee inside out, was drafted in from his vacations in Yessentuki to restore these aircraft. He arrived in Moscow on 26 June but he was not allowed onto the airfield. He was told that raids by German aircraft were expected and the 'iron line' was giving away that this was an airfield. In view of this all the aircraft would be crushed by a tractor and all the scrap removed. Ivanov began to call anyone he could in order to stop the 'massacre'. The GU GVF offered him assistance, promising engines and spare parts. All the PS-43s were towed away to a site with flat ground between the airfield and the Vsekhsvyatskoe cemetery. Ivanov put a team together, which, working in a field conditions with the minimum of equipment and tooling managed to assemble 14 aircraft in the course of a little over two months. They worked from dawn to dusk, eating dry rations (the airport's canteen was two kilometres away), before workers began to be fed at the neighbouring collective farm.

Time was of the essence, and the PS-43s were ferried without any testing. Pilots P.S. Gusev, V.N. Ilyin, V.S. Mineev performed these ferry flights. The Vultees began to be concentrated in the 2nd Squadron of the MAGON, which was based on the airfield at Sukovo in the Moscow region. In July, eight aircraft arrived there, in August – four more, and in September – a further eight. Pilots were converting to the American aircraft under the leadership of P.S. Gusev.

The Vultees for the most part carried post, special messengers, and sometimes staff officers. On 13 August 1941, pilot Mineev was flying a PS-43 that was carrying a special military courier when a German fighter attacked the aircraft. The pilot managed to evade the German for half an hour, and eventually got away. Given the enemy's air superiority, losses were constantly being incurred by the group – one aircraft was shot down in July, and another in August. In September, as the enemy was approaching Moscow, the group was drafted in to carry out reconnaissance of enemy troops near Maloyaroslavets, Mozhaysk, Volokolamsk, and Kaluga, and with some success. By that time, the PS-43s were already carrying defensive armament, which had been fitted from August onwards, when this had been done to the first aircraft. The aircraft mechanics or passengers acted as the air gunners. Nevertheless, in September a further two aircraft were lost.

On 25 September 1941, a Special Liaison Air Group (OAGS, *Osobaya Aviagruppa Svyazi*) was formed from the 2nd Squadron of MAGON and the 200th Detachment of the Moscow Directorate of the GVF, and this new group was based at Myachkovo airfield in the Moscow region. All the remaining PS-43s were transferred there; on 1 October there were 16 of them. They were all listed in the 3rd Squadron under Captain Gvozdev. Along with the male pilots, two women served in this unit – Lieutenants Streltsova and Chugunova. In the following month the group lost another aircraft.

On 9 November pilot Mineev's aircraft was intercepted by a MiG-1 fighter, which, menacingly, escorted the aircraft to Kalinin airfield. There the Vultee was strafed from the ground by machine gun fire. Mineev, who was injured in the leg, turned the aircraft back, and once he was sure that it was the Soviet forces on the ground, he made an emergency landing. The PS-43 was burnt out, and the pilot and flight engineer Kobylko sustained burns.

The final PS-43 arrived at the OAGS in December, and that same month German anti-aircraft gunners shot one down. By the end of 1941, all the Vultees were in front line air groups, there were none left in the rear.

In winter 1941–1942, the PS-43s took part in the 'air bridge' into Leningrad that had been encircled by the Germans. The aircraft flown by M.G. Skrylnikov was hit over Lake Ladoga and had to make an emergency landing. The undercarriage had been broken, and the tail unit had been completely torn off. Ten days later, however, the aircraft was returned into service and I.I. Tukish flew this airplane up until the end of the war.

In the spring of 1942, a sharp increase in the numbers of accidents was recorded. This was linked to the fact that the group had lost its most experienced pilots, who had been sent to the front at the start of the war. In the second quarter there were eight accidents, and moreover one airplane was completely destroyed.

On 1 May 1942, three PS-43s were listed in the Kiev Air Group, and 13 in the OAGS. On 16 May 1942 the airplane flown by pilot Gershbeyn from the Kiev Air Group was shot down by German fighters; the pilot, mechanic, and four passengers were killed. Another aircraft landed in Grozniy during the evacuation from Kiev, where it was appropriated by the Air Force flying school. After some protracted correspondence a Vultee was returned to the North-Caucasian Air Group of the GVF. This aircraft, however, turned out to be unlucky. On 27 June 1942, the undercarriage had failed to deploy on landing, and the aircraft went for repair. On 24 October on landing at Sochi, two German fighters were lying in wait. The PS-43 crashed into the sea and pilot Nikonov and the passenger were killed.

In 1942, what had been initially an original, but highly impractical, shock absorber system of the undercarriage was acknowledged as unsuitable for service. These shock absorbers began to be replaced with Soviet ones of oleo-pneumatic type. By autumn the shock absorbers had been replaced on all of these airplanes. Another novelty was the use of frost-resistant lubricant in the landing gear retraction mechanism. American oil had been used in the system, which thickened at temperatures below -15 degrees Celsius. Then, the American oil ran out. As a result, the aircraft flew with extended undercarriage in winter and lost 25–30km/h of maximum speed. Engineer I.A. Ivanov put together a non-freezing mixture of Soviet oils that were used from that point onwards.

The tail wheel leg would often break, and furthermore, the rudder would usually be damaged, as it extended significantly underneath. The tail wheel legs from LaGG-3 fighters began to be fitted instead, at the same time strengthening the rear part of the fuselage with metal profiles. The base of the rudder was trimmed slightly which had almost no effect on the handling but the ground clearance had increased.

There was a shortage of the M-62IR engines, and for this reason the airplanes would sometimes stand idle. As the engines arrived, they were immediately fitted to the aircraft on right at the front-line bases.

During the battles on the approaches to Stalingrad the OAGS maintained communications with the front in the south, which was cut off from the rest of the country. Three PS-43s came under the flight led by Major Pakhomov, which was based in Astrakhan, along with three R-5s, and a single U-2. They delivered mail and passengers in a relay to Astrakhan, and from there these were distributed around the various cities. They flew to Tbilisi, Sukhumi, Krasnodar, Grozniy, Mineralniye Vody and to other locations. They were often crossing the Caucasus Range through passes, which were frequently covered with clouds.

They also flew to Stalingrad. It was the PS-43 flown by pilot Savchenko that made the last flight into the city. The aircraft landed as the Soviet troops were leaving the airfield. German airplanes had bombed the landing ground, and the splinters had damaged the PS-43s, mechanic Miroshnichenko suffered from contusion. The pilot was able to get the aircraft into the air and returned to base. In Mineralniye Vody pilot Mishchur had already realised there were Germans below them as they were approaching the airfield. He was strafed but turned back and departed. Pakhomov's flight was later re-deployed to Makhachkala.

On 10 December 1942 the OAGS was transformed into the 3rd Independent Liaison Division made up of two regiments and a transport air unit. The number of the PS-43s in this division was reducing gradually, but at quite a slow pace. If on 1 January 1943 there were 14 aircraft, on 1 December there would be 12. The losses were explained, for the most part, by accidents and crashes, although the Germans did destroy some aircraft. Thus, on 12 March, pilot Yegupov flew into a ship's mast during a flight along the Don River at low-level. Everyone on board the aircraft was killed. On 29 April a Messerschmitt strafed V.I. Timofeev's aircraft on take-off in Krasnodar. The aircraft caught fire, the pilot and flight engineer ended up in hospital with burns.

By 1 June 1944, only nine PS-43 aircraft remained in service, and by the end of the year this figure was eight. Three

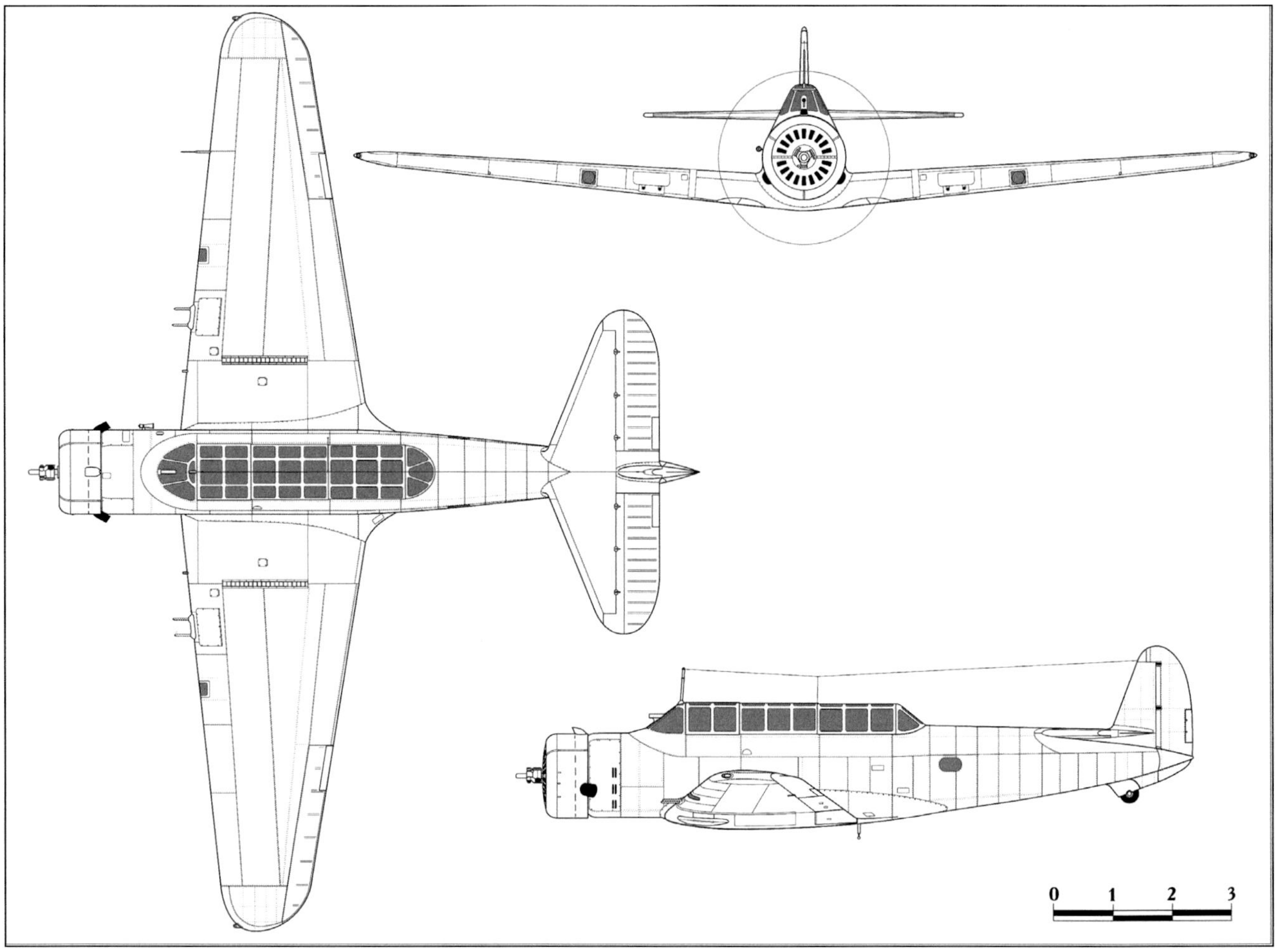

Three-view drawings of a BSh-1 airplane.

aircraft were based in Lvov in January 1945. They carried mail to the 1st and 4th Ukrainian, and the 1st Belorussian fronts. One airplane each was based in Kaunas and Minsk, which served the 1st Baltic and the 2nd and 3rd Belorussian fronts.

Before the war, the service period between major overhaul for the PS-43 was set at 1,500 flying hours. Many aircraft had flown more than 2,500 hrs during the war. A report on the combat service of 3rd Liaison Division noted the following about the Vultee: 'the aircraft flew perfectly'.

From the beginning of 1945, the 3rd Liaison Division began to introduce into service more modern A-20 and B-25 aircraft, which enabled the old and worn-out PS-43s to be gradually written off. By September, not one such aircraft remained in service in the Soviet Union.

And what was the fate of the two aircraft purchased in the USA? The V-11 serial number 33 crashed in July 1938 during tests at the Scientific Testing Range of Aircraft Armament. The engine failed unexpectedly on take-off, and the pilot Captain Andreev tried to land but ran off the end of the airfield and crashed into a peat mound. It then emerged that the fuel gauge had failed, and the pilot had switched to an empty tank by mistake.

This aircraft was later repaired, and it was operated by an aviation unit of aircraft engine Factory No.19 in Molotov (now Perm), with the registration number СССР-И294. By that time the airplane had been fitted with an M-62IR engine, it was unarmed, and a locally made starboard undercarriage leg replaced the one that had failed before. On 17 July 1943, pilot V.N. Truntsev was to fly the aircraft to Sverdlovsk (now Yekaterinburg) with six passengers. The undercarriage, however, collapsed on take-off. Nobody was hurt, but the aircraft was sent for repair. This time, two new main undercarriage legs were fitted in October. On 31 October, however, they collapsed again, this time on landing in Kuybyshev (now Samara). After that, the Vultee was written off.

Information on the fate of the other Vultee purchased in America has not yet been found.

4.9 The GST – Catalina from Taganrog

During April-May 1936 a representative delegation of Soviet aviation specialists led by the well-known aircraft designer A.N. Tupolev made a visit to the USA. At that time Tupolev was not only in charge of the design bureau but he was also the chief engineer of the GUAP. The delegation visited around a dozen factories, as well as various scientific and research organisations, and the Wright Field airbase. During a tour to the factory of Consolidated Aircraft Corporation, the representatives of the company management made a series of proposals that related to the new flying boat, work

The *Guba* as it was flown in the USA and Canada. The flying boat was already considered Soviet and carried the registration number URSS L-2.

The *Guba* in Leningrad, the airplane still carries its old registration, 1938.

The *Guba* at Zakharkovo air base of GUSMP, July 1938.

The *Guba* was given the Polar Aviation registration number H243.

on which had only just been completed. The flying boat they had offered was designated 'Model 28'. This flying boat soon was accepted into service with American naval aviation under PBY-1 designation, and subsequently, this aircraft began to be exported to Britain, where they were given the name 'Catalina'.

This was a large, all-metal twin-engine monoplane with a wing that was raised above the fuselage on a pylon and supported by pairs of struts.

The Soviet Union at that time desperately needed to modernise its hydroaviation. The mainstay of the country's fleet of the flying boats were comparatively small wooden single-engine MBR-2 and MBR-4 airplanes. They could not boast excellent flight-performance characteristics, and their range and flight duration meant they could only operate close to shore. The functions of long-range reconnaissance aircraft continued to be fulfilled by the long-obsolete Dornier Wal airplanes (these were designated DVs in the USSR), which had been purchased in Italy at the end of the 1920s. These aircraft were gradually handed over to the aviation service of the GUSMP.

Soviet designers had tried on more than one occasion to create a more advanced long-range maritime reconnaissance aircraft. Tupolev achieved the greatest degree of success as he had managed to take his ANT-27bis (MTB-1) to the series production stage. A small series of these flying boats was manufactured by Factory No.31 in Taganrog. The new Factory No.30 in Savyolovo on the Rybinsk Reservoir was also preparing to produce the MTB-1.

It is sufficient, however, just to look at the MTB-1 and compare it to the Catalina, so to appreciate immediately that they are aircraft that belong to different generations. Tupolev's angular-shaped machine with its corrugated sides is more typical of the beginning of the 1930s, while graceful reconnaissance aircraft of Consolidated company featured a whole set of innovations, which were inherent to the second half of the decade. Tupolev's engineers were designing a new aircraft, the four-engine ANT-44 (MTB-2), but production of its prototype had only just begun.

Back when Tupolev had been in America, in April 1936, the STO took a decision to acquire examples of new aircraft, as well as engines, in the USA, together with licences for them, and to conclude agreements with American companies for assistance with arranging their production. A significant sum of money in hard currency was allocated for this purpose. On the initiative of the Head of the GUAP M.M. Kaganovich, the Model 28 was included on the list of airplanes to be purchased.

Initially, the GUAP had planned to acquire a single flying boat, and, after copying it without a licence, to put it into production at Factory No.126 in Komsomolsk-on-Amur. Under pressure from the UVVS, however, Kaganovich agreed to hold talks on provision of a licence.

The tail fin of the H243.

The pilot's cockpit of the H243.

The radio-operator's station in the H243.

An underwing float of the H243 in the deployed position.

On 9 January 1937 Amtorg signed an agreement with Consolidated to provide a licence for a cargo and passenger version of the flying boat. This aircraft was described as an 'Arctic' machine and strengthening of the hull and provision of drawings for a ski undercarriage were stipulated specifically. There was no mention of any military application. Under the agreement, Amtorg acquired one fully assembled aircraft, as well as engineering drawings, strength and aerodynamic calculations, the results of wind tunnel and towing tank tests, test reports, specifications, various instructions, estimates, and a large volume of documentation on the aircraft production technology. Apart from that, the Americans committed to familiarise the Soviet specialists with their factory in San Diego, and, where necessary, send their engineers to the Soviet Union for consultations. It was envisaged that Consolidated, over the course of three years following the agreement signing, would be sending materials to the Soviet Union on all the changes made to the series production flying boats. The total cost of the agreement was set at 237,000 US Dollars. In an additional letter, Amtorg requested a further two flying boats in a dismantled condition without engines, instruments and equipment. For all three airplane examples the deadline was set no later than 1 November 1937.

In August–October of that same year, from 10 to 40 sets of the most important units and assemblies were ordered from the company. Consolidated, however, did not manufacture all of these in-house, but did take responsibility for their delivery. The acquisition of technological equipment at different enterprises around the USA was also arranged through this company.

The export version of the type was given the designation Model 28-2, but more often it was simply called the 'Russian cargo and mail flying boat'. In essence it was a PBY-1, but without any armament, and fitted with R-1820-G3 engines (the US Navy flying boats were fitted with Pratt & Whitney R-1830 engines). This engine was chosen because it was very similar to the Soviet M-62. All the combat equipment was also removed from the flying boat. The turret had disappeared from the nose section and this was replaced by a bulb-shaped fairing. In all other respects the Model 28-2 copied the PBY-1.

Before the company had fulfilled the Amtorg order, however, another airplane of this type had ended up on the list of aircraft of Soviet civil aviation. On 12 August 1937 the crew of the famous pilot S.A. Levanevskiy took off from Moscow in a DB-A aircraft with the registration number H209, in an attempt to complete a long-range flight to Fairbanks in Alaska via the North Pole. After the aircraft had flown over the Pole, however, one of the engines failed, and then communication with the crew was lost. The Soviet Government organised a search – ships and aircraft were sent

One of the power plants of the *Guba*, with open cowling panels.

The view of the flying boat tail section from inside.

to the north. As there existed a possibility that the aircraft had disappeared close to the coastline of northern Alaska or Canada, the search operations began in that area as well. In addition to the Soviet airplanes that had arrived in Alaska, the decision was taken to acquire aircraft in the USA and to hire crews to fly them. Already on 18 August 1937, a Model 28-1 flying boat was purchased in America in order to search for the missing Levanevskiy's crew. This was a disarmed PBY-1, which had been prepared by American scientists for an expedition to New Guinea. At that time there was only one civil aircraft of this type in America, and it carried its

The H243 near the Northern riverboat station in Moscow.

The H243 following removal of the canopy in the nose section.

own name of *Guba* (the New Guinea Hiri Moutu word for a tropical storm, in honor of his preceding aircraft, Fairchild 91B, that sank in Guba storm). This flying boat was the best match for the requirements of the expedition that was being organised – it was fitted with improved instrumentation and radio equipment, as well as additional fuel tanks. The Soviet Embassy went to great lengths to acquire this aircraft, as the owner of this flying boat Dr. Richard Archbold was adamant and he was not going to sell it. The Ambassador K.A. Umanskiy personally led the negotiations, and he was supported by the American Government, as well as by Consolidated. As an exception, the US Department of the Navy lifted the export ban on the PBY-1, which had previously been imposed until 1 November 1937, and agreed to move the delivery deadlines of these hydroplanes for the Navy units, so that a new flying boat could be manufactured for Archbold outside of the production schedule. Consolidated offered Archbold a discount of 20,000 US Dollars on a new aircraft if he agreed to sell *Guba* to the Russians. The Soviet Embassy initially wanted just to rent the aircraft, but Kaganovich intervened and convinced everyone that the aircraft needed to be purchased. In the end, the owner agreed to concede this flying boat to the Soviet Government for 230,000 US Dollars.

The Canadian crew led by Hubert Wilkins was to fly the Guba, and Wilkins himself would perform the role of navigator. Herbert Hollick-Kenyon was selected to pilot the aircraft during the search. On 17 August, even before the documents had all been drawn up, the Canadians collected the aircraft from Archbold. Two days later the flying boat took off to the north, having made two intermediate landings for refuelling – in Toronto (where they also picked up their co-pilot S.A. Cheesman) and in Fort Smith. On 23 August the *Guba* made its first flight in search of Levanevskiy's crew.

The flying boat was already considered Soviet and carried the registration number URSS L-2. Wilkins' crew performed five long flights in the *Guba*, with a total distance of 20,000km. In mid-September the lakes and bays of northern Canada had begun to freeze. On 19 September the Canadian pilots made their last flight in the hydroplane, and on 25 September the aircraft returned to the USA. A new airplane, Lockheed L-10E Electra, which could be put onto a ski undercarriage, was acquired for Wilkins.

According to the conditions of sale the *Guba* was not to arrive in the USSR before 1 November 1937, and the US Department of the Navy was insistent on this. The deadline was maintained, but back on 17 August the Soviet Government had decided that the flying boat would be taken to the Soviet Union following the conclusion of the rescue operation. In December 1937 the airplane was returned to the Consolidated factory for minor repairs and for modifications required for operating in the Arctic. In particular, the volume of the de-icing mixture tanks was increased, from which the mixture was spilled onto the propellers. The *Guba* was then dismantled and sent by sea from New York to Leningrad. Some 150,000 US Dollars had been spent on the repair, crating, and transportation.

In June 1938, 16 crates with dismantled *Guba* were unloaded in the Grebnoy Port in Leningrad. The flying boat was intended for Polar Aviation, which provided the crew for it. M.I. Kozlov was appointed commander of the airplane, and his crew included co-pilot E.K. Pusep, navigator A.P. Shtepenko, radio-operator B.I. Anufriev, and two flight mechanics – B.M. Kosukhin and V.V. Makarov. It was they who was tasked to assemble the *Guba* (in the USSR the aircraft was often named the 'Consolidated'). The drawings and descriptions were not provided; there were just two photographs of the airplane and an English-Russian dictionary, which was used to translate the inscriptions on the placards. In fact, the assembly was conducted exclusively on the intuition of the experienced flight mechanic Kosukhin, and the entire crew helped him. A month later the hydroplane was ready for flight, and on 5 November it was ferried to the Polar Aviation base at Zakharkovo in the Moscow region. There, the airplane was subject to detailed study by specialists from Factory No.156 (the former Factory of Experimental Designs of TsAGI), and the military aspects of the aircraft design were of particular interest, as the *Guba* was a disarmed series production PBY-1 and retained the locations of military equipment attachment. Soviet engineers estimated how the armour and armament could be fitted.

A prototype of the Model 28-2 in the USA prior to the start of testing, December 1937.

Test flight of the Model 28-2 in America.

The aircraft was highly marked, and there were noted many innovations of its design (for instance, small hatches in the fabric skin closed by zippers) and the sensible layout and ease of use of the various items of equipment.

Subsequently, after receiving registration number H243, this aircraft operated for a long time by the Moscow Air Unit of the GUSMP. The airplane even managed to catch some of the 1938 season, carried out ice reconnaissance flights and transported passengers and cargoes. At that, the crew did not manage to fully master the new aircraft, and much of it remained unknown to them. Kozlov, for example, suggested that the engine speed governors were failing which led to the propellers going into over-speed, but nobody knew how to adjust them. The autopilot was already showing signs of corrosion when it arrived from the USA and did not work properly.

Overall, however, the attitude towards this aircraft was good. At a conference of the Directorate of Polar Aviation of the GUSMP on 9 January 1939 Kozlov said: 'The Consolidated aircraft demonstrated how important it is to have airplanes with a long range in the region of the Northern Sea Route'. The flight range was considered the main advantage of the American flying boat. At that same time the conclusion was reached that stability on water of this flying boat was inferior to the one of the old Wal, which up until that time remained the main hydroplane for the Directorate of Polar Aviation. It was also harder to taxi the 'Consolidated' around on water. Apart from that, some

The Model 28-2 in flight.

Frame of the flying boat hull during assembly at Factory No.31 in Taganrog.

of the bays that had been used by the polar aviators were inaccessible for H243 – the American flying boat had a draft of approximately a metre and could catch on the bottom in the places where the MP-1s (the disarmed MBR-2s) and Wals could pass. The cost of the aircraft operation would also 'bite' – the operation of the Wal cost 2,000 roubles per hour, and of this new machine it was 5,000 roubles.

In autumn the flying boat underwent repair. As it later turned out the unfamiliar engines could not be brought up to an operational condition. This had an effect on the operation of the *Guba* in 1939. Already on take-off from Moscow, Kozlov drew attention to the reduction in take-off power. A short while later the thermocouples and thermostats began to fail. One of the magnetos on the port engine had failed in one of the flights at the end of that season. This led to a decision to return to Dikson, after dumping off more than two tonnes of fuel. During another flight from Igarka to Krasnoyarsk a ball bearing in the supercharger of the port engine disintegrated. Without boosting, the engine itself failed a short while later. There were no logbooks for the engines but according to estimates they had already served 700 hours. Nevertheless, on 18 September Kozlov arrived in Krasnoyarsk.

The aircraft was sent for repair, and when the engines were disassembled a crack was discovered in the master connecting rod. The former *Guba*, which was a disarmed PBY-1 flying boat, was fitted with the standard 14-cylinder, twin-row radial Pratt & Whitney R-1830-64 engines. No spare parts for these engines were found in Krasnoyarsk, and there were none in Moscow, or in the entire USSR. The problem was solved drastically – the engines were replaced with the American Wright R 1820 G103 engines that were available in storage. This engine, however, had nine cylinders in a single-row radial layout, was shorter but had a larger diameter. Therefore, new engine mounts were manufactured, their attachments to the wing centerplane were re-designed, the pipelines had to be reconfigured, and the cowlings were modified. As a result of this large volume of modifications, the release of this aircraft into service was delayed: instead of 1 June the H243 left the factory on 16 August. In the 1940 season, Kozlov's crew used this airplane from Dikson base for purposes of ice reconnaissance.

Lower part of the flying boat hull during assembly.

Nose section of the GST civil version, which was made using the example of the American Model 28-2. Note the figure 1 identifying the hatch for the anchor.

The power plant of the GST with the cowling removed.

A prototype of the GST military version.

The nose-mounted turret of the GST military version with the ShKAS machine gun fitted.

With the outbreak of war with Germany the aircraft was armed. The *Guba* was lost at the end of November 1942, after being strafed by German U-601 U-boat off the south-west coast of Novaya Zemlya. The German submarine had unexpectedly surfaced in the bay where two flying boats were anchored and had opened fire on them. One of the aircraft caught fire and sunk. Along with the aircraft one of the mechanics also perished. Pilot Kozlov, in saving himself, swam approximately 500m in icy water. The Germans also strafed the tent that the other crewmembers were in but they managed to get away and hide.

Returning to the licencing story – arrangement of the Model 28-2 series production was entrusted to Factory No.31 in Taganrog, which had specialised in hydroaviation. The group of specialists led by A.K. Belenkov, that visited Consolidated company in the USA in February 1937, included engineers of the factory and of the Central Design Bureau of Maritime Aircraft headed by G.M. Beriev, which was based at the factory as well. In America they studied equipment and technological processes that were new to them, helped to translate technical documentation into Russian, and converted the data into metric system.

In the autumn of that same year Consolidated engineers travelled to Taganrog, bringing with them the necessary documentation. The factory directorate specially created a department of foreign specialists in order to support the cooperation. The work was started with assembly of aircraft that had been shipped from America as sets of parts.

The first flying boat was fully completed in the United States, and it underwent testing in California at the end of 1937 in the presence of Soviet representatives. The airplane was then partially dismantled and sent by sea to the USSR. Two other hydroplanes were shipped as sets of units and subassemblies.

The first flying boat was assembled from American parts in Taganrog in May 1938, and it was fitted with American R-1820-G3 engines. On 3 June factory testing began. The

Bomb racks under the wing of the GST.

The side-mounted machine-gun position with a sliding hatch, which was similar to the American original but accommodated a ShKAS machine gun. Such were fitted to series production military GSTs.

A GST flying boat during state testing in Sevastopol.

factory pilot A.I. Smolovik initially flew the airplane and was joined by E.M. Koshelev from the eighth flight onwards. Specialists from the NII GVF arrived for the testing as well, and the flights concluded on 20 July. The recorded characteristics of the aircraft powered by the Wright engines ended up being a little lower than of the airplane with the Pratt & Whitney power plants, and the maximum speed and service ceiling reduced. Koshelev's overall feedback can be summed up as follows: 'The flight-performance characteristics of this aircraft are good; it is easy for pilots to master and to fly'.

In the Soviet Union the Model 28-2 was given the designation GST (*GydroSamolyot Transportniy* – transport hydroplane), which was suggested by A.K. Kupreev, the Head

A mechanic, standing on a folding platform, carries out maintenance of one of the engines on the GST. Note emblems on the propeller blades indicating that this airplane is fitted with the original American propellers.

Three FAB-250 high-explosive bombs on the wing bomb racks.

Smaller FAB-50 bombs could be carried on the bomb racks in pairs.

of the Department of Procurement and Supply of the VVS Naval Aviation Directorate. As was the case with the other American flying boat, the Martin M-156, the Soviet side was primarily interested in a possible military application for this aircraft. The airplane was considered as both a long-range reconnaissance aircraft and a naval bomber, and only then as a transport aircraft. The works on the development of a Soviet military version had begun back in 1937, but initially

A DAP-100 smoke generator mounted on one of the bomb racks. The aircraft could carry two of these devices.

The GST could also carry two VAP-500 chemical spray devices on the bomb racks under the wing.

the progress was sluggish, as the factory was producing a few other aircraft types in parallel and the small design bureau was overloaded.

One of the aircraft delivered from the USA was converted into a prototype of a military version. The GST received an armament that consisted of four 7.62mm ShKAS machine guns which were positioned in the same locations as on the PBY-1. Interestingly, machine-gun side mounts on the prototype military GST were made not with sliding hatches, but with small round blisters. This was rejected, however, when it came to series production, and the preference was given to the initial American solution. The GST had six points for carrying the bomb load, and the largest bomb the aircraft cold carry was the FAB-500 that weighed 500kg. The ability to carry torpedoes, in contrast to the American design, was not envisaged, but on the other hand it was possible to fit the chemical weapons – two VAP-500 spray devices, which contained 500l of toxic agent each. The flying boat was also capable of carrying the DAP-100 smoke generators.

The leadership of naval aviation were full of enthusiasm with respect to this new aircraft, and demanded an acceleration of its entry into production. A variety of projects appeared that involved non-traditional uses for this

A series production GST, which sank following an accident during a test flight at the factory in Taganrog, 28 October 1940.

The crashed GST was lifted out of the water but the factory was not able to repair it

A GST that has been built from American subassemblies, which operated in Polar Aviation with the registration number H275.

airplane. For example, a version of 'flying aircraft carrier' was considered – the idea was to carry two I-15bis fighters on the hydroplane's wings. This project, however, remained just on a paper.

In 1938 preparation of the full set of engineering drawings of the Soviet military version was completed. It was this version, designated 'airplane M', that was to become the main one in series production.

According to the plan, the series production was to commence in 1939, and the factory was set the plan for the year at 30 GST flying boats, of which 16 were to be handed over in the fourth quarter. However, the attitude of the factory management towards this aircraft has changed

The H275 near the shore.

A crew of I.I. Cherevichniy standing in front of the H275.

markedly, as they already understood that the type was complex and expensive. To manufacture this aircraft would mean mastering new technological processes, such as forging and stamping large-scale parts. Many of the aircraft components could not be found in the USSR or were only just being introduced into series. Ten American specialists were drafted in to this work, but they were not employed effectively.

The management of Factory No.31, who were supported by some officers at navy headquarters, were counting on the new flying boat design by I.V. Chetverikov, the MDR-6 (which was subsequently renamed the Che-2). It was significantly simpler in manufacturing, and consequently, cheaper. Back in November 1938 the People's Commissariat for the Navy, reporting to the government on the successful testing of the MDR-6, suggested to reject manufacturing of the flying boats under licences from Consolidated and Glenn Martin companies.

The GST production was now explained only as a way of mastering the advanced American technology, and also as a way of using imported materials, parts and units. In 1939 the design work on the refinement of the aircraft was all but stopped.

Nevertheless, the factory began manufacturing of all 30 (according to other sources 29) planned flying boats. Their production was accompanied by multiple delays, which were explained by objective reasons. The factory workers had to master new lathes, which had been brought from America, to study new technological processes, such as casting large parts from aluminium alloys. Many problems were linked to the manufacture of conical gears and internal gears. Some of the manufactured parts had to be scrapped because of their low quality. The design of the Consolidated flying boat utilised a number of large duralumin forgings, which had been purchased in the USA for 22 airplanes. For the next aircraft, manufacturing of these parts was planned to be arranged at Factory No.95, but the factory had hard times to master this technological process. Up until the end of 1939, 16 fuselages and 18 wing centerplanes had been handed over for final assembly.

At the factory warehouse, however, there were just four engines! According to the plan, the M-62R engines (a geared variant of the M-62) with variable pitch VISh-21AK propellers were to be fitted on the GST, but manufacturing of the M-62R had only just started at the factory in Molotov. The first engines of this type were not known for their excellent reliability. They suffered from smoking, pressure surges in the oil system, jamming of the pushrods in the valve timing system, and what was the main shortcoming – quick wear out of the friction discs in the speed changing mechanism of the supercharger. But even such engines were of short supply. The first two power plants suitable for installation on the aircraft were delivered by Factory No.19 in mid-August, and a further two were added in November. That was all there was for 30 aircraft! There was a shortage of autopilots, radio compasses, and some of the instruments as well. The factory badly needed stainless steel, duralumin rods, and duralumin pipes. Even ordinary screws and bolts were in short supply. In August 1939 the People's Commissar for the Navy N.G. Kuznetsov reported to the Committee of Defence about the delays in the delivery of the GST airplanes to naval aviation, indicating that the main reason for this was the shortage of engines.

The first aircraft took to the skies on 25 August, and by the end of the year three airplanes had been presented to the military acceptance commission. Only the first of these was actually fitted out in full – it received M-62R engines and an autopilot and became the only example to be accepted by the Navy in 1939. It was expensive as well – 1,396,101 roubles were paid for it, while the MDR-6 was twice as cheap, and almost an entire squadron of obsolete MBR-2s could be produced for that money (each of them cost less than 130,000 roubles).

The leading GST flying boat was handed over to the NII VVS of the Navy in Sevastopol for state testing, and the aircraft was flown by N.P. Kotyakov. In one of the flights the flying boat began to shake because of the buffeting. As a result, the skin on the upper surface of the wing had blistered in places, the rivets had popped, and tearing had appeared in the sheets of the skin where the rivets had remained in place. The GST had to be returned to the factory for the extensive repairs. Subsequently, limitations were imposed on some flight modes.

Testing had shown that the GST was a little heavier than its American prototype, which in conjunction with the reduced engine output at altitude led to decrease in the flight-performance characteristics.

In January 1940, the factory had 22 completed fuselages, 25 sets of wing outer sections, 20 wing centerplanes, and 19 sets of tail fins. The plans relating to the use of this stock changed several times. Initially the NKAP, which now encompassed aircraft production, issued an order to manufacture eight flying boats in the civil version, which were known as MP-7s. Five of these were intended for the GVF routes, and three for the Polar Aviation of the GUSMP. The factory began to convert of what was almost completed aircraft. Then, a new order came through – to restore four flying boats back to a military configuration. In view of this, in the first three months of 1940 the factory was not able to present a single aircraft for acceptance.

This leapfrog was compounded by changes in the requirements, which were presented by the Naval aviation. Among them were installation of armoured pilot seat backs and fitting of a fuel tank pressurisation system using a neutral gas. The design of engine cowling was changed several times. The final variant of the cowling envisaged installation of front panel with adjustable shutters for winter operation. These works were drawn up using additional order to the factory and were paid for separately. At that, the aircraft handed over at the start of the second quarter did not get all these changes. In total, the armoured seat backs and the neutral gas system were fitted to 15 flying boats.

The situation with supply of engines remained tense, and it was planned that airplanes manufactured in 1940 would be fitted with the M-62IR engines. This version of the power plant, with an output of 1,000hp, differed from the M-62R by the single-speed supercharger and the inertia electric starter in place of the pneumatic starter system, as well as by a number of small refinements borrowed from the later M-63 engine. In reality, however, only the M-62Rs were delivered, and in small quantities as well. The workers had to assemble the flying boats with the so-called 'mock up' engines, which were unsuitable for flight operations, by removing them from one aircraft to fit to another. Similar situation happened to the wing struts, which were being manufactured from tubes of a teardrop cross-section. These tubes had not been available for a long time, and the airplanes were fitted with temporary struts made of standard steel tubing.

A civil version of the GST, registration number H308, which was built in 1940 and entered service with Polar Aviation.

Flying boats of Polar Aviation anchored in the bay at Igarka. Note GST H308 in the foreground.

An attempt was made to solve the engine problem by replacing the power plant type. It was suggested that an M-87 engine be fitted. This was a twin-row radial engine, which in fact was a modernisation of the French Gnome-Rhone 14K. Manufacture of these engines was arranged at Factory No.29 in Zaporozhye. The M-87 had slightly lower output than the M-62R (950hp versus 975hp) but had a smaller diameter and good altitude characteristics.

On 27 September 1939 the People's Commissariat sent a direction to the factory, stating: 'To oblige comrade Trukhan *(Director of Factory No.31 – author's note)* to commence preparations for installation ... M-87 engine on the Consolidated airplane'. This work was actually undertaken at the end of 1939, and a pair of M-87 engines was installed on the second series production airplane. Prior to the New Year this aircraft made a few flights but did not undergo official acceptance. An increase in speed was observed, as well as a rise in service ceiling, but the reliability of the engines left something to be desired.

A GST airplane at anchor in Zakharkovo air base.

In March 1940 an order arrived to cease production of the GST and transfer to the manufacturing of the MBR-6. A decision was taken to complete 15 GSTs which were at the most advanced stage of assembly, and to scrap the assemblies of the remaining aircraft. Corrections, however, were subsequently made, and in total the factory assembled 22 aircraft in 1940. Of these, 12 were accepted in the second quarter and six in the third quarter of the year. After May 1940, no further components for the GST were manufactured, the only work was the completion of the ready airplanes which were handed over as the engines arrived. At the end, the long-awaited M-62IRs arrived; the final eight engines arrived in October, and in November the final GST left the factory.

One of the flying boats crashed during acceptance tests. This took place on 27 October 1940, and prior to the crash the airplane had only amassed 42 mins of flying time. After lifting off from the water the aircraft began to gain altitude whilst banking to port. At an altitude of 25–30m the flying boat suddenly 'pitched' onto its nose and hit the water, initially with the port wing, and then the nose impacted. The aircraft sank up to the leading edge of the wing, and the fuselage broke from the impact. Pilot Smolovik sustained a head injury and concussion, and the sole of his left foot was also broken. Representative of the acceptance commission *Voentekhnik 1-go ranga* (Military Technician 1st rank) A.S. Pozdnyakov was killed as the flying boat hit the water. The pilot was blamed for the accident, and the destroyed flying boat was raised from the water but was later written off at cost to the factory.

The GST did not become a widely used aircraft; in total 27 flying boats of this type were built, including the ones which were made from imported subassemblies.

The Directorate of Polar Aviation of the GUSMP was the first to receive these new hydroplanes – the Moscow Air Group that was based in Zakharkovo was augmented by a single flying boat, assembled from American parts. On 4 July 1939 this airplane (registration number H275) with a crew headed by I.I. Cherevichniy flew to the North for the first time, where they were conducting ice reconnaissance. Over the entire season just a single incident was recorded with this airplane: on 24 July 1939 the flying boat turned back due to bad weather and made an emergency landing in Bulun.

According to the plan for 1940, the Directorate of Polar Aviation was to receive three airplanes built in Taganrog, and in fact four arrived, which received the registration numbers H304, H307, H308 and H309. Airplane H307 flown by the crew of pilot Syrokvasha took part in ice reconnaissance in 1940 season. For this purpose, the flying boat was ferried from Taganrog to Naryan-Mar (some 4,260km).

From April 1940, the GST began to be mastered by naval aviation units. The first airplanes were sent to the Black Sea Fleet, to the 80th Squadron, which was based in Matyushenko Bay in Sevastopol. The overall assessment of the airplane by the crews was positive, as the GST was a huge leap forward as compared to the obsolete MBR-2.

From July 1940, the GST began to enter service also with the Northern Fleet, and on 24 July the first flying boat participated in a parade there in honour of Naval Forces Day. In September, as part of the 118th Reconnaissance Air Regiment, the 4th Squadron was formed that flew these flying boats. By the outbreak of the war with Germany there were 11 GSTs on the Black Sea, and seven in the Northern Fleet. These airplanes, however, never represented a significant portion of the Soviet hydroaviation fleet: on the Black Sea they amounted to around six percent, and in the North – around 12 percent.

The GU GVF also counted on the arrival of the MP-7 flying boats, and in June 1938 the Economical Council under the Council of People's Commissars decreed that five flying boats be delivered to civil aviation in 1939 and a further 10 the following year. As the plan was being drawn up for the third five-year plan, more modest figures were entered – up until the end of 1942 they wanted to receive 12 these airplanes. The intention was to put them into service on the coastal routes, as well as along the big rivers of Siberia. On the basis of these plans, in 1939 the GU GVF signed an agreement with Factory No.31 to supply five MP-7s the following year. One flying boat was to be delivered in the second quarter of 1940 and a further four in the third quarter. They were intended for flights on the routes Irkutsk–Yakutsk and Krasnoyarsk–Igarka. Then, due to the reduction in the GST production, the portion for civil aviation was cut to two airplanes. In reality only one was received, in the summer of 1940. In October this airplane, with registration number A3454, had already commenced operations with the East Siberian Directorate of the GVF, and a crew of U.K. Bergstryom flew this flying boat. Subsequently, this airplane was handed over to the Yakutsk Air Group, where it served them well until mid-1943 when it was also handed over to the polar aviators.

Preparing a GST for take-off. The aircraft belonged to the 82nd Squadron, Black Sea Fleet Air Force.

From the very beginning of the war with Germany the GST was drafted into combat operations. They flew reconnaissance missions, carried out both day and night bombing, transported passengers and cargoes, as well as performed special sorties.

In the Northern Fleet these airplanes served with the 4th (Long-Range Reconnaissance) Squadron of the 118th Reconnaissance Air Regiment headed by Captain V.I. Boyko, which was based in Gryaznaya Bay. They were used very intensively as they had two important advantages – a long range and a significant bomb load. Thus, on 27 June a GSTs bombed Linakhamari, and on 29 June they were sent to Petsamo. The airplanes carried 10 FAB-100 bombs each. One pair of GSTs was intercepted by six Messerschmitts as they were taking off. Captain Boyko was killed and the uncontrollable aircraft crashed into a hill and burnt out; the entire crew perished. The flying boat flown by the crew of Senior Lieutenant V.A. Merkulov landed in the Kola Bay beyond Salniy Island with their port engine on fire. The engine did not cut out, and the burning fuel was spreading out on the surface of the water. The crew abandoned the aircraft and were picked up by a motorboat. Prior to this, however, the injured gunner Sergeant Bogatyrenko, firing from the burning GST, managed to hit a German fighter.

The crew of a GST of the 118th Separate Reconnaissance Air Regiment (from left to right): navigator A. Zaikin, pilot L. Elkin, co-pilot Vorobyov, flight engineer A. Skvortsov, and gunner A. Kruglov.

On 11 July six SB bombers, as well as five GSTs and nine I-153s participated in a raid on German positions close to Zapadnaya Litsa. Significant damage was inflicted on the enemy, but they in turn shot down a flying boat flown by N. Talalikhin. On 13 July a pair of MBR-2s and a flight of GSTs attacked enemy destroyers and damaged one of them.

Special missions were also carried out. Commander of the 118th Reconnaissance Air Regiment Vasilyev was to have delivered a group of reconnaissance personnel behind enemy lines onto Lake Odezhyar. During a night landing the airplane ran into an obstruction and was holed. Repairs were not successful and the airplane had to be blown up. The crew crossed the front line safely and returned to their unit.

On the Black Sea the GST carried out reconnaissance along the Bulgarian and Romanian coastlines. Active participation in combat operations led to significant losses, and fighters were especially dangerous for the slow flying boats. From autumn 1941 onwards they gradually began to transfer to night bombing and transport flights.

As of 1 January 1942, just five GSTs remained on the Black Sea. They were part of the Sevastopol group and were used to deliver especially important cargoes to this besieged city. By 22 April only three airplanes were left, which were re-deployed to the coast of the Caucasus, to Gelendzhik. From there they participated in the evacuation of Sevastopol, and then supplied partisans in the Crimea. From there the aircraft also undertook reconnaissance on the open sea, but no further than the longitude of Yevpatoria, as their range would not allow them to go beyond that point. Then, the number of these airplanes grew less and less. Nevertheless, the GST made its contribution to the conclusion of the war in this theatre. On 8 September 1944 the last surviving GST on the Black Sea, along with the Catalinas that had been supplied through the lend-lease program, landed an assault by marines on Varna (Bulgaria).

In the Northern Fleet one aircraft of that type served until the end of the war in the 16th Transport Air Unit. The flying boat performed reconnaissance missions, escorted

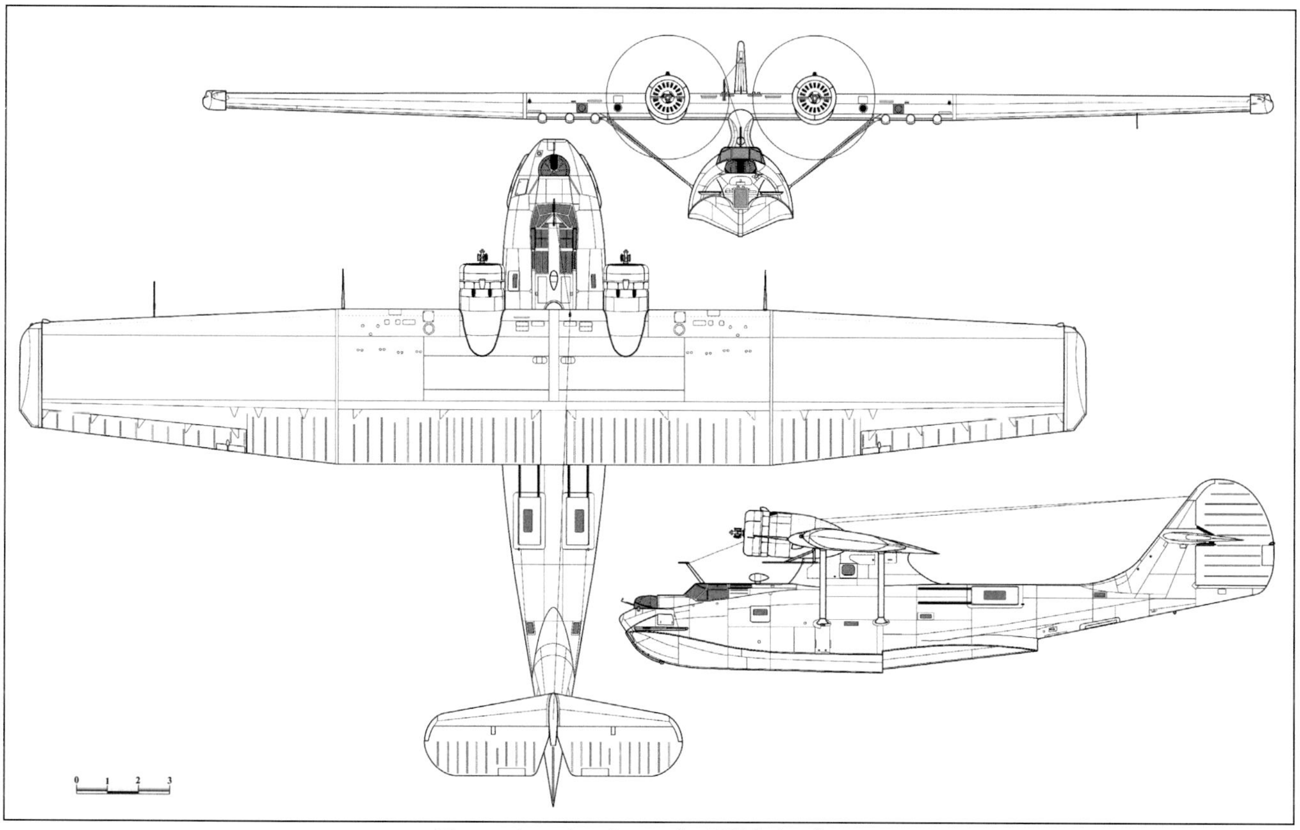

Three-view drawings of a GST flying boat.

convoys, carried out anti-submarine patrols, and was used to transport passengers and cargoes.

The Polar Aviation GSTs participated in the war effort as well. In August 1941 they were armed similarly to the combat version and were drafted in to operations in the Northern Fleet. Some of the GSTs came under the 2nd Separate Air Group of the GVF, which was commanded by the famous Polar aviation pilot I.P. Mazuruk. Aside from their usual missions – ice reconnaissance and carrying whatever was needed to the remote winter locations, airplanes of this unit patrolled Barents and Kara Seas in search of submarines and surface targets. It was two Polar Aviation GSTs (flown by the crews of Cherevichniy and Zadkov) that delivered a group headed by M.M. Gromov to Alaska in August 1941, which was accepting combat aircraft for the further delivery to the USSR.

The GSTs serving in Polar Aviation actively participated in escorting Arctic convoys and in ensuring shipping navigation in the North. In the 1942 season, four of these aircraft were operating in the Arctic skies. In September 1942, one of these flying boats, registration number H275, participated in the search for the German pocket battleship *Admiral Scheer* that had been operating in the Arctic region. It was the crew of this aircraft that found stoker P.I. Vavilov – the only crewman from the steamer *Sibiryakov* who had escaped captivity. The steamer had been sunk by the Germans, and Vavilov had survived for a month on the uninhabited island of Belukha. In mid-October of the following year this same airplane supported navigation of two icebreakers to the west. The GST was always renowned for its reliability but the American engines had by that time used up their service lives, and there were no spare engines available.

In June 1943 a decision was taken to replace the power plants with Soviet M-62IR engines. This work was entrusted to the Central Aircraft Repair Base which belonged to the Directorate of Polar Aviation in Krasnoyarsk. There was little time left before the start of the shipping season so extraordinary steps were taken. The workers were confined to barracks, so they spent 14–15 hrs a day in the workshops. The first modified MP-7 airplane, registration number Λ3454, was handed over from GVF to Polar Aviation (it received registration number H313), and it was followed by another aircraft which received registration number H275.

In 1943 Cherevichniy had to land his flying boat not on water but on ice in Tiksi Bay but nothing came of it, the airplane was undamaged. In that same year Factory No.477 in Krasnoyarsk carried out the armament modernisation on a GST operated by the Polar Aviation. The ShKAS machine guns were replaced by large-calibre UBTs, and bomb racks were fitted for bombs of calibre up to 250kg.

By the end of the year, however, the conclusion had been reached that aircraft which belonged to the Directorate of Polar Aviation no longer required armament. In the course of annual winter overhaul, the machine guns and bomb racks were removed and the firing apertures were covered over. At the same time, a modernisation of the equipment was carried out – new Bendix radio compasses were fitted, as well as autopilots and additional instruments. For aircraft registration number H309, a glazed canopy was manufactured for the navigator's cockpit. All these works have been completed by the end of April 1944.

The repairs on the H309 were poorly carried out: at the start of the season this airplane flew to Igarka and returned back to the Central Aircraft Repair Base to eradicate defects. Flying boat H275 did not get very far either as the engines were just 'eating' oil. An inspection revealed a defect made by the engine Factory No.19. In order to find a quick way out of this situation, the M-62IR was fitted with cylinders, pistons and piston rings from the G2 version of Cyclone engine. At that, the engine output dropped but its operation became a little more reliable.

In July 1945 the aircraft H309 was involved in an accident: pilot Smirnov was landing on the Yenisey River at a high speed and damaged the flying boat. A month later, however, the aircraft returned to operations.

In Polar Aviation the GST also operated after the end of the war. In August 1949, four flying boats of this type remained in service there including the 'old' H275, and they flew along with the new US-supplied Catalinas. At that, the majority of the American flying boats were standing idle because of the absence of spare engines, while the old airplanes were operating very intensively. The airplanes were flown by the Moscow, Chukotka, and Igarka air groups of the Polar Aviation. They were fully superseded only after the US-built flying boats had been converted to fit the Soviet ASh-82FN engines by the end of 1950.

In 1946 a single MP-7 was returned back to Aeroflot, to the Krasnoyarsk Directorate, where it operated at least up until 1949. Another flying boat of this type served with departmental aviation under the Ministry of Ferrous Metallurgy. How long this airplane was flown, and where, is not known.

4.10 Douglas Airplanes

Douglas Aircraft Company built a multitude of airplanes but if to choose a symbolic aircraft from all of them, it would definitely be the DC-3. Perhaps there is not a single country in the sky of which this aircraft would not have flown. The Soviet Union is no exception, where this airplane was often known simply as a 'Douglas'.

The family of successful passenger airplanes manufactured by Douglas attracted the attention of Soviet specialists right from the beginning. To get the first-hand experience with this airplane, a single series production DC-2 (serial number 1413) was acquired via Amtorg in August 1935. The aircraft arrived in Moscow in 1936 and was handed over to the GVF. The airplane was introduced into the list of aircraft operated by the EON which was based at the Moscow Central airfield. The EON pilots, along with specialists from the NII GVF, tested the DC-2. In course of the testing, on 6 May 1936, the airplane undertook a flight Moscow–Tbilisi–Moscow and was piloted by Timashev and Gurevich. The aircraft was also closely studied by TsAGI and NII VVS specialists, and it gained excellent feedback.

In parallel, a delegation of Soviet aviation specialists led by A.N. Tupolev also familiarised themselves with these airplanes. During a visit to the Douglas factory, the DC-2 was demonstrated to the delegation both in the air and on the ground. The Soviet specialists were given a tour at the company workshops with demonstration of manufacturing processes of the main components, as well assembly of the units and the aircraft as a whole. The aircraft design was

A Soviet DC-3 at an airfield in Berlin. Note *Aeroflot* inscription on the nose.

The only Soviet DC-2, registered URSS–M25. The letter 'M' denotes that this airplane belongs to the UMVL.

Assembly of one of the DC-3s from the first Soviet order at the Douglas factory.

The first DC-3 to arrive in the USSR was given the registration number M132.

DC-3 registration number M132 at an airfield in Stockholm.

The Deputy Head of the VVS Ya.V. Smushkevich (on the right, without cap) and a group of fighter pilots, who had experience of air combats in Spain and China, had been delivered to Khalkhin-Gol on three DC-3 airplanes.

well suited to mass production and a number of what were advanced technologies for that time was used. Engineers Taits and Kvitko intentionally purchased tickets on a flight that was operated by a DC-2. In their report following this flight they remarked on the airplane's high reliability, multitude of equipment to serve the passengers, and comfort in the passenger cabin (thermal and sound insulation, ventilation, heating, elaborate lighting, and comfortable seats with reclining seatbacks).

The DC-2 received by the GVF was not just intended for study. The airplane got the registration number M25 ('M' indicated that the aircraft would be operated on the international air routes) and commenced its service with the Soviet-German company *Deruluft*, to which the airplane was leased temporarily. The DC-2 served one of the sectors on the Moscow–Berlin route. Then, the time came to put this airplane into service on the Soviet route, which was only one at Aeroflot at that time – to Prague. This route had been opened in May 1936, but only began to function properly after the DC-2 M25 had replaced the obsolete PS-9. The

A military DC-3 on a landing ground in the area of combats at Khalkhin-Gol. The aircraft wears a characteristic camouflage made up of small paint spots.

route was under responsibility of the EON, so it was served by the airplanes and crews of the special purpose squadron.

The DC-2 flew 54 flights before it was involved in a fatal crash on 6 August 1937. On its return journey from Prague the aircraft made an intermediate landing in Cluj (Romania) for refuelling. A few minutes after leaving Cluj, there was an explosion in the Douglas. The burning aircraft could still be flown for some time; the pilots were preparing for an emergency landing – they lowered the undercarriage and deployed the flaps. Then, the flames engulfed the canvass on the elevators, the airliner went into a dive and flew into the ground. The pilot Gurevich, co-pilot, flight mechanic, and two passengers were killed. A commission led by I.F. Petrov from the NII VVS was sent to Romania to investigate the reasons behind this tragedy. Initially, they suggested sabotage. In order to investigate the location, above which the explosion had happened, the Romanian side sent 2,000 people. The collected wreckage enabled them to build up a picture of what had happened. Sabotage was not the case – the reason for the explosion was a build up of fuel vapour in the aircraft toilet; this vapour ignited when one of the passengers decided to have a smoke in there.

The second DC-2 appeared in the USSR much later. This was an airplane operated by Polish LOT airline, which had been ferried to Latvia as the Germans invaded Poland in September 1939. The aircraft was interned, and less than a year later Soviet forces entered the Baltic states. The former Polish aircraft was introduced into service of the Baltic Military District Air Force but was later destroyed on take-off.

The Douglas company, following the DC-2, released a more modern DC-3, which immediately aroused interest in the Soviet Union. On 11 April 1936 the STO issued a decree on acquiring an example of this airplane. This was a DC-3-196 (serial number 1589) fitted with Wright SGR-1820-G2 engines. Excello company had acted as an intermediary in the acquisition of the airplane. On 1 December the dismantled DC-3 was shipped to Europe and arrived in the USSR at the beginning of 1937. The aircraft was also handed over to the GVF and received the registration number M132. It underwent testing at the NII GVF, and then was transferred to the Directorate of International Air Routes (UMVL, *Upravleniye Mezhdunarodnykh Vozdushnikh Liniy*) that had been set up not long before this took place. On 27 June 1937 this aircraft opened a new air route to Stockholm, and the pilots were Timashev and Dyomchenko.

The Soviet Union acquired a licence to build the DC-3, but in parallel with the arrangement of the serial production, new batches of this airplane continued to be acquired in America. It will take some time for the Soviet 'Douglases' to emerge, while contemporary passenger and military transport airplanes were needed immediately. The twin-engine PS-9 was obsolete, and the PS-35 proposed by Tupolev was inferior to the DC-3 in lifting capacity and in the number of passengers it could carry. As a result, in 1937 a further three aircraft were acquired in the USA – the DC-3-227s. The formal customer for these aircraft was the non-existent (or nominally created) Mongolian Air Transport company. Naturally, none of these airplanes ended up in Mongolia, and they were entered into the Aeroflot list under registration numbers M135, M136 and M137.

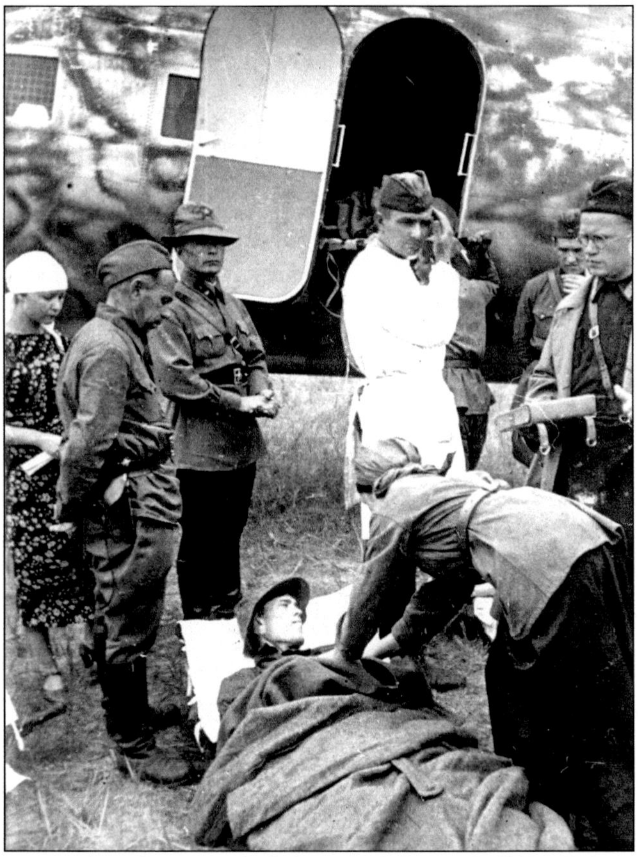

Loading the wounded aboard a DC-3 at Khalkhin-Gol.

One of these aircraft joined the service on the route to Stockholm. This route was constantly operated by two DC-3s in 1939–1941, and in total they flew 718 flights. Two other airplanes were involved in the 'Operation Z' – the re-deployment of Soviet military aircraft and entire air units to China. The Douglas aircraft were considered leased by the VVS from civil aviation. The first airplane flew the Alma-Ata–Lanzhou route in October 1938, and the commander of that aircraft was pilot F.M. Korshunov. The civil pilots worked on this route alongside their military colleagues (they operated TB-3RN and converted DB-3 airplanes) and were transporting the ground crews, as well as spares, equipment and much more. By the end of the year a second DC-3, flown by pilot V.S. Lebedev, had appeared on this route.

In January 1938 the Deputy Head of the VVS Ya.V. Smushkevich suggested to the People's Commissar for Defence K.E. Voroshilov to send an additional batch of SB bombers to Spain. These were to be manufactured by the Moscow-based Factory No.22 in place of the PS-40 postal aircraft, which were planned to be delivered to the GVF (these were the same SBs but they were unarmed). Instead, Aeroflot was offered to purchase 30 DC-3s in the United States.

This pilot has every right to play the harmonica happily following the end of hostilities at Khalkhin-Gol – he earned himself two Orders of the Red Banner – a Soviet one and a Mongolian one.

Preparing a civil DC-3 for flight, 1939.

It is possible that the new orders for Douglas airplanes were initially dictated by these ideas. On 2 March 1938, an agreement was signed for the delivery of nine DC-3-196As, costing 120,800 US Dollars each. One of these airplanes was fitted with anti-icing equipment, and on the others the possibility of fitting this equipment was just envisaged. The North-Western Company acted as intermediary in this deal. On 31 March, the agreement was accompanied by the Amtorg order, and on 4 April permission for export was secured from the American authorities. Nine airplanes with serial numbers 2031–2033 and 2042–2047 arrived in the Soviet Union by sea in June–August 1938.

Not one DC-3 from this batch entered Soviet civil aviation, however – three aircraft were transferred to the Reconnaissance Directorate of the RKKA, and six entered service with the VVS. Three aircraft of these six were used by special purpose squadron (later a regiment) which transported the upper military command. One ended up at the Air Force Academy, one served the XI-th Department of General Headquarters, and the last was sent to the Far East. Civil pilots undertook the training of the first crews from the VVS, and UMVL specialists serviced the airplanes.

One of the military DC-3s was destroyed in September 1938 in the course of the search for the ANT-37 *Rodina* airplane after its long-range record flight by female crew had ended in an emergency landing in the taiga. The DC-3 collided with a TB-3RN during a manoeuvre not far from the *Rodina* landing site, killing everyone on board.

The number of airplanes purchased, however, again turned out to be low. On 16 September 1938, in the name of the non-existent Far-East Fur Trading Company, Amtorg ordered six DC-3s (serial numbers 2096–2101). Soviet commission, which included engineers Borisenko and Kozlov, completed acceptance of these airplanes in February 1939. The commission carried out a check of the weight and the available equipment, tested the operation of the power plant and propeller, undercarriage, flaps, and other important systems. They were also responsible for observing the flights undertaken by the company crews. The aircraft began to be shipped from the USA starting from 28 February 1939, and by 27 March four DC-3s had already left.

Another batch followed almost immediately after this one, and also consisted of six airplanes. On 16 December 1938, Amtorg placed another order through North Western Company for six DC-3-196B airplanes. Aircraft from this batch differed by second electrical generator, second battery, interphone (intercom system), Bendix radio set, and radio compass. All these airplanes were fitted with Goodrich pneumatic de-icing system, and each airplane cost 114,000 US Dollars. Aircraft from this batch had serial numbers 2112–2117.

On 22 March 1940, a Soviet commission, led by the Head of Baltic Fleet Support Services *Kapitan 1-go ranga* (Captain 1st rank) N.I. Moskalenko, arrived in Finland on this military DC-3, to accept a territory for the future Soviet military base at Hanko.

Of the 12 DC-3s that had arrived in the Soviet Union in 1939, only two were allocated to civil aviation, while all the others were transferred to the military. All three special-purpose air armies received one airplane each, as did the headquarters of the Transbaikal, Leningrad and Belorussian military districts. A single DC-3 was transferred to the 1st Separate Red-Banner Army, and two went to the 2nd Separate Red-Banner Army in the Far East. One airplane became part of the Air Force of the 57th Special Rifle Corps, which had been deployed to Mongolia.

Since May 1939, hostilities began between Soviet–Mongolian and Japanese forces in the region of the Khalkhin-Gol River. There were no railways in that region and all the supply for the 57th Corps (subsequently re-formed into the 1st Army Group under the command of G.K. Zhukov) from the Transbaikal region was carried out using road transport and aviation. Air transportation was performed using TB-3 bombers and a group of three to five DC-3s airplanes, including those re-deployed specially from Moscow. The Douglas airplanes were based at Chita.

They were flown by the country's best pilots, such as A.E. Golovanov (who later became a Marshal of Aviation, commanding Long-Range Aviation), famous test pilot M.A. Nyukhtikov, and V.G. Grachyov (it was Grachyov who flew Stalin to the Tehran conference). The aircraft delivered spare parts, as well as ammunition and medical supplies to Khalkhin-Gol. In total, over the period of these battles DC-3s transported 350 tonnes of cargo. They also carried passengers – Douglas airplanes flew the best fighter pilots to the front and transported wounded on their return flights.

Up until August the airplanes flew with up to 18–20 wounded sitting in the seats in the passenger cabin, which restricted the potential to carry seriously wounded servicemen. Then three airplanes were converted right on the spot into special medical transports, by fitting stretchers in three tiers enabling them to transport 18 wounded in each. The assessment of this conversion was very high: 'This modified Douglas airplane is very convenient for medical evacuation: the engine noise is well dampened, the ventilation and heating work, the wounded are accommodated in such a way that it is easy for medical staff to monitor them and to offer them the required assistance where necessary; and an oxygen supply is arranged at each stretcher'.

A 'millionaire' pilot (who has flown one million kilometres) I.M. Skorokhodov stands next to his DC-3, 1940.

These airplanes flew singly, without fighter cover. They were camouflaged with small patches of khaki colour and the flat steppe enabled them to fly at very low level. The Douglas flown by Grachyov was fitted with defensive armament. A paired ShKAS machine gun protruded from the entrance door, and another machine gun was positioned in one of the windows on the opposite side. The Head of the Main Political Directorate of the RKKA L.Z. Mekhlis, who had been sent to Khalkhin-Gol as Stalin's representative, and for whom this aircraft was made available, categorically refused

Flight mechanic I.S. Molyarov inspects the propeller on a DC-3 airplane serving under the UMVL, 1940.

Pilot G.M. Garmash, who distinguished himself in the war with Finland, stands next to a DC-3.

to fly in an unarmed airplane, so the aircraft had to be fitted with these impressive looking but not very effective machine-gun mounts, within one day.

In the last few days of the battles, these airplanes would land directly onto the steppe, close to the front line, and would pick up the wounded from the front. In August, Japanese forces suffered a defeat, and the combat activities ceased. The DC-3s had not seen any losses in this campaign, and pilots Golovanov, Grachyov, Nyukhtikov, Lebedev, Kubyshko, and the navigator Ivanov were all awarded the Order of the Red Banner.

For the Douglas aircraft, however, this period of peace turned out to be short. In November 1939 the war with Finland began. The DC-3s also operated in this location, after they had been dispersed into different separate air groups under the GVF, which were attached to the front-line armies. One Douglas saw action in the Karelian direction, and two in the Petrozavodsk direction. For the most part they transported the wounded to hospitals in the rear. In January 1940, however, they also flew at night to drop provisions to the forces of two divisions that were surrounded in Karelia, and also dropped leaflets behind the front line.

In the winter of 1939–1940 the tire inner tubes on these airplanes would often rupture. Due to this, their material began to be replaced with Soviet rubber, which was more frost resistant. At the same time the sealant in the hydraulic system was replaced as this would leak when the temperature hit 20 degrees below zero. Insulated spinners were placed onto the propeller hubs.

Since 1939 the PS-84 airplanes began to enter service with civil aviation, which were the Soviet copies of the DC-3. The import of airplanes from the USA ceased, but the examples that had been purchased continued to operate intensively.

In November 1939 Chairman of the Council of People's Commissars V.M. Molotov asked the VVS to hand over four Douglas airplanes to civil aviation to serve planned international air routes to Berlin and Sofia. This request was equated to an order, and on 1 January 1940 the UMVL had eight DC-3s, and a further three belonged to the Moscow directorate of the GVF and flew on the Moscow–Ashkhabad route. The last, twelfth airplane was at the Flight centre in Moscow, where the new aircrew were being trained.

Subsequently, one of the DC-3s was handed over to the Georgian Directorate, and this example performed flights around the Transcaucasian region and periodically flew to Moscow.

Four UMVL airplanes operated on Moscow–Berlin route which had been re-opened following the liquidation of the *Deruluft* airline. The first flight to the German capital took place on 8 January 1940. On 14 March a DC-3 flown by pilot Krichenko opened the route to Sofia. The route had stopovers in Kherson and Burgas, and on the return journey the aircraft only stopped in Burgas. At the end of 1939 a Sino-Soviet *Khamiata* company commenced operations – it

A DC-3 registration number M136 was operated by the UMVL.

received two Douglas airplanes from the UMVL, which were put into service on Alma-Ata–Hami route. The registration numbers of these airplanes remained Soviet. Another air route passed between Moscow and Stockholm.

In view of a shortage of airplanes there would occasionally be long interruptions between flights. For instance, the airplane registration number M132 did not fly to Stockholm for two months due to the maintenance works.

In 1940 the registration system used by the UMVL changed, and now airplanes were identified using Latin letters (such as URSS-A, URSS-B and so on). On international routes, the DC-3s deserved very high reputation. In comparison with them, the indigenous PS-35s, which were also operated by the UMVL, had a number of shortcomings: a cramped passenger cabin, unreliable engines, inferior instruments and radio equipment. This culminated in the Douglas airplanes superseding the PS-35 completely on international routes. DC-3 flights to Europe continued right up until the outbreak of war with Germany. The last airplane returned from Berlin on 21 June 1941, and on the morning of the following day German forces crossed the state border.

The Air Force also retained these airplanes in service. For example, in March 1940 DC-3 serial number 2099 was serving the headquarters of the Far Eastern Front, and Lieutenant Gerasimov's crew flew this airplane.

With the outbreak of war, the majority of the Douglases became military transport aircraft. Many of the UMVL airplanes were transferred to the MAGON – there were six DC-3s in its 1st Squadron in July 1941. They participated, for example, in flights to transport provisions into the besieged city of Leningrad. Douglas aircraft also flew to the Soviet rear, delivering urgent cargoes and passengers. In particular, they operated between Moscow and Kuybyshev (now Samara), to where in autumn 1941 many of the departments and the diplomatic corps were evacuated. They would occasionally transport foreign delegations as well.

One of these aircraft, which had previously belonged to the UMVL, was used in autumn 1941 when filming the movie 'The Air Cabby'. The airplane featured the original registration URSS-M and the added CCCP Λ-3431 imitating that this aircraft was operating on scheduled flights for the territorial directorates.

As of 13 May 1942, four DC-3s remained in the GVF, and five in the VVS. The number of these aircraft was reducing for the most part due to accidents, wear, and a shortage of spare parts. On 9 June 1943, the airplane registration number URSS-N of *Khamiata* crashed due to icing during a flight on Urumchi–Hami route some 30km south of Yanchi; the crew and all passengers perished.

Following the re-formation of the GVF special air groups into regiments and divisions, the DC-3s joined the

1st Regiment of the 1st Transport Air Division, which was deployed at Vnukovo airfield just outside Moscow.

In the VVS, the Douglas served, for the most part, in the Special Purpose Air Regiment in Monino. They were also in the strength of the Long-Range Aviation (ADD, *Aviatsiya Dalnego Deystviya*). A.E. Golovanov, whilst transferring from the GVF to the VVS in February 1941, 'grabbed' a single DC-3. This airplane served with the 212th Long-Range Bomber Air Regiment as a 'flying classroom' to train pilots in blind flying. At least one airplane joined the 1st (Transport) Air Division of the ADD, where it flew alongside Soviet PS-84s.

In military aviation the American Douglases were used right up until the end of 1943, when their remote descendants the C-47s had begun to arrive under the Lend-Lease.

The DC-3s, which remained in civil aviation, continued to operate partly on international air routes, for example Alma-Ata–Hami. From summer 1943, a single DC-3 and a C-47 flew on this route. From July 1942, two Douglas airplanes served the route to Tehran, flying via Guryev, Krasnovodsk, and Baku. From October, in view of the approaching front line, the route was changed, and it began to pass via Aktyubinsk, Dzhusaly, and Ashkhabad.

The Douglases continued to operate in the USSR for the entire duration of the war in ever decreasing numbers. In November 1944, the aircraft registration number URSS-A, which had been previously flying to Tehran, was written off after becoming worn out. At least one airplane continued to operate after the war – this was a DC-3 that carried the serial number 2046. In July 1946 it made an emergency landing on Yegoryevsk airfield. This aircraft was written off on 14 January 1947.

The American DC-3s did not make a big contribution to the volume of air transportation in the GVF or in military aviation, as there were very few of them. On the other hand, they did train flight and ground crews to operate the Soviet copy of the Douglas – PS-84, which for a long time became the main transport aircraft in the Soviet Union.

4.11 The PS-84 also known as the Li-2

In the mid-1930s the flagship of Aeroflot was the PS-9 – a twin-engine version of the Tupolev ANT-9, a slow airplane with a fixed undercarriage and an old-fashioned corrugated skin. It did not correspond to the requirements that had changed since the end of the 1920s, not in terms of its flight-performance characteristics or its level of comfort. Apart from that, the majority of these airplanes have been completely worn out. The report by the Main Directorate of the GVF for 1937 states about the PS-9s: ' ... they are in operation at the present time only because we have nothing to replace them with'. The Soviet aircraft production was not able to offer anything to replace this airplane that was in any way a significant improvement. The development of the PS-89 (ZIG-1) and the PS-35 (ANT-35) passenger aircraft were protracted, and their performance characteristics lagged behind those of the rest of the world. A solution was found in

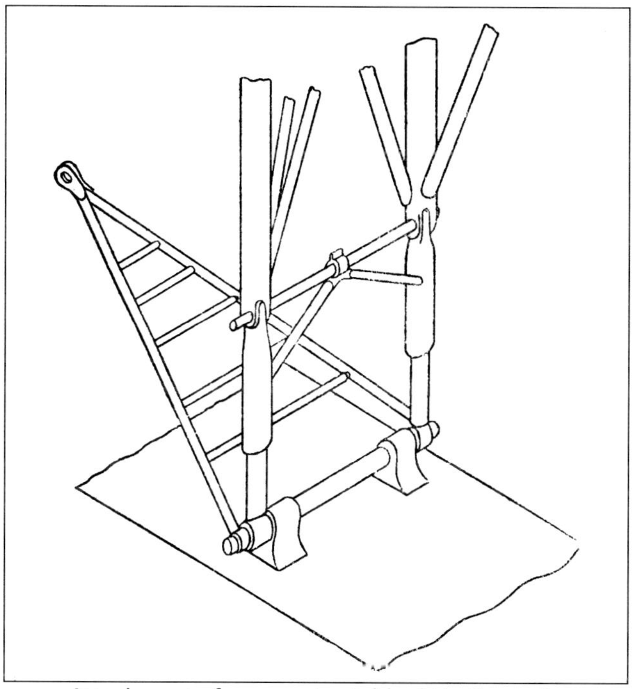

Attachment of a non-retractable ski to the main undercarriage leg on a PS-84. Note the wide rear winter support, which was very different to the summer one.

An early example of the PS-84 with a non-retractable ski undercarriage.

Flight mechanic/radio-operator P.S. Lalaev checks that the cabin equipment in a PS-84 is functioning properly, 1941.

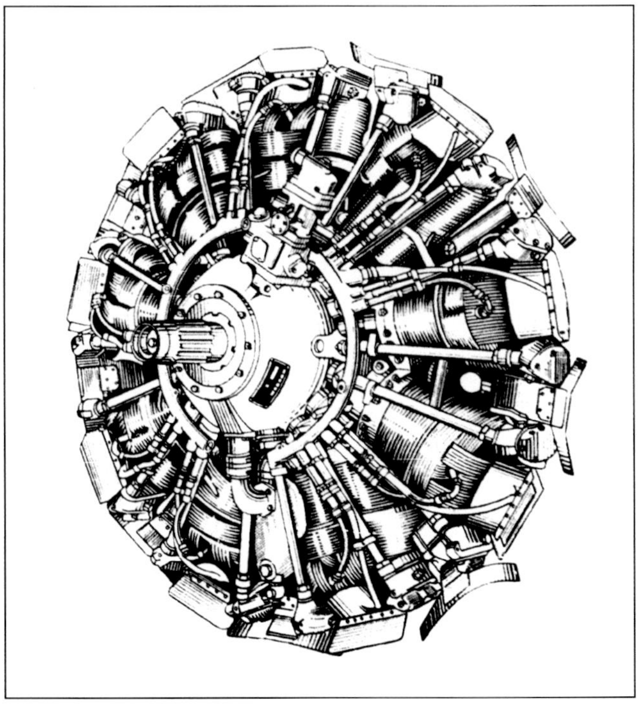

An M-62IR engine (which was later re-designated the ASh-62IR).

Early examples of the PS-84 had main undercarriage that were similar to that on the DC-3.

selecting a successful foreign design, and the choice fell on the American airliner produced by Douglas Aircraft Company.

Initially, the DC-2 option was carefully scrutinised, and by spring 1936, following an exchange of views between the GUAP NKTP, the GU GVF, and the UVVS the decision had all but crystallised around arranging production of this type in the USSR. The GUAP initially wanted avoid buying a licence, limiting the scope to a careful study of an example. The Head of the UVVS Ya.I. Alksnis, on the contrary, suggested acquiring the company's technical assistance to accelerate a resolution of this objective. The opinion of the military carried quite some weight as the Douglas was considered in no small way as a potential military transport aircraft. Apart from that, in April 1936 it was proposed that the Soviet aviation industry would be introducing both civil and military versions of this airplane in parallel (in the documents the word 'bomber' is mentioned). By military version, evidently, they were referring to the DB-1 (the B-18 Bolo), which was standardised with the DC-2. The B-18 was reviewed by a delegation led by A.N. Tupolev at the Douglas factory at the beginning of 1936. With the creation of the indigenous long-range DB-3 bomber designed by S.V. Ilyushin, the interest in the B-18, however, fell away. In 1939 this aircraft came up again (the company proposed this) but it was decisively rejected as being obsolete.

After the appearance of the more advanced DC-3, the focus shifted in favour of this airplane and even more serious plans began to be made. The search began for a suitable factory that could master what was a more complex airplane from a production perspective. In March 1936, in his report to the People's Commissar K.E. Voroshilov, the Head of the VVS Headquarters V.K. Lavrov proposed to arrange production of the American airplane at Factory No.18 in Voronezh, having taken the TB-3 out of production at this site. Subsequently, plans emerged to erect a special factory in Kuybyshev for this purpose.

On 11 April 1936 the STO issued a decree on the acquisition of a licence for the DC-3 production. The order was issued – and it had to be carried out. A commission was sent to America led by N.M. Kharlamov.

606-607. The first example of the PS-84K military transport aircraft during testing.

The negotiations with Douglas Aircraft Company were successful, and on 15 July 1936 an agreement was signed through the Amtorg for a licence to manufacture the DC-3 in the Soviet Union. From September of that year groups of specialists began to be sent to Douglas to accept the technical documentation and to master new technologies. According to the report written by A.A. Senkov, who travelled to the USA with the very first group on 4 September, the carried-out work included: acceptance of the drawings, translation of the inscriptions, technical manuals, US standards, maintenance and flight manuals, and compiling lists of the required materials. The company was to provide a set of engineering drawings, specifications, and photographs of the parts and joints at different stages of manufacture and assembly, and descriptions of the manufacturing processes. The specific version of the DC-3 had not yet been selected at this stage, and some time later the choice fell on the DC-3-196. By 15 January 1937, the Americans were to have completed the transfer of the drawings into the metric system, and to hand over to Amtorg two sets of drawings on tracing paper and 10 sets of blueprints.

The search for a factory for the Douglas finally came to an end, and on 26 September 1936 the STO issued a decree, in accordance with which the production of the DC-3 was assigned to Factory No.84 in Khimki in the Moscow region. On 10 January of the following year a corresponding order was issued by the GUAP, placing the responsibility for this work on the factory director Murashov and chief designer V.M. Myasishchev. At the time this factory was engaged in repair and modification of civil aircraft, as well as assembly of the PS-9 airplanes from the stock made at Factory No.22. In April 1937, the Myasishchev design bureau KB-6, which was formerly a Design Department of the Experimental Aircraft Development Sector of TsAGI.

The final scope of work of the American side was recorded in an Amtorg specification dated 30 November 1937. In accordance with this, all technical documentation on the DC-3-196 version as of 3 June would be handed over,

The first example of the PS-84K with FAB-100 high-explosive bombs on a removable bridge with bomb racks under the wing centerplane. Basing on the shape of the engine cowlings it can be defined that this airplane was assembled from imported subassemblies.

Two 45mm anti-tank guns with their limbers in the cargo compartment of the PS-84K.

A second example of the PS-84K during state testing, May 1940.

together with all the changes introduced into the drawings prior to 1 December. The configuration of this airplane included the use of the Wright SGR-1820-G2 engines, Hamilton Standard propellers, and an autopilot. Apart from that, Douglas company was to supply one complete airplane in a dismantled condition, one airplane in a condition ready for assembly (a set of units and sub-assemblies), two sets of pre-forms (castings, forgings, etc) and bought-out finished items. A separate clause in the agreement envisaged assistance by the company to master the hydraulic forging technique in the USSR.

By the time the documentation had arrived from the USA, V.M. Myasishchev had been arrested as the 'people's enemy' and never returned to his work on the Douglas. Chief Designer of the factory A.A. Senkov (he had been appointed to this position already before the arrest of Myasishchev) and the Chief Engineer B.P. Lisunov led the work on the arrangements of the DC-3 series production at Khimki.

It should be noted that the program of introducing DC-3 into series production in Soviet Union had its own opponents, who were sceptical about this very possibility. For example, a group of NII GVF specialists had prepared a report, which stated: 'The airplane cannot be manufactured from Soviet materials according to the standards of strength for civil aircraft in the Soviet Union, as this will seriously deteriorate all the technical and economic characteristics of the airplane'. The optimists, however, outnumbered them.

This aircraft was to be built in two versions – a civil (passenger) and a military transport. On 16 February 1938, a full-scale mock-up of the 'Soviet Douglas' was presented to the mock-up commission, which had two chairmen – Grebenyov from the UVVS, and Zakharov from the GU GVF. The mock-up was accepted, although a number of changes were requested. The commission noted that the designed flight range of 1,220km was not sufficient for the needs of the GVF, the strength of the airplane did not meet the standards applicable in the USSR, and dimensions of the airplane subassemblies did not fit into the railway envelope. As

The benches for paratroopers were placed on the PS-84K along the airplane's axis.

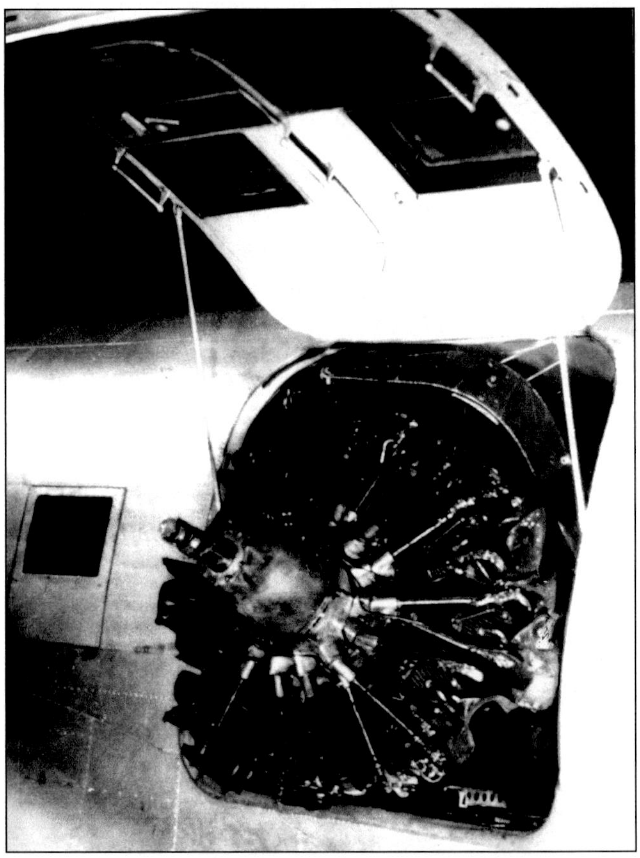

Loading an aircraft engine to the PS-84K. The wide opened cargo hatch is clearly visible.

A 76mm model 1927 regimental gun before loading into the aircraft.

The stretchers for the wounded were placed in three tiers in a medical PS-84I.

PDBB-100 tanks (for fuel or oil) with their parachutes on a bridge under the wing centerplane of the PS-84K.

A PS-84 of Polar Aviation on a non-retractable ski undercarriage, 1941.

the further improvements, it was recommended to fit frontal engine panel with adjustable shutters, to change the location of the radio set to the position of the American original, to fit an AVP-12bis autopilot (a copy of the Sperry one), and to put canvas sleeves on the apertures of the emergency fuel drain in the same manner as on the German Ju 52/3m. The first series production airplane was to have the possibility of using ski undercarriage, and this was to be made retractable starting from the series of 1939.

Following introduction of a range of changes, the mock-up was presented to the commission once again on 11 January 1939, almost a year after the initial demonstration. In accordance with the government decree, the production began with the passenger version, which was closest to the American original. This airplane, which was complex to manufacture, and which envisaged an unfamiliar loft-template production technology, took a long time and was difficult to appropriate. The engineers had adapted the airplane to use indigenous materials, a metric assortment of rolled products, as well as other equipment and instruments built in the Soviet Union.

In 1938–1939 the employees of OKB 1 design bureau at Factory No.84 re-calculated almost all the units and sub-assemblies taking into account the changes in materials and other strength standards. The airframe of the Douglas, however, was barely altered at all, since according to American standards it was considered extraordinarily strong, and only in certain calculated cases did it fall short of the Soviet standards. It is just that when converting inch sizes into the metric, the parameters were rounded up almost everywhere. For example, the attachment bolts in the wing centerplane were selected of 7mm in diameter instead of 6.35mm in the original.

The airplane was fitted with Soviet M-62IR engines with an output of 1,000hp on take-off, and its dimensions and attachment points were similar to the original SGR-1820-G2. Indigenous automatic VISh-21 propellers were also selected. Layout of the crew and passenger cabins was slightly reconfigured, and the wheels were replaced with Soviet ones, of a larger size. Shock absorber struts were redesigned for heavier loads.

Refuelling of a PS-84. This airplane was built in 1941 and is distinguishable by the propeller spinners with clutches to start the engines using a starter vehicle.

Despite the initial expectations, not one airplane was completed in 1938. The plan was changed, the deadline was shifted into the first quarter of 1939, but it was not maintained either. In reality, by the summer one airplane had been completed from the imported subassemblies and fitted with American engines and propellers. Following a brief factory testing, this airplane was handed over to the NII GVF for state testing. The aircraft, which had been listed for some time in the documents simply as the 'Douglas', was given a designation of the PS-84. Testing was conducted from 3 September till 17 December, and the airplane flew 166 flights, amassing 73 hrs 45 mins of flying time.

Loading leaflets onto a PS-84 airplane.

The aircraft was sent to the front straight from testing, as the war with Finland was underway. For the entire winter, the airplane was used to transport injured to hospitals in the rear. The series production plan was amended once again: the new version prescribed to deliver two PS-84s in October, two in November, and then three in December. The customer for all these airplanes was the VVS. In reality, six such aircraft were handed over in a year (including the first one).

All these 'Douglases' contained a significant proportion of imported components. The first four airplanes were assembled almost entirely of the imported items. Even on the later stages some of the PS-84s were fitted with Bendix wheels, Hamilton 3E50 propellers (which were interchangeable with the VISh-21s), Fairchild radio compasses, and imported electrical equipment.

The production process utilised temporary technologies as the manufacturing fixtures were not yet fully ready. The assembly jigs were due to be completed by the beginning of 1940. Not all the lathes brought in from America were put into operation. Some items of the electrical equipment

A cargo hatch, which was introduced on series production PS-84s in August 1941.

A glazed MV-3 turret with a 7.62mm ShKAS machine gun.

A fixed mount in the nose with a ShKAS machine gun.

An MV-3 turret, fitted on top of the fuselage of a PS-84.

A view on the ShKAS machine gun mount in the nose with raised upper fairing. Note the cartridge case ejection tube running below.

A hatch mount on the fuselage side with a ShKAS machine gun.

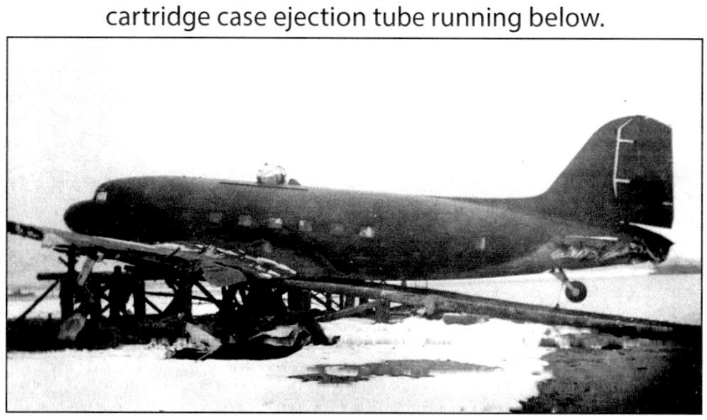

Field repairs of a PS-84 on the bank of the Volga River. On 29 October 1941 female pilot V.F. Stoyanovskaya, flying from Moscow to Saratov at low-level in bad weather, caught the water by the aircraft wing, close to the Island of Kazachiy. The aircraft armament corresponds to early configuration, as just an upper VUS-1 gun mount is fitted.

were not produced at all in the USSR, so they immediately began to be copied from American examples. The M-62IR engines, although being built in series, were produced in small numbers, and their reliability left much to be desired. A batch of indigenously produced wheels that had arrived at the factory was rejected out of hand.

The factory was only just starting series production, while the designers were already thinking about modernising the airplane. In 1939 Senkov put in a proposal to reinforce the airframe and fit two more powerful water-cooled 1,350hp AM-35 engines. The People's Commissariat supported the designer and ordered that two aircraft prototypes be manufactured. After careful consideration, however, it emerged that a great deal of conversion work would have to be undertaken. The undercarriage kinematics and the load-bearing structure of the wing centerplane would need to be changed, and the equipment layout would need to be re-configured because of the significant shift in

A result of forced landing by a PS-84 from an NKAP transport unit, on 17 November 1941. The airplane was flown by pilot V.N. Kuzmichyov who flew from Rybinsk to Ufa, evacuating equipment from an aircraft engine factory. Due to icing the airplane was forced to land on a frozen marsh, into which the airplane partially sank.

Typical appearance of a civil aviation PS-84 in 1941 – no camouflage, and a red star insignia has been painted over the registration number.

The gunner mans the side-mounted ShKAS machine gun.

During the winter counterattack outside Moscow several airborne assaults were landed using PS-84s. In this photograph a unit of paratroopers with skis prepares for boarding a MAGON airplane.

Landing airborne troops from a PS-84.

the aircraft centre of gravity. And this had to be done at a time when arranging production of the original variant was proving difficult! The designers, however, did not relent. In September 1940 I.P. Mosolov proposed a project of the PS-84A fitted with 2,000hp M-71 engines. This airplane differed from the standard PS-84 by the reinforced airframe, wheel fairings, engine cowlings with adjustable flaps, and a larger wing area. The number of seats in the passenger cabin was increased to 26–34, and the speed was to have increased by 120–130km/h. Mosolov's design was supported by the leadership of the GVF, and in December 1940 they proposed adding a corresponding clause to the state plan of the experimental design work. In response, two people's commissars came out against this – K.E. Voroshilov (for defence) and A.I. Shakhurin (for the aviation industry). They were insisting that creation of this new version would slow down the arrangement of series production of the PS-84 itself. In essence, they were proved right, as the M-71 was not refined to a level that would justify series production.

The KB-29 design bureau was also examining the possibility of equipping the 'Douglas' with a pressurised cabin, but this work was ceased at the stage of the first estimates.

The VVS RKKA did not want to have standard passenger airplanes, but specialised versions. The first requirements for these had been developed at the NII VVS back in December 1937. In accordance with these requirements, two versions were to be designed – transport and medical. The first would carry 15 persons plus 450kg of cargo, and the second would carry 17–18 stretcher cases and two accompanying medical staff. The crew in both cases comprised a pilot, navigator, and a gunner. The latter would operate two firing points: an upper

Airborne troops offload a mortar from the airplane.

A PS-84 delivered boxes with butter to sieged Leningrad in the winter of 1941–1942.

A crew of pilot D. Kuznetsov from the MAGON stand next to their PS-84 airplane.

Loading the wounded onto an airplane at Smolniy airfield near Leningrad, the end of 1941.

A pre-flight inspection of an M-62IR engine by mechanic Gordov.

mechanised turret, and a ventral machine-gun mount similar to one used on the SB bomber. In both locations, ShKAS machine guns were installed with an ammunition load of 500 cartridges for each. In April 1938, the requirements for a transport version were detailed and somewhat tightened. The total payload was raised from 1,680kg up to 1,800kg, and there were arranged the external carrying of the PDBB-400 fuel tanks (air droppable, with parachute), transportation of oversize cargoes (such as cannons and engines) inside the fuselage, mechanical assistance for the loading and moving cargoes inside the cabin, and installation of a special cargo door (either opening inward or sliding to the side).

Loading of the engineers with the modification of the passenger version, which had been declared as priority, slowed down the work on the tasks set by the VVS. The first project

Pilot T.A. Taran explains to his friends how he deceived a German fighter.

Loading provisions onto a PS-84. The airplane is wearing the so-called 'springtime' camouflage: the temporary winter white paint on top of the airplane has been washed off by the snow and the rain, but underneath it remains in place.

Preparing a PS-84 from the Karelian-Finnish Air Group of the GVF for a night flight, 1942.

At the site of a fatal crash of a PS-84 that happened on 12 May 1942. During a flight Kuybyshev–Nizhniy Tagil the aircraft crashed into Shaytan mountain and everyone on board the airplane was killed.

A PS-84 of the 36th series with its bomb armament, July 1942.

of the military transport version was presented by Senkov in June 1939, and on 29 July Committee for Defence issued a decree mandating Factory No.84 to make a prototype of this version available for state testing in December of that year. In November, one of the first series production PS-84s was converted into a transport and airborne troop-carrying PS-84K version, and factory testing was undertaken. However, during the ferry flight to the NII VVS on 4 January 1940 the aircraft was involved in an accident. The factory urgently completed another prototype. This time there was no factory testing, as they were conducted alongside the state testing at the NII VVS. Captain Predeyn and navigator Major Marin-Fyodorov flew this aircraft.

The PS-84K differed from the series passenger version by the reinforced floor of the cabin, the wide hatch on the port side with a hatch door that opened upwards, and the availability of a lifting crane to make loading easier. The cabin accommodated 26 airborne troops seating back-to-back on benches positioned along the airplane centerline. The troop commander sat on a separate seat which was equipped with intercom system. When cargoes were being carried, all the seats would be removed. The internal volume of the fuselage enabled to accommodate 10 barrels of fuel, two 45mm anti-tank guns with their limbers, or one 76mm field gun. Oil cans could also be carried, as well as aircraft engines and ammunition.

Carrying cargoes externally was also envisaged – a special bridge for bomb racks, developed in November 1939, could be attached for this purpose under the wing centerplane. A variety of loads could be carried on Der-19 or Der-31 bomb racks – PDMM parachute bags, PDBB fuel tanks with a capacity from 100l up to 400l, and universal containers (carrying 300kg of cargo in each). These loads were dropped with the help of an ESBR-3 electric bomb release mechanism, and there was also an ASBR mechanical bomb release as the reserve. This bridge was detachable, and five workers were able to fit this in just seven minutes.

The total payload for the PS-84K was 2,400kg, which was 400kg more than of a standard PS-84.

State testing of the PS-84K was satisfactory, and it was recommended for service in the VVS RKKA. At that, the revealed shortcomings had to be eliminated – the position of the port side door had to be changed (this door had been built into the cargo hatch door), the floor had to be covered in rubber, the seats for the airborne troops had to be made to fold back, the armament needed to be fitted ('not less than two machine guns'), and seatbelts were to be installed for the paratroopers. During the aircraft taxiing the engines cooled down, so they were in need of the winter frontal panels with shutters, and the spinners had to be fitted to the propeller hubs (the first PS-84s did not have spinners, just like the DC-3).

The bridge with four Der-19 bomb racks is attached under the wing centerplane.

Four FAB-250 high-explosive bombs were a maximum bomb load of a military PS-84.

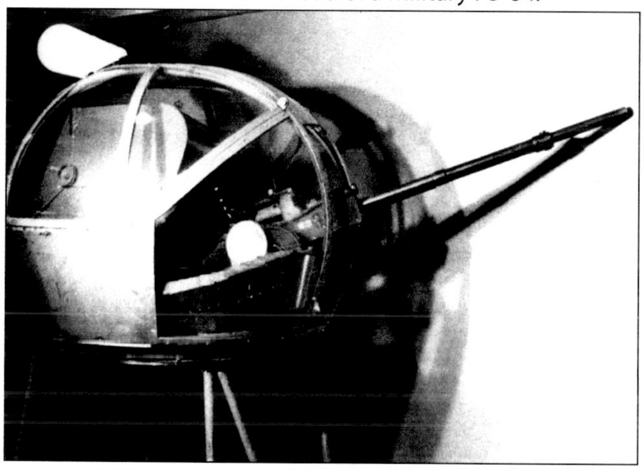

A PS-84 airplane with an upper UTK-1 turret.

An experimental installation of a VISh-21-D-22 propeller with wooden propeller blades, September 1942.

The glazed UTK-1 turret with a 12.7mm UBT machine gun, introduced on the PS-84 in September 1942.

The instrument panel of a PS-84 that was built in July 1942.

On 31 May 1940 this airplane was demonstrated to the People's Commissar for Defence K.E. Voroshilov at Moscow Central airfield, and the Marshal was happy with this aircraft.

During the course of service testing on 17–18 June, an airborne assault involving troopers of the 201st Airborne Troop Brigade was carried out from the PS-84K at Relbitsy airfield just outside Leningrad. The paratroopers jumped out of the airplane through both doors – port and starboard; this took 12–14 seconds. Boarding these paratroopers took approximately one and half a minute. The conclusions to the test report stated: 'The PS-84K airplane in troop carrying version is significantly better than the TB 3 aircraft ... '

According to the available records, the plan was to build the PS-84Ks for the VVS (both in armed and unarmed versions), as well as to convert standard passenger airplanes into military configuration where necessary, having envisaged this possibility in the aircraft design. In July 1940 the Head of the NII VVS A.I. Filin wrote: 'All PS-84 airplanes should be manufactured taking into account all the changes required to convert them into military variants ... '

The second military version of the Soviet 'Douglas' was the medical PS-84I. When designing this aircraft, Factory

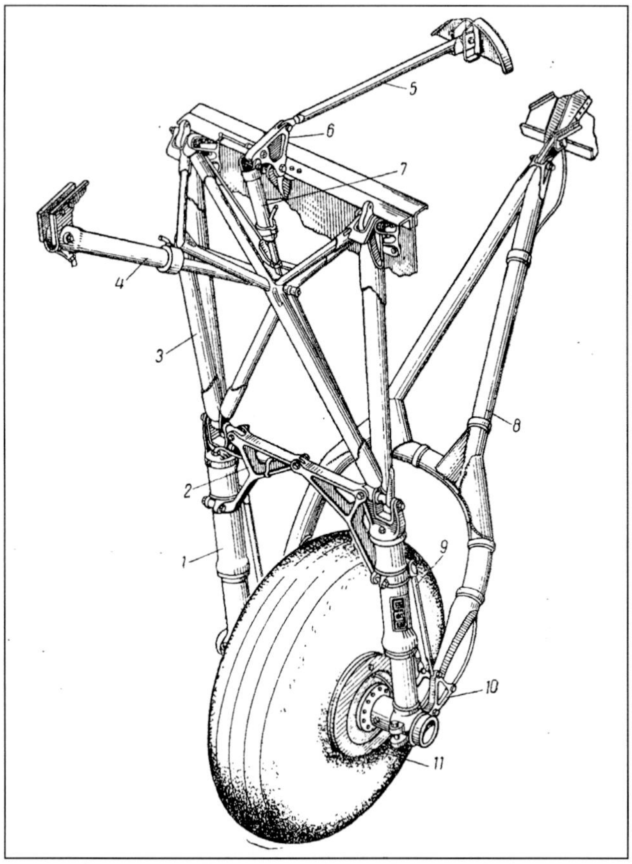

The main undercarriage leg with a doubled rear strut, introduced onto the PS-84 in summer 1942.

An additional summer nine-inch oil radiator, which was installed on the outside of the engine nacelle.

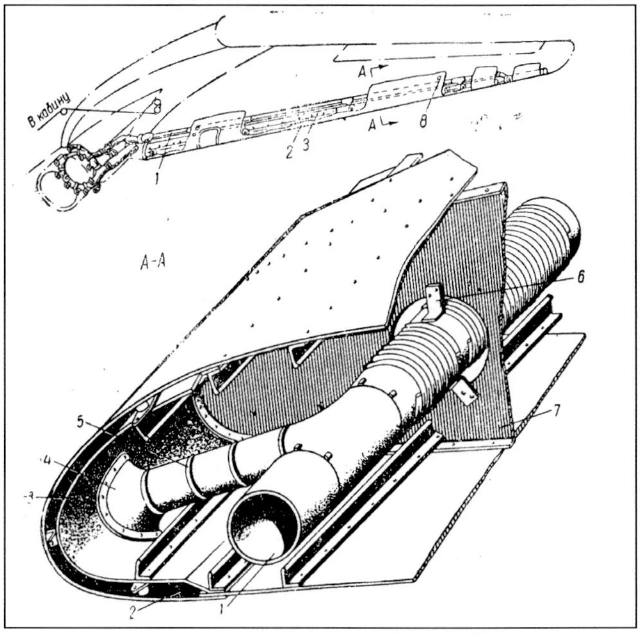

Thermal anti-icing of the wing, introduced on the Li-2s of the 62nd series.

No.84 used the experience of modifying three DC-3s, which were utilised to carry wounded in Mongolia in August–September 1939. The bulkhead between the passenger cabin and the baggage compartment was removed, leaving a large space where stretchers were placed in three tiers. In total, the airplane could accommodate 18 stretcher cases, three wounded sitting in the seats and a single medic.

In reality, neither the PS-84K nor the PS-84I airplanes were put into series production prior to the outbreak of war with Germany, but many design solutions of these versions were introduced subsequently on airplanes built in wartime.

The aforementioned Mosolov's project of the PS-84A also had a military transport version. It was designed to carry between 40–45 airborne troops or three tonnes of cargo on a distance of 400–500km. Medical and staff versions were also envisaged.

Projects also emerged to transform the PS-84 into a bomber – the first such variant was proposed by designers at Factory No.84 (approved by Deputy Chief Designer Khavkin

An Li-2 (as it is known from now on) of the 37th series, Tashkent, November 1942.

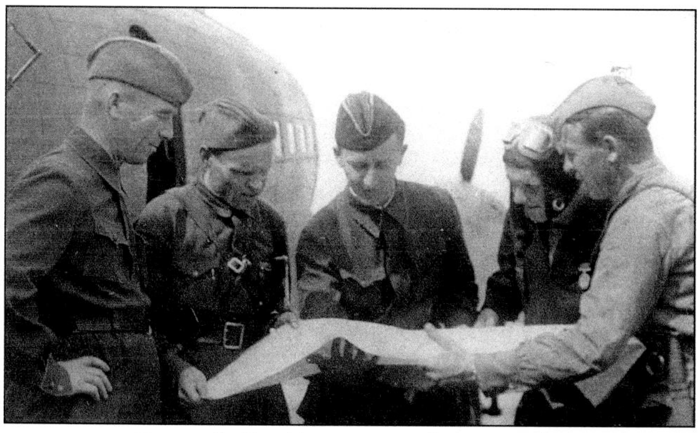

Crew of pilot Yeromasov discusses the route for their combat sortie.

Boarding a group of paratroopers onto an Li-2.

Mechanic Shkurov inspects the starboard M-62IR engine.

Loading fuel for delivery to the Western Front.

Pilot Skrylnikov, who evacuated the Black Sea Fleet Military Council from Sevastopol prior to the fall of the city.

Airfield of Factory No.84 in Tashkent, November 1942.

in September 1938) before any of the Soviet 'Douglas' had actually been produced. The project included the use of the wing, tail fin, and undercarriage from a passenger airplane, combined with a new fuselage. The power plant should also be different – more powerful M-88 engines which had better altitude characteristics. The bomber defensive armament comprised two 20mm cannons in the nose and rear gun mounts and a single hatch-mounted ShKAS machine gun firing below and to the rear. The standard bomb load comprised 2,000kg, and the maximum was 4,000kg. The bombs were accommodated internally, in bomb cassettes with 22 locks, and externally on six bomb racks under the wing centerplane. Inside the bomb bay, bombs of up to 100kg could be accommodated, and externally bombs of up to 1,000kg calibre could be carried (on two central bomb racks). The airplane had a crew of four: a navigator, a pilot, a gunner/radio-operator, and a gunner. The maximum calculated air speed without external bomb load was 445km/h, and the service ceiling was 9,900m.

In 1939 the NII VVS developed tactical-technical requirements for a night bomber based on the 'Douglas'. There were two proposals based on these requirements. The first was limited to minimal modifications: the PS-84K was to carry FAB-100 bombs on external racks on a cargo bridge. The second variant was a new project of a bomber fitted with M-63 engines. The airplane was to have three machine-gun mounts and to carry 1,200kg of bombs internally. In view of

The GAM-10 silencer during factory testing. Note the additional ventilation apertures over the engine cylinder heads.

A collision of two Li-2s at an airfield in Tashkent, the end of autumn 1942.

Offloading Li-2 at the sieged Leningrad.

An Li-2LL flying laboratory aircraft in flight.

Mechanic Teplitskiy prepares an airplane for a combat sortie.

estimated poor flight-performance characteristics, however, it was not considered viable to build this version.

In April 1939, designers Makarov, Malyshev, Pesin and Fedotov at the factory in Khimki prepared a project of 'airplane Ch' – 'a heavy ultra-high-altitude bomber'. This was the PS-84 with a new fuselage of smaller diameter and with the bombs carried internally. The flight-performance characteristics with a service ceiling of up to 13,000m were ensured by the use of a pressurised cabin and a centralised system of the main engines boosting provided by compressors driven by two 270hp MV-6 engines. The Head of the VVS A.D. Loktionov, however, considered the 'airplane Ch' unrealistic.

Mosolov designed a bomber project based on the PS-84A fitted with M-71 engines, which was not a modification of the passenger airplane, but used a large number of units from the original aircraft. Later, a preliminary project of PS-84M version was prepared which had an even greater estimated flight range provided by the use of the 1,500hp M-30 diesel engines, but all this remained on paper.

The aviation industry at that time was slowly increasing production of the standard PS-84s as the country required a great number of them. In October 1939 the VVS set their requirement at 510 airplanes, and by January 1943 they wanted to increase their fleet of 'Douglases' to 815 aircraft. Aeroflot appetite was growing too, as they were counting on having up to 100 PS-84s by the same date.

The Factory No.84 of course could not keep pace with this demand, and to increase PS-84 production a range of immediate measures were undertaken. The plan envisaged modernisation of the factory in Khimki, taking its production

An Li-2 of the 119th series, December 1943.

A folding hatch in the glazed emergency exit door on an Li-2 of the 119th series.

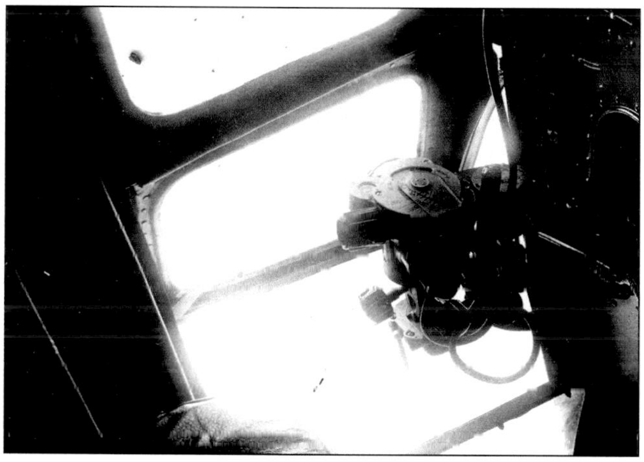

An NKPB-7 night bombsight in the deployed position, the hatch of the emergency exit door is open.

The port side of the pilots' instrument panel in an Li-2 of the 119th series.

The starboard side of the pilot's instrument panel.

rate up to 500 airplanes per year, and construction of a new factory in Tashkent, which was to build PS-84s and DB-3Fs in parallel. On 11 January 1940, the Committee for Defence issued a decree on the arrangement of series production of the PS-84 at Factory No.124 in Kazan (this factory was given a plan for 100 airplanes), but in reality at this enterprise, in view of the resumption of production of TB-7 (Pe-8) heavy bombers, only 10 airplanes were built. Factory No.84 was immediately allocated new lathes, assigned additional specialists, as well as more financial resources were given, and from the second quarter of 1940 onwards output was significantly increased.

The airplanes which were built at the end of 1940 and in the beginning of 1941 differed externally by spinners with clutches for the auto-starter mechanism, and the engine frontal winter panels. Internally, the airplanes had almost fully received the indigenously manufactured instruments and equipment, including the Soviet VISh-21 propellers, RPK-2 radio compasses, and wheels of larger diameter (the latter began to be fitted starting from airplane serial number 316). The empty weight of the PS-84 following the introduction of a series of changes increased from 7,060kg up to 7,200kg.

Over the course of 1940, 64 airplanes were manufactured (and 51 were accepted out of this number), all of which were passenger versions. The standard crew of the PS-84 comprised five persons: two pilots, a radio-operator, flight mechanic, and a stewardess (at that time the latter was known as a 'buffet girl'). Twenty-one passengers could be accommodated in the passenger cabin, but with a full fuel load only 13 passengers were taken on board.

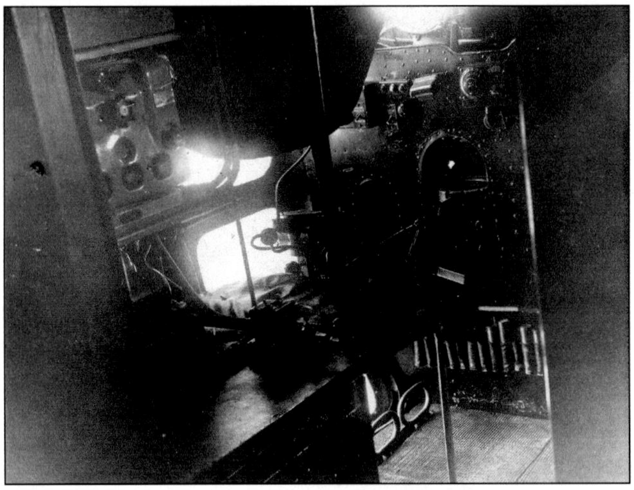

The navigator's workstation.

The navigator's instrument panel.

The radio-operator's workstation.

The commander of the aircraft Kulikov explains the combat mission to the crew.

The airplanes produced in 1940 suffered from a number of defects. For example, it emerged that the brakes were jamming in the activated position. The reason for this turned out to be a simplification of the valve design by Soviet manufacturers in comparison with the American original. Leaks in the hydraulic system and in the shock absorbers were a constant headache, as were radio equipment failures, and defects in the carburettors. The engines continued to be the 'Achilles heel' of the PS-84. The crews of the Soviet version were envious of those who flew the American DC-3s with their Wright engines.

The defects and the further modifications that accompanied them led to a significant increase in production costs. Instead of the planned 1,498,000 roubles, the early series PS-84s cost 3,950,000 roubles each, which represents a 264 percent increase on the original figure.

By 1 January 1940 Aeroflot had put the first PS-84 into service on the Moscow–Irkutsk route, and a further three airplanes had been prepared for operations on this route but the war with Finland got in the way. On 15 June 1940 the number of PS-84s in the GVF had exceeded the quantity of their DC-3s (12 airplanes against 11). Further to the route to Irkutsk, the Soviet 'Douglases' entered the routes to Tbilisi and Ashkhabad. In total in 1940 nineteen PS-84s entered service with Soviet civil aviation. One of them was lost on 7 August – the aircraft registration number Л3409 flew into the ground in bad weather close to Novosibirsk. The crew of four led by pilot M.I. Tyutyaev and 14 passengers were killed, and a further three passengers were injured. Along with the airplane, government bonds worth 600,000 roubles that were being sent with the mail were also destroyed in the fire. Another PS-84 flown by pilot N.V. Kazhentsev on a flight from Moscow to Tbilisi crashed into a mountain close to the village of Voronilovskaya on 26 November also in poor weather conditions. The entire crew were killed along with four passengers.

Operations of the PS-84s were limited by the short service lives of the M-62IR engines. They had to be changed frequently, and their spare parts were of short supply. As a result, the airplanes stood idle.

Gradually, however, 'Douglas' operations in the GVF were expanded, and by 1 December 1940 there were 23

A group of paratroopers boarding an Li-2.

Starting the engines of an Li-2 using a starter vehicle.

An Li-2VP bomber during testing, December 1944.

The open bomb bays of an Li-2VP.

The forward Der-21 bomb racks.

The rear Der-21 bomb racks.

airplanes of this type in seven territorial directorates. For example, the Northern Directorate in Leningrad received its first PS-84 on 19 November, which was soon joined by another example. The airplanes were used on the Moscow–Leningrad route that opened on 20 January 1941. Seven aircraft operated on the Moscow–Irkutsk route which was so called the 'trunk route'. By summer 1941 the PS-84s were already operating on 12 Aeroflot routes. In six months, they had amassed 18,000 hrs flying time (over the entire course of 1940 – 9,500 hrs).

The production rate at the factory in Khimki was growing gradually; they built 40 PS-84s in the first quarter of 1941, while in April Factory No.84 handed over its 100th airplane of this type. By the outbreak of war with Germany, Aeroflot had 72 PS-84s in service. A further 49 airplanes belonged to the VVS, five – to naval aviation, and several aircraft served with the People's Commissariat of Internal Affairs.

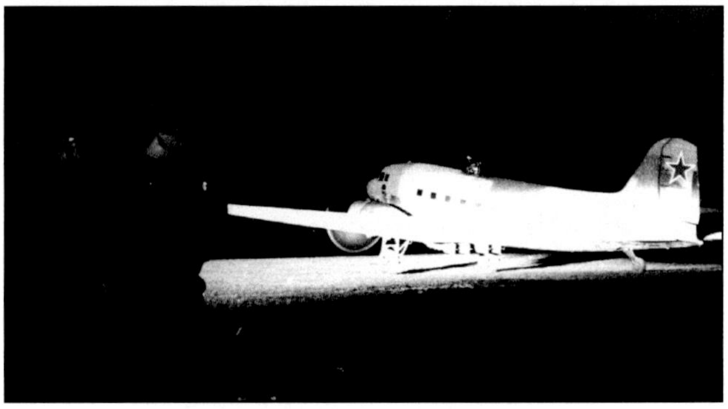

A night bombing sortie, the 18th Air Army, 30 December 1944.

Offloading ammunition from an Li-2 at a front-line airfield.

An accident with an Li-2 on landing in Molotov, December 1944. Pilot V.A. Simakov ran off the end of the runway in the fog and skidded into a gulley. This airplane belonged to the NKAP and operated exclusively in the rear; therefore, it did not have any armament.

Training paratroopers at an airfield in the rear.

An Li-2T transport airplane during state testing, September 1945.

Immediately after Germany's attack on the Soviet Union, most of the PS-84s were brought into separate air groups and air units of the GVF, which had been supporting operations on the front line and of the navy fleets. On 25 June there were 68 PS-84s and DC-3s in their service, including 51 in the MAGON, while by 29 July already 96 PS-84s operated in five air groups and three air units. These aircraft participated in a number of important operations in the initial stage of the war, delivering cargoes and reinforcements to the front line and taking away wounded and evacuees. The first flight of four airplanes serving in the MAGON was undertaken on 23 June 1941, delivering 7,800kg of ammunition to Kishinev. They also had to fly behind enemy lines, paradropping reconnaissance and sabotage groups, cargoes for encircled formations, and leaflets.

In October 1941 MAGON airplanes participated in a hurried re-deployment of the 5th Airborne Corps to the Oryol area – the PS-84s transported 5,440 combatants and 12.5 tonnes of cargo. At the beginning of October 'Douglases' flew to the island of Dagö in the Baltic Sea, transporting fuel and ammunition to the island and evacuating the wounded, and flying only by night. In total, some 11,200kg of ammunition and 1,600kg of fuel were transported to Dagö, and 160 people were evacuated over 15 days. Operations of this nature were undertaken on different sectors of the front by VVS and naval aviation formations.

In conditions of German air superiority, these unarmed airplanes sustained heavy losses. For example, on 7 July 1941 in the area around Rogachyov, German fighters attacked and burnt an airplane that was transporting a KS self-igniting mixture, which was used against tanks. Two days later,

Disembarking passengers at an airfield in Riga, 15 May 1945. The airplane still carries its two-tone wartime camouflage.

by Soviet fighters and anti-aircraft defence. Thus, on 8 July 1941, in the area around Murmansk, the anti-aircraft artillery shot down two PS-84s.

The pilots sometimes demonstrated real heroism, saving their aircraft. For instance, a bottle containing KS liquid ruptured inside the aircraft flown by pilot Frolovskiy, and a fire broke out in the cabin. The crew threw the burning boxes out of the airplane and put out the fire.

During the retreat, damaged airplanes had to be blown up or set on fire. GVF air units alone had lost 16 PS-84s by 1 August 1941, and six of those were shot down or destroyed on the ground by the Germans, three by retreating troops, and seven had to be written off after accidents.

whilst returning from Velikiye Luki, a PS-84 piloted by Andreev was intercepted. The pilot managed to land safely the burning aircraft, and the crew was rescued. On 13 July, directly over the Velikiye Luki airfield, German fighters strafed an airplane that was loaded with ammunition, which exploded in mid air. Losses from direct action by the enemy were added to those from accidents and from mistakes made

The unarmed airplanes initially flew in the day, even across the front line. The crews were evading fighter attacks by flying at low level, dropping to 50–75m altitude. The level of the pilots' qualification allowed for such manoeuvring, since at the beginning of the war the best aircrews were sent to the front line. This tactic, however, led to an increase in losses from

Li-2T airplanes following a landing of paratroopers at a captured Japanese airfield in Mukden, August 1945.

Assembly of the first Li-2T airplanes at Factory No.126 in Komsomolsk-on-Amur, 1946.

An Li-2, which was landing in fog at an airfield in Saratov, bumped into two parked Yak-3 fighters, November 1945.

A result of an Li-2 forced landing in Samarkand, April 1946.

ground fire. The vulnerability of the airplanes also increased because of the habit among civil pilots of using motorways and railway lines as navigation aids, since the German columns had sufficient air defence means in their strength. A particularly high number of PS-84s were lost over the Varshavskoye shosse. Subsequently, routes began to be selected that passed over sparsely populated areas, the front line was crossed at an altitude of 2,000–2,500m, and the pilots began to use cloud and fog banks for cover. Gradually, the pilots gained experience in manoeuvring and started to make use of sharp turns and dives for escaping form the attacks.

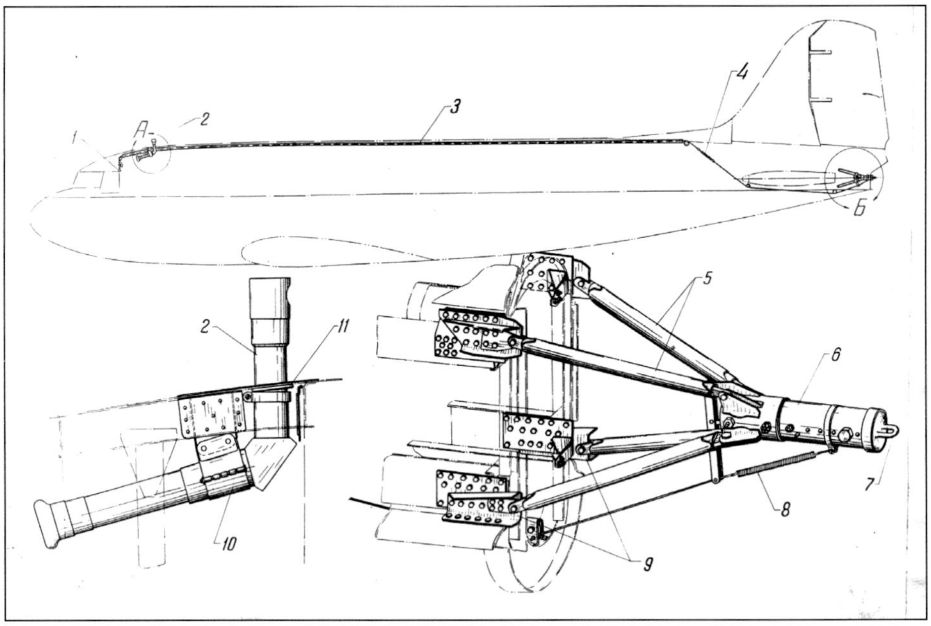

The periscope (on the left) and a glider towing device (right), introduced in the airplanes of the 277th series.

A line-up of paratroopers standing next to Li-2 airplanes.

At the end of July, engineer M.M. Kulik of the aviation repair base at Vnukovo airport where the MAGON was based designed the VUS-1 gun mount for the PS-84 airplane. The mount was based on the series production MV-3 turret with a ShKAS machine gun, and was positioned on top of the fuselage. At the same time, installation of DA machine guns on swivelling mounts in the baggage compartment was envisaged. They fired through hatches in the sides of the airplane. A single aircraft was modified at Vnukovo and underwent testing, being flown by pilot M.A. Nikiforov. In the first flight, buffeting set in because the enormous turret disturbed the airflow around the fuselage. Therefore, the gun mount had to be re-designed. The refined version was accepted as standard on 17 September.

An armament workshop headed by V.N. Chitaev was established at Vnukovo base, which was used not only for the aircraft belonging to the GVF but also to the VVS. Along with the armament, the PS-84s were also receiving the armoured seat backs and seat pans for parachutes. This work has been started already before approval of the modification standard. Over the course of August 30 airplanes were armed this way. A short time later the set of armament on the 'Douglas' was augmented by a fixed ShKAS machine gun in the nose part of the fuselage.

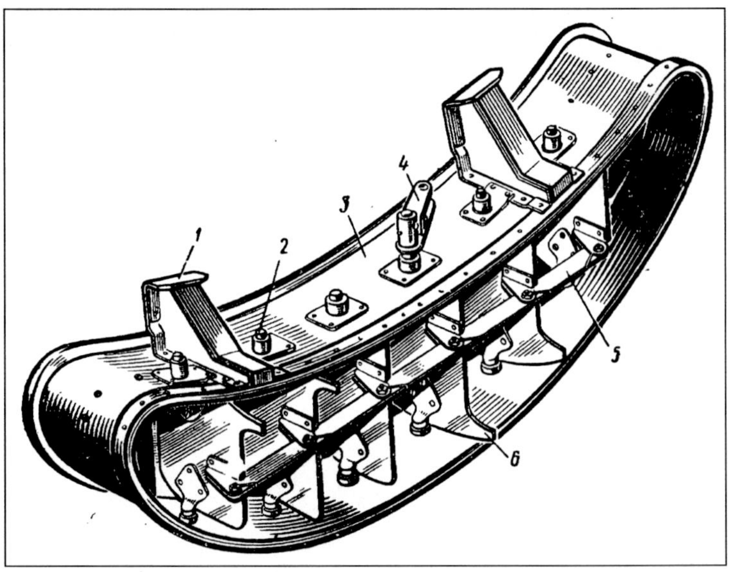

A new Type 812 oil radiator, introduced in the aircraft of the 300th series in 1948. Its installation led to the characteristic 'lip' view under the engine.

Air landing of paratroopers from Li-2T airplanes during exercises.

The installation of the armament changed the tactics – in day flights, in case of enemy fighters' attack, the pilots would put the aircraft into a steep dive, directing towards a nearby forest or into the folds of the landscape. In this way only the airplane's upper hemisphere needed to be defended. Another variant was to go into a spiral or a turn, making the work of the gunner easier. For instance, an airplane flown by pilot Ilyin was attacked by Ju 88 close to Liski. The pilot performed a turn, exposing the enemy to the machine gun of gunner Yatsuk, who set the enemy bomber on fire and shot it down with a long burst from 200m. The PS-84 also came back with a number of bullet holes and some of the crew were injured.

The armed PS-84s arrived on the front line already in September 1941. On 6 September four German fighters were chasing aircraft flown by pilot Pantelli over Lake Ladoga. The Germans brazenly approached the airplane, coming right up to it. The upper gunner Novitskiy shot down a single Bf 109 and it crashed into the forest. A second fighter tried to get closer in still but was driven away by flight mechanic Dumnov, who was firing from the side-mounted machine gun, and a further two Messerschmitts turned away after sustaining damage.

Several other incidents are known about where the defensive armament was used successfully. Gunner Tolokonov shot down a single Bf 109 just outside Kharkov, and gunner Shanga – in the area around Volkhov. Pilot Bibikov landed at the position of an encircled unit whilst under fire from mortars, and even from small arms fire. He was assisted by aircraft flown by pilot Sukhorkin, who descended and neutralised enemy fire. With the air assistance of the second airplane, Bibikov took off successfully, taking the wounded away from the battlefield.

The drawings prepared by Kulik were handed over to Factory No.84 and soon the machine guns began to be fitted right at the workshops. According to Kulik's design, the base of the turret was a tubular truss, while the factory variant stood on a riveted panel, which provided for greater arcs of fire downwards. These modification works, however, did not last long. The Germans were approaching Moscow, and the enterprises from the capital and the Moscow region began to be evacuated to the east. Evacuation of Factory

An Li-2 serving in Polar Aviation. The airplane is fitted with new retractable ski undercarriage.

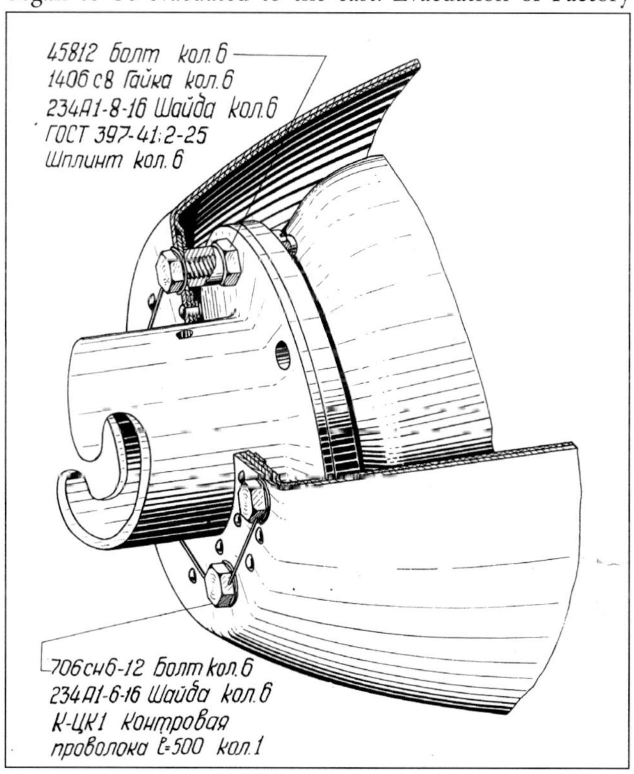

A new propeller spinner, introduced on the aircraft of the 301st series.

Passengers boarding an Li-2P airplane.

No.84 began on 15 October. That month the factory in Khimki managed to complete only 11 PS-84s. The production equipment was transported by trains to Central Asia, and the design factory was relocated to the site of the uncompleted aircraft Factory No.34 in Tashkent (where, incidentally, PS-84s were to be built before the war).

At the beginning of October, the PS-84s began to see action in the 'air bridge' into the besieged Leningrad. On average, in one day the airplanes carried approximately 150 tonnes of provisions, and occasionally up to 200 tonnes. Usually, the crew would fly two sorties a day: on the first flight they would take off before dawn, and the second would land in twilight. On the return flights, the airplanes transported women and children, as well as highly valued specialists, and also armament and mortars that continued to be manufactured by Leningrad factories. In order to save

An Li-2 serving in aviation of the Ministry of Internal Affairs (MVD, hence the inscription on the nose), Syktyvkar, the beginning of the 1950s

The participants of a long-range propaganda flight in honour of the 30th anniversary of the All-Union Leninist Young Communist League (VLKSM, or Komsomol), standing next to the Li-2P on which they made this flight, Riga, October 1948. Note special inscriptions on the fuselage – 'Inter-republican flight of the Central Committee of the Komsomol and the Voluntary Society of Assistance to the Air Force (DOSAV)', and '30 years of the VLKSM'.

Two Li-2s from one of the air units of the Ministry of the Aviation Industry at an airfield in Saratov, June 1950.

A prototype of the 'flying classroom' UchShLi-2 during testing, April 1947.

The layout of desks for students in the UchShLi-2 cabin.

The leading series production UchShLi-2, February 1949.

The workstation under a transparent blister for astronavigation.

Antennae under the fuselage of a series production UchShLi-2.

as many people as possible, the airplanes flew mercilessly overloaded – the PS-84 would sometimes carry 35–38 persons which was almost double of the standard capacity. The flights were carried out even when German aircraft had been grounded by bad weather. The MAGON alone rescued more than 29,000 people from the besieged city.

The airplanes were flown at low level, in groups of up to 10 aircraft formed into a wedge shape, flying in a close formation. Sometimes such group would be accompanied by fighters, and sometimes not, while German fighters were operating from ambush landing grounds near Lake Ladoga. The GU GVF reported to the Kremlin: 'The heavy losses among PS-84 airplanes are to a large extent attributable to insufficient fighter cover on flights in the frontline area. Thus, in the first half of October there were just 10 fighters available to escort PS-84 aircraft that made 30–50 flights into Leningrad'. The PS-84 flown by pilot Taran came under fire from anti-aircraft artillery close to Mga; the nose of the airplane was destroyed and both pilots were seriously injured. Taran flew for 18 minutes with a broken leg and still managed to take the airplane to Leningrad. By 1 October 1941 overall losses of the GVF stood at 36 PS-84s, and by the end of the year this figure raised to 69 (with 40 of those were destroyed by the enemy action). Large-scale flights to Leningrad continued until the end of January 1942, when the columns of trucks broke through into the city across the ice of Lake Ladoga.

In November 1941, in the Smolensk region partisans captured a new German six-barrel rocket mortar. Stalin had personally ordered this to be delivered to Moscow. Several pilots had attempted to fulfil this order but had been unable to do so. The weight of the mortar caused the wheels of the PS-84 sinking into the deep snow. Finally, pilot Kalina found a nearby earth road and landed on it. The mortar was dragged up to the airplane, loaded into it, and Kalina managed to take off from this road.

As the delivery of new aircraft by the aviation industry had come to a stop, by the end of 1941 almost all the PS-84s from civil aviation were sent to the special air groups and

The layout of a staff version of the Li-2.

air units to offset the losses. In January–February 1942, during counteroffensive near Moscow the PS-84s delivered a number of large groups of airborne troops behind enemy lines, specifically, close to Vyazma. Each airplane carried 25–27 combatants, and the air drops were done during daytime with a fighter escort. The airplanes flew from forward airfields one by one at intervals of 10–15 mins. They would circle two or three times over the target to drop the paratroopers, who jumped from altitudes of 200–400m. Enemy fighters would loiter over the drop zones, and it would be rare for a transport airplane to return without bullet holes.

The flights were also carried out at night, the crews made up to four sorties per night.The intensity was defined, for the most part, by the time it took to refuel and load the airplanes. After the landing sites were captured by the airborne troops, the aircraft delivered assault forces along with artillery. The paratroopers succeeded in partially halting traffic on the railways and roads in the enemy rear, disrupting the deliveries of supplies and reinforcements, and capturing important strongholds.

Then, aviation supplied the units of the 4th Airborne Corps headed by General A.F. Kazankin, and the 1st Guards Cavalry Corps under Lieutenant General P.A. Belov behind the enemy lines. The airplanes flew by night, making from two to four sorties, and the crews were spending from eight to ten hours in the air each night. The PDMM parachute bags and PDBB-100 parachute fuel tanks were dropped manually from the open doors. The cargoes were dropped in special packages without parachutes from an altitude of 70–80m.

From 21 January to 24 February 1942 alone, the GVF air groups lost 25 PS-84s, and of those figure 16 aircraft plus seven damaged were lost over the week of 29 January to 4 February in the area around Kaluga.

On 20 January the Head of the GU GVF V.S. Molokov reported to I.V. Stalin: 'A particularly difficult situation has developed in the air groups equipped with PS-84 airplanes that are flying to the front and to the enemy-occupied territory. The fleet of these air groups has experienced losses from enemy fire in amount of 50 percent of their total number of airplanes. For instance, the Moscow air group lost 64 airplanes. The only way that the losses of the PS-84s can be compensated is by restoring and repairing damaged airplanes, as the deliveries of any new ones, following the evacuation of Factory No.84, has ceased'.

On 7 January 1942, however, in Tashkent, the first 'Douglas' was manufactured from subassemblies that had been delivered from Khimki. In total, six airplanes were handed over in January. In view of the evacuation of a whole range of subcontracting factories there were shortages of many components – wheels, propellers, RSB-bis radio sets, autopilots, gun sights, and on-board machine-gun mounts were in short supply. As a result, heating system was not fitted to all airplanes, and radio compasses were installed to every second example.

Production was gradually increasing at the new location, and 25 airplanes were built in April, in May this figure reached 30, and by August it had risen to 58. Subsequently, the factory consistently maintained a production rate of 40–60 airplanes a month.

A.P. Golubkov was in charge of the PS-84 modernisation in Tashkent. The passenger cabin interior design was significantly simplified. For instance, the seats were not usually fitted. While the pre-war passenger airplanes were not painted, retaining the natural colour of the duralumin, now the airplanes were painted as per the VVS standard – green on the top surfaces and light blue on the underside. In service, this scheme was often augmented by patches of black or brown paint, without any kind of a standard template. Airplanes of the earlier series were also camouflaged. The GVF aircraft began to carry the red star insignias which were sometimes applied straight over the civil registration numbers.

The airplanes built in the war years were equipped with defensive armament. Initially, this corresponded to Kulik's design and consisted of an upper MV-3 turret, movable side mounts with DA machine guns and a fixed ShKAS machine gun in the nose. The conclusion was reached fairly quickly, however, that the firepower of this arrangement was insufficient for beating off attacks by German fighters. Back in December 1941 a proposal appeared to replace the ShKAS machine gun in the upper turret with a large-calibre

A standard example of the UchShLi-2 during testing, March 1950.

This Li-2 during testing at the NII GVF in March 1952. The aircraft is fitted with anti-dust filters designed at OKB-30 for operations in Central Asia.

An OKB-30 filter on the port engine of an Li-2.

UBT (12.7mm), and replace the DA in the side mounts with a ShKAS machine gun that was capable of a higher rate of fire. By the beginning of April 1942, the GVF workshops experimentally fitted a UTK-1 turret with a UBT machine gun on two airplanes. The UTK-1 represented a re-design of the MV-3 turret for more powerful armament. The results of testing turned out to be acceptable, so a similar modification was carried out at Factory No.84. An aircraft with new set of armament built in Tashkent successfully completed testing at the NII VVS and was approved. From 15 September all the PS-84s were fitted with UTK-1 turrets, and from October the conversion of the earlier-built airplanes began.

Initially, the airplanes were fitted with two DA machine guns installed in cargo hatches on retractable brackets, with the ammunition supplied from disks. These mounts made it possible to fire not only to the side direction but also to the rear. An attempt was made to replace these with ShKAS machine guns in hatches in the baggage compartment. The firepower was enhanced, and the cartridge feed from a belt increased the practical rate of fire but the arc of fire decreased.

The weight of the armament along with the ammunition was 134kg, but given an equal flight weight, the armament caused 14–17km/h of the maximum speed decrease at various altitudes (the maximum speed fell to 281km/h). Correspondingly, the range also fell (down to 2,350km), the rate of climb deteriorated (a climb to an altitude of 5,000m took 10 minutes longer), and the service ceiling was reduced by half a kilometre.

The side-mounted ShKAS machine guns were introduced on series airplanes much later, in March 1943. In the air force units, the armament was occasionally augmented by installation of machine guns in the windows of the passenger cabin. One instance is known when a 20mm ShVAK cannon was fitted in one of the windows on the starboard side. In one of the VVS units, an upper turret was fitted with this cannon and ammunition load of 200 cartridges, so the weight turned out to be 40–60kg more than that of a UTK-1.

Complaints were received from the air force units on the complexity and inconvenience of servicing the forward fixed machine gun. At the MAGON, an experimental movable machine-gun mount was arranged in the cockpit canopy; the navigator would fire this machine gun. Factory No.454 was developing a new on-board 'Blister' machine-gun mount as well as a hatch mount for firing below and aft, but no information was found about realisation of this project.

From the spring of 1942, bomb armament also began to be fitted to the PS-84s as well, and even before this there were attempts to fit bomb racks in the units themselves. For example, two airplanes of the Karelian-Finnish Air Group of the GVF were converted into bombers. On 8 March 1942, a crew of I. Churikov flew one of these aircraft on a bombing raid on the port of Oulu in Finland. This time the question arose on a mass conversion of the majority of the remaining PS-84s. As the airplane was very slow and clumsy, its use in the daylight was inexpedient, so it was planned to operate it by night. A project of transforming the transport airplane into a bomber was developed at OKB-43 under the leadership of A.I. Shulgin. The bombs were only carried externally, under the wing centerplane. The maximum load was 1,000kg, and only the bombs of 250kg and 500kg calibre were to be carried, while the smaller munitions were to be positioned inside the RRAB-3 rotating-cluster bombs (single-use bomb cassettes). The airplane could also carry two VAP-500 chemical spray devices. An electric bomb release mechanism and an emergency mechanical bomb release were fitted, as well as the NKPB-3 (night) bombsight which was mounted externally next to the starboard window of the pilot's cabin. For bomb aiming, the navigator, sitting in the co-pilot's seat, would have to put his head out the side. This version is known in some documents as the PS-84NB.

On 23 April 1942, the People's Commissar of the Aviation Industry A.I. Shakhurin wrote I.V. Stalin that the bomb armament had already been fitted to the PS-84 and had been tested in one of the ADD regiments. Installation of this armament on series production airplanes was planned to start from 25 May. Shakhurin requested the VVS to allocate 10 airplanes for this conversion, and supply for this purpose the same number of the NKPB-3 bombsights from military stores.

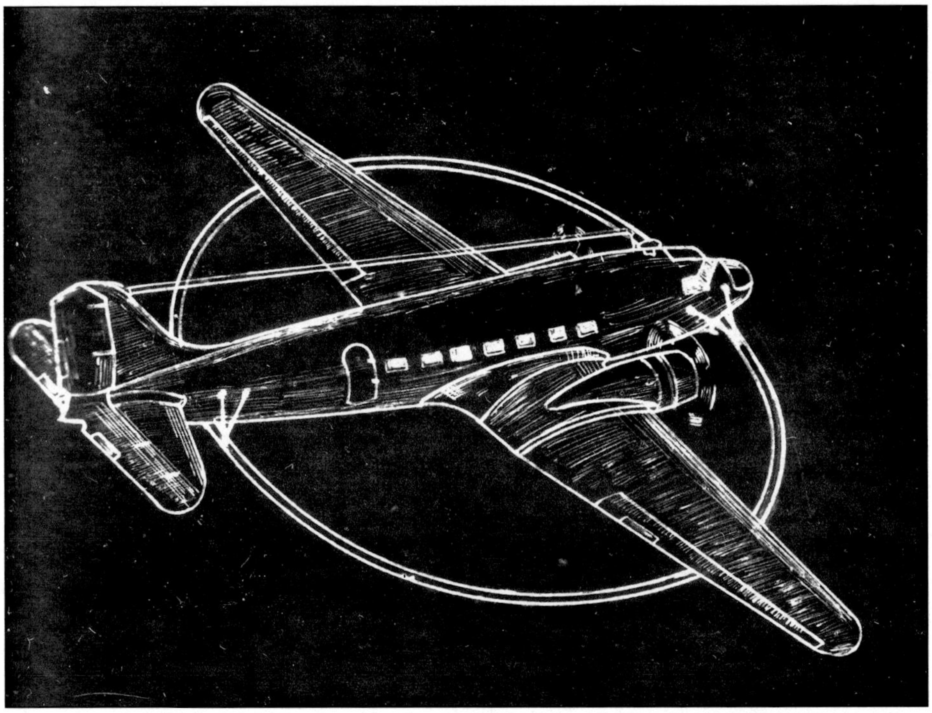

A PS-84T minesweeper of magnetic mines, the project of 1943.

OKB-43 handed over the engineering drawings simultaneously to Factory No.84 that was to fit the bomb armament on new airplanes, and to Factory No.89 that had to convert the earlier-built aircraft. At that, both Air Force and GVF airplanes were due to be converted in parallel and in approximately equal proportions. The design of modification developed at OKB-43 turned out to be not very successful, as the equipment installation was complex while the wiring to the bomb racks disturbed the operation of the fuel system. Therefore, designers of Factory No.89 slightly refined the drawings. The first two modified airplanes left the workshops of the factory on 23 May. A little later Factory No.81 was drafted into this conversion work, having received the documentation from Factory No.89.

Factory No.84, however, did not diverge from the original documentation received from the OKB-43. Also from May 1942, the factory began to fit the bomb racks, bomb release mechanisms and bombsights (including the NKPB-3 night sight) to the PS-84s starting from the airplanes of the 32nd series. The military acceptance commission, however, refused to accept these airplanes, as they were not fitted with Der-19 bomb racks for large calibre bombs. As a result, the rollout of fully equipped bombers began there in June.

The PS-84 in the bomber version went through several other changes – the maximum fuel reserve was increased up to 3,110l as the additional fuel tanks were mounted inside the fuselage (in fact such tanks had been fitted earlier, in the air force units themselves), the airframe was strengthened, and doubled rear struts of the main landing gear were installed. As a result, the take-off weight of the airplane exceeded 11,500kg (given a pre-war standard of 10,900kg). The armed earlier-series airplanes, which had not been strengthened, operated with limitations on their flight weight and maximum speed.

A fire of the port engine on a cargo Li-2T on landing in Ufa led to the explosion of a fuel tank during the landing run, February 1950.

Testing of this 'stop-gap bomber' (in fact, a multi-purpose airplane of 36th series) was undertaken at the NII VVS from 28 July to 11 August 1942. The aircraft could carry 25 persons on folding wooden benches or up to 3,000kg of cargo. When special attachments were fitted in the cargo compartment, 18 stretchers with wounded could be positioned with a further two persons carried on folding seats. The bridge under the fuselage enabled to carry 1,000kg of bombs or artillery gun (including those dropped by parachute). Among the innovations, this airplane also featured a system of fuel tanks pressurisation with the exhaust gases, and additional oil radiators. The aircraft armament still consisted of four ShKAS machine guns. Pilot V.V. Lisitsyn and navigator A.I. Starykh flew this PS-84 in course of the testing. Further to the tests completion, the NII VVS approved the aircraft modifications.

As of 13 May 1942, the GVF had 83 PS-84s in its strength, while the VVS operated 53 airplanes. Almost four

At the beginning of the 1950s the Li-2 was the most widespread passenger airplane in the USSR.

On 22 April 1942, the first two aircrews flew a sortie out to the partisans. In July 1942, however, it was considered necessary to transfer this division to ADD.

Thus, the PS-84 became a dual-purpose airplane, having been given the ability to carry bombs it retained the capability of operating as a transport aircraft. Now, these airplanes were no longer known as PS-84 but Li-2. It is still is unclear why, of all the persons who participated in the arrangement of series production and modernisation of this type, it was decided to reference B.P. Lisunov, who was not actually a designer. The new designation was officially introduced in

fifths of the latter quantity was concentrated in the special purpose air regiment, and the others were attached to the headquarters of the fronts or used by the training centres. The NKAP was the third in terms of number of PS-84s in service, which had 26 airplanes. They were used for urgent transportation of components to the aircraft factories. A comparatively small number of such airplanes were at the disposal of the GUSMP, the People's Commissariat of Internal Affairs, the People's Commissariat of the Tank Industry, and other departments.

In April, formation of the VVS transport regiments began, and this meant cardinal changes to the concept of military transport aviation in the USSR. Earlier, in peacetime, military transport aviation did not exist as such – there was only a special purpose squadron (later a regiment) that was based in the Moscow region, which partially performed air transportation functions, and small transport air units in the districts. When necessary, the military rented aircraft from civil aviation. In the event of war, it was planned to mobilise all the available GVF airplanes for transportation flights, while the responsibility for airborne assault operations was entrusted to bomber aviation. By the beginning of the 1940s, the experience acquired in course of military campaigns led the VVS to the need to have its own transport aviation, equipped with special aircraft and crews, trained to transport troops and airborne assault forces. The shortage of contemporary airplanes, however, meant that this idea could be realised only in 1942.

Two regiments were formed – the 101st and the 102nd, with a standard compliment of 20 PS-84s in each of them. The regiments were combined into the 1st Transport Air Division, which was commanded the GUMP famous woman pilot A.S. Grizodubova. It is worth noting that she used not a PS-84, but an American-built DC-3 as her flagship airplane.

September 1942, but the documents for some time referred to the old and new designations alternately, while for the majority the airplane was still known as the 'Douglas'.

Three spheres of use were defined for these airplanes: transporting urgent cargoes in the rear (these were provided by the GVF and departmental aviation), transport flights to the front and beyond the front line (these were provided by both the special air groups of the GVF which were later transformed into regiments and divisions, and the VVS), and night bombing (which became the main objective of the ADD, but occasionally GVF airplanes were drafted in for this).

Comparatively few Li-2s remained in the rear, where the main burden fell on the obsolete aircraft types that could no longer operate on the front line – the G-2s (disarmed TB-3s), PS-9s, and others.

Considerably more PS-84s were used on the front line. In June 1942 almost the entire MAGON was re-deployed to Krasnodar, from where these airplanes began to fly to the encircled city of Sevastopol, where the landing ground near to the Khersoness lighthouse was strafed by German artillery. The airplanes were given signals made up of seven 'Bat' type kerosene lamps laid down on the ground. The main objective of these flights was to evacuate the garrison, and in total 2,174 people was rescued by air from Sevastopol. On the night of 19–20 July, the Li-2 flown by pilot Shangin caught a beam of an aircraft shelter on landing. Under the enemy fire, the ground crews managed to change the wheel and began to straighten out the bent propellers. They repaired one, but a German shell hit the workshop building and destroyed the second one. The following night the enemy succeeded in setting an airplane on fire.

The Li-2s made their debut as the night bomber airplanes in summer 1942 – on 24 June the airplanes of the 1st

Transport Air Division bombed the Shchigry station. As bombers the Li-2s had their pros and cons. They could not boast a high speed or excellent manoeuvrability, but on the other hand the crew could work in significantly more comfortable conditions than on an Il-4 bomber for example. The spacious cockpits, dual controls, which enabled pilots to take over from one another, the passenger cabin, where crews could take a nap on the covers should they need to, the cabin heating (in an Il-4 in the winter it was not much warmer than it was outside the airplane), the ventilation, and the excellent instruments made this airplane very comfortable for long-range sorties.

Refuelling of an Li-2 in Surgut, mid-1960s. As a result of the on-board equipment modernisation, the airplane featured a number of new antennae.

Alcohol based anti-icing agents were used to combat icing, and this fluid was spilled onto the propeller blades and glazing of the cockpit canopy. In reality, the poor manufacturing quality of the wartime introduced its own specifics. 'As a result of the insufficient sealing in the window frames ... the alcohol seeps through into the pilot's cockpit and often drenches the pilot's clothes ... During changes in altitude the alcohol comes out from the filler cap and floods the radio-operator'.

The behaviour in the air of this slightly inert but responsive former passenger airliner differed advantageously from the unstable Il-4, which would cause fatigue among its pilots. In terms of defensive armament, the Li-2 and the Il-4 were more or less equal, although on the 'Douglas' the space behind the tail and under the fuselage was not covered at all by defensive fire.

Operations with the Li-2 in the ADD steadily expanded, and in 1942 long-range aviation received 221 airplanes in total. In August–September, regiments of the 53rd and 62nd Air Divisions, which had previously been equipped with the TB-3, began to convert onto this new type.

Li-2s were operating actively as night bombers in November–December 1942 during the battles for Stalingrad. After taking off from the forward landing grounds they approached the Volga River under cover of darkness, where searchlights at the left bank illuminated the target zone for the bombing on the other bank. Soviet forces held only a narrow strip along the river, so the airplanes immediately began to release their bombs. The bomb load of 1,000kg was standard for the maximum range, while on these 'short haul' trips the airplanes could carry significantly more. The crews took small-calibre bombs inside the fuselage in addition to the main bomb load, and these were dropped by hand through the door. When the bombs ran out, the airplanes carried all sorts of metal scrap (for example, the railway spikes were dropped), as well as hand grenades.

Crews of the 102nd Regiment of the ADD destroyed the important crossings across the Don River, disrupting the enemy supply lines. There was a case when the night bombers flew a sortie by daylight – the 62nd Air Division received an order to attack Pitomnik airfield inside the ring of the encirclement to prevent a possible escape by 6th Army Command under *Feldmarshall* Paulus. The order was carried out but the division lost five airplanes shot down by fighters and enemy anti-aircraft defence.

In those same battles for Stalingrad the PS-84s performed transportation of urgent cargoes, as well as carried troop reinforcements and took out the wounded. Just the 102nd Air Regiment delivered 800 tonnes of cargo and 1,448 people to the front and evacuated 5,220 injured personnel on their return flights. Transport aviation was involved in supply of fuel for tank units that had made significant breakthroughs during the course of the counterattack.

The number of airplanes arriving from the factories was already significantly outweighing the losses, and in total in 1942 some 423 airplanes were completed. During this period the ADD lost 52 Li-2s (of those 29 were for combat reasons). From the middle of the year onwards the airplanes, for the most part, fell victim to anti-aircraft artillery. As a result, not only the bombing sorties but also transport flights in the combat area began to be made at night, and the altitude of these flights was increased.

Li-2s would frequently fly out to the partisans, and airfields, albeit relatively primitive, were constructed for this purpose behind enemy lines. The partisans did not have any special construction equipment so they did everything by hand. The airplanes carried armament, ammunition, explosive charges, medical supplies and mail, returning with wounded and sick, as well as children.

Servicing an Li-2T of one of the VVS regiments at an airfield in Vinnitsa, 1962.

During such flights, amazing stories sometimes happened. Li-2 flown by Captain Yurkov unexpectedly collided on take-off with two horses running out of the forest. As a result, the wing centerplane was damaged, as were the starboard undercarriage leg and the starboard propeller. The airplane had to be pulled into the bushes and hidden. On the next day a second Li-2 arrived carrying spare parts and a repair brigade. Yurkov's Li-2 was being repaired over two days, and then the weather deteriorated. The crew made four attempts to take off but each time they were unsuccessful. The batteries ran down and one of the engines began to play up. These problems were resolved 'using every available ingenuity'. Finally, Yurkov took off, taking the repair staff back. All the participants were later awarded orders and medals for saving this airplane.

In the winter of 1942, Stalin wanted to gather at a meeting in Moscow the commanders of the large partisan units from the Kursk, Oryol, Bryansk, and Gomel regions. The small U-2 biplanes brought 18 people from different places out to the Vypolzovo partisan airfield, from where an Li-2 took them to the capital. When the partisans explained this to Stalin, he did not believe that deep behind German lines there were landing sites capable of receiving large twin-engine airplanes. The leader ordered them to describe the airplane, and only then was he convinced that the partisan commanders were right. After the meeting they were all taken back to where they had come from.

In 1943 the intensity of Li-2 participation in combat operations grew, first and foremost because there were simply more of these airplanes. In one year, the industry handed over 618 aircraft, of those the ADD received more than half – 369 airplanes. The re-equipment of the ADD regiments, which had previously been equipped with TB-3s, was completed in July–October 1943. Formation of new regiments with the Li-2 began as well. Losses also increased, first and foremost this affected ADD, which lost 160 airplanes, 105 out of these were destroyed by the enemy. The GVF suffered to a much lesser extent, losing 42 Li-2 airplanes on the front line. On the other hand, 46 airplanes were lost in crashes in the rear, and the reason for this was that the best crews had been sent to the front. Behind the lines, on the whole, were the pilots whose training had been rushed through in wartime. In fact, the GVF had far fewer airplanes in service – the entire fleet of this department in December 1943 consisted of 90 Li-2s. The priority of the ADD and VVS in the delivery of aircraft led to the GVF receiving three times less airplanes than the planned figure.

In the majority of cases the Li-2 bomber operated in small groups against area targets. They would fly as a column up to the target for the bombing run, with short intervals between them. The leading airplane would illuminate the target with SAB bombs dropped using parachutes. Every crew carried out aiming independently of one another. In the event of the presence of anti-aircraft defence over the target, the Li-2s would often come back with damages, but overall the airplane was distinguished by its outstanding survivability.

In September 1943, the Li-2s from the ADD and GVF landed a large airborne assault on the Bukrin bridgehead on the right bank of the Dnieper River – three brigades were dropped by night by parachute. The loss of orientation by the aircrews and the intensive anti-aircraft fire led to the airborne troops being scattered over a wide area, or actually falling into the river itself. As a result, they sustained heavy losses.

Further growth in production of the Li-2s was slowed down, for the most part, by a lack of components, including engines. This led to the idea of acquiring these from the USA under Lend-Lease program. On 15 July 1943, the State Committee for Defence took the decision to order 2,000 R-1820-G2 engines in the USA, which were very similar to the M-62IR. The Wright Company, however, refused, as these engines had been withdrawn from production back at the beginning of the year. There were 120 of these engines found in the stores, of which the Soviet acceptance representatives identified 52 that were serviceable. During their transportation by sea, 10 of these engines went to the bottom along with the vessel carrying them, and the rest were used as spare engines for the US-made airplanes, which still remained in use; thus, they were not fitted to the Li 2s.

In place of the G2s, the Americans offered Soviet side the more powerful G202, so the designers in Tashkent examined the possibility of fitting them. It turned out that the engine mount would need to be changed, as well as the oil radiator, engine cowling, and the exhaust manifold. On 7 October the Soviet side officially rejected the offer of the R-1820-G202 engines. Variants of equipping the Li-2 with the R-1820-71, R-1830-92, and R-2600 engines were examined, but they were all rejected as significant changes to the airframe had to be introduced. For example, if the R-1830-92 were fitted, the power plant layout would have

An Li-2P at an airfield in Kherson, the mid-1960s.

to be completely re-designed, the wing, centerplane, undercarriage, and part of the fuselage would have to be strengthened.

Another direction for the improvement of the Li-2 in the war years was its complete modification into the night bomber. Two obstacles limited the airplane's potential in this respect: firstly, the capability to carry bombs only externally limited their number and calibre and also reduced already low speed of this passenger airplane. Secondly, the bombing accuracy suffered a great deal because of the poor downward visibility for the navigator and from the primitive bombsight fitted to this airplane. Therefore, the next stage in modification was to accommodate the bombs inside the fuselage, and to give the navigator the capability of downward visibility and use a more contemporary bombsight.

In February 1943, the Li-2NB version appeared at the NII VVS – the airplane was flown by a single pilot, with the navigator occupying the seat next to him. An NKPB-4 night bombing sight was provided for the navigator, and another important difference for the Li-2NB was the possibility of carrying the bombs internally in a bomb bay under the cabin floor. The Li-2 serial number 1845408 was used for this modification; the airplane was tested at the NII VVS but was rejected. The reasons for this included the unsatisfactory bomb armament and the need in complex re-design of the fuselage. Moreover, the specialists were afraid that introduction of this new design would have an effect on the production rate. Another example of such version was manufactured, which featured certain refinements, but it was rejected by the NII VVS as well.

Instead of the extensive modification, the process of adapting the original transport version for night bombing was continued. By the end of summer 1943, the aircraft received GAM-10 flame dumpers, enlarged oil radiators and anti-icing equipment (thermal ones on the leading edge of the wing, and electric – on the stabiliser).

Nevertheless, the idea of arranging the possibility for carrying the bombs internally continued to be developed. In December 1944, another variant, the Li-2VP, was put forward for testing. The airplane featured much more simple way of carrying the bombs – Der-21 bomb racks for 100kg-caliber bombs were fitted right in the cabin, and the bombs were dropped through tunnels in the floor. The external bomb racks, moreover, were retained. When FAB-100 bombs were carried internally, the bomb load increased to 2,500kg. Defensive armament remained as standard – a single upper UTK-1 turret and two ShKAS machine guns in the side-mounted hatches. The nose-mounted machine gun was considered useless and was removed. Two bombsights were envisaged for the navigator: an OPB-1r (day sight) and an NKPB-7 (night sight). The crew of pilot V.I. Zhdanov tested this airplane. The transition to carrying the bombs internally enhanced the flight-performance characteristics somewhat, so the Li-2VP was recommended for series production.

This airplane, however, did not enter production because the preference was given to a significantly simpler re-design of the basic Li-2, which was again designated the Li-2NB. This modification was done to the airplane serial number 18411906. The bombs were still carried externally, and the load included four 250kg bombs. The layout of the crew positioning in the cabin was changed: the radio-operator was seated in the place of former forward baggage compartment behind the co-pilot, and the navigator sat on the left-hand side, close to the emergency exit door, which had now been completely glazed over, turning it into a large window. The door itself had been made bulbous, and behind it was the NKPB-7 bombsight, which was directed through the lower part of the door, the glazing for which opened outwards to enhance the view. The radio-equipment was refined – in place of the indigenous RPK-2 radio compass an American Bendix MN-26C was fitted instead, and the RSBbis radio set was replaced with the RSR-1.

The new Li-2NB was tested at the NII VVS by a crew of pilot M.A. Nyukhtikov and navigator N.P. Tsvetkov. The flight-performance characteristics compared to the Li-2 remained unchanged, but the field of view for the navigator was considered unsatisfactory. As the proposed changed were considered minimal as comparing to the airplanes leaving the production workshops, the Li-2NB entered series production. These aircraft participated in many of the operations in the closing period of the war both as bombers and as transport airplanes.

Starting from 1944, some of the Li-2s received thermal anti-icing equipment, which was mounted on the wing and stabiliser. Their leading edges were covered in a paste that was based on graphite crumbs, through which a current was passed. By 5 November 1942 the workshops in Vnukovo fitted two airplanes with this system, and by the end of the year a dozen more airplanes had been equipped for operational testing. Subsequently, the conclusion was reached that such anti-icers were not very effective, and on the majority of airplanes this system was shut down.

At the same time a decision was made to order Goodrich pneumatic de-icing equipment from the USA, which had proved itself well on DC-3 and C-47 airplanes. On 13 March 1944 the State Committee for Defence issued a decree for the purchase of 250 sets. Protracted negotiations followed, which were made all the more complicated by the fact that the Soviet side refused to provide detailed engineering drawings for the wing of the Li-2, emphasising that this was similar to that of the DC-3. Finally, agreement was reached, and deliveries were to be made in June 1945. Evidently, in view of the partial freezing of the Lend-Lease program following the victory over Germany this cargo never arrived. A certain number of these sets, however, were received, and these were possibly spares for the C-47 airplanes. In any case, in 1948 Factory No.48 fitted two Li-2s with this equipment.

At the end of the war, Li-2s were manufactured in the version of night bomber-transport (with an empty cabin designed for cargo), as well as unarmed cargo and medical versions. These airplanes had a reinforced cabin floor and a cargo hatch on the port side, as on the PS-84K. The folding plywood seats were placed along the fuselage sides. In the cabin of the medical version, the stretchers were placed in three tiers. In total such airplane could carry 18 stretcher cases, two wounded in the seats, and a medical orderly. The medical version had the heaviest empty weight – 8,114kg.

Some of the airplanes were equipped with American MN-26C radio compasses, and the type of the main radio set was changing constantly – initially this was an RSB-1, followed by RSB-3, RSB-3bis, RSR-1 and RSR-2. In addition, RSI-3 VHF station sets were fitted in the air force units, together with a second radio mast above the fuselage on the port side.

In winter the Li-2s often flew on ski undercarriage but these were not retractable, creating additional drag. An alternative was jettisonable ski undercarriage proposed by the NII GVF – the airplane would either be towed into these boot-shape skis by a tug along special gangways or taxi into them under its own power. To fit the tail ski, the rear part of the airplane was raised up using a lifting jack. After take-off, the skis, which were not fixed in any way to the wheeled undercarriage, would simply fall away. The airplane would land on its wheels. These jettisonable skis were manufactured in a small batch but they were not used widely.

The Li-2s in passenger version were not built in a war time, while the only exception were five airplanes with the pre-war style passenger cabins, which were specially manufactured in Tashkent in June 1943 for transportation of Soviet delegation to Tehran conference. These airplanes were assembled with greater care and were accepted by a special commission. Another example (other sources indicate three aircraft) was converted into passenger version by the workshops of the 1st Air Regiment of the People's Commissariat of Internal Affairs in Bykovo in the Moscow region. This airplane featured fewer seats than the standard passenger airplane, it had more spacious cabin, and the finish was even luxurious. Stalin, however, decided not fly on any of these airplanes as he preferred the American C-47 above any of them – this airplane was not particularly comfortable but it was faster and reliable.

By February 1944, the Li-2s were already operating in three ADD Air Corps – the 5th, 6th, and 7th, and they were used for massive bomb raids on Finnish cities. Helsinki alone was bombed three times in a row, and the Li-2s from airfields on the Karelian Isthmus would fly up to three sorties per night. The airplanes would set off for the target in small groups with intervals between them, and the crews were tasked with not achieving mass destruction but inflicting prolonged psychological pressure, since talks were being held at the time around Finland exit from the war. In September 1944, the raids by large formations of bombers, including Li-2s, were carried out against targets in Hungary.

The Li-2s flew behind the front line for the entire duration of war, dropping intelligence agents and delivering cargoes to encircled formations and partisan units. Under orders from the Reconnaissance Directorate of General Headquarters, they flew over occupied territory and even farther – to Poland, East Prussia, Czechoslovakia, Romania, Bulgaria, and Austria. The 1st Transport Air Division alone (the former MAGON) delivered 850 agents behind enemy lines. For these sorties, four pilots were awarded the title of Hero of the Soviet Union.

The first flight to the partisans with a landing behind enemy lines was flown in September 1942, and the mass transport flights began in 1943. The chronicle of these flights contains a number of memorable pages. The pilots were always looking for ways to cross the front line as safely as possible – they raised the altitude, gradually reaching the heights of 4,000m, launched flares imitating the flares launched by German pilots, and flew over occupied territory with their lights on, as if they were flying over their home base. Pilot Taran who is mentioned above, was changing the propeller pitch achieving the sound inherent to German aircraft engines.

By no means did this help every time. On the night of 18–19 August 1943, five enemy fighters attacked aircraft flown by pilot Bogdanov on his return back to base. He evaded the fighters and landed on his home base but the

An Li-2P with GVF registration numbers, beginning of the 1970s.

mechanics counted 1,500 bullet holes in his airplane, including 12 that were left by shells. The Li-2 returned with the rudder jammed, a failed hydraulic system, a leaking oil tank, and a non-functioning port aileron and trim tabs. On the port side the outer skin was hanging off in clumps. On 27 May 1943 two night fighters shot down airplane flown by pilot Dubrovskiy in the area around Lyudinov. Li-2 of pilot Bulatnikov, which had been damaged by anti-aircraft artillery, performed a belly landing among marshes behind enemy lines. The crew repaired the airplane over the course of a week and took off in it as the Germans were approaching the landing site.

In September 1944 three divisions of the ADD played their part in organising an 'air bridge' into Slovakia that had risen up against the enemy. Starting from 16 September these airplanes began to land regularly at Tri Duby airfield located on the other side of the Carpathian Mountains. The Li-2s were delivering around 80 tonnes of cargo per day, transporting anti-tanks cannons and guns, rifles, machine guns, cartridges and grenades, as well as provisions and medical supplies. On 28 September, several companies from the Czechoslovak airborne brigade together with their artillery were landed in an Li-2, and they immediately went into battle. As this attack was not anticipated, the Germans pulled back some 30km. These flights were hounded by German fighter aviation, but the Li-2s incurred fewer relative losses than the unarmed C-47s.

The most significant losses were incurred by the ADD regiments in December 1944 when the Li-2s participated in raids against cities in East Prussia. The powerful and well organised German air defence was shooting down up to 20 airplanes per night!

The GVF was also losing aircraft, albeit in much smaller numbers, and in the whole of 1944 just 15 Li-2s were written off, and of these nine were from front line regiments. In the main, the airplanes were destroyed on their airfields. Thus, on 7 September 1944 a pair of German FW 190 fighters attacked Beloverzhishki airfield, where the 120th Air Regiment was based. A single Li-2 was among those airplanes that were burnt out but there were also aircraft that were destroyed in the air. On 8 March 1944 the Germans hit two airplanes at once, one of them managed to land and caught fire on the ground and another crashed, killing its entire crew.

The losses, however, were recouped by arrivals from industry, and therefore the numbers of airplanes grew, both in military and civil aviation. As of 1 April 1945, there were 546 Li-2s in the ADD. In that month they again bombed Konigsberg, and moreover on 7–8 April they bombed this target in daylight. By the end of the war the Li-2s had become the most widespread airplane in the 18th Air Army (the ADD transformed into this army), and 19 regiments flew within it. In total over the entire course of the war the long-range aviation received 1,214 of these airplanes.

At the end of the war, however, Li-2s were used as bombers much less frequently. These aircraft were gradually transferred to cargo flights, and in operations against Japan they were only used as transport airplanes. Two divisions, which had been re-deployed from the west, plus units from the Transbaikal region and the Far East landed troops at airfields in Manchuria and supplied forward mechanised units with fuel. Aviation also transported cargo to the south of the Island of Sakhalin.

Back in the course of the war thought began to be given to post-war operation of these airplanes. The GVF aircraft repair bases began to convert these 'cargo aircraft' into passenger airplanes – the armament was removed and seats were fitted in the cabin. The cargo door, however, was retained, as a rule. Although from spring 1945 Li-2s conceded their position in terms of the number of airplanes in civil aviation to the American C-47, this position could not be maintained for long, as deliveries from the USA had stopped.

After the war series production of these well-proven airplanes was continued. The main variant became the cargo version, the Li-2T. This airplane differed from transport

The last Li-2 in flying condition in Russia, at an airshow at Zhukovskiy, 1995.

enhanced comfort, and the so-called 'economy' with 24 seats, where the distance between the seats was reduced. The Li-2T was manufactured in the same configuration for the military as it was for civil customers. All the changes were being introduced on both versions at almost the same time, with a slight delay at Factory No.126 relatively to the factory in Tashkent.

In 1946 the old AVP-12bis (hydraulic) autopilot was replaced with an AP-42 (electric), which was also copied from the American example, but was more advanced, developed in wartime.

The most important step in the refinement of the post-war Li-2s happened in 1947, when, starting from aircraft of the 231st series, the position of the oil radiators was changed. Earlier, these two large cylinders were installed almost vertically in the engine nacelle. Now, they were lowered down, closer to the engine suction pipe, and were suspended horizontally and covered with a single cover. The adjustable shutters previously were positioned at the air inlet, and now they were relocated to the air outlet. As a result of all these modifications, the characteristic 'lip' appeared under the engine cowling.

On the aircraft of the 250th series, the changes only affected the Li-2T version, and they were all aimed at enhancing the effectiveness of the airplane during the air dropping of airborne troops. Previously, the main entrance door (on the starboard side) opened outwards, but now it was changed to inwards opening. Inside the cargo cabin, two steel cables were mounted to clip the parachute static lines onto.

On the airplanes of the 252nd series (in May 1947) a refined AP-42A autopilot was fitted, and on the 257th series an RPKO-2B radio compass was installed, which allowed the navigator to take bearings from the broadcasting radio stations in the same manner as from radio beacons.

Starting from the aircraft of the 262nd series the Li-2T was modernised once again: a door was fitted to the cargo hatch and this also opened inwards. Now the paratroopers could exit the airplane twice as fast. At the same time, easily detachable seats were installed for the paratroopers, which were simple benches made from wood and plywood, each could seat two persons. The paratroopers sit back to back, and the commander's seat was positioned on the port row, closer to the doors. When cargoes were being transported, these seats were removed so the airplane was not carrying excess weight, or they were simply folded back. On the airplanes of the 266th series, a corrugated metal floor better suited to

planes produced in wartime for the most part by the absence of armament. On the Li-2T, the thermal and sound insulation was only to be found in the pilot's cockpit, and the airplane was not fitted with heating system at all. The cargo compartment was expanded by the removal of the forward baggage compartments (as with the PS-84I). The crew comprised four persons – two pilots, a radio-operator, and a flight mechanic, as had been the case before the war, but without a stewardess, who was not required in the absence of any passengers.

On 22 April 1945 a decree arrived from the State Committee for Defence on the introduction of the Li-2T into series production. Testing of the prototype that had been built in Tashkent was undertaken at the NII VVS in September–October 1945. The series was initially produced at Factory No.84, but in small numbers because in the autumn of 1945 production was restarted there of the passenger Li-2P version with a cabin that could accommodate 19 seats. From the end of 1946, Factory No.126 in Komsomolsk-on-Amur had begun to arrange series production of the Li-2T, having ceased manufacturing of the Il-4 bombers. These airplanes were supplied, first and foremost, to military transport aviation, specifically, into transport and airborne troop-carrying regiments, which were formed intensively in 1946–47, for interaction with airborne forces.

The post-war evolution of the Li-2s was significantly influenced by familiarisation with the American C-47s delivered in the war years, which contained multiple improvements as comparing to the pre-war DC-3s. Operating the C-47, Soviet crews had cause to wonder why all these features could not be introduced onto the Li-2.

Starting from 1946, the Li-2Ps and Li-2Ts were built in parallel, and the passenger airplane was produced in three versions: one designed for 15-21 seats, one for 15 seats with taking the concentrated loads replaced the plywood one, and rubber walkways were placed on top of it.

In the second half of the year changes were made to the electrical equipment, a hydraulic balancing shock-absorber was put in place of the rubber one for the main undercarriage legs, and the RSI-6 VHF radio set was fitted as standard. All these modifications copied the improvements of the C-47 precisely. The Li-2 received heating system for the crew cabin, and from the 277th series onwards a device was fitted for towing military gliders. At that, a part of the tail cone had to be cut away, and the airplane began to resemble a C-47 more closely. The crew would monitor the glider position through a periscope (re-designed OP-2LM bomb sight), which was mounted on the ceiling over the places of the flight mechanic and radio-operator.

In October 1947, the airframes of the Li-2P and Li-2T were unified, and the layout of the forward part of the fuselage in the cargo airplane was changed similarly to the passenger version. At that, the capacity of the cargo compartment was reduced slightly by the arrangement of three baggage compartments. Right at the end of the year, the feathered AV-7N-161 propellers appeared, which made flying on one engine much easier. On 31 October 1949 the Council of Ministers issued a decree ordering installation of these new propellers to 238 airplanes of early series. Conversion kits for such modification were also sent abroad.

In the following year of 1948, the Li-2s were fitted with windscreen wipers on the forward glazing of the pilot's cockpit, which were electrically operated, in spite of the fact that the C-47 featured more powerful hydraulic ones. On the 300th series airplanes, RV-2 radio-altimeter was fitted, as well as a marker radio receiver, an ARK-5 automatic radio compass, and the electrical system was made single-wire. Subsequently, the Li-2 underwent minor changes to its equipment. Only three significant changes can be identified in later series airplanes: the transfer to a calorific heating, replacement of the electro-thermal anti-icers with thermal ones, and the installation of a single large horseshoe-shaped oil radiator instead of two circular units. The removal of the old steam boiler came as a great delight to the flight mechanics who had to fuss around with them. This capricious and unreliable device would frequently fill the airplane with clouds of steam, which meant the flight mechanics were dubbed 'stokers'. Now, petrol fuelled BO-10 or BO-20 calorific heaters were fitted instead. Another such heater would warm the air passing through the leading edge of the stabiliser. The wing leading edges were warmed by air passing through sleeves around the exhaust pipes. In May 1950, a prototype aircraft with such changes underwent testing at the NII GVF. The new equipment was not only introduced at Factory No.84 but was also retrofitted to the earlier-built airplanes. By 20 December 1950, 204 Li-2s had been fitted with the BO-20 heaters. Initially, the incidents occurred where the petrol-fuelled heaters would catch fire, but these were dealt with relatively quickly.

Everything described above can be defined as the general line of the Li-2 evolution. There were, however, so many other modifications, prototypes, and unrealised projects! In 1948, the UchShLi-2 (*Uchebno-Shturmanskiy*, navigator trainer) version was manufactured for the VVS. Ten workstations fitted out with the required instruments and bombsights were arranged inside the cabin. These airplanes were used to train both navigation and bombing and were utilised for a long time at a number of military schools, such as at Chelyabinsk for example.

The second, less successful, military version of the Li-2 was the minesweeper designed for detonating magnetic bottom mines. The first project of such airplane, which was designated PS-84T, was proposed by Golubkov back in 1943. Under the wings and the fuselage there was mounted an enormous ring with an electric winding inside, and it was supported by a system of bracing wires. The current in the electric winding was created by an electrical generator, which itself was operated by an auxiliary engine. Development of the PS-84T, which was later designated the Li-2MT, had been slowly progressing for the entire duration of the war. In June 1946, the Ministry of the Aviation Industry ordered LII to test the prototype of 'Golubkov's minesweeper'. The commander of the test crew was P.E. Genaev. Two of these airplanes were due to be demonstrated at an aviation parade in August 1948, but it is not known whether this did actually take place or not. The final mention of the Li-2MT was in 1949, when a project was prepared that saw the installation of the new 260hp M-14 as the auxiliary engine.

At the end of the war plans emerged to modernise the Li-2 by fitting significantly more powerful engines, and this work was led by Golubkov at Factory No.30. In 1945, an Li-2 fitted with ASh-82FN engines (also known as the Li-4) was transferred for testing. Despite the increase of the take-off weight up to a total of 13,700kg the speed increased up to 418km/h, and the service ceiling to 8,800m. On the basis of this prototype, the T-82M project was developed, which saw reinforcement of the airframe. This airplane was designed to carry 30 passengers and the take-off weight was designed to increase to a total of 15,600kg (other sources put this total at 16,150kg). The Il-12 appeared, however, and the T-82M was not developed further.

In 1953, Antonov Design Bureau developed the high-altitude Li-2V version fitted with TK-19 turbo-superchargers. This airplane was intended for operation on Dushanbe–Khorog route in the Pamir Mountains, as well as for weather reconnaissance. The aircraft was fitted with oxygen equipment for the crew and passengers, and a small batch of the Li-2V were built.

Many versions of the type appeared as a result of modifications at the aircraft repair bases and repair factories. One of them was the Li-2Gr, a hybrid of passenger and cargo

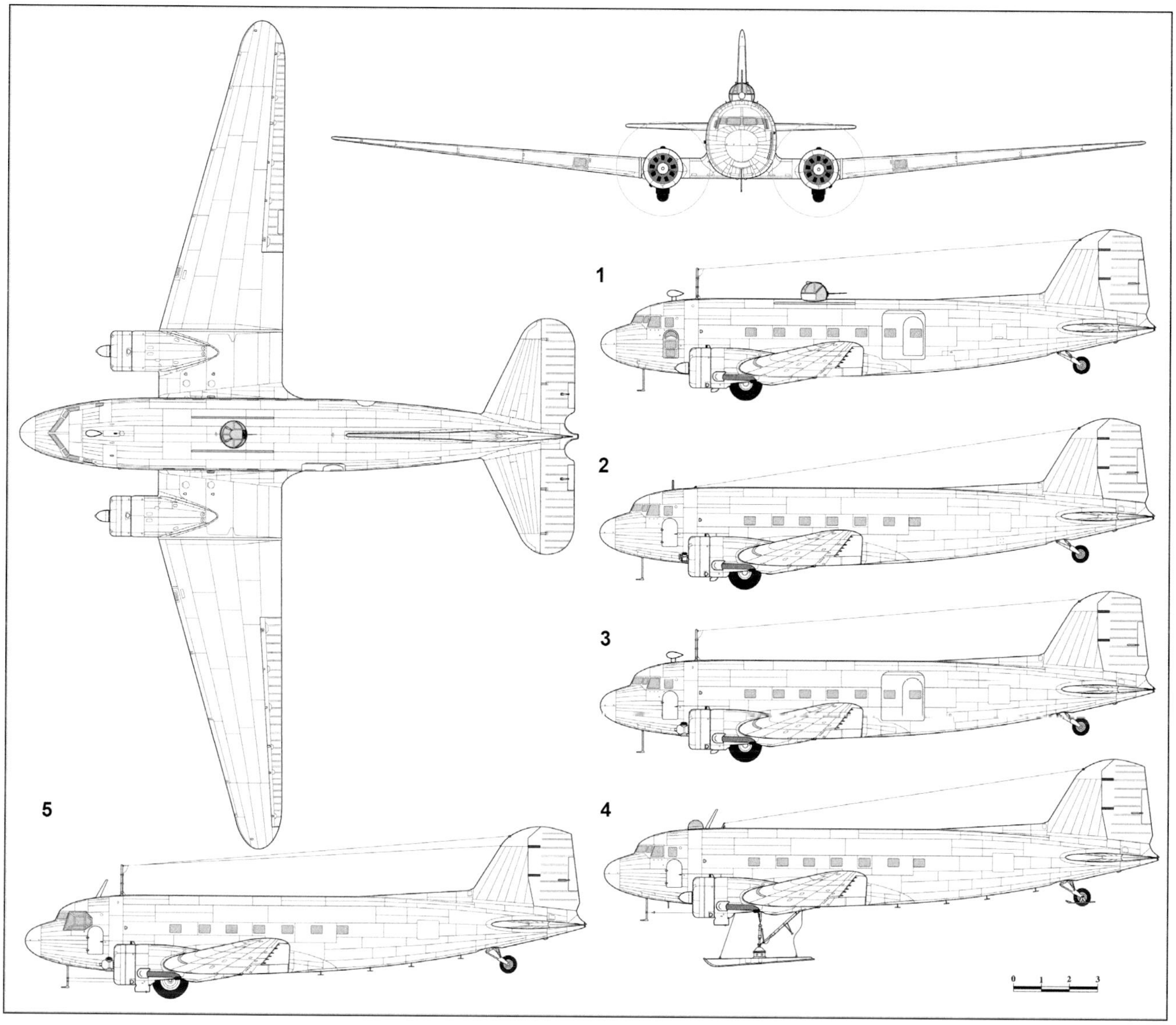

1. Three-view drawings of a Li-2NB night bomber with a UTK-1 turret.
2. Side view drawing of a PS-84 of early series.
3. Side view drawing of a Li-2 in military transport version.
3. Side view drawing of a Li-2 user by Polar Aviation.
4. Side view drawing of an UchShLi-2 navigator trainer version.

variants, which could accommodate 10 persons and 1,200kg of cargo. The Li-2F aerial photography versions was equipped with two aerial cameras, additional fuel tanks in the passenger cabin, glazing that protruded out from the pilot's cockpit on the starboard side, and a blister for the cameras on the port side. The Li-2RP fishing reconnaissance variant was made for the interest of fishing industry and was modified in such a manner that an observer was seated in the glazed nose part of the airplane and could monitor the movements of the shoals. Some airplanes of this version were later fitted with radar.

Li-2s were also used to take air samples during the testing of the first Soviet nuclear bombs. The cockpit remained unpressurised, and the efforts were made simply to seal it. Such airplanes carried cigar-shaped containers with a special porous content.

Different Soviet ministries ordered 'saloon' Li-2s for their leadership, with a luxurious finish, huge seats and tables, as well as broad sofas. Velvet and leather, oak and Karelian birch were all used in the finish for these aircraft.

Polar aviation did not pursue luxury but they were concerned with the comfort of their crews, as with additional fuel tanks in the cabin the Li-2 could stay airborne for up to a day, and on some airplanes the capability to top up fuel tanks from barrels carried on board was envisaged. This variant was known as an 'expedition' version. Each crew flying airplanes of the Polar Aviation Directorate always included a navigator, for whom a workstation was fitted out in the cabin with a desk and the required instruments. Subsequently, a number of Li-2s flying for this department received another feature, which was similar to the C-47 – an astronavigation blister in the ceiling in the forward part of the fuselage.

The polar aviators continued to use ski undercarriage after the war, and at the end of 1949 engineer Mostovoy from the design bureau of the Directorate of Polar Aviation developed retractable ski undercarriage for the Li-2. This undercarriage was manufactured in a small series by the Factory No.477 named after Pobezhimov in Krasnoyarsk. From spring 1950, this type of ski undercarriage began to be fitted to airplanes.

The Li-2s participated in many polar expeditions, such as the large high-latitude expeditions of 1948 and 1950. In the first case, six airplanes of this type were used, and in the second – 10 aircraft, and some of them were put onto ski undercarriage. These expeditions did not just have a scientific importance but a military one too (they explored Arctic operations and flights from temporary ice airfields) therefore approximately half of the aircraft was supplied by the VVS. Subsequently, Li-2s also flew in the Antarctic.

Production of the Li-2s at the factory in Komsomolsk-on-Amur was ceased in 1950, and in Tashkent in 1953. In total, 4,863 examples were produced, but story of this legendary airplane, however, by no means ended there.

By January 1948, the numbers of the Li-2s had again superseded the C-47s in Aeroflot – 323 airplanes vice 228, and they continued to arrive, so by the end of the year civil pilots already had 522 of these aircraft. The most prestigious airplane in the GVF at that time became the new Il-12, and there were more than a hundred of them in service. In the VVS, a greater proportion of the 'Americans' were retained because the air force had collected quite a large number of spare engines. They also received the Il-12 airplanes but the tried and tested Li-2 remained the most widespread transport type in the VVS.

Subsequently, the Il-14 appeared, and then came the new generation of turboprop and turbojet airplanes, which superseded the obsolete aircraft. The 'old timer' Li-2, however, continued to fly on regional routes, while in the VVS it was used for training purposes and also for secondary transport flights.

The aircraft and equipment were gradually improving, but the 'Douglases' all continued to fly. To keep them in step with the new requirements, the instruments and radio equipment were replaced – various VHF radio sets were installed (R-802Ts, R-860-IIs, and others), improved intercom systems, AP-45 autopilots, and an SP-50 blind landing system. More and more antennas appeared on the aircraft, but the airframe of the Li-2 was not refined any further.

In the post-war period, this type managed to participate in combat activity abroad – the airplanes were drafted in to support Soviet aviation units active in South China in the early 1950s. A little later the Li-2s operated for a short time during the Korean War, and in 1956 they were used during the suppression of the uprising in Hungary.

In the post-war period, the Li-2 saw service in 10 countries. The first five airplanes were handed over to the Polish military formations in the USSR in 1944. In July 1945 the Council of People's Commissars made a decision to supply 20 airplanes to Poland in both passenger and cargo versions. A little while later deliveries of Li-2s to other East European countries began, and at the end of the 1940s China received a large number of these airplanes. The aircraft also found their way to North Korea, and later to Cuba and North Vietnam.

The Vietnam War was the last for the Li-2 – in summer 1968 the Vietnamese airplanes would fly by night to the south of the country to drop cargoes and paratroopers. The crews were Soviet as well as of mixed descent, and some were purely Vietnamese. The Li-2s did not incur any losses, even though they would come back with holes from enemy fire.

In course of the modification work abroad, original versions of the Li-2 appeared. In Poland in 1947 there was built their own military training version, which was nothing like the UchShLi-2. This airplane was used to train navigators and radio-operators, and for this purpose the photographic equipment was fitted in the cabin, as well as an RSB-3bis radio set, radio compass units, and two OPB-1R bombsights. In 1949, four beams were placed under the fuselage of this airplane with bomb racks taken from the Po-2 (U-2) light night bomber. As a result, the aircraft could carry a dozen practice bombs of 15kg each. Subsequently, bomb locks from MiG-15 fighters were fitted, so the airplane could carry eight bombs of up to 50kg each. In 1948, also in Poland, eight airplanes were modified to spray agricultural chemicals. The container with chemicals was housed in the cabin and was loaded through a hatch in the ceiling, the spray equipment was located underneath the fuselage. In Poland an aerial photography version was also built, with Swiss equipment.

The decorated veteran survived in service until the 1980s when the final airplanes were cut up for scrap. At the end of the 1990s, a single Li-2T was restored to flying condition in Russia, but on 26 June 2004 this airplane crashed on take-off from Myachkovo airfield in the Moscow region. At the same time, many 'Douglases' are still exhibited in aviation museums around Russia.

4.12 The Electras

In April 1934, Amtorg representatives were demonstrated a Lockheed Model 10 Electra twin-engine airplane, and the possibility of turning it into a light bomber. The first mention of the Electra in Soviet documents can be traced to a report by a delegation led by A.N. Tupolev. During a trip to the USA in 1936 the delegation was shown the L-10 at the Lockheed factory in Los Angeles.

In July 1937, the Head of the NII VVS N.N. Bazhanov visited Britain with a delegation, attending demonstration of new aircraft at Hatfield airfield. Amongst other new types, Bazhanov was shown the twin-engine Lockheed airplane owned by Lord Beaverbrook. The hospitable owner offered the Russian a ride in this airplane. Bazhanov wrote in his report: 'In the air I took the controls and after the third steep turn Beaverbrook requested clearance to land'. This airplane was very highly marked – Bazhanov wrote that it was easier to control than a fighter because of the excellent balancing. After this, evidently, a decision was made to purchase the airplane.

In 1938 this airplane arrived at the EON GVF, but initially was not flown. Operations began only from 1939, and the records indicate: 'occasional flights of the command'. In that same year the airplane underwent a short testing at the NII GVF, which was undertaken on 26–29 June. Pilots Miloslavskiy and Taborovskiy flew the Electra, and with a take-off weight of 4,000kg a maximum speed of 312km/h was attained, as well as a service ceiling of 4,340m.

In 1938, another Electra arrived in the Soviet Union, and it had been acquired under extraordinary circumstances. Following disappearance of S.A. Levanevskiy's crew during the long-range flight to the USA, widespread search operations were organised, and Hubert Wilkins and his crew from Canada also flew in this search. In September, however, the sea froze over, and Wilkins was not able to operate his flying boat. The Soviet Ambassador in Washington Umanskiy suggested acquiring an airplane equipped with a ski undercarriage for Wilkins so he could resume the search. On 19 September he wrote from the USA: 'The airplane type and its cost are being clarified'. The Head of the GUSMP O.Yu. Schmidt reported to Stalin about this personally the following day.

The L-10E version of the Lockheed Electra, with more powerful engines and additional fuel tanks, was selected for this expedition. This particular aircraft was originally manufactured under order of the millionaire Vanderbilt. In May 1937, Merril and Lambie flew the Electra on a round-trip crossing of the Atlantic Ocean. Merril was asking 50,000 US Dollars for the airplane and they reached a deal on 45,000 US Dollars. On 3 October Schmidt sanctioned the purchase of the Electra, and on 11 October the airplane was accepted by the new owners – representatives of the Soviet Embassy. The aircraft was given a temporary registration number 'USSR 214', and its crew comprised Hubert Wilkins (commander and navigator), Herbert Hollick-Kenyon (pilot), S.A. Cheesman (co-pilot) and A. Dine (flight engineer).

A post-war Li-2T at the Museum of the Great Patriotic War in Moscow. An attempt was made to pass this aircraft off as a wartime machine, after fitting a mock-up of an MV-3 turret.

A Li-2T standing as a monument in Ivanovo.

A Li-2, which once served in Polar Aviation, at the Central Museum of the Russian Air Force in Monino.

Inspection of an Electra acquired for Hubert Wilkins.

Hubert Wilkins (centre) at the airplane handover ceremony, 11 November 1937.

Wilkins' Electra at an airfield in the USA.

On 22 October the expedition left New York, while Amtorg drew up the payment order only on 16 November when the airplane was already in Edmonton in Canada. There the aircraft was put onto a ski undercarriage, but in view of poor weather conditions began to fly only from 14 January, in the midst of the polar night.

Winter operations raised a range of issues – landing gear skis were freezing to the snow, the cabin windows got covered in an icy crust in flight, so the pilots had to fly with one small side window open and freeze. On 6 February 1938, the port engine failed, but Pratt & Whitney immediately sent a new engine from their stores in Montreal. An airscrew was delivered from Montreal as well by an airplane of local Mackenzie Air Service company, and the pilot of this aircraft helped to repair the Electra. On 11 March, whilst taxiing, the L-10E got into a snowdrift and the tail skid almost broke off completely. The airplane was repaired again, and the fruitless search for Levanevskiy continued until the end of March. On 25 March this airplane returned to New York.

The Electra was dismantled, crated and shipped to the USSR. The assembly, evidently, was undertaken in Leningrad, from where the L-10E was ferried to Moscow. In summer 1938, the airplane was already at the Moscow Air Group base under the Directorate of Polar Aviation of GUSMP in Zakharkovo. The Electra was given a new registration number 'H214' and the markings of Polar Aviation – a banner in a circle on the fin. The airplane was tested, and the excellent flight-performance characteristics were recorded. The airplane was then used for training flights and was flown, for the most part, by S.I. Antyushev (commander) and I.P. Mazuruk (co-pilot). Antyushev was the one who crashed this airplane in the autumn of 1938; the crew were unhurt but the airplane was no longer able to fly.

The aircraft was handed over to Factory No.156 for study, where it was dismantled, measured and weighed, and every subassembly was analysed. The elaborated overall layout of this airplane was noted, as was the limited assortment of used metal profiles and outer skin panels. The undercarriage was particularly notable: 'The undercarriage is worthy of attention from the point of view of strength and simplicity', – the report noted. The 'smooth and excellent retraction' was singled out.

The ski undercarriage was studied separately, and this had a different, more reliable undercarriage leg and a second oil-pneumatic shock absorber that was attached to the cabane

Electra H214, of the Moscow Air Group under the GUSMP, at Zakharkovo airfield outside Moscow.

The port engine with the cowling removed.

In 1938, the Electra was thoroughly studied on arrival from the USA. This photograph shows the open hatch in the fuselage nose part.

of the ski. The design of the skis was assessed as 'compact and simple'.

The shortcomings of this airplane were mentioned as well – the joint between the wing centerplane and outer sections was noted as ineffective: the landing flap was sectioned not in the plane of the joint, so it had to be removed before the wing outer sections could be detached. Some of the fuel tanks were difficult to remove.

At the beginning of 1939, aircraft H214 turned up in Krasnoyarsk at the aircraft repair Factory named after Pobezhimov where it was restored to serviceable condition. Crew of pilot V.M. Makhotkin, which also included co-pilot I.S. Kotov, flight mechanic N.L. Kekushev and radio-operator V.F. Bogdanov, flew the airplane to Taymyr.

On 31 March 1939, the Electra took off from Dikson for the trading post at Ust-Pur close to the Pyasina River to rescue a sick member of the overwintering staff at this location. Once there, Makhotkin discovered that the runway they had been

The view from the former passenger cabin into the pilot's cockpit of the Electra.

invited to land on was unsuitable: it was short, had large snow ridges and was incorrectly marked with thelanding sign 'T'. After flying a circuit, the pilot found a more suitable location but even this was not ideal. After rolling for approximately 100m the airplane's starboard ski hit a snow ridge. The rivet holding the cabane in place was severed in the impact and the ski began to bend. After a second impact this bend in the ski increased and after a third impact the ski folded in half. The Electra spun round and two struts broke on the starboard undercarriage leg, and the end of the ski punctured the wing outer skin. The port undercarriage leg was also damaged following the impact with the snow ridge. It emerged that the lower spar boom in the wing had also sustained damage.

Then the conclusion was reached that in this accident, aside from the pilot, the repair staff were also at fault. When the ski was being repaired in Krasnoyarsk, they had, for some unclear reason, removed four steel strips with a triangular cross-section from the ski base. These functioned as guides and also acted as reinforcing ribs. As a result, the strength and rigidity of the skis in the longitudinal direction had decreased significantly.

The aircrew, however, did not lose hope, and they somehow patched the airplane up in a primitive way in situ, and in place of the starboard ski they adapted a dummy ski that was cut from four logs. In this configuration, the H214 landed at Dikson, and moreover, Makhotkin was planning to take off on such aircraft for an ice reconnaissance mission, and even with an overload of 900kg! Only the protests of the mechanic Kekushev, who had sent the radiogram to Moscow from the winter hut himself, stopped this brave pilot.

The return to Moscow 'under the aircraft own power' was permitted to Kekushev, however. Later on, the Directorate of Polar Aviation was offering excuses that the pilot did not fully report the condition of the airplane. Everything after that resembles such a chain of recklessness and irresponsibility that it could not fail to end in an accident. The airplane flew via Amderma and Arkhangelsk and was already using its wheeled undercarriage. Following a landing in Arkhangelsk, the landing flaps could not be retracted as the battery had run down. It emerged that due to a failure of some kind in

The port main undercarriage leg.

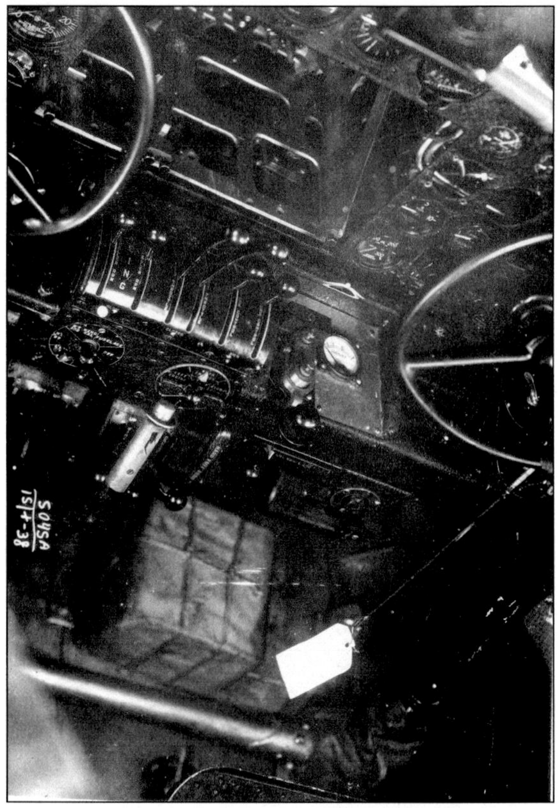
The pilot's cockpit.

the electrical system the battery was not being charged while the engines were running. Nobody, however, had thought to search for this defect, and the battery was just topped up whilst on the ground, but not fully, and instead of being on charge for five or seven hours it was only charged for no more than 50 minutes.

As a result, on 22 May, half an hour after take-off from Arkhangelsk the power supply cut off, and the radio set no longer worked. Makhotkin asked Kekushev whether the remaining charge was sufficient to lower the undercarriage and flaps on approach to the airfield in the Moscow region. He answered: 'It might be enough'. The pilot decided to lower the undercarriage using the emergency method, without resorting to the electrical supply.

The airplane had an AK-50 emergency unit on board with its own small engine. This could top up the battery but the exhaust passed into the cockpit, and from there, through to the cabin. They had long wanted to route the exhaust pipe outside the airplane but had not got around to it. Nevertheless, Kekushev and Bogdanov prepared to start the AK-50 (but did not start it, as they were concerned about the exhaust gases in the cabin).

There was fog at the airfield in Khimki, and Makhotkin saw the landing sign only on his second approach, after he had descended to below 100m. He immediately came in to land as the undercarriage was lowered in advance. His co-pilot Kotov primed the flaps and their position indicator activated, showing 10 degrees. Kotov decided everything was in order, whereas in fact the flaps were stuck in this position. At a high-speed, the Electra overshoot the landing sign 'T' approximately half a kilometre and rolled along the runway. The brakes had no effect on the wheels; they had failed a long time prior to this and had been deactivated. The airplane skidded past the boundaries of the airfield and ended up in a ditch. Makhotkin managed to switch off the engines before this happened. As the airplane hit a mound next to the ditch the undercarriage broke, and the airplane spun round approximately 45 degrees and lay on its belly; the crew were unhurt. The results of the investigation established that the undercarriage was destroyed, as were the airscrews and two oil tanks; the skin of the wings, fuselage and tail fin was damaged. The Head of the Directorate of Polar Aviation characterised Makhotkin as 'an arrogant, self-satisfied individual who had forgotten how to be subordinate to discipline'. There was an intent to bring him to justice but subsequently the authorities sympathised with him and this was limited to a strict reprimand, and a demotion of his pilot status to 2nd class.

Any further trace of the H214 is lost at this point, and evidently this Electra did not fly any more. The other airplane, which had joined the EON, continued to be used, albeit not very intensively. In 1940, this aircraft amassed more than 88 hrs of flying time, and this was partially linked to the fact that from June the airplane was unserviceable and stood idle for more than six months at a Moscow airport.

By that time there were not one but two Electras serving with the EON, and the second airplane was a trophy from the Polish campaign of September 1939. According to Polish records, two unserviceable L-10As belonging to the LOT airline were left at the territory occupied by the Red Army –

Electra H214 at an airfield, August 1938.

April 1942 became unfortunate for the Electra – on 11 April pilot V.V. Osipov tore off the tail wheel on landing at Stalingrad: it fell through some black ice into a deep puddle. The airplane was repaired in situ but 10 days later there was an accident on take-off in Astrakhan when the airplane's undercarriage was torn off.

In mid May, however, following a major overhaul, the Electra resumed operations and flew successfully for almost a year. In April 1943 the airplane once again required repair. The Electra got through the aircraft repair bases Nos.400 and 401, and the latter in Novosibirsk managed to complete the repairs. The airplane flew in the rear up until June 1944, when it was written off because its worn out condition.

one in Horodenka, and another in Kolomiya. A record about the second airplane can be found in a report by the trophy commission of the VVS of Ukrainian Front, which was headed by *Voeninzhener 1-go ranga* Znamenskiy.

As of 21 February 1940, there were two Electras listed on the inventories of the GVF – the first was the earlier example, and the second – the one which had been transferred from Western Ukraine. Another ex-LOT airplane remained at the disposal of the military and in May 1940 it was in the list of trophy equipment of Kiev Special Military District.

The former Polish airliner has been repaired only by March 1941 – the issue was with availability of the Wasp Junior engines as there were none in the stores. The GU GVF approached the government for permission to import several such engines but evidently this request was declined. The engines of the H214 airplane, which had been kept at the EON stores since 1939, came to their aid. Factory No.89 fitted them to the L-10A, and on 31 March–12 April 1941 the aircraft underwent testing at the NII GVF, flown by pilot Tabarovskiy. The additional 300hp, as compared to the original power plant, increased the aircraft cruising speed from 260km/h up to 275km/h and reduced the take-off distance. The ex-Polish Electra was given the registration number Λ3451.

Whether the L-10A that had been at the EON stores was actually repaired is not known. Since May 1941, there is no mention of this airplane in any records.

After the outbreak of the war with Germany, the Electra Λ3451 was transferred from the EON to the Moscow Directorate of the GVF, which was engaged in transport flights in the rear along the entire European part of the USSR. In August 1941 this airplane was involved in an accident but was repaired.

There was another Electra in the Soviet Union but this was a completely different airplane – the L-14H Super Electra. Initially, this airplane also belonged to the Polish LOT airline, and in September 1939 it crossed the Estonian border and landed there. After the Baltic states became part of the USSR in May 1940, all the aircraft that was in these territories was subject to a census. In August of that same year, Major General R. Tomberg, the Head of the air defence of the newly formed Estonian SSR, reported to Moscow: 'An interned Polish Lockheed and a medical RVD have been found at Jagola airfield'. For some time, the Super Electra was registered with the VVS of the Baltic Military District. The intention was to hand this airplane over to the Baltic Directorate of the GVF and to put it into service on the Riga–Velikiye Luki–Moscow route. No information, however, on civil operations of this Super Electra in the Baltics has been found.

In May 1941, the military nevertheless handed over L-14H to representatives of the GVF. The aircraft acceptance was undertaken in Riga, and it was test flown by pilot Lebedev. Then, Lebedev and the Deputy Head of the GU GVF M.F. Kartushev ferried the airplane to Moscow, where the Super Electra was given the civil registration number Λ3435.

Following the outbreak of the war with Germany, this ex-Polish airplane was transferred to the MAGON, and it completed two trips: Moscow–Simferopol–Moscow and Moscow–Khabarovsk–Moscow. After the second, a failure was noted in the port engine, and in October 1941 the aircraft was grounded for repairs. Two pistons were changed in the port engine, together with one cylinder and a ball bearing in the magneto drive. In the starboard engine one piston was changed and grinding was undertaken on the valves. Despite the work of the repair crews, the port engine vibrated from time to time and smoked heavily. As a result of this, on 18 November Kartushev, who by that time had been awarded the title of regimental commissar, decided to carry out a test flight of the Super Electra. The following day he had to fly to Kazan and then further east to Uelkal with the aim of inspecting the future route of the ALSIB.

The airplane took off from the Moscow Central airfield, and apart from Kartushev the Chief Engineer of MAGON Ostretsov and flight mechanic Pustotentsev were on board. At an altitude of approximately 100m, the port engine failed and the airplane entered a spin, hit the tops of the trees, crashed into the ground in Petrovskiy Park behind the building of the Air Force Academy, and caught fire. The soldiers who had run up to the airplane pulled those on board out of the Super Electra and extinguished the fire with snow. Kartushev had broken his right hand and sustained severe bruising, while Ostretsov and Pustotentsev were killed. The airplane, which had been destroyed and burnt out, was written off.

The commission that investigated the accident came to the conclusion that there were two factors behind this disaster. The first was the technical condition of the airplane (the reliable operation of the port engine on the ground had not been achieved), and the second was the lack of familiarisation on the part of Kartushev with the Super Electra (his previous experience for the most part had been on the PS-84). The regimental commissar did not have any experience of flying on one engine at all. Taken as a whole this meant an accident was inevitable.

5

The Trophies

Following the end of the Civil War there was a relatively long period of calm for the Red Army. Correspondingly, there were no trophies to be gained either. Combat activities in Northern China against the troops under Marshal Zhāng Zuòlín in 1928 were very one sided with respect to the air war. Although the marshal did have airplanes, they did not play a part in any air combat.

The first trophies after a long break were captured on foreign soil in a foreign war. From autumn 1936, Soviet volunteer pilots began to fight in Spain, and a year later in China. Their enemies were using aircraft of Italian, German, and Japanese derivation, but they also encountered airplanes created in other countries.

At the very start of the Spanish Civil War, the forces of General Franco were using British de Havilland DH.84

Gloster Gladiators, abandoned by Soviet forces during the retreat in June 1941.

A German soldier inspects the Gladiator in the hangar

Dragon passenger biplanes quite actively. These airplanes were utilised as light bombers and transports, and one such aircraft was taken to the USSR in a dismantled condition. In the records of the NII VVS, this airplane is listed as a 'trophy', which, evidently, should have indicated that this biplane was captured from the Nationalists. The lists of the Reconnaissance Directorate, where the trophies were recorded, (German, Italian, Japanese and later Polish) do no mention a Dragon. In memoirs, it is often said that the biplane was gifted to the Soviet Union by the leadership of the Communist Party of Spain. But there is no confirmation of this to be found in the documents.

The date of this airplane's arrival in the Soviet Union is not known, and it is also unknown whether the Dragon underwent a full state testing program at the NII VVS. A number of pilots, however, test flew this airplane, including the well-known test pilot P.M. Stefanovskiy. The feedback on piloting this airplane was very advantageous. The biplane was used for several years by a liaison flight of the NII VVS, at least up until March 1940.

The Dragon gave rise to a great deal of interest among Soviet specialists, as it fitted in very well with the indigenous aircraft production concepts – it was more of a basic design, it was cheaper and it was designed for pilots without a high degree of experience to fly. At the beginning of 1940, the leadership of the VVS tasked the aviation industry with creating an indigenous copy of the DH.84 in a medical version, and to put it into series production in place of the Yakovlev twin-engine Ya-19 monoplane. However, the Soviet 'Dragon' was never produced, and moreover, the Ya-19 did not enter series production either.

When the Red Army entered the eastern regions of Poland in September 1939, they captured a variety of different airplanes but they were Polish-designed or Polish-manufactured types. The only British items they found were

A Hawker Hart from a Latvian order prior to delivery from Britain; these airplanes also ended up among the Soviet trophies.

engines. As far as American airplanes are concerned, they only found two Electras mentioned above.

On the other hand, the aircraft that were captured after the Baltic states of Latvia, Lithuania and Estonia were joined to the USSR in summer 1940, was for the most part of foreign origin. American airplanes were not used in this region but a great number of British aircraft were in service there. Representatives of the VVS carefully reviewed the entire fleet of the air forces' units, airlines and aeroclubs, while the civil airplanes were likewise processed by the representatives of the GU GVF.

On 25 August 1940, the Head of the VVS Headquarters of the newly formed Baltic Military District Major General S.P. Sinyakov reported to Moscow from Riga which aircraft types had been found, and where. Of the British airplanes, the most common was the Gloster Gladiator biplane fighter: 14 airplanes were in Lithuania (of those 12 were serviceable), and 25 (with 23 serviceable) in Latvia. In Estonia and Latvia, four old Bristol Bulldog biplanes each were also found.

Only one twin-engine bomber was found in the Baltic region – it was Avro Anson at Yagola airfield in Estonia. In total, a little more than a dozen British light bombers and reconnaissance airplanes were collected. In Estonia, there were seven Hawker Hart light bombers (four were found in Rakvere and three in Yagola), while in Latvia three Hawker Hinds were found. Latvian aviation also had four Fairey Seal reconnaissance floatplanes.

Among the trainers in use in Baltic states, there were a number of ancient types. Thus, the Estonian Air Force left seven Avro 504Rs, four Avro Avians, two Avro 626s, and an Armstrong Whitworth Siskin. Two DH.82As and a DH.60 of Lithuanian aeroclub transferred to their new owners. In essence, very few captured aircraft represented any real value, and only one contemporary training airplane – an Estonian Miles Magister, was found across the whole Baltic region.

A large proportion of the military aircraft had become hopelessly obsolete and had gone for scrap, such as the Fairey Seals that were used as targets on the weapons range.

The Air Forces of Estonia, Latvia and Lithuania that had been significantly cut back were reduced to separate squadrons, and attached to rifle corps, into which the former national armies had been reformed. They received the most contemporary and serviceable airplanes from those that were available. Thus, all seven Harts and Magister along with other airplanes joined the 22nd Squadron (Estonian), and the Anson and one of the Gladiators joined the 29th Squadron (Lithuanian). In Latvia, at least three Gladiators were operating for a short time. The number of airplanes in the national squadrons significantly surpassed the usual standard complement of 10 airplanes in the Soviet units.

Following the German invasion, these units, which had been deployed relatively close to the border, were the first to come under attack from the Luftwaffe. Many airplanes were destroyed on the first few days of the war. The loss of records

Two Lithuanian military DH.89Ms.

A military DH.89M with red stars.

during the Red Army retreat means it is not possible to trace the fate of many these aircraft. It is known that a Lithuanian Gladiator managed to perform just one combat sortie, which was a reconnaissance mission. Other fighters of this type that remained in long-term storage in Siauliai were either destroyed or captured by the Germans.

Civil airplanes from the Baltic region served in the Soviet Union for a longer period. There were two DH.89Ms in the Lithuanian Air Force, which were military versions of the Rapide, that could be used as reconnaissance aircraft, light bombers or transports. In Lithuania, two such aircraft in civil version were found. Initially, the VVS got their hands on all four airplanes but a GVF commission under the leadership of Ya.I. Artamonov that had been sent to the Baltic republics immediately started to press for their handover to civil aviation. Artamonov, having inspected the biplanes in Riga wrote to Moscow: 'these aircraft are excellent – they have two engines, and can carry six passengers each. If we get these airplanes, we can ensure air communication between the republics'. The military did not give away the armed Lithuanian DH.89Ms but two ex-Latvian Rapides were transferred to the Baltic Directorate of the GVF. One biplane was accepted at the beginning of November 1940, and the second in March next year. They were based in Riga, served the Riga–Tallinn route, and periodically operated on other routes.

The further fate of the four DH.89s is not entirely clear – the German records indicate that they captured three or even four airplanes of this type in summer 1941 in the Baltics. One of these was even used by an Estonian squadron that had become part of the Luftwaffe in 1942–1943. This, evidently, refers to ex-Lithuanian two DH.89Ms and a single civil DH.89.

The second civil DH.89, airplane which received the registration number Λ20, in December 1941 was in the strength of the Moscow Directorate of the GVF. This airplane was evacuated during the retreat and operated in the rear, carrying mail, passengers and different types of cargoes over a relatively long period of time. On 7 April 1942, the Rapide was involved in an accident at Stalingrad. Whilst it was taxiing, the aircraft fell into a track that had been left on the soft ground by a truck and got stuck, breaking the port undercarriage semi-axle. The biplane, however, was quickly repaired and was used without interruption up until May 1943, after which it was under repair up until December. Then the airplane flew for a short time again but in February 1944 it was written off as 'obsolete and worn out'.

Two Lithuanian Percival Q.6L airplanes served until the Soviet invasion on an internal route Kaunas–Palanga. These airplanes had been given their own names, *Darius* and *Girenas*, in honour of two Lithuanian pilots who in 1933 made a transatlantic crossing. After the change of owners in autumn 1940, they were also transferred to the Baltic directorate of the GVF. According to the plan, these airplanes were to be based in Riga and they were to operate from the beginning of 1941 on a route Riga–Kaunas but in fact they also flew on routes Riga–Velikiye Luki–Moscow, and Velikiye Luki–Vitebsk. On 19 June 1941, the Percival flown by pilot Lodzing spun round on take-off from Moscow and the undercarriage had to be repaired. It is possible that it was this airplane that was destroyed in a crash in July 1941. The fate of the second Q.6L remains unknown and it is more than likely that it was destroyed by Germans during their invasion.

Colour section 2

Color views by Andrey Yurgenson

NOT TO SCALE

Fleetster which was flown by M. Slepnyov to the *Chelyuskin* camp, Vankarem, Chukotaks, April 1934.

Fleetster of the Yenisey air group of Polar Aviation, Krasnoyarsk, November 1934.
Aviaarktika inscription on the nose was used for Polar Aviation aircraft.

Northrop 2ED ground attack aircraft during testing at the OELID TsAGI, end of 1936.

NOT TO SCALE

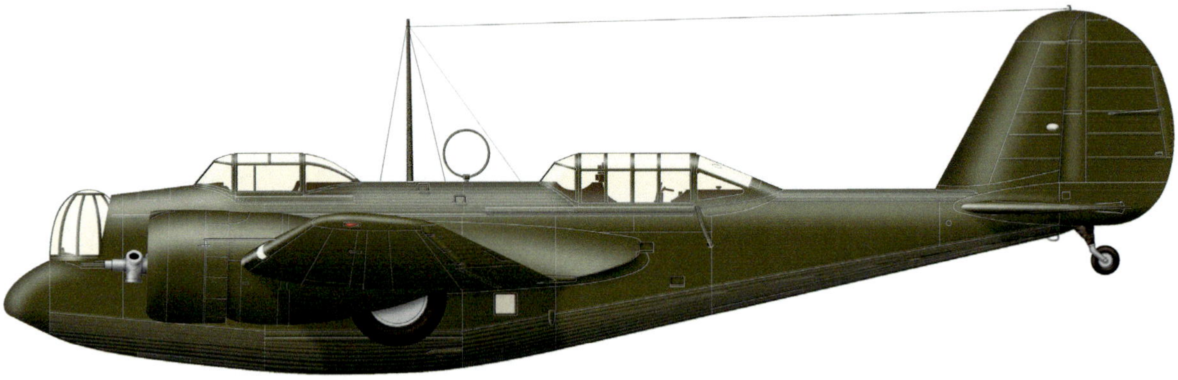

Martin 139WR bomber during testing in USSR, Leningrad, Komendantskiy airfield, February 1937.

Sikorsky S-43A amphibian at the Polar Pilots School, Nikolaev, May 1937.

Sikorsky S-43A amphibian, registration number H207, during search of the missing DB-A airplane of S.A. Levanevskiy, Fairbanks, 1938.

NOT TO SCALE

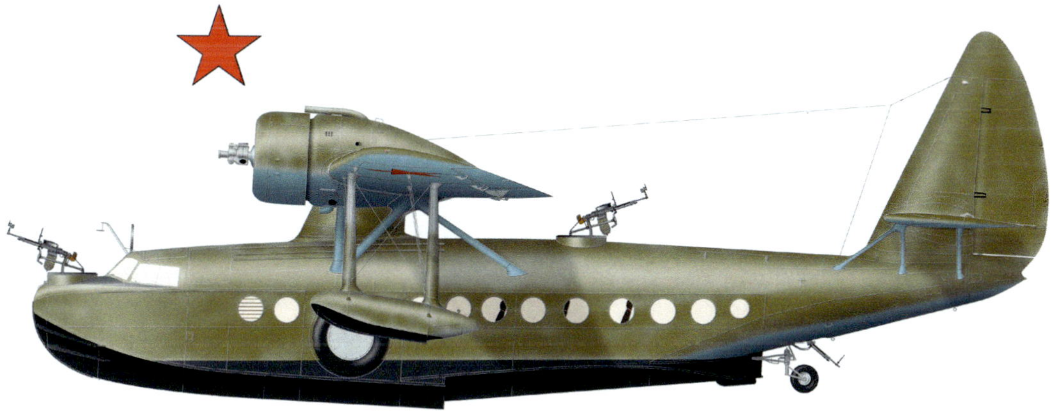

Sikorsky S-43A after repairs and installation of the armament in Krasnoyarsk, Tiksi Bay. August 1942.

Douglas DF flying boat, registration number H205, after arrival in USSR, Leningrad, Grebnoy Port, March 1937.

Vultee V-1AS airplane on floats, which was ordered by the Soviet Union. Alameda hydro-port, San Francisco, August 1936.

NOT TO SCALE

Vultee V-1AS on wheels at Shchelkovo airfield outside Moscow after completion of ferry flight from the USA, September 1936.

Seversky 2PA-A amphibian during a test flight in the USA, Long Island, March 1938.

Seversky 2PA-L two-seat fighter during testing at NII VVS, June 1938.

NOT TO SCALE

Martin M-156 flying boat during testing in the USA, Baltimore, November 1937.

PS-30 flying boat of the Far Eastern Department of Civil Air Fleet, Khabarovsk, 1940.

A project of GM-156 military version, based on Martin M-156.

NOT TO SCALE

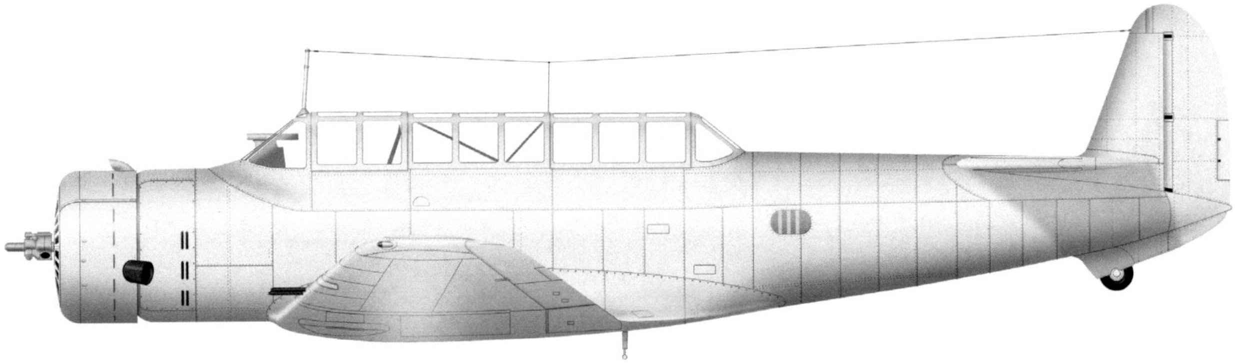

A leading series-build BSh-1 ground attack aircraft during state testing at the NII VVS, 1939.

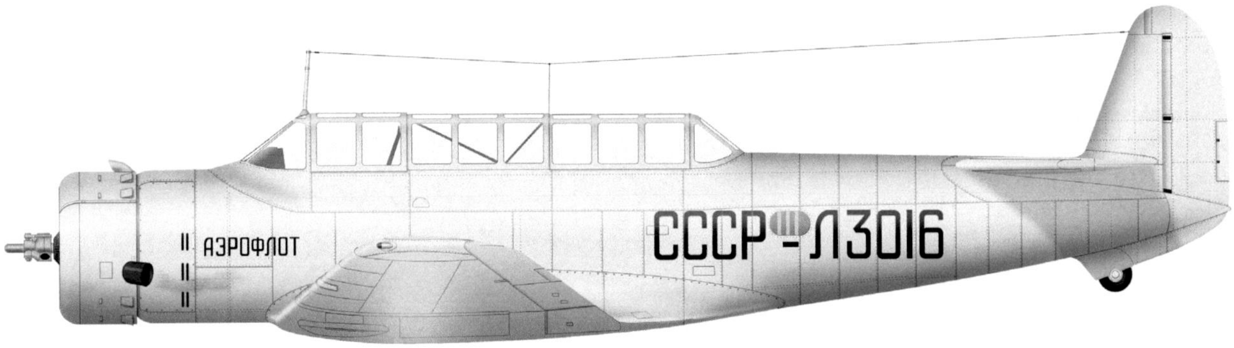

PS-43 postal airplane.

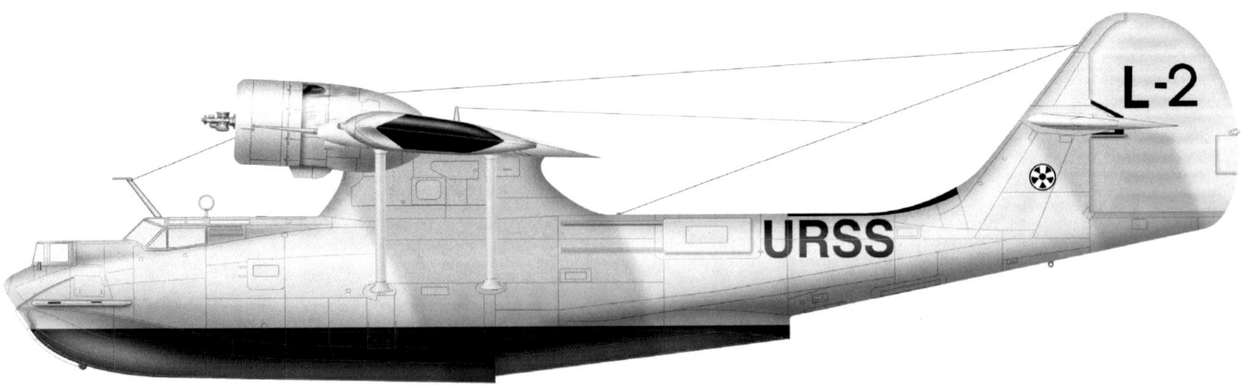

The *Guba* flying boat after arrival to the USSR, March 1938.

NOT TO SCALE

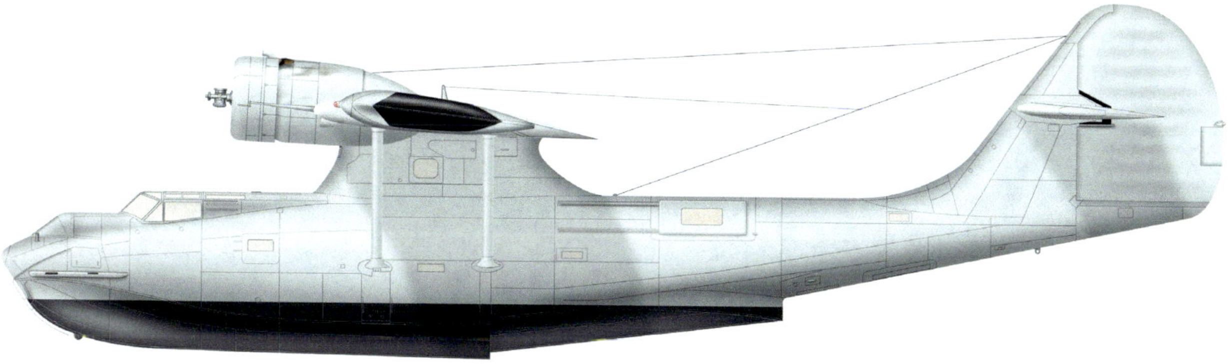

Prototype of the Consolidated Model 28-2 flying boat during testing in the USA, 1937.

Leading series production military version of the GST flying boat. The armament is not yet installed.

One of GST airplanes of Polar Aviation, registration number CCCP H308.

NOT TO SCALE

GST flying boat of the 80th Squadron, Black Sea Fleet Air Force, Sevastopol, 1941.

GST flying boat of the 4th (Long-Range Reconnaissance) Squadron of the 118th Reconnaissance Air Regiment, Northern Fleet Air Force, August 1941.

MP-7 civil flying boat, registration number СССР-Л3454, of the East Siberian Directorate of the GVF, flown by the crew of U.K. Bergstryom.

NOT TO SCALE

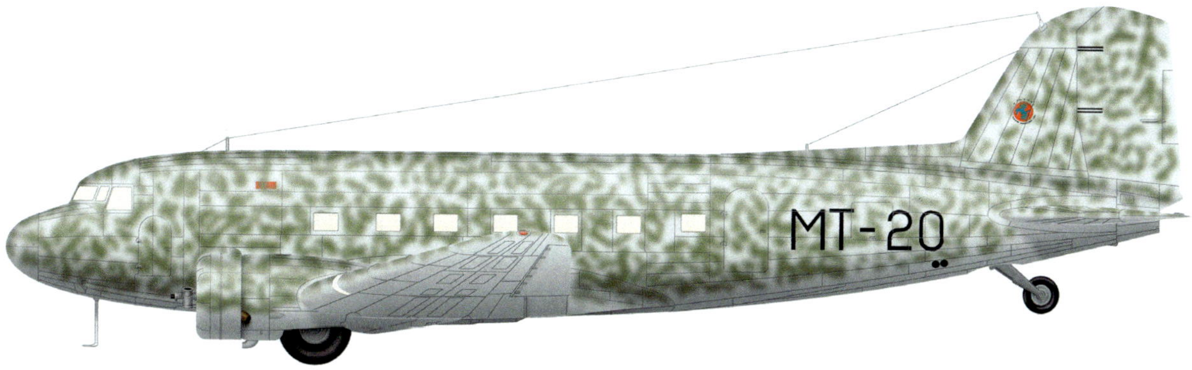

Camouflaged DC-3 which was used for air transportation to Mongolia during hostilities at Khalkhin-Gol, summer 1939.

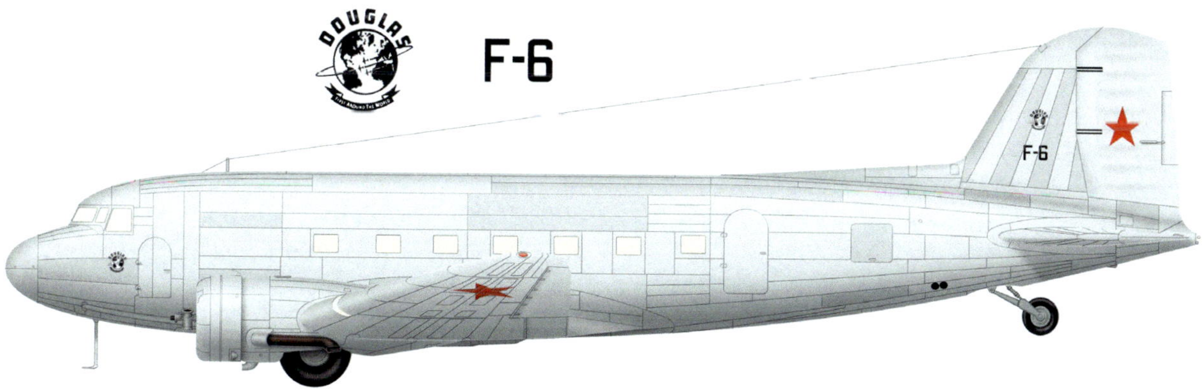

DC-3 airplane of the Baltic Fleet Air Force which transported a Soviet military delegation to Finland in March 1940.

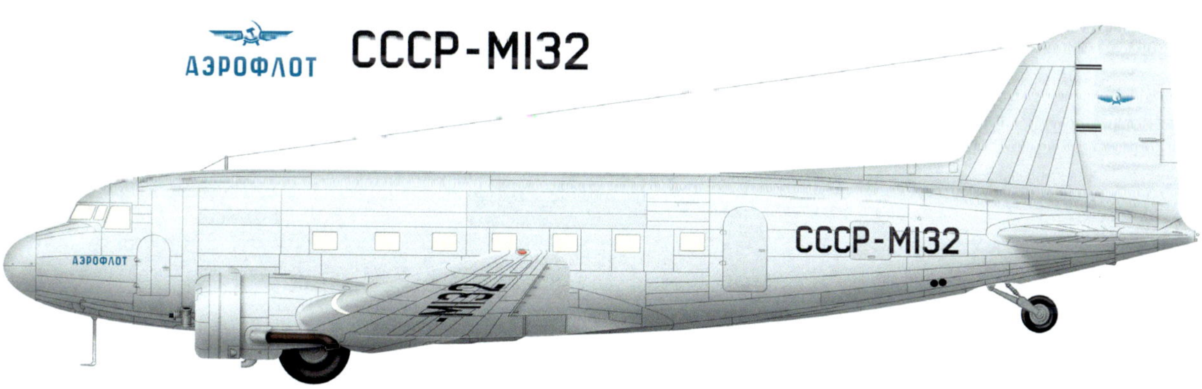

DC-3 of the UMVL which operated on Moscow–Stockholm air route.

NOT TO SCALE

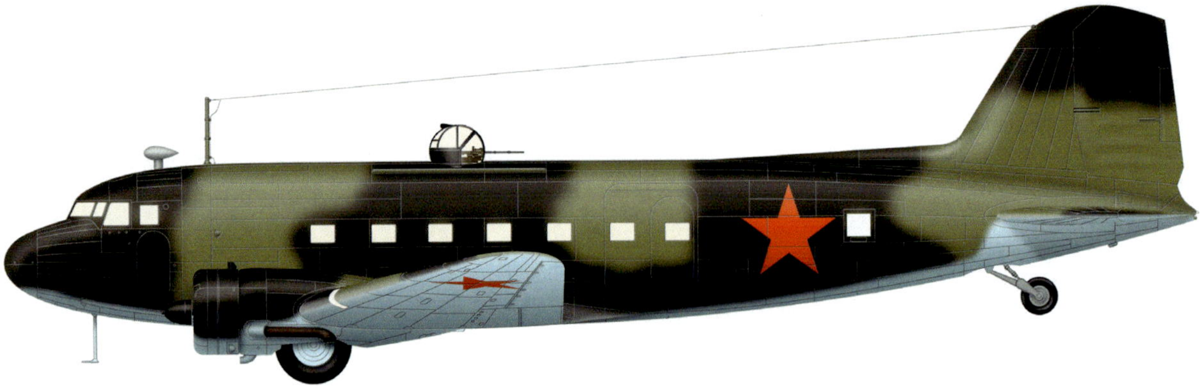

PS-84 of the Moscow Special Purpose Air Group, Khvoynoe airfield, October 1941.

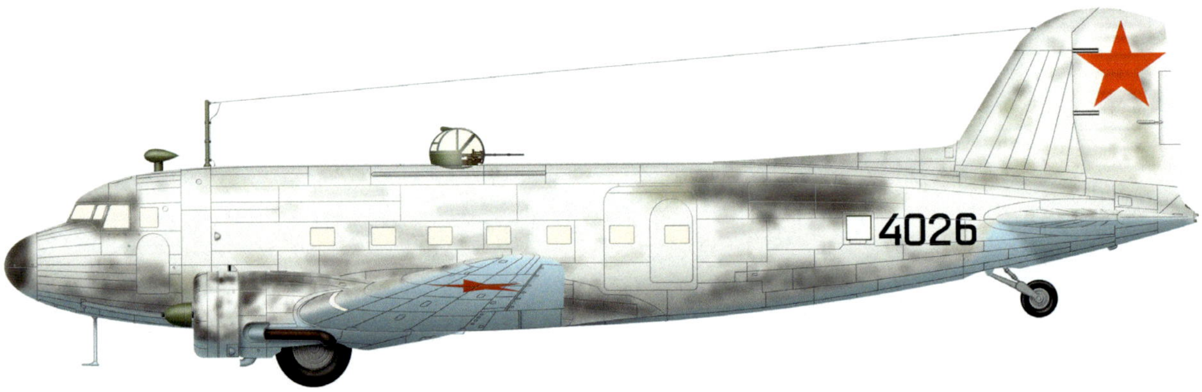

PS-84 which took part is transportation of supplies to besieged Leningrad, winter 1941-1942.

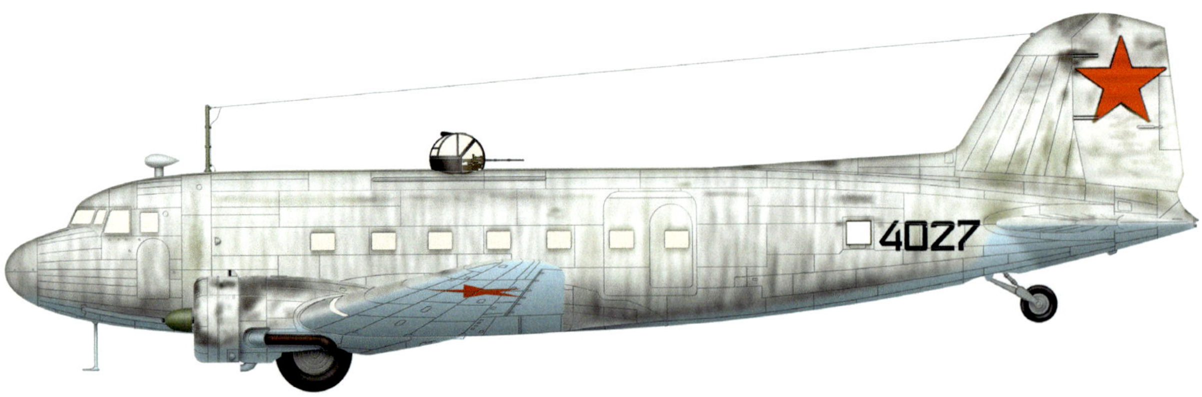

PS-84 which took part is transportation of supplies to besieged Leningrad, winter 1941-1942.

NOT TO SCALE

Li-2NB night bomber.

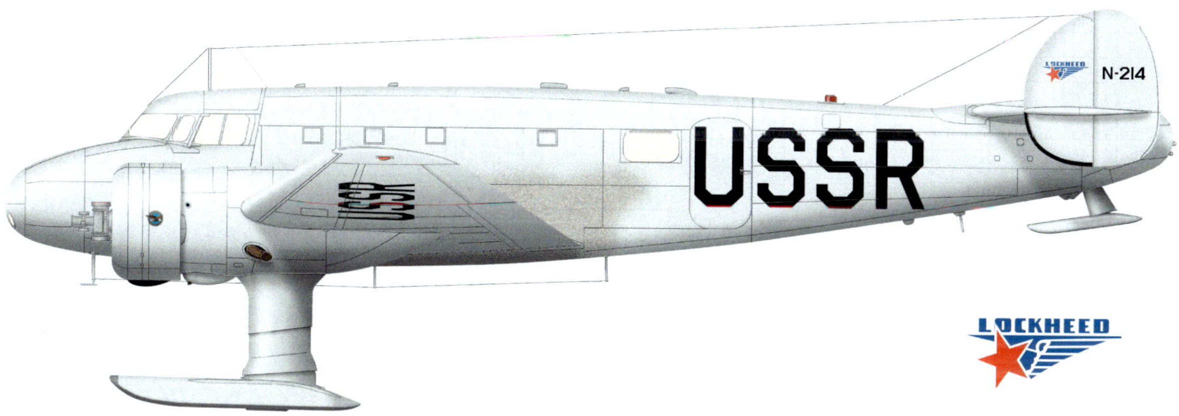

Lockheed L-10E with non-retractable ski landing gear.

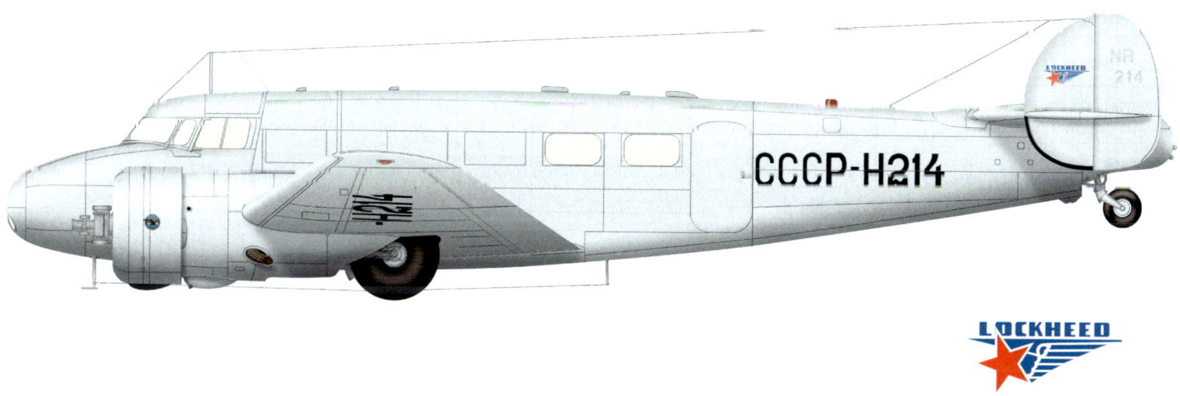

L-10E in service with Moscow Air Group under GUSMP, Zakharkovo airfield.

NOT TO SCALE

Soviet Gloster Gladiator I, which originally have seen service with the 123rd Squadron of Latvian Air Force, Spilve airfield near Riga, June 1941.

Ex-Estonian Miles Magister I of the 22nd Corps Squadron of the Soviet Air Force, 1941.

Appendix

Military Ranks in Imperial Russia and the Soviet Union

Within this volume various military ranks are often mentioned, which were used in Imperial Russia and in the Soviet Union. The author will attempt to explain their meaning to the reader.

By the beginning of the 20th century in Russia five systems for military ranks were in use, which were retained right up to the October revolution of 1917. The 'Table of Ranks' defined how they corresponded with ranks for those in the civil service. Four were in existence in the army, depending of which branch they belonged to: they were for the infantry, artillery, cavalry, and Cossacks. Moreover, the names of these ranks did partially coincide. The infantry system was the most widespread. This was how it appeared:

Ryadovoy
Yefreytor
Mladshiy Unter-Ofitser
Starshiy Unter-Ofitser
Feldfebel
Podpraporshchik
Zauryad-Praporshchik
Praporshchik
Podporuchik
Poruchik
Shtabs-Kapitan
Kapitan
Podpolkovnik
Polkovnik
General-Mayor
General-Leytenant
General ot Infanterii
General-Feldmarshal (this was no longer used from 1912).

The *Praporshchik* was considered the first officer's rank and in contrast to other officers this did not elevate individuals automatically into the personal nobility. From 1884 onwards this rank was only introduced in wartime and following the conclusion of military activity those still serving were promoted to *Podporuchik*, while all the others were sent to the reserves.

In Russia there were three ways to become an army officer. Firstly, a person could graduate from the Schools of *Praporshchiks*, and typically *Unter-Ofitser* or new recruits who had the appropriate education would be sent there. The standard military education would be gained in the Military Schools, graduates of which would receive the epaulettes of a *Podporuchik*. Along with these epaulettes a young officer would be given a certificate of personal nobility (if they were not a hereditary nobleman). In the third instance, a recruit with good education would be offered volunteer status. If they agreed they would prepare to take the exams of School of *Praporshchiks* or School of Cadets independently. The commander of a military unit in which a volunteer was serving was obliged to spend time with them to give lessons, and to provide textbooks as well as acting tutor officer or officers.

Senior officers (from *Podpolkovnik* upwards) once they had been awarded the appropriate rank would gain hereditary nobility, which would extend to their wives and children.

In the artillery the names of the ranks differed somewhat for privates and non-commissioned officers:

Kanonir
Bombardir
Mladshiy Feyerverker
Starshiy Feyerverker
Feldfebel

From this point onwards they all corresponded to the infantry ranks, culminating in a *General ot Artillerii*.

In the cavalry, instead of the rank of *Ryadovoy,* cavalry nomenclature would be used – *Gusar, Dragun, Kirasir*. From this point on the career ladder corresponded overall to that of the infantry, but a *Feldfebel* was known as a *Vakhmistr*, a *Podporuchik* was a *Kornet*, a *Shtabs-Kapitan* was a *Shtabs-Rotmistr*, and a *Kapitan* was a *Rotmistr*. The top rank was a *General ot Kavalerii*.

The system of cossack ranks displayed the greatest diversity, in order of rank these were as follows:

Kazak
Prikazniy
Mladshiy Uryadnik
Uryadnik
Starshiy Uryadnik
Vakhmistr
Podkhorunzhiy
Khorunzhiy
Sotnik
Podyesaul
Yesaul
Voyskovoy Starshina
Polkovnik

That is to say a *Podkhoruzhniy* corresponded to a *Praporshchik* and from that point onwards the system was the same for the rest of the cavalry and culminated in a *General ot Kavalerii*. In two cossack imperial guard regiments, the cossack ranks were not used, in favour of the ordinary cavalry ranks.

Pilots graduated from the flying schools with the rank of *Praporshchik*. This was not the case with officers who had voluntarily transferred to aviation from other branches of the armed forces. They retained the ranks they had been awarded previously, and as they progressed through their service they would be awarded ranks in accordance with the old system. Therefore, *Poruchik*, and *Kornet*, and *Yesaul* would be encountered in the air fleet. They would only differ from their previous colleagues in the infantry or the cavalry in terms of the increments in their pay, which were set at a significantly higher level. In contrast to other countries, there were very few *Unter-Ofitser* pilots in Russia. They were usually re-trained mechanics, or engine specialists. The point being that at the time it was permitted for pilots to be trained in a combat unit directly. The commander of the unit had the right to arrange training and set exams, and subsequently sign the pilot's certificate.

Naval aviation formed part of the navy, and was not subordinate to the Military Ministry, but to the Ministry of the Navy. Therefore, naval pilots had fleet ranks and the career ladder for sailors was much shorter than in the army. Moving up the chain of command these were as follows:

Matros 2-oy statyi
Matros 1-oy statyi
Kvartirmeister
Botsmanmat
Botsman
Konduktor
Michman
Leytenant
Starshiy Leytenant (introduced in 1907)
Kapitan-Leytenant (introduced in 1907)
Kapitan 2-go ranga
Kapitan 1-go ranga
Kontr-Admiral
Vitse-Admiral
Admiral
General-Admiral

The first officer rank was the *Michman* and this was awarded to graduates of the Naval Corps. This was an educational institution for the nobility that only accepted hereditary noblemen. Representatives of the technical services (mechanics, electricians, navigators) were trained at special colleges and were considered second-class officers. For a long time, they were not awarded naval ranks but infantry ranks with the addition that they were 'under the Admiralty'. They were later distinguished by the colour of their epaulettes – which were not gold but silver. The land forces ranks were also to be found among the border forces and the military shipbuilders.

Following the October revolution in 1917, the military ranks were discontinued. For almost 20 years in the army and the navy there were only job titles and categories. It was the latter that defined the rights and responsibilities, as well as the insignia and the wages. In aviation only two formal ranks were in existence for pilots: the *Krasvoenlyot* (which was a syllabic abbreviation of *Krasniy Voenniy Lyotchik*, or Red Military Pilot) and the *Starshiy Krasvoenlyot* (which was a Senior *Krasvoenlyot*). Furthermore, a *Starshiy Krasvoenlyot* could just be an experienced pilot (such as the commander of a heavy bomber, for example), as well as the Head of a Department in the UVVS. For flight observers the *Krasvoenlyotnab* (*-nab* from *Nablyudatel*, or Observer) and *Starshiy Krasvoenlyotnab* respectively were used. *Krasvoenmorlyot* (*Krasniy Voenno-Morskoi Lyotchik*, or Red Naval Pilot) served in naval aviation, and flying school student was known as *Uchlyot* (an abbreviation of *Uchenik Lyotchika*, or Apprentice Pilot).

In autumn 1935 the system of military ranks in the Soviet Union was restored. It differed from that used in Tsarist Russia, and moving up the chain of command it was as follows:

Krasnoarmeets
Otdelyonniy Komandir
Mladshiy Pomkomvzvoda
Pomkomvzvoda
Starshiy Pomkomvzvoda
Starshina
Leytenant
Starshiy Leytenant
Kapitan
Major
Polkovnik
Kombrig
Komdiv

Komkor
Komandarm 2-go ranga
Komandarm 1-go ranga

Under the new system, the first officer rank was *Leytenant*, and furthermore it turned out that a *Kapitan* of Tsarist army was the equivalent not of a *Kapitan* under the new system but a *Major*. This system was subsequently changed over time. In 1936 the top rank of *Marshal* was introduced, and this was followed in August 1937 by the *Mladshiy Leytenant*. In May 1940 the Soviet *Komdiv* (Division Commander), *Komkor* (Corps Commander), and *Komandarm* (Army Commander) were re-classified as *General*. The *General-Major*, *General-Leytenant*, *General-Polkovnik* and *General Armii* appeared and the *Kombrig* (Brigade Commander) rank was discontinued. Special commissions reclassified the minority of the former *Kombrig* as *General-Major*, while the majority were reclassified as *Polkovinik*. This process took until the end of 1941. In July 1940, the rank of *Podpolkovnik* was introduced. At the same time *Pomkomvzvoda* was reclassified as *Serzhant*, and a *Yefreytor* began to follow the *Krasnoarmeets*.

On graduation from flying schools, students would initially be awarded the rank of *Leytenant*, and from 1940 onwards, as per the German example, young pilots began to graduate as *Serzhant*.

The technical personnel in the VVS had their own ranks, and *Mladshiy Leytenant* corresponded to the *Mladshiy Voentekhnik* (Junior Military Technician). Then came the *Voentekhnik 2-go ranga* (Military Technician 2nd rank), *Voentekhnik 1-go ranga* (Military Technician 1st rank), *Voeninzhener 2-go ranga* (Military Engineer 2nd rank), *Voeninzhener 1-go ranga* (Military Engineer 1st rank). The latter was the equivalent of a *Polkovnik*. Higher still were the ranks of *Briginzhener* (Brigade Engineer), *Divinzhener* (Division Engineer), *Korinzhener* (Corps Engineer), and *Arminzhener* (Army Engineer). In 1940 the rank of *Briginzhener* was discontinued.

The political workers also had their own ranks, up to and including company level they were known as *Politruk* (*Politicheskiy Rukovoditel*, or Political Leader), and higher still as various levels of *Komissar*. There were their own ranks for supply officers, military doctors, veterinary surgeons, and lawyers but they hold no interest for us. In naval aviation, during the Soviet era standard army ranks were employed, which was also the case for the VVS.

Bibliography

Archival

Central House of Aviation and Cosmonautics
Central Museum of the Russian Air Force
Russian Aviation Research Trust
Russian State Archive of Economics
Russian State Archive of Social and Political History
Russian State Military Archive
Scientific and Memorial Museum of N.E. Zhukovskiy

Published Sources

Aviatsiya Krasnoyarskogo Kraya v Dokumentakh Arkhivov, Publikatsiyakh i Fotografiyakh (Krasnoyarsk, Sibirskiy Federalniy Universitet, 2016)

Aleksandrov A.O., *Amerikanskie Gidroplany v Rossii 1912–1917* (St. Petersburg, 1999)

Altunin E.V., *Ocherki Istorii Lyotnogo Dela* (Moscow, Gosoboronizdat, 1940)

Amiryants G.A., *Lyotchiki-Ispytateli* (Moscow, Kuchkovo Pole, 2008)

Danilenko V.F., *Krylya Dalnego Vostoka* (Khabarovsk, Khabarovskoye Knizhnoe Izdatelstvo, 1979)

Duz P.D., *Istoriya Vozdukhoplavaniya i Aviatsii v Rossii do 1914* (Moscow, Mashinostroyenie, 1979)

Dyomin A., Makarov N., *OAO 'Duks'* (Moscow, Rusavia, 2003)

Dyomin A.A., *Khodynka: Vzlyotnaya Polosa Russkoy Aviatsii* (Moscow, Rusavia, 2002)

Eliseev S.P., *Organizatsionnoe Stroitelstvo Sovetskikh Voenno-Vozdushnykh Sil (1921–1923)* (Moscow, VUNTs VVS, 2012)

Gorshkov M.F., *Ispytanie Samolyota Martin 139WR* (Moscow, TsAGI, 1939)

GosNII GA Za 60 Let (*GosNII GA, 1990*)

Gratsianskiy A.N., *Uroki Severa* (Leningrad, Gidrometeoizdat, 1979)

Istoricheskiy Perelyot Levanevskogo (Moscow, Pertizdat, 1936)

Istoriya Otkrytiya i Osvoenie Severnogo Morskogo Puti, Volume 4 (Leningrad, Gidrometeizdat, 1969)

Kak My Spasali Chelyukintsev (Moscow, Pravda, 1934)

Karpiy V. *Geniy Neba Vladimir Kokkinaki* (Moscow, 2007)

Kondratyev V., Khayrulin M., *Aviatsiya Grazhdanskoy Voyny* (Moscow, Tekhnika-Molodyozhi, 2000).

Krasniy Vozdushniy Flot Na Sluzhbe Revolyutsii (Moscow, Voenniy Vestnik, 1923)

Kratkiy Ocherk Istorii Korabelnoy Aviatsii (Moscow, Aviatsiya VMF, 1982)

Mirniye Krylya v Gody Voyny (Moscow, Vozdushniy Transport, 1995)

Moiseenko V.L., *Opisanie Samolyota DN.4 s Motorom FIAT A-12 240H.P.* (Moscow, Vestnik Vozdushnogo Flota, 1923)

Morgunov N.N., *Samolyot Li-2* (Moscow, Transport, 1968)

Muravyov V.K., *Ispytateli VVS* (Moscow, Voenizadat, 1990)

Osnovniye Sobytiya iz Zhizni Instituta 1930–1990 (Moscow, GosNII GA, 1990)

Pesterev V.I., *Khroniki Aviatsii Yakutii (1921–1987)* (Novosibirsk, 1997)

Pochtarev A, Goncharov L., *Polyarnaya Aviatsiya Rossii 1914–1945,* Volume 1 (Paulsen, 2011)

Regulirovka Biplana Avro tip 504 (Moscow, Vestnik Vozdushnogo Flota, 1923)

Rukovodstvo po Lyotnoy Ekspluatatsii Samolyota PS-43 (Moscow, RIO Aeroflota, 1940)

Samolyot DC-3 (Moscow, RIO Aeroflota, 1939)

Samolyot DH.9 Daimler (Mercedes) 260h.p. (Moscow, Vetsnik Vozduhsnogo Flota, 1923)

Samolyot Martinsayd F.4. (Moscow, Vestnik Vozdushnogo Flota, 1923)

Samolyot PS-84 (Moscow, Redizdat Aeroflota, 1940)

Sbornik Byulletenei po Izmeneniyu Konstruktsii Samolyota Li-2 v 1947 (Moscow, Oborongiz, 1948)

Shavrov V.B., *Istoriya Konstruktsii Samolyotov v SSSR* (Moscow, Mashinostroenie, 1978)

Shcherbakov A.A., *Lyotchiki, Samolyoty, Inspytanie* (Moscow, Aviko-Press, 1998)

Siniktsiyants A.M., *Otechestva Krylatie Syny* (Moscow, Mozaika, 2002)

Smirnov B.A., *Nebo Moey Molodosti* (Moscow, Voenizdat, 1990)

Sobolev D.A., *Nashi Sootechestvenniki v Zarubezhnom Aviastroenii* (Moscow, Libri, 1996)

Sovetskaya Armiya: Gody Reform i Ispytaniy, Volume 1 (Moscow, IstLit, 2018)

Tikhomolov B., *Romantika Neba* (Tashkent, Izd-vo Literatury I Isskustva 1985)

Veygekin K.E., *Ocherki Istorii Lyotnogo Dela* (Moscow, Gosoboronizdat, 1940)

Voenno-Vozdushniye Sily Rossii. Neizvestniye Dokumenty (Moscow, Vestnik Vuzdushnovo Flota, 2005)

Volovich V.F., Razuvaev V.K., *Lyotnaya Ekspluatatsiya Samolyota Li-2* (Moscow, Redizdat Aeroflota, 1946)

Zinger M.E., *Put Geroya* (Moscow, DOSAAF, 1958)

Zinger M.E., *Sigizmund Levanevskiy* (Moscow, Izdatelstvo GUSMP, 1939)

Andersson L., *Soviet Aircraft and Aviation, 1917-1941* (London, Putnam, 1994)

Barnes C., *Shorts Aircraft since 1900* (London, Putnam, 1967)

Blowers P., *Curtiss Aircraft 1907–1947* (London, Putnam, 1979)
Flintham V., *Truculent Tribes, Turbulent Skies 1919–1939* (Air Britain Historians Limited, 2015)
Francillon R., *Lockheed Aircraft since 1913* (London, Putnam, 1982)
Jackson A., *De Havilland Aircraft since 1909* (London, Putnam, 1965)
Jackson A., *De Havilland Aircraft since 1909* (London, Putnam, 1987)
Lamberton W., *Fighter Aircraft of the 1914-1918 War* (Letchworth, 1960)
Smith J., *Gone to Russia to Fight* (Chalford, 2010)
Taylor H., *Fairey Aircraft since 1915* (London, Putnam, 1974)

Journals

Aero
Aero i Avtmobilnaya Zhizn
Aviatsiya i Khimiya
Aviatsiya i Kosmonavtika
Aviatsiya i Vremya
Biblioteka Vozdukhoplavaniya
Dayosh Motor
Grazhdanskaya Aviatsiya
Khronika Vozdushnogo Dela
Krylya Rodiny
Samolyot
Vestnik Vozdushnogo Flota
Vozdukhoplavanie
Vozdukhoplavatel
Technical bulletins of TsAGI
Technical bulletins of Factory No.156